D1444753

Implementing Routine and Radical Innovations

The Issues in Organization and Management Series

Arthur P. Brief and Benjamin Schneider,
Editors

Implementing Routine and Radical Innovations

Walter R. Nord

School of Business Administration
Washington University in St. Louis

Sharon Tucker

Hay Management Consultants

Lexington Books

D.C. Heath and Company/Lexington, Massachusetts/Toronto

The views expressed in this book are not necessarily those of the Hay Group, Inc.

Library of Congress Cataloging-in-Publication Data

Nord, Walter R.
  Implementing routine and radical innovations.

  Bibliography: p.
  Includes index.
  1. Organizational behavior. 2. Organizational change. I. Tucker, Sharon.   II. Title.
HD58.7.N67 1987   658.4′063   84–48504
  ISBN 0–669–09565–6 (alk. paper)

Published simultaneously in Canada
Printed in the United States of America
Casebound International Standard Book Number: 0–669–09565–6
Library of Congress Catalog Card Number: 84–48504

The paper used in this publication meets the minimum requirements of American National
Standard for Information Sciences—Permanence of Paper for Printed Library Materials, ANSI
Z39.48–1984.

86 87 88 89 90 8 7 6 5 4 3 2 1

Contents

Foreword

Arthur P. Brief
Benjamin Schneider

Healthy organizations appear to maintain the vitality of their youth; their growth and development never seem to plateau. Such vigor often is attributed to an environmentally sensitive management. This sort of management is not only responsive to the ever-changing demands made by the marketplace, but it is a management which takes initiative by innovating in ways that create favorable conditions in the marketplace. These innovations cannot be described as meek; rather, they are bold, sometimes even radical. Implementing radical innovations is a risky business. Successful implementation requires a management that has discovered the pathway through hazardous terrain to nirvana on the other side. Failure to map the route to nirvana not only results in stagnation, it may place the very survival of the organization in jeopardy.

Is the picture we have painted of the healthy organization more a reflection of fact or fiction? *Implementing Routine and Radical Innovations* is very much concerned with answering this question. Through careful scholarship, Nord and Tucker attempt to separate the realities of managing the innovation process from currently popular mythologies. For example, they address issues surrounding what makes an innovation a radical innovation, the defining properties of successful implementations of innovations, and, most of all, the alternative pathways to such successes.

Readers concerned with understanding and managing the innovation process will find *Implementing Routine and Radical Innovations* refreshing as well as both reassuring and challenging. This book is not standard "how to" fare; it is a meaty portrayal of how some organizations implemented innovation more successfully than others. The book is reassuring in that it demonstrates that managers can innovate successfully by following a variety of paths, which are shaped by complexities in and around their organizations. On the other hand, the book is challenging because Nord and Tucker do not shy away from treating these complexities in detail.

Those concerned with studying the innovation process will be impressed with Nord and Tucker's creative research approach. The study reports on a "natural" experiment. The innovation investigated was the NOW account. Nord and Tucker unmasked how twelve banks and savings and loan associations coped with this "constant" through a comparative, in-depth analysis. This book is rich in data, and the authors' interpretations of their results reveal aspects of implementation previously undetected in the literature.

In sum, both as a candid guide to practice and as a scholarly work, we are pleased to have *Implementing Routine and Radical Innovations* as a part of the Issues in Organization and Management Series. The book, like the others in the series, shows that practical advice and solid scholarship need not be incompatible. We hope, in reading the book, you concur.

Preface and Acknowledgments

This book began with our curiosity about how innovations get from the design stage to the "doing" stage. Much has been written about the necessary conditions for creating new products or new organizational routines and about implementing government policy. Some people have written about the processes and stages of innovation. As pragmatic social and organizational psychologists, we have found in organizations a big lag between developing strategy and actually putting that strategy into practice. As consultants and students of organizational change, we have seen how organization structures and social factors sometimes interfere with and sometimes facilitate changes we hope to help an organization make. Our quest has been to increase understanding of what makes a change effort "take," and what makes it possible for some products to move from conception into the market while others lag behind or are unsuccessful.

As we began to think about implementation and how to study it, we decided we needed a field study in which we could see examples of organizations that varied in how successfully they implemented some innovation. From this we could get ideas about the differences between those organizations that were more successful and those that were less so, and we could begin to clarify what contributed to successful innovation. We needed comparable innovations, though. It would not do to compare organizations implementing new advanced computer technologies with those implementing quality circles or a new brand of cereal.

Initially, the study was rooted in the existing literature on organizational innovation, which draws heavily on concepts from an applied, interdisciplinary field called organizational behavior. Organizational behavior has two complementary parts: a micro focus dealing primarily with individuals and groups and a macro focus dealing mainly with matters of organizational structure and design.

As we read the innovation literature, we found it drew more heavily on the macro material. Because this literature was our foundation, our investigation was oriented more to macro than to micro issues. This emphasis is most clear in our review of the literature presented in chapter 1. As will be seen, however, when we compared the twelve organizations we studied empirically, we found the micro-level concepts were at least equally helpful for comprehending what happened. Thus, there is a discontinuity between our conceptions developed from the literature and our findings. Some of the discontinuity is more apparent than real, because in many ways organization structure is simply one way to conceptualize organizational influence on human interaction. On the other hand, this discontinuity frames what we believe to be the major contributions of our work to the innovation literature. In essence, the focus on structure proved to be too static to describe the dynamics of the processes that took place in the firms we investigated. Indeed, our conclusions point to the need for students and managers of innovation to focus on a variety of ways to produce the type of social arrangements that aid in implementing innovation. Structure in this view is but one element of process.

Our research was conceived in the winter of 1981. On January 1 of that year, NOW accounts—interest-bearing checking accounts—had become legal for financial institutions outside the New England area. Federal approval of NOW accounts was the first step in a continuing deregulation of the financial industry.

A study of NOW accounts offered several advantages for learning about implementation of innovation. First, most financial institutions decided to offer them, but because information from the New England experience was widely disseminated, none outside of New England had to design the product from scratch. Consequently, differences in the design stage would be less likely and less critical than for other innovations, allowing us to see the implementation process without excessive contamination from the design process. Second, almost without exception, all firms that intended to offer NOW accounts felt the need to begin on the date they became legal. Because they were all implementing at exactly the same time, the external conditions (markets, the economy, and broad social or cultural factors) were apt to be similar for all financial organizations located within a given region. Third, both savings and loan associations (S & Ls) and banks were implementing NOW accounts but their previous experiences differed in ways that provided an opportunity to study a central distinction made in the innovation literature—the distinction between routine and radical innovation.

Banks had offered checking accounts for years, whereas savings and loan associations had no experience with demand deposit accounts whatsoever. Checking accounts have significantly different requirements than passbook savings accounts do. Among other things, checking accounts generate high volumes of transactions and result in much greater lobby traffic compared to savings accounts. In short, we expected NOW accounts to be a radical departure from past practices for S & Ls but a rather routine one for banks. Therefore, by comparing the two, we could examine the differences in implementing radical and routine innovations postulated in the literature. With all these advantages, NOW accounts appeared to be a fruitful innovation to study.

Our next step was to select a random sample of banks and savings and loan associations of various sizes and interview representative people at all levels who were significantly involved in implementing NOW accounts. The results are the twelve case studies presented in the book. The case studies communicate in a concrete way the exhilaration and the agony of implementing innovation.

The book is organized into three major sections. The first two chapters set the stage. Chapter 1 puts the study in context by describing historical changes in the innovation process, reviewing the building blocks of organization theory that we used for understanding the events we heard about in the interviews, and reviewing the literature on innovation. Chapter 2 describes the methods we used and the reasons we chose these methods.

The case studies make up the second section of the book. Chapters 3 through 7 describe what happened in the large organizations; chapters 8 through 10 treat the medium-sized firms; and chapter 11 describes all the small organizations. These cases were developed from two steps that we took more or less simultaneously: using the core concepts from previous work to classify what we found and inductively using categories that emerged to classify data from this study. In each chapter, we portray the events that took place and conclude, as much as possible, by putting the empirical findings into the conceptual framework defined in chapter 1. A special appendix at the end of part II is included to allow the reader to examine a summary of all the findings together.

Finally, in part III (chapters 12 through 14) we draw implications from the case studies for students of innovation and provide clues for successful implementation for managers. Our findings do not allow us to say definitively what will lead to success and what will lead to failure. The state of current knowledge in this field is too primitive and organizational dynamics are too complex to make such sweeping statements. However, we were able to arrive at conclusions about what the critical factors appeared to be for these companies, leading us to define some of the clues to success. We believe the clues can help managers focus their attention on significant factors when they attempt innovation and give scholars the basis for further research.

Our study benefitted from the ideas and support of numerous people. Jane Dutton helped us to define our approach at the outset and made extensive and insightful comments on an earlier draft of the manuscript. The final product owes much to her. Marilyn Sargent, Gail Buss, and Jim Hanley contributed to the development of the interview guide and interviewed a number of the participants. Kerstin Sonnerup, Pat McGee, and Arif Nasib assisted in the data analysis. Jerry Mueller provided us a background in demand deposits and NOW accounts. Elizabeth Case made much needed editorial revisions to the manuscript. Drew Weiss, Vicki Simon, Jess Yawitz, Glenn Detrick, Bev Stroup, Elizabeth Doherty, Joe Dobson, and Eliot Asser all gave us useful ideas, feedback, and support. Many people were involved in transcribing our interview notes and in typing and retyping numerous drafts. They were Mary Blair, Linda Clemons, Phyllis Janish, Donna Langlois, Eveline Mohr, Ruth Scheetz, Victoria Siegel, and Carla Stricklin. Their competent work and courteous responses to our requests are greatly appreciated. Victoria Siegel was especially helpful in our stretch drive. Finally, Martha Cleary, Susan Cummings, and Bruce Katz at Lexington Books were patient, supportive, and extremely helpful.

We reserve a special thanks for the many people who participated in our study. They contributed their time generously and helped our search by sharing their views and understandings with clarity and depth. We deeply appreciate their commitment and very special contribution to our knowledge about implementing innovation.

I
Background and Research Design

1
The Organizational Dynamics of Implementing Innovation

I nnovation in modern organizations is a complex and little understood process. Creating something new and useful is difficult and unpredictable, requiring special conditions that foster both imagination and the synergistic use of ideas. In addition, implementing or putting a newly created product or service into use may be even more difficult than discovering and refining it. This book is about implementing innovation in organizations, about making something happen. It is about taking ideas from conception to reality in complex systems with values, routines, and interpersonal relations that affect the destiny of the dream. It is about the tortuous path a new idea for a product or service has to travel, tortuous because at any point the idea may be modified or even destroyed due to encounters with existing values, practices, preferences, or incompetencies.

Our search was for some clues about differences between organizations that implemented well and those that implemented poorly. Even though much has been written about innovation, to date there has been little systematic research about implementation in organizations; our research was undertaken in the spirit of exploring nearly uncharted territory. We worked back and forth between considering organization theory and other people's research, collecting data, and interpreting our data until we felt confident that the patterns we saw were clear, strong, and meaningful.

The heart of the research is the discovery of four organizational characteristics that distinguished successful from unsuccessful implementation in the twelve financial organizations we studied. Each organization began offering some version of a particular new product—a Negotiated Order of Withdrawal (NOW) account—on the same day. In this introductory chapter, we set the stage by examining some fundamental dimensions of modern organizations that affect their ability to implement, and we review current research on these dimensions.

Implementing within Organizations

In the past century or so, large complex organizations have become the basic economic units in this society. Increasingly, it appears that if society is to innovate as successfully in the future as it has in the past, organizations need to improve the ways they develop and implement new ideas; most of this innovating will depend upon organizations—often, large complex ones. Although there are some similarities, implementing innovation in large, established organizations and in a society dominated by large organizations is very different from the process of innovating in a society consisiting of many smaller organizations. These constrasts are clear from history.

In the nineteenth century, innovative products often came from new companies formed especially to produce and market a particular new product. Describing that process, Schumpeter (1961) wrote: "[N]ew combinations are, as a rule, embodied . . . in new firms which generally do not arise out of the old ones but start producing them; . . . In general, it is not the owner of stage-coaches who builds railways" (p.66). The new, being an improvement on the old, then replaced the old through the operation of the "invisible hand" of a decentralized market.

Large multiunit business firms came into existence and have replaced smaller firms as major actors in the economic system, over the past hundred years. Whereas multiunit enterprises simply did not exist in the United States as late as 1840, by World War I, they had become the dominant form in many industries; by the middle of the twentieth century they were pervasive (Chandler, 1977). Economic functions (such as research for innovative products or processes) that once did not exist or were performed by several independent firms now are all often contained within the boundaries of one firm. As Chandler put it so well, the "visible hand" of managerial actions now plays an increasingly important role.

In some ways the deliberately managed bureaucracies that these developments produce make innovation difficult. People who have the vision and missionary zeal of the classical inventor/entrepreneur often chafe under the visible hand and its discomfort with uncertainty. Although entrepreneurs still play a major role in developing new products and services, today the concern is with "intrapreneurs" who create and implement within the constraints of a large organization (Pinchot, 1985). Even when a discovery is made by an individual or a small firm, often a much larger organization is needed to develop and disseminate it nationally and globally.

It is not surprising, therefore, that Kanter (1983) focused almost exclusively on ways to foster innovation in large organizations. Her insightful anaylsis of the processes that foster successful implementation by "corporate entrepreneurs" emphasized coalition building and mobilization within the boundaries of a firm. While innovators in the past perhaps faced similar challenges to those of today, they were resolved and implemented in simpler organizations; a large bureaucratic firm presents a very different set of challenges. How similar are corporate intrapreneurs to the classical entrepreneur? Kanter suggested they are quite different. Whereas the classical entrepreneurs were rugged individualists, the corporate intrapreneurs are more likely to be good builders and users of teams. They must manage internal organizational processes.

Innovators in the past often established a new organization to realize the potential of their ideas. In essence, they were operating in new territories. Their ideas did not disturb the routines of others or trigger "turf" battles with established units within their firm. They had only to build. The situation is often different when established large organizations implement a new product or service. Complex institutional arrangements often must be dismantled before new ideas can be nourished. Established interests may need to be persuaded, coopted, or removed. This dismantling or "unlearning" can be very difficult for an existing organization to do (Nystrom and Starbuck, 1984). It clearly involves different social and political skills than the dogmatic, unidimensional passions of the legendary inventors and industrial pioneers of yesteryear.

In sum, there exists more and more a society of large organizations. In tandem with this trend has been a tendency for large organizations to become relatively more important in the innovation process. As a result, implementing innovation in organizations has become increasingly important. However, little is known about how to improve this process.

Innovation and Implementation Defined

As a practical matter, the newness or innovativeness of something is not absolute. Something that is new to members of one system or subsystem often is not new to others. The metal axe, for example, could still be new to some primitive cultures.

In addition, implementation of the same or similar innovations, in different organizations will be different. For example, consider two firms, organizations A and B, each introducing a product that represents a radical departure from past practices—that is, it is equally new to both in all respects. However, organization A has always made only one product, whereas organization B has introduced so many new products that it has established set routines for innovation. What must each firm do to introduce the new product successfully?

If we were to observe success at A, we would probably conclude that it depended on entrepreneurial activity. We would see success stemming from individuals who were creative, took risks, and fought standard operating procedures (SOPs). In contrast, B might be successful because members followed SOPs established to promote innovation. In short, what constitutes innovation and what it takes to implement successfully are relative to the particular characteristics of the organization doing the innovating.

In view of the relativity of the concept, it is not surprising that theoretical development is not very advanced. Most writers agree that knowledge and theoretical understanding of innovation are rudimentary (Downs and Mohr, 1976; Ettlie, Bridges, and O'Keefe, 1984). Downs (1978) went so far as to label the concept of innovation a very dangerous reification. At this point, it is safe to say that no coherent theoretical or conceptual framework exists. Consequently, we found the need to create a new conceptual framework for this book that was based on previous work on the implementation of innovation and organizational change, fitting research from different perspectives into our framework.

Defining Innovation

Although there is a lack of agreement about what innovation is, two definitions are common. According to one definition, innovation is the first or a very early use of an idea by any organization (Becker and Whisler, 1967, p. 463). The second definition is more frequently used in research on organizational innovation. It views innovation as the first use of an idea *within* an organization (Aiken and Hage, 1979), whether or not the idea has been adopted by other organizations already.

In this book, we used the second and more encompassing definition. Innovation refers to a technology, product, or service being used for the first time by members of an organization, whether or not other organizations have used it previously. There are some problems with this choice. Defining innovation in terms of newness to the organization mixes the special case of the first or very early user with a far larger group of later users. Certainly the experience of being the first and only operator of a complex process is very different from that of being even the second user, because the second user can benefit from observations of the first. For example, the organizations we describe in this book were introducing a product that had been offered for some time elsewhere in the country. Consequently, their managers avoided many pitfalls by learning vicariously from the experiences of these earlier innovators. Equally important, the first user may have helped to educate suppliers and potential customers—and thereby provided a new and perhaps more facilitative environment for second adopters. For example, vendors of computer software may have a much better understanding of users' requirements for later innovations than they did in working with the first user; they and the first user learned much as they worked together. If we were to restrict our inquiry to first or very early users only, though, we would exclude the vast majority of organizations shaping and developing path-breaking technologies, products, and services. The difference between first and later adopters is more sharply defined during the design of an innovation; when it comes to implementing innovation, the idea is still very new to late adopters and implementation creates many of the same challenges for late users as it does for the first adopter.

Once an innovation is designed, an organization can do many different kinds of things to implement it. Relatively little research has been done on implementation (Kimberly, 1981), and most of what we do know is based on individual case studies (Eveland, 1981). Since collectively these involve so many different types of projects, undertaken at different times and under very different environmental conditions, they provide only preliminary understanding. The idea that implementation is "an important phenomenon (not merely noise, error variance, endogenous irrelevance, or individual perversity) has been slow to be incorporated into models of innovation" (Tornatzky et al. 1983, p. 134). As a result, important components of the process, such as interpersonal influence, have been neglected (Aiken, Bacharach, and French, 1980). This is unfortunate because implementation activities have much more to do with the innovation's success than do design activities, yet so little is known about them (Tornatzky and Solomon, 1982). The focus on the design stage of innovation has resulted not only in a lack of attention to implementation, but an overemphasis on the objective properties of adopting units, such as their size and structural complexity. The study of successful implementation requires an investigation of processes as well as structure.

Defining Successful Implementation

Most previous research has given inadequate attention to what constitutes *successful* implementation. People have generally been concerned with whether the new idea has been installed and institutionalized (for example, Tornatzky, Fergus, Avellar, and Fairweather, 1980; Neal and Radnor, 1973; Yin, 1979). It has been rare to consider things as basic as the quality of the installation or institutionalization.

Part of the problem in defining standards of successful implementation is that the standards are so intimately bound with the organization's goals for the innovative idea that organizations will measure themselves by very different yardsticks. An appropriate standard of success for one organization is necessarily different than it is for another. For example, in one study, Radnor and Neal (1973) used project backlog as a measure of implementation success. As will be seen, backlog for the organizations in our investigation was a clear indication of poor implementation.

Our pilot work and knowledge of organization change led us to conceive successful implementation in broad terms. We wanted to look at such factors as how customers or users judged the new product once it was in place, as Radnor and Neal had done. We expected those judgments to be tied to the design, but also to tell us how well the new idea was implemented. We also wanted to know if the innovative idea accomplished what managers had hoped for when they adopted the innovation. Did it increase profits or market share? Did it change the image of the firm? Did it maintain the firm's existing position by preventing losses? What were the long-term consequences of the implementation for the organization and its members? Also important was what the implementation process did to employees—the level of stress from confusion, overtime, and conflict; the amount of excitement and challenge; and the level of motivation and new learning. Finally, we wanted to know how much, at least in general terms, it cost to implement. Even though these seem to be obvious criteria of successful implementation, they are not found in most existing research. To us, they seem necessary for extending understanding about how to implement effectively.

Effects of Design on Implementation

Understanding implementation requires understanding the whole process of innovation, from conception or selection of the idea through institutionalization. In addition, the specific characteristics of the innovative idea are important for implementation. The nature of the new product or service has a profound effect on the implementation process. Differences in the complexity and newness of the product or service will require differences in implementation processes.

Much has been written about the processes of designing and adopting innovative ideas. We have chosen to discuss only the small portion of those writings that seemed particularly relevant to the process of implementation, beginning with a general discussion of the stages of innovation in order to develop the rationale for looking at the design stage first.

Stages of Innovation

There have been numerous attempts to classify the stages of innovation. Although most models have several stages, almost all of them distinguish between two main stages. The first, design, consists of a series of early events in which members of the organization create, search, evaluate, and decide about the innovation; the later phase, implementation, consists of steps taken to introduce innovation (Normann, 1971; Hage and Aiken, 1970; Zaltman, Duncan, and Holbek, 1973; Utterback, [cited in Rosenbloom, 1978]; Pelz and Munson, 1980).

We adopted the approach of Pelz and Munson (1980, pp. 4–5) because it links the stages systematically to particular types of innovation and because our pilot work suggested their model fits well with the particular innovation we studied. The following are their four stages:

Diagnosis is the translation of a sense of unease or an aspiration into a problem so that action toward solving it may be undertaken.

Design is the development, adoption, or borrowing of an innovating solution.

Implementation is the "payoff" stage of the innovating process; the innovation is put in place, and the process of embedding it in the organization becomes the central activity.

Stabilization is the period in which the innovation proves itself either a success that becomes the status quo or a practice that disappears in some shift of organization priorities.

Although Rogers (1983) reported that organizations often go through such stages in order, because many uncertainties cannot be resolved before an innovation has become operative, there is a recycling process among the four stages (Nelson and Winter, 1977). Many decisions made during the design stage need to be modified. Thus, the stages are not discrete. Rather than thinking of these "redecisions" as moving an implementing organization back into the design phase, we suggest that it is more reasonable to consider them as part of implementation. A key element for effective implementation may well be the organization's ability to be flexible, not only with respect to well-established routines, but with respect to very recent decisions made for the particular innovation. In short, we consider this behavior as part of implementation, although we recognize that at any point in the process the organization may decide to stop innovating.

Levels of Development

A second important characteristic of an innovation is how well developed it is when the organization tries to introduce it. Technologies, processes, and products differ with respect to how widely used and how well understood they are at the time they are adopted. This is a major reason for the distinction we made earlier between first and later adopters. Pelz and Munson (1980) captured this distinction by postulating three levels of development of an innovation. First, initiation refers to an innovation where "no solution to a problem is known to exist elsewhere." Adaption refers to cases "when a few prototype solutions exist, but are not well packaged." Third, borrowing applies to cases where "many well-packaged innovations exist; the organization copies one and applies it with little modification." (p.3).

When the Pelz and Munson stages are put into a table with their levels of development (as shown in figure 1–1), twelve conceptually distinct conditions emerge. Of course, a recycling process occurs here as well; during innovation the various stages are apt to be overlapping in time, with the organization attending to the various stages simultaneously.

Our study focused primarily on cell 11 of figure 1–1—implementation of a well-developed product. Because our organizations were late adopters, they had ample opportunity to observe what other organizations had done to design and implement NOW accounts. Thus, much of what the banks and savings and loans (S & Ls) we studied did is best described as borrowing: taking existing ideas, technology, and assumptions and introducing them into their organizations. However, some of them did attempt to so some things that had not been done before and many of them modified the innovations they borrowed considerably. Therefore, to some degree, they are both adapters and borrowers.

This mixture of borrowing and adapting means that, despite its usefulness, the Pelz and Munson framework did not allow us to locate the level of development of this inovation precisely, because we found that not all organizations adapt or borrow in the same way. An important finding of this study is that no firm had a NOW account exactly like another firm's, even though the NOW account was a fairly straightforward and well-packaged innovation. However, many were very similar. Moreover, it is possible to borrow at one stage and adapt at the next (or vice versa). For example, an organization may do exactly what another firm has done to get the innovation going; but when it comes time to tie the innovation in with other features of the organization, it may modify what it has borrowed substantially. Not only did we find such mixtures, but we also saw that there were variations *within* stages. For example, in the design stage, an organization might need to develop its own computer software and simultaneously borrow general notions about the product (pricing, for example) from others.

Level of Innovating Process	Stage of Innovating			
	I. Diagnosis	II. Design	III. Implementation	IV. Stabilization
A. Initiation	1	2	3	4
B. Adaptation	5	6	7	8
C. Borrowing	9	10	11	12

Source: Adapted from Munson and Pelz, 1979.

Figure 1–1. Intersection of Stages and Levels of Innovation

Characteristics of the Innovative Idea

A number of characteristics of an innovative idea may have important effects on the implementation process. These include how radical the innovation is, whether it is administrative or technical, and whether it is part of the major tasks of the organization or peripheral to those tasks. These characteristics are determined during the design stage.

Routine versus Radical Innovation. Routine innovation is the introduction of something that while new to the organization is very similar to something the organization has done before. A radical innovation, in addition to being new to the organization, is very different from what the organization has done previously, and is therfore apt to require significant changes in the behavior of employees and often the stucture of the organization itself.

It is widely believed that the requirements for successful routine and successful radical innovation are not the same. The more radical the innovation, the greater the disruption of the status quo and, other things being equal, the more changes there will be in information, values, incentives, power, and other elements. This distinction is central to our research and we will examine it in depth.

A major purpose of the present study was to compare the dynamics of implementing these two types of innovation. In essence we asked: Are different stuctures and processess needed for radical versus routine innovation? If so, what are the differences? Previous research has provided a guide to this inquiry.

Normann's (1971) comparison of the requirements for routine innovations (what he called "variations") and radical innovations (what he called "reorientations") in product development has been extremely influential. According to Normann, variations involve only minor changes in the task system which can be accommodated without major adjustments within the existing political system. They can be handled with few changes in the cognitive orientations of organizational members. In contrast, reorientations involve basic changes in the task system; they necessitate new types of knowledge and new specialists. As a correlate, new values, goals, power structures, and cognitive systems (such as attention, decision, and interpretation rules) are needed. Normann suggested that reorientations introduce more uncertainty and therefore require more organizational change, more entrepreneurship, and greater involvement of top management than variations do.

In the recent literature, variations are most commonly called "routine innovations" and reorientations are termed "radical innovations." As defined by Zaltman et al. (1973), the more an innovation differs from existing alternatives, the more it is said to be radical. The closer the innovation is to what the organization has done or experienced before, the more it is said to be routine. This particular characteristic of innovations is a key factor in influencing the way the organization implements. The more radical an innovation, the more learning and unlearning must take place, and therefore the more modificatioins must be made in exisiting structures and processes. In short, the degree of radicalness is likely to have a major impact on what organizations must do to implement successfully.

Technical versus Administrative. Innovations also differ with respect to what parts of an organization they affect most directly and intensely. This distinction has been conceptualized by Daft (1978) as the contrast between technical and adminstrative innovations. Technical innovations tend to originate in the technical core and include ideas for a new product, process, or service. Administrative innovations, on the other hand, originate in the organization's administration and pertain to specific policies of recruitment, resource allocation, and the structuring of tasks, authority, and rewards. Based on this distinction, Daft proposed a dual-core conceptualization and suggested that different principles might apply to innovations in the different cores. Most importantly, innovations in the technical core are apt to be enhanced by low formalization, by decentralization and by a distribution of power that allow the professional employees to handle the innovation. Consequently, they are best handled by loose coupling of the technical and adminstrative cores. On the other hand, administrative innovations are best served by high formalization, centralization, and rather tight structures. Of course, administrative innovations often affect the technical core as well; therefore, tight coupling of the two is required.

As we began our research, it seemed clear that the introduction of NOW accounts was clearly a technical innovation. However, as we observed what actually happened, we found an overlap between the two kinds of innovation. Particularly for radical innovations, as we will see, implementation of the technical innovation of NOW accounts requried many administrative innovations.

Central versus Peripheral. To date, most studies of implementation have examined secondary concerns of the units involved rather than the central or primary tasks. For example, research on implementation by Beyer and Trice (1978) and Marino (1982) centered on the adoption of personnel policies by line units. Not only are such innovations administrative, but they deal with matters that have secondary importance to the major work of the line units. Similarly, the operations research/management science studies (for example, Radnor and Neal, 1973) appeared to involve specific and limited projects with individual units; they did not appear to have a central impact on the whole organization or a critical impact on the work units.

In contrast, the research reported in this book focuses on a central innovation, one that is integrally related to major tasks a unit exists to perform. It deals with an innovation that took place in a central function. Central innovations differ from more peripheral ones because they affect the major day-to-day work of the organization and involve activities critical to the performance of almost all concerned. They are apt to be viewed as extremely important to everyone; and because they affect the well-being of the entire firm, their consequences are perceived as more significant than peripheral innovations initiated in staff units.

The motives and orientations of employees implementing central innovations are likely to be quite different from those implementing peripheral innovations. If a peripheral innovation fails, different units can defend themselves by showing someone else is at fault. For example, the staff department can blame the line operators for resisting change and line operators can blame the staff for not understanding the business. The benefits of successful peripheral innovations are less likely to be experienced commonly than in the central case. In contrast, in a central innovation, the assignment of blame serves no one especially well. In social psychological terms, superordinate goals may emerge more readily and any consequences may be more evenly shared. The "we–they" orientation Sapolsky (1967) found in an organization attempting to diffuse an innovation throughout different units is less likely when the innovation is central, because an innovation that affects the whole organization pulls everyone together as a group through a joint reward system.

In sum, these are the characteristics of the innovative idea and the design process that affect implementation. These characteristics interact with the another set of characteristics—those of the organization doing the implementing. We turn now to an examination of the factors that directly affect implementation.

Effects of the Organization on Implementation

Organizations can vary in so many ways that a myriad of organizational characteristics could potentially affect implementation. Our data led us to focus on only a limited number of those, because they were the characteristics most important to the banks and savings and loan associations we studied. A number of aspects of the organization as a whole were critical. Structure, history, strategy, size, culture, the ability of an organization to learn, and the nature of a firm's relationships with its environment were especially important. Of these, structure has been studied most systematically. We treat it separately first then review the other factors in less detail.

Organization Structure and Implementation

The relationship between implementation and organization has received considerable attention, if not considerable research, at least since Burns and Stalker published *The Management of Innovation* in 1961. We also found it to be a significant factor in explaining implementation, especially when structural explanations are supplemented with the patterned processes that make up the structure. Given its centrality both for us and previous researchers, we examine it in some depth.

Organic and Mechanistic Structures. Burns and Stalker's most lasting contribution to knowledge about innovation was their distinction between organic and mechanistic organizations. These concepts have proven to be so useful that they are used almost reflexively to classify organizations. The result has been that the terms have come to take on a simplified meaning for many who use them—mechanistic organizations are bureaucratic; organic organizations are flexible, with open, cross-functional communication that facilitates mutual adjustment. For many purposes, this simple distinction is adequate. However, when the concepts are analyzed in more depth, problems with thinking of them in such a simplistic fashion emerge.

Burns and Stalker's analysis was more fine grained. They viewed mechanistic organizations as classic bureaucracies. In these organizations, work tends to be divided into many subtasks; individuals who perform the subtasks are unlikely to see the relevance of their work for the whole task. Moreover, the duties and powers of each person's role are defined in very precise terms. Hierarchical relationships are stressed—communication lines are vertical and people's work is controlled by decisions and directives of their superiors. In many ways, these systems are exactly what the classical writers advocated—human actions planned and directed with the predictability of an efficient machine.

Organic systems are different on every one of these dimensions. Although organic structures are hierarchical, hierarchy plays a less important role in direction and control. Moreover, top-level managers are not assumed to be omniscient; and formal definitions of approaches, duties, and power are less important in defining what people do than are ongoing interactions among individuals working on a task. The accepted communication patterns are continually redefined as work proceeds; lateral communication and consultation across levels are typical. All employees are committed to the organization as a whole rather than their functional specialities, and they put energy into solving problems for the organization rather than defending their own turf and their own status. Burns and Stalker concluded that these systems can innovate more easily than mechanistic ones, primarily because individual members have less parochial interests and are less concerned with protecting their status.

Overall, mechanistic and organic systems represent two quite different ways of getting things done in organizations. Burns and Stalker suggested that these differences could be analyzed by using one concept, which they called the code of conduct. The code defined what individuals would perceive as "feasible, acceptable, worth taking into account" (p.10). As they used the term, the code of conduct was synonymous with the organization, defining the essence of the organization's culture.

In explicating the organic form, Burns and Stalker *legitimated* a new type of organization. Although they stated explicitly that this form was superior for change and not for stability, students of modern organizations have often championed the organic form, arguing that change characterizes almost all organizations today. Therefore, to be effective now and in the future, organizations need to be more organic than most currently are. However, the organic form is appealing for other reasons than its effectiveness for implementing innovation. The characteristics of organic structure are so consistent with the values of democracy and humanistic psychology that the term *organic* takes on considerable surplus meaning which may have contributed both to a failure to scrutinize the construct fully and perhaps to overestimate its merits. Although Burns and Stalker cannot be blamed for any misuse of their term, we believe that part of the problem does stem from a deficiency in their work that contributes to difficulties in using the concepts precisely.

Burns and Stalker asserted that mechanistic/organic structures represent poles of a continuum. However, a closer look at their work, particularly their description of organic structures, suggests that they have not defined the extreme poles of the continuum, that more extreme organizational structures can and do exist. For example, when discussing organic firms, they noted that even though they are not hierarchic in the way mechanistic systems are, they are stratified (p. 22). Logically, a system composed only of equals is the relevant extreme. At this point, proposing this logical extreme may seem to be merely academic hairsplitting. However, its importance will become more obvious later when we see that one of the large organizations in our study had less concentrated power than that described by the organic structure, and in fact, this dispersion interfered with its ability to design and implement the innovation. On the other end of the continuum, power can certainly be more closely and personally held than it is in the mechanistic structure in which certain amounts of power are delegated to each "office" or position in the organization. Similar issues could be raised about other dimensions in their framework. Burns and Stalker did not describe logically extreme forms, although they and their followers have proceeded as if they had.

Another problem is that there is no logical or empirical reason for any combination of the dimensions of the two forms to occur together. It is certainly possible for organizations to be both decentralized and committed to functional specialties; or to be both centralized and have undefined roles and communication lines. Such possibilities suggest the Burns and Stalker framework is often used in ways that obscure the complexities and dynamics of the events it purports to explain. Such oversimplification may have had significant negative effects on current understanding of how innovation is implemented; so much of the relevant work on implementation has used Burns and Stalker as the foundation in ways that lead us to focus on a simple dichotomy of structures. In this book we use the concepts of organic and mechanistic as Burns and Stalker did in order to be consistent with other work on implementation. However, as will be seen, the ambiguities noted above will cause some difficulty in treating our results. We attempt to rectify these problems in our conceptual chapters following the cases.

Although there is some controversy, a large body of literature supports the conclusions of Burns and Stalker (1961) and Hage and Aiken (1967) that organic structures are needed during the design stage of innovation. For example, Gerwin (1981) observed that organic structures are superior during design because they stimulate proposals, new sources of information, and insights. Shepard (1967), Sapolsky (1967), and Normann (1971) all provided additional support for this view. Zaltman et al. (1973) argued that design stages involve high degress of complexity and therefore require low formalization and low centralization to perform the gathering and processing of information which is crucial at this stage. In contrast, they asserted that implementation is advanced by the absence of conflict and ambiguity. Consequently, high levels of formalization and centralization and low complexity are best for implementation and stabilization. Duncan (1976) captured the essence of this view by asserting that organizations need to be *ambidextrous* if they are to innovate successfully. "[T]he organization has to shift its structure as it moves through the various stages of innovation" (p. 179). It must be relatively organic during design and relatively mechanistic for implementation. Rogers (1983) went so far as to conclude that the basic reason that correlations between organization structure and innovativeness are low is the failure to recognize the need postulated by Zaltman et al. for different structures at different stages. Because this view has such acceptance in the innovation literature, we will consider the evidence for it at some length at a later point.

While there is support for the view that organic structures facilitate the design of innovation, there are also some conflicting views (Baldridge and Burnham, 1975; Corwin, 1972; Radnor and Neal, 1973; Evan and Black, 1967; Ettlie et al., 1984; and Marino, 1982). Marino observed that the conflict appears to be explained by variations in the importance of the initiation stage. Organic structures tend to be less important when only adoption and implementation are required than when the design process requires the generation of new ideas and proposals. While Marino's own findings are consistent with this resolution, Aiken et al.'s (1980) finding that organic structures did *not* generate more proposals is inconsistent with Marino's thesis.

Overall, while the literature does suggest it is reasonable to expect that organic structures will be useful in the design phases, there are some significant exceptions. In particular, organic structures may not be important for highly developed innovations. Even more serious challenges to the ambidextrous view appear in the limited amount of research that exists on the implementation stage.

Opinions about the best structure during the implementation stage are more polarized. Those who work out of the organizational change tradition assume that organic structures, including participative processes and free-flowing communication, are the most conducive to implementation. Those working out of the innovation research tradition assume that mechanistic structures are best for effective implementation.

A major reason for the emphasis on relatively organic processes in the change literature may have been the dominant concern with motivating individuals to change. Such motivation is often produced by activites that reduce resistance by identifying dissatisfaction and bringing it to the surface, and that build ownership, provide appropriate rewards, and help "unfreeze" or disengage people from the present state. Participation is often a useful tool to accomplish such motivational objectives (Nadler, 1983).

Whereas the change literature, because of its focus on motivation, may have overemphasized the organic requirements for implementing change, the innovation literature may have overemphasized the mechanistic aspects. For example, Duncan's (1976) argument that mechanistic structures will be best able to implement change centers on issues other than motivation. Low complexity is helpful because it reduces the chances of conflict. Formalization is useful because "singleness of purpose is required" (p. 175). Rules and procedures reduce ambiguity, provide clear guidance, and reduce potential conflict. Duncan also argued that, while the research was less clear, centralization also is apt to aid implementation because it provides a specific line of authority and responsiblity that helps to reduce role conflict and ambiguity and to increase the organization's ability to influence individuals with differing priorities.

Simple Structures. While organic and mechanistic structures have been the focus of attention in the study of innovation, there are other ways of conceptualizing structures that are potentially fruitful. Simple structures as defined by Mintzberg (1979) tend to be small and relatively undifferentiated.

When a simple structure characterizes a whole organization—not just an operating unit—the organization is usually young, small, and technically unsophisticated. Power and decision making are concentrated in the hands of the very top managers, who process all the important information; because the tasks are often simple and the organization is small, the top managers can control and coordinate the efforts of the lower-level participants. Mintzberg calls this type of coordination "direct supervision." Simple structures lack formally developed procedures and announced specialties. They are extremely flexible because the power, expertise, and communication flows are centered in one place. Of course, since decisions are typically made where power, information, and expertise meet, decision making in these organizations is highly centralized.

Clearly, simple structures should make it easier to implement an innovation. They require less communication, less coordination, and less influence to gather the necessary support. Since they are usually small organizations, though, the way they behave would not seem to be very instructive for larger organizations that attempt innovation. On the other hand, Mintzberg points out that simple structures may characterize units of larger organizations, so a simple—perhaps temporary—structure within a more complex structure may hold the key to successful implementation of change.

Parallel Structures. This bifurcation of structures is similar to the concept of parallel structures (Kanter, 1983; Stein and Kanter, 1980). Stein and Kanter suggest that a formally sanctioned but temporary organization—the parallel organization—existing side by side with the more permanent formal organization can aid implementation of innovation. Parallel structures are formed by taking people from the host organization, assigning them an innovative task, and then reintroducing them into the host unit after they complete the task. (Often the task is to design a procedure to be implemented in the host organization.) The structures are parallel in the sense that they coexist in the same organization with the traditional structure but are separate from it. The informal organization is temporary and it is characterized by decentralization of power, freedom from the normal written rules and procedures of the formal organization, and simplicity. These characteristics allow the organization to create a change without becoming overwhelmed by the pressures of the formal organization to maintain the status quo. They allow the flexibility needed for innovation without costly disruption of existing routines. Kanter's model assumes a mechanistic organization that adopts a temporary and informal organic structure when it needs to innovate. Two elements are important to the operations of parallel structures. One is appointing a steering committee to link the two units. The second is

buffering participants in the new structure from established routines. In fact, the success of the parallel organization is reduced by competing responsibilities faced by all participants. Like Duncan, (1976) Kanter argues that a more mechanistic structure is desirable at the implementation stage, though in our view her own data do not clearly support that assertion.

In sum, most of the work done to date suggests that different structures within the same organization are desirable for making change happen. The arguments are of three types: different structures at different stages of the innovation, different structures existing simultaneously, or both. However, the approaches we have considered so far tend to characterize organizations in fairly coarse ways. A more fine-grained perspective that considers specific characteristics of structures will further clarify the issues.

Structural Characteristics Associated with Implementation

Structures differ from each other on a number of dimensions. Where an organization stands on these dimensions has major implications for almost everything it does, including implementation. What may be particularly interesting is the configuration or patterns these dimensions form in given organizations. These characteristics may not always co-occur to make up the prototypical organic, simple, or parallel structure theorists envision, making it important to examine all of them as separate constructs.

Centralization. Centralization seems to describe an important fact of organizational life, but it is a difficult concept to describe and use. Our definition of centralization, borrowed from Mintzberg (1979), is the degree of concentration of power and decision making, regardless of where in the hierarchy the concentration occurs. This definition differs from the more common one of centralization as the concentration of power at the top of the formal hierarchy. Of course, organizations where power is centralized at the top will not be the same as those where power is concentrated elsewhere. In the latter case, we still speak of centralization because the decision is made by one or a very small number of persons. However, because this power is apt to have been delegated or at least can be constrained by actions of those higher in the organization, we refer to this as constrained centralization.

Zaltman, Duncan, and Holbek (1973) defined centralization using two dimensions: the locus of authority and how decisions are made. First, the higher in the hierarchy the decisions are made, the greater the centralization. Second, the less the participation in decision making, the greater the centralization. Based on this definition, they concluded that research provided evidence that centralization was associated with more successful implementation. In support of this conclusion, they used Wilson's (1966) conceptual argument that diversity makes it difficult for the organization to influence participants. Moreover, building on the work of Corwin (1969) and Gamson (1966), they indicated that decentralization increases the opportunity for different groups to express disagreement. They did, however, acknowledge Corwin's observation that participation might increase the expression of conflict and could facilitate change under some conditions.

In our view, this reasoning provided equivocal support for the view that centralization is conducive to implementation, particularly if centralization implies concentration of authority at high levels. For one thing, as Zaltman et al. (1973) realized, Corwin's (1969) position on the role of conflict in aiding change can easily be seen as an argument that decentralization can aid implementation. Moreover, if one assumes that implementation may require recycling through the design stages (as we suggested is often the case), disagreement and diversity may continue to be needed. In addition, to the degree that implementation per se requires attention to issues of motivation and meshing new ways with old routines, ongoing mutual adjustment will be needed. Decisions made close to the areas where the adjustments must occur will often be more rapid and effective.

Two studies have reported evidence that certain elements usually present in decentralized structures do indeed aid implementation. In a study of twenty-nine innovative educational projects, Greenwood, Mann, and Mc-Laughlin (1975) defined successful implementation in terms of perceived success, change in behavior, and fidelity of implementation. They observed that the projects implemented most successfully were those "that fostered mutual adaptation and permitted it to take place" (p. 65). They included: frequent meetings of project personnel, training, local development of project materials, intangible professional or psychological incentives, a sufficiently large group to provide mutual support and sharing of ideas, a flexible administrative approach, and open channels of communication. Many of these features are more likely to be present in decentralized than centralized structures.

Results from one of the best conducted studies in the field directly contradicted the predictions of Zaltman et al. (1973). Beyer and Trice (1978) studied the implementation of two personnel policies—EEO and alcoholism policies in installations of the federal government. They found that decentralization was associated with successful change efforts; formalization and centralization appeared to inhibit implementation as measured by supervisors' use of and receptivity to the policies.

Clearly, the available evidence on the relationship between centralization and implementation effectiveness is extremely sparse. The research that has been done is too limited to make broad generalizations, but particularly if all the research on the introduction of change is included, it appears to lean slightly toward a conclusion that implementation is best accomplished in a decentralized structure.

Differentiation and Integration. Of the particular characteristics of structure, differentiation and integration have received the most attention in the study of designing and implementing innovation. Lawrence and Lorsch (1967a, 1967b) laid the foundation by examining the relationship between an organization's ability to adapt to change in the environment and the degree of its internal differentiation and integration. Differentiation was defined as "the state of segmentation of the organizational system into subsystems, each of which tends to develop particular attributes in relation to the requirements posed by its relevant external environment" (1967a, p. 3–4). Integration was defined as "the process of achieving unity of effort among the various subsystems in the accomplishment of the organization's task" (1967, p. 4).

Lawrence and Lorsch's research resulted in a contingency theory: In stable environments, less differentiated structures are appropriate; in more dynamic environments, more differentiated structures are appropriate. In effect, those organizations that have to innovate to survive in their environments require more differentiation to gather the external information they need to define the best innovations for them. In addition, high levels of integration are needed in all organizations. This fact creates a problem for the more highly differentiated firms because, given their diversity, they are harder to integrate. More resources must be devoted to achieve the integration to pull the organization together to implement the innovation. One of the ways to achieve integration in a highly differentiated organization is to use the structures and processes of the organic organization, though there are other ways.

Much of the research that has examined the relationship between innovation and structure has focused on complexity, which in our view is another term for differentiation. Zaltman et al. (1973) suggested that high complexity has a negative impact on implementation. A major source of their empirical support was Sapolsky's (1967) study of innovation efforts in department stores. Sapolsky concluded that structural arrangements that induced managers to attempt to persuade rather than exercise their authority to order adoption were responsible for the failure of these organizations to implement innovation proposals. It is important to note that Sapolsky's data came from extremely decentralized organizations with limited integrating mechanisms. In his words, "Each merchandise department . . . is run almost as if it were an independent business" (p. 501). Further, Sapolsky speculated that managers in one department saw what had happened to managers in another department and became more resistant to the change, and as Beyer and Trice (1978) pointed out, it is not clear that top management ever intended to implement the ideas. In essence, Sapolsky's findings tell little about the influence of the structure of individual departments on implementation; he attributed the problems to the nature of the relationships between units. Zaltman et al. (1973) used these results to show that structures low in complexity and therefore mechanistic were needed for implementation. We suggest that such a conclusion is questionable. To us, Sapolsky's findings do show that integration was a problem but are silent as to what type of structure would have been best. It seems just as logical to argue that a common commitment and high levels of mutual adjustment—that is, organic structures—between the units would have provided adequate integration.

In addition to Sapolsky's work, Zaltman et al. (1973) drew on rather equivocal findings from Hage and Aiken (1967). Also, they cited Carrroll's (1967) study of innovation in medical schools, which found that whereas diversity was better for generating proposals, it was low centralization, not complexity, that was associated with a failure to implement. From these studies they concluded: "at the *implementation* stage high complexity [differentiation], because of potential conflicts, makes it more difficult for the organization to actually implement the innovation" (p. 137). In our view, the evidence provides almost no support for this position. Furthermore, when complexity is considered using the Lawrence and Lorsch framework, it is clear that complexity per se is not the issue, but rather whether the organization has ways of integrating the complexity.

Formalization. Following Shepard's (1967) position, Zaltman et al. (1973) argued that formalization was a third feature of mechanistic organizations that aids implementation. Their primary support for this proposition consisted of unpublished papers by Radnor and Neal—later published as Radnor and Neal (1973) and Neal and Radnor (1973)—on the introduction of operations research/management science (OR/MS) acitivities. Neal and Radnor (1973) found a strong positive correlation between establishing policy and procedural guidelines and the success of the OR/MS group. (Success was defined as the OR/MS group's own perceptions of how well they and their projects were accepted by others in the organization.) In another paper, Radnor and Neal (1973) found that the greater the orientation of the OR/MS managers to the whole organization, the more liaison activities, meetings, and reports employed by the organization. Although Neal and Radnor's findings did not emphasize formal communications only, Zaltman et al. (1973) concluded from this evidence that formalized procedures provide both information and the specific techniques that organizational personnel need to utilize the innovation. They argued: "The lack of these more formalized procedures at the implementation stage is likely to lead to both role conflict and role ambiguity" (pp. 140–41).

To us Radnor and Neal's published results show a more complex pattern than Zaltman et al. (1973) presented. First, Radnor and Neal (1973) reported that older, well established OR/MS groups tended to be moving toward less formalization. They suggested that as OR/MS practitioners developed understandings and friendships, more informal activities and fewer mechanical procedures were used, with no apparent decline in effectiveness. In addition, there were other factors beside formalization that influenced implementation. For example, in a paper based on the same survey, Neal and Radnor (1973) indicated that some of the structural changes over time may have been associated with changes in the nature of the projects. The older groups might have been doing different types of tasks: perhaps skimming over projects certain to succeed; alternatively, buoyed by their past successes, undertaking far less certain projects. Thus, the evidence provided by Radnor and Neal does not show a consistent pattern of a positive relationship between fomalization and success. In fact, even if such a pattern was found, it could very easily have been due to unknown changes in the nature of the work involved.

The final bit of evidence Zaltman et al. (1973) provided for the importance of formalization at the implementation stage stemmed from the findings of Gross, Giacquinta, and Bernstein (1971). Their research on educational innovation revealed that role ambiguity, (resulting from teachers not being clear about what was required to carry out an innovation) and role conflict (which resulted when teachers faced requirements contrary to the requirements of the innovation) caused poor implementation. Obviously, formalization is one way role ambiguity can be reduced. However, in the Gross et al. study, one of the problems was that teachers did not get the necessary materials, because the director did not have authority to spend the money to obtain them. It was not the absence of formalization but inappropriate bureaucratic process that got in the way of implementation. Moreover, in their conclusions, Gross et al. stressed the issue of incompatibility between the existing arrangements and the innovation. Although more attention to formalized relationships might have helped to reduce the incompatibility, it is not clear that more formalization was the only or necessarily the best way to do this.

As with centralization and complexity, additional evidence on the relationship of formalization to implementation provides little resolution. Some of the evidence does suggest that formalization improves implementation. In a study of school systems, Baldridge and Burnham (1975) found that larger, more complex districts had an advantage in implementing because they had staff, specialized resources, and other support available; and because they had career lines that gave administrators incentives to innovate. Evan and Black (1967) reported that successful proposals (those that had been implemented or were *on the verge of being implemented*) had more formalized rules and centralized decision making. Since their measure of success included innovations that had not even been implemented, though, it is questionable whether it is a useful indicator of successful implementation. In a study of the introduction of affirmative action, Marino (1982) found that formalization was positively associated with compliance, but he cautioned that the nature of affirmative action may lend itself to a control strategy based on formalization. What is clear from the evidence available is that clarity of tasks and relationships is important for implementing change. There are likely to be a number of ways to do this, and the findings of our research will bear this out. Formalization is one way of establishing that clarity, but it is not the only way.

Structural Requirements for Radical and Routine Innovation

Just as there is an argument that different structures are appropriate at different stages of innovation, there is also an argument that different structures are appropriate for radical and routine innovation. One point of view is that radical innovation requires an organization to be even more ambidextrous than does routine innovation (Duncan, 1976), requiring even more organic properties during the design stage.

A second perspective, more extreme but consistent with Duncan's, is that few organizations can perform radical innovation without, in essence, forming a new organization. Hage (1980) argues that organic structures can only innovate incrementally, because power during the implementation stage is shared. In such systems change is slow—the successful innovator must, via recruitment, change the balance of power within the dominant coalition. While a number of small moves, over time, may add up to substantial change, innovators in organic systems may become fatigued and discouraged by the struggle. Thus, although organic structures are apt to have higher rates of innovation, they are also more likely to follow incrementalist strategies—and incrementalist strategies do not produce radical change.

On the other hand, mechanistic organizations, according to Hage, may be a fertile ground for revolutionary change. For one thing, only a relatively few specialists are involved in planning and development; an individual is likely to have the substantial power needed to revise the structure. Moreover, mechanistic organizations are prone to crises, and crises may be necessary to motivate sweeping changes. Hage concluded, however, that radical innovation is not probable in mechanistic systems either, because the authoritarian approach produces great resistance, preventing the necessary cooperation. In other words, neither organic nor mechanistic structures are ideal for producing radical innovation in an established organization.

Consequently, support for radical innovation requires the creation of a new unit "in which new personnel are recruited and which has its own source of resources and enough time to work through the implementation stage" (Hage, 1980, p. 244). The new units need to be distant from the organization, allowing them to recruit new personnel on the basis of commitment to the innovation. Resistance and vested interests can be bypassed. These new units are organic structures composed of a "dedicated bank of true believers who can work out the mechanics of the technology without having to make concessions to existing staff with more traditional conceptions" (p. 245). Quasi-charismatic leadership to inspire others is also important. In sum, Hage is proposing organic structures for both the design and implementation of a radical innovation, but the organic structure is of a special type. It is a powerful, resource-rich parallel organization.

A third and similar perspective uses parallel structures. A comparison of two companies—General Electric Medical Systems and Chipco—shows how parallel structures can allow organizations to be ambidextrous (Kanter, 1983). Both companies generated valuable new ideas. However, Med Systems achieved the balance between the low formalization needed for initiation and higher centralizaton required for implementation through a system "in which centralized planning mechanisms ensure sufficient focus for innovations to be developed which can and will be implemented" (p. 172). The balance was aided by: (1) headquarters' ability to provide unified guidance by giving strategic direction and controlling large expenditures, (2) effective short- and long-range planning at the middle levels of management, (3) a clear financial results orientation in evaluating requests for major products, (4) the role played by higher-level managers in exercising their power when needed, and (5) stability and formality at lower levels. In contrast, Chipco lacked these five features and was less able to implement. While there were other major differences between these companies, including their states of development, their cultures, and the degree of difficulty in isolating projects, Kanter's work provides a useful guide to the requirements for radical innovation. Parallel structures combine elements of both organic and mechanistic structures: the flexibility of the organic, plus the clarity of direction and concentration of power of the mechanistic. The combination occurs in a context that buffers the new from the old long enough that the novel, fledgling ideas are not crushed by the established routines.

For the most part, the available literature on the requirements for routine versus radical innovation is quite speculative and lacking support. Although Kanter did provide some supporting evidence, her findings are open to alternative conclusions. Systematic research on the routine–radical dimension is extremely sparse.

To our knowledge, the most systematic effort to study the relationship between the radical–routine dimension and requisite structure was reported by Ettlie et al. (1984). In a study of process and packaging innovation in food processing firms, they found that radical process adoption was most likely to have occurred frequently in organizations that were centralized and had informal structures. For less radical innovations (new product introductions), complex, decentralized structures were most typical. These patterns held up when the impact of size was controlled. Finally, concentrations of technical specialists appeared to support both types of innovations.

The writings on radical and routine innovation are valuable in several respects for our efforts to understand organizational innovation. A useful resolution can be achieved by keeping several thoughts in mind. First, while they support the view that organic structures are necessary to produce the richness of ideas required for radical innovation, they also reveal that such structures need not be decentralized. Some of the literature we have just summarized suggests that centralized structures may be better able to provide the motivation and focus required for designing and implementing radical innovation. The findings by Ettlie et al. that decentralized structures tended to be associated with incremental innovations while centralized structures were associated with radical innovation are particulary noteworthy in this repect. It appears then that successful radical innovation *within* larger organizations may be similar to what Mintzberg (1979) described as simple structures—centralized and organic. Except for the fact that these units are subsystems of larger ones, they appear to have much in common with the organizations developed by the entrepreneurial types of the past.

Second, motivation and focus can certainly be achieved in a variety of ways. Motivation can be achieved by a strong central authority, charismatic leadership, or widespread participation; focus can be created by clear roles and procedures or a common vision and shared mission. Procedures can be clarified either through formalization or through frequent communication through an open network. Likewise, clear roles and common vision can be achieved by both centralized and decentralized structures. In short, there are many paths for creating the conditions for successful implementation.

Third, it is possible that there is a curvilinear relationship between innovation radicalness and the degree of centralization needed. Centralization can clearly have contradictory effects on innovation (Corwin, 1972). On one hand, it can enforce implementation. For example, for extremely radical innovation, the existing system may be incompatible with what is needed; here strong focus and direction from a powerful person or group may be the only way to successfully initiate the process. Somewhat less radical innovations may be able to build very effectively on existing organizational routines using a decentralized decision process which will enhance motivation and reduce resistance. On the other hand, centralization may retard innovation because those who have power concentrated in their hands may resist change while less powerful actors with needed expertise may be unwilling or unable to influence those powerful actors.

Finally, routine innovation may benefit from a more centralized structure because existing routines and resources are quite compatible with the new requirements; all that is needed is to focus them coherently on the new activities. Even here there is disagreement, though. Ettlie et al. (1984) found that decentralization was associated with effective routine innovation. Perhaps some of the conflict among the writers is because they have focused on different levels of radicalness.

Much needs to be learned about the structural requirements for radical innovation and how they differ from those of routine innovation. This section has shown that speculation, including our own, far outweighs available data. The research reported in this book seeks to clarify the dynamics of routine and radical innovation by investigating different organizations introducing the same new product, the NOW account, which was radical for some organizations and routine for others.

Other Organizational Influences on Implementation

As we indicated, of all the dimensions that describe the entire organization, structure has received the most attention in studies of innovation. However, a number of other features are also known to affect the ability of organizations to design and implement innovations. These include an organization's history (distant and recent), strategy, size, culture, ability to learn, and relationships with its environment.

History and Concurrent Events. To some degree all organizations, like all people, are idiosyncratic. Previous experiences have been stored in each organization in a pattern that makes it different from other organizations that on the surface appear to be very similar. Kimberly (1979) used the metaphor of organization biography to describe these differences. Theory and research suggest that many biographical elements have a significant impact on how individual organizations innovate. In reality, these elements blend together; we treat them separately here only to aid exposition.

One way of examining the organization's biography is to consider its history. Many elements of an organization's history will influence all aspects of its current behavior (Greiner, 1972; Mintzberg, 1979). The impact of organizational history on innovation has been treated in case and cross-sectional studies. From case treatments by Burns and Stalker (1961), Gibson (1975), Kanter (1983), and Yin (1979, 1981), it is safe to conclude that what happened in the organization prior to the innovation and the history of any particular innovation mutually affect the results achieved. Moreover, cross-sectional research has demonstrated that experiences of organizations with previous innovation are related to more recent innovation. For example, Hage and Aiken (1979) found a strong positive correlation between past and present adoptions of innovation, although they observed that the reasons for this relationship are complex. In short, history makes a difference, but the dynamics of how and why are not known.

Strategy. Organizational strategy, defined as the organization's major objectives, purposes, goals, and essential policies (Rosenbloom, 1978), is another element that affects the adoption and implementation of innovation. There is good reason to believe that strategy influences almost all critical aspects of an organization (Chandler, 1962; Miles, Snow, Meyer, and Coleman, 1978). In fact, Miles et al. indicate that the nature of the innovation will be a function of a firm's strategy. For example, some firms ("defenders") seldom innovate at all—they prefer to compete in a narrow domain by improving how they do what they have always done. By contrast, other firms ("prospectors") emphasize being early users as a core component of their efforts to compete. Such strategic differences are associated with different structures for approaching innovation (when it is attempted) as well as different degress of experience with and attitudes toward innovation.

Because strategy is a convenient way for summarizing so many of the diverse components of an organization, Rosenbloom (1978) argued that it may be a useful way "to reduce the multitude of apparently relevant factors" that might affect innovation "to a parsimonious few" (p. 223). However, because strategy is itself multidimensional, most empirical efforts to link strategy and innovation have focused on only a small number of the possible aspects.

Even though each study has examined only a small number of the relevant elements, the results have been promising. For example, Hage and Dewar (1973) found that elite values—the preferences about desired organization outcomes held by an inner circle of members—was a strong predictor of innovation. Of course, elite values are not necessarily the same as strategy, but they do seem likely to play a similar role in orienting the behavior of members. In addition, Ettlie (1983) and Ettlie et al. (1984) found that certain elements of firms' strategies—especially their policies about technology—were associated with innovation. Additional support for the possible importance of aspects of policy (such as policies toward innovation, technology, and relationships with external actors such as suppliers) on innovation was provided by Weiss (1983). We too considered only a limited part of the strategies of the firms we studied. When we speak of strategy, we are referring to the particular aspects of the strategy that were relevant for designing and implementing the NOW account. The organization's overall strategy was beyond the scope of this study, although the investigation of the organization's NOW account strategy often revealed much about its general strategy. In fact, in some cases, the NOW account was a major part of a firm's approach to the future. Our focus, though, was simply on NOW account strategy.

Size. Another dimension of organizatons that is thought to influence innovation is size. Of all the variables that might relate to organization innovation, size has been one of the most frequently studied and most frequently found to have some association with innovativeness. Most of that research has focused on adoption—frequency of innovating—rather than on implementation. The frequency with which an organization adopts innovations can affect implementation, through such factors as experience in making changes as well as structures and procedures that support change. Therefore, the research on size, though rarely directly applicable to implementation, is important.

It would be a serious mistake to assume that today innovation is exclusively or primarily the province of the large organizations that dominate the economy in so many other ways. Large organizations have, it is true, many of the resources that should aid innovation, such as large pools of resources to sense consumer demand, conduct basic and applied research, and develop new products. Despite these advantages and contrary to the conventional view that innovation has increasingly become the province of large entities, many observers argue that such organizations have very limited capacity for innovation. Some evidence supports this contrary view. According to Stein (1973), for example:

> There is every reason to believe that smaller firms or private individuals have as much, or more, opportunity in this regard as the giants. In fact, there are probable diseconomies of scale in the large entities due to the difficulty of accepting or implementing change (p. 58).

Similarly, Mintzberg (1979) argued that even when the multidivisional firms employ structures that involve only a minimal amount of coupling of the parts, the existing control systems often impede innovation. Finally, as organizations grow, they tend to accumulate large, fixed investments in technology and operating structures and procedures. Thus, they may prefer slow, step-by-step changes over rapid, sweeping changes that might "make their processes obsolete" (Abernathy, Clark, and Kantrow, 1981, p. 78).

However, it cannot be assumed that small firms are necessarily more able and/or willing to innovate than large ones. The matter is more complex than that. While small firms may have certain advantages in the early stages of development of an industry due to their flexibility, they do not have the technical and financial resources to play an important role in innovation as the industry matures (Rothwell and Zegveld, 1982). At this point, large size can be a necessary condition for innovation, at least in terms of successful implementation. For example, some innovations may involve such extensive capital outlays and development that they can be attempted only by the very largest firms. (Abernathy et al., 1981).

Investigating the relationship between size and the design and implementation of innovation is difficult. First, much of the research on the relationship between size and innovation has been cross-sectional; it has investigated the frequency but not the process of innovation. Second, organizational researchers have tended to use size as a variable out of "empirical pragmatism" rather than for clearly articulated theoretical reasons (Kimberly, 1976). One consequence is that there are a variety of measures of size, (such as assets, revenues, number of employees, and number of divisions or units) that may operationalize various aspects of organizations, such as complexity or resource availability. As result, the findings on size are different and sometimes contradictory. For example, using asset size to predict innovation may find a positive relationship because large assets provide slack, and slack facilitates innovation. On the other hand, research using number of employees might find a negative correlation because control and integration are difficult with large numbers of employees. Size is probably a surrogate measure for a number of dimensions (such as total resources, slack resources, and organization structure) that might promote innovation (Rogers, 1983). These dimensions and the role they play in innovation need greater specification.

The conceptual and methodological confusion surrounding size has led to arguments and research findings that support *both* the expectation that small organizations adopt innovations more readily than large ones and the expectation that large organizations innovate more readily than small ones. In a study of one thousand hospitals, Moch and Morse (1977) found small but significant positive correlations. Also, in a study of diffusion of innovations involving credit card and data processing services in banks, Malecki (1977) found that large firms had advantages over smaller ones in adopting innovations due to their abilities to raise capital, bear risk, and afford managerial and technical specialists, as well as due to the positive relationship between size and the magnitude of potential use of the innovation. In contrast, a number of studies have not found significant relationships between size and measures related to innovation such as the number of new proposals or the rate of program change (Aiken et al., 1980; Petersen, 1976).

Recently, several scholars have developed what amounts to a contingency approach to explain the effects of size on adoption. Kimberly and Evanisko (1981) found that size was a predictor of adoption of both technological and administrative innovation, but the factors that accounted for the relationship depended on the type of innovation. For technological innovation, size was one of several organizational characteristics that were related to innovation. (The others were specialization, functional differentiation, and centralization, the last being negatively related.) On the other hand, size alone was the only organizational variable significantly related to adminstrative innovation. Kimbery and Evanisko suggested that adminstrative innovations were adopted to help meet the control and coordination problems created by size. Ettlie (1983) found that size was related to product innovation in a curvilinear manner—the relationship was positive, but only up to a certain size. Finally, Rothwell and Zegveld (1982) have proposed that the relative advantages or disadvantages of size are a function of the state of a given industry. For example, when an industry is in its early, fluid phase, small organizations may have advantages; at later stages, the characteristics of large firms may give them advantages. In short, the dynamics of the relationship between size and innovation can be understood only in the context of the problems faced by people who decide whether or not to adopt an innovation.

One additional problem in considering the effects of size on innovation is knowing at what point an organization is small and when it becomes large enough that the dynamics of large organizations take over. Size probably is not a continuous variable; at some point one can probably detect a major qualitative difference between the dynamics of small and large organizations (Tornatzky, et al. 1983). It is not clear what the nature of "smallness" is or where it ends and "largeness" begins. As we studied the implementation of NOW accounts, we broke our organizations into three sizes (large, medium, and small), expecting qualitative differences between these three groups. We did find those differences, though our medium organizations were very similar to the large ones.

Culture. Recently it has become fashionable to account for innovation by analysis of organizational cultures. An organization's culture—its shared key values and beliefs (Smircich, 1983)—may play an important role in innovation. Among other things, culture may serve some of the functions that elements of mechanistic structures have been assumed to serve in reducing ambiguity. Aspects of culture may help people develop shared meanings, goals, and commitments, making it possible for focused efforts to occur at times when the novelty and uncertainty involved in innovation precludes formal procedures or even moderately firm guidelines. Like strategy, structure, and leadership, culture may function to help people attend to certain important variables and ignore others. Moreover, the shared meanings, goals, and commitments may facilitate integration.

Unfortunately, attention to organizational culture is a relatively new development; existing studies have not tried to operationalize the concept, although it is possible to draw out examples of how culture affects innovation from nearly all of the vast number of case studies in the literature. Reviewing that literature for evidence of the effect of culture on innovation is not fruitful, since it is indirect and speculative. Nevertheless, we took culture to be an important part of this study.

Organizational Learning. Innovation often requires more than creativity, motivation, and focus. It demands new skills and behaviors of individuals and new means of coordination. Organizational learning, defined as organization members' shared new understandings about the relationship between actions and their outcomes (Duncan and Weiss, 1979), has to be a part of effective implementation. There are but a few studies examining the function of organizational learning in implementation. For example, Jelinek (1979) revealed the way innovation was advanced at Texas Instruments by an institutionalized set of systems that provided "rules for learning"—a set of adminsitrative systems that fostered paradigm changes. Other research has revealed the role of more ad hoc learning. For example, Ettlie and Rubenstein (1980) found that imitation and modeling played important roles in the implementation process, particularly for the first use of the technology by an organization.

Although data are scarce, organizational learning must be considered an important factor in implementation. Without the ability to learn as a group, members of the organization will have great difficulty in developing the technical and social competence needed to embrace successfully something new in their midst. They will be constrained by the way they have done things in the past, whether those ways were successful or not. Organizations that learn quickly and well have a distinct advantage in implementing change.

Relations with the Environment. Finally, an analysis of the organization as a whole is incomplete without examining the organization's relations with its environment, particularly since innovation is, in many respects, an interorganizational process (Tornatzky et al. 1983). Although many dimensions of this relationship are potentially important, the ones that have received the most attention in the innovation literature concern how organizations transcend their boundries to obtain information about what is needed and what innovations are available. While most of the work has examined the design and adoption of innovation, many of these ideas are applicable to implementation as well, in that an organization can learn how to implement from other organizations.

Perhaps the most useful construct that has been employed is boundary spanning. According to Adams (1980), boundary spanning encompasses those "activities of members or agents of an organization that serve to functionally relate the organization to its environments" (p. 328). These activities include: acquisition of inputs, disposal of outputs, filtering inputs and outputs, information search and collection, representation of the organization, and protecting and buffering the organization from external threat. These activities will be crucial in innovation, although their importance may not be the same at all stages. For example, search for information, even information about implementation, is apt to be most important at the design stage. Other boundary-spanning activities such as filtering inputs and outputs or disposing of outputs (for example, through dealing with customers) may be more important during implementation.

Because individuals play boundary-spanning roles, the way the organization perceives its environment will be a function of individual perceptions and actions as well as of social processes within the organization. The dynamics of this process become critical for understanding innovation. Boundary spanners screen and interpret information and thereby introduce two types of error into the design of the innovation and decisions about how to implement. The first type of error is a false positive (FP)—people accept into the organization information that appears to be relevant and useful for designing and implementing their innovation, but it really is not; or they release information or products to the outside that are inaccurate or unacceptable. The other type of error is a false negative (FN) in which useful information is not perceived as such and information and products that should have been put out of the organization are not.

False positives are likely to occur under different conditions than are false negatives. For example, organizations doing routine innovation are apt to be susceptible to FN errors in their search process, because people assume that they already know how to design and implement and so fail to heed valuable information that may be available. Those doing radical innovation have few standards by which to judge the value of information and are therefore likely to accept without question poor advice (FP). During implementation, radical innovators are susceptible to both FNs and FPs. FNs will occur as the existing routines lead individuals within the organization to screen out important information that is incompatible with those routines, while FPs will occur as people are unable to discriminate among the information that was able to penetrate the organization anyway.

Routine innovators are usually not subject to the confusion introduced by false positives; they have learned to screen out irrelevant data. In addition, they may have fewer difficulties than radical innovators because they have already established effective boundary-spanning patterns (Tushman, 1977; Weiss, 1983). By contrast, organizations implementing radical innovations are faced with developing a new boundary-spanning system to access an unknown environment. They have little clear idea of where they can go for the information they need and how to separate information from noise. Consequently, their attempts to innovate contain a variety of ill-advised trials and a large number of errors.

Another aspect of the environment that will affect innovation is the set of organizations with which a focal organization has direct linkages. These include suppliers, customers, distributors, and trade associations. For example, we found that radical innovation radically affects the relationships with members of the organization set. Suddenly, the old suppliers of information and materials are no longer providing what is needed, while the focal organization may no longer be supplying what it has traditionally provided to customers and others and must look to different markets.

In sum, established relationships with people and organizations in the environment can have a major effect on implementation. If communications and expectations are clearly established and there are definite criteria for judging the value of information, as is usual with routine innovation, implementation will proceed much more smoothly with fewer false starts and amendments to the plan. If these factors are not present, the organization must grope blindly for a period of time until it can establish them.

Obviously, there are a number of organizational characteristics that will influence all stages of innovation. Our primary concern is their effect on implementation, though the interdependence of the design and implementation stages has led us to consider both from time to time. Given the number of these organizational characteristics, their ill-defined nature, and the nature of their possible interrelationships, it is easy to understand why knowledge about organization innovation is so amorphous. In this context, our research objective of finding "clues" to implementation success may seem less modest than it first appeared. So far, we have left out one major aspect that adds additional complexity to the matter—the role of interpersonal processes.

Interpersonal Processes in Implementation

While the characteristics of the organization explain many of the differences in how well organizations design and implement innovation, the picture is incomplete without looking at what goes on between and among particular people. How involved are they in the change process? How do they feel about the process? How is the political game played? What is the nature of the communication among people? How flexible are they in changing direction? All of these are significant micro processes that much more directly explain implementation than structural variables. People, not organizations, make change happen or keep it from happening.

Employee Involvement

The organizational change literature emphasizes the social processes and the dynamics of group interaction that lead people to take the actions they do. (For useful summaries of these perspectives, see Beer, 1980, and Trist, 1981.) The way decisions are made is seen as critical, with those who have been involved in the decision process having more commitment to implement the decision and having more understanding of the reasons for the change. The *way* change is introduced, not just the substance of the change, is viewed as critical to the success of the change because the process itself affects the motivation, perception, and learning of those involved. For the most part, writers have tended to assume that if individuals who are affected by the change are allowed to participate in decisions regarding the change itself, they will be less apt to resist the change. Involvement in the process will contribute to psychological involvement in the substance.

While this perspective continues to have considerable support and is widely accepted, the evidence for the value of participation is mixed. After a detailed and critical look at the evidence, Locke and Schweiger (1979) concluded that participation can indeed have these positive effects on both productivity and satisfaction, at least under some circumstances. In addition, they concluded that the benefits of participation in decision making are much more likely to be revealed in satisfaction than in productivity. They concluded that there are a variety of mechanisms that might account for these effects, including: goal clarity, greater understanding, ego involvement, and increased value attainment. They argue that while participation leads to satisfaction, it often does not lead to the best decision, is not equally valued by all individuals, and is only one of a variety of approaches to motivate employees.

More recently, Nadler (1983) has divided the requirements of organizational change into three parts: motivating change, managing the transition, and shaping the political dynamics for the change. The latter are likely to require managers to orchestrate resource flows, develop and run transition structures, win the support of key power groups, and build in stability. We speculate that employee involvement, while not unimportant for responding to these requirements, is only one aspect of motivating change, which involves surfacing dissatisfaction with the status quo, helping people to disengage from the present, and encouraging participation in the change.

The possible effects of involvement and participation on implementation have received some attention in the innovation literature. For example, Berman and McLaughlin (1978), Yin, Heald, and Vogel (1977) and Gross et al. (1971) have all found that participation by those closely affected was related positively to successful implementation. Tornatzky et al. (1983) note that these effects are generally attributed to "ownership" of the innovation. However, they observe that ownership is often associated with modifications of the innovation. We speculate that employee involvement may increase the use and duration of an innovation, because it results in the innovation being modified to suit the needs and interests of those who will use it. This increase in fit, however, stems from modification of the innovation. While such modification may or may not have an impact on the value of the innovation for the organization, it certainly means that two organizations that at first appear to be installing the same innovation are often not. Thus, employee involvement not only may influence the success of implementation, it may reshape the innovation itself.

Here we have summarized only an infinitesimal amount of the vast literature on the role of employee involvement in change and innovation.

Clearly, from this brief review of the change literature, it is obvious that the process used during innovation must be considered in any complete account. Equally obvious is the fact that the degree of employee involvement is one aspect that should be examined, although its importance can be expected to vary widely between stages of the process and among organizations. We designed our research to develop a detailed understanding of these matters.

Politics and Influence

A second micro-level factor affecting implementation is the organization's politics, defined as individual pursuit of self-interests within the organization, whether or not those self-interests are in conflict with larger organizational interests. Many standard treatments of organizations have recognized, at least implicitly, that conflict among individuals and units is a way of life in organizations, but they have nevertheless proceeded to give little attention to the role it plays in determining organizational processes or outcomes. Often it is assumed that agreed upon goals exist in an organization and the fate of an innovation within the firm will be determined by its objective contribution to these goals.

In contrast to this orientation, Gibson (1975) proposed that implementation be conceived as a complex multivariate process of interpersonal influence. The issue is that agreed upon goals often do not exist; or if they do exist at some abstract level, they have only limited impact on a number of decisions and actions (Pfeffer, 1981), because the goals are not uniformly shared. Individuals and groups, particularly groups that form functional units, have different and conflicting preferences for what outcomes the organization should seek. Under these conditions, rational decision procedures do not yield a clear course of action, and organizations must use other means to establish the basis for coordinated action by their participants. These other means are labeled "power"; the use of power in this way is "politics."

Conflict stems from several interrelated elements. Among other things, differentiation leads to heterogeneous goals among people and departments. People within a department see their own well-being as tied to their department's well-being, and they are therefore motivated to try to increase the department's resources and influence. Differentiation also causes members of different departments to perceive the relationship between specific actions and their consequences in different and often conflicting ways. Since people in these departments see the world differently, when called upon to implement an innovation, they will proceed in unique and often opposing directions.

Innovation introduces many of the elements that contribute to conflict. Because it often involves moving resources from some units to others, some people will be faced with giving up resources. Moreover, when new specialties are added, differentiation will increase, leading to greater heterogeneity in

goals, perceptions, and beliefs. At the same time, some units may find themselves needing to work much more closely with others, heightening the sensitivities aroused by resource reallocation and increased differentiation. In the midst of this uprooting of power arrangements, the organization faces greater task ambiguity than usual and previously powerful actors may not be able to act as authoritatively as they did under more traditional circumstances. Implementing the innovation may force the organization to decentralize power as it incorporates the expertise of various specialists. Alternately, it may need to find ways to bypass previously powerful people, including replacing them. Clearly, innovation is at heart a very political process.

Other Processes

The impact of employee involvement and political influence were the two major interpersonal processes we set out to explore here. However, we did find other aspects of interpersonal relations to be important in the implementation of NOW accounts. In particular, communication frequency and methods are extremely important in gaining employee commitment not only to implementing the designed innovation but also to improving upon that design once implementation has begun. Leadership style and motivational methods are important for similar reasons. Those who use punishment implement differently than those who use reward. Moreover, the climate surrounding interpersonal relationships varies. For example, organizations in which people are comfortable reversing decisions gain flexibility. All of these additional elements appear in our findings. Though these were not initially central to our work, none of them are counterintuitive and most have been discussed at length by students of organizational behavior.

The Search for the Cutting Edge

Building on the existing research and advancing knowledge about implementing innovation is a challenge, because there are thorny conceptual and methodological problems in studying innovation. Downs and Mohr (1976) suggested that it is impossible to generalize the findings from one organization to another, because people in different organizations perceive the objectively same innovation differently. The same innovation, such as a NOW account, means different things to people in different organizations, so they take different actions on it. Consequently, there will be different explanations for the same level of success in implementing the same innovation. Among other things, this view indicates the importance of studying innovation by developing an in-depth understanding of what the particular innovation means to a particular organization at a particular time. Rather than focusing on the objective properties of an innovation, knowledge will be advanced by exploring the perceptions of people within a particular organization implementing a particular innovation. This view has been widely interpreted as suggesting that a theory of innovation is at best premature.

Tornatzky and Klein (1982) presented an extremely insightful response to Downs and Mohr. Although they acknowledged that research has yielded few useful generalizations and accepted the importance of perception in the innovation process, they rejected the notion that attempts to build typologies of innovations are fruitless or premature. They proposed that it is possible to develop a taxonomy based upon perceived innovation characteristics that can be related empirically to aspects of design and implementation. For example, how complex an innovation is perceived to be or the degree to which it is seen as compatible with existing values can be measured across organizations. Many other perceived characteristics could also be measured. These percieved characteristics can then be related to alternate measures of success, making it possible in principle to construct theoretical statements. The difficulty in making general statements, according to Tornatzky and Klein, does not arise from the nature of the phenomenon, but from a more mundane problem—poorly designed studies.

This debate strongly influenced our study of implementation. We assumed the importance of the study of perceived innovation characteristics and the relativity of innovation to particular organizations at particular times. Nonetheless, we sought to find processes that might generalize across organizations.

Given our conceptual orientation and the scarcity of accumulated knowledge about implementation, we chose qualitative case studies to further our understanding. Many others find this a particularly useful method given the state of knowledge about implementation (Nelson and Yates, 1978; Eveland, 1981). Yin (1978) has been the staunchest advocate of this view. He sees innovation as a particular type of organization change and advocates employing cross-case comparisons for uncovering the key organizational events that influence innovation (1981b). He suggested that such studies are likely to be most fruitful "where, for instance, a critical factor or two appear to be of enormous importance" (p. 63). Yin's view is similar to the earlier position of Becker and Whisler (1967) that innovation is not a single variable but is "an attenuated and complex process in which a number of critical variables are likely operating. Under these circumstances, longitudinal analysis—even at the level of single case studies—seems to be most appropriate" (p. 469). Likewise, Pellegrin (1978) argued the need for research on the natural history of innovation—particularly of successful innovation. He observed: "especially needed are studies that concentrate on how the capacity to innovate is affected by authority and status systems, power struggles and status games, and the integration and coordination of the roles of organizational members" (p. 25). Gibson (1975) made a similar point. Finally, Kimberly (1979) stressed the need for detailed longitudinal studies guided by the metaphor of organizational biographies. In short, there is considerable agreement that we know little about what makes for successful implementation and that in-depth studies of individual cases would be useful.

Case studies, of course, have major limitations; the most serious ones come when attempts to aggregate them or generalize from them are made. In order to reduce the strength of these difficulties, we opted for a comparative case study—we selected an innovation that allowed us to look closely into twelve different firms at some of the significant issues other people had reported. The innovation we chose was one adopted within a whole geographic region at one time, allowing us to examine how perceptual issues influenced the implementation of the same product. And because it was adopted at the same time in the same region, we could rule out some factors that plague efforts to aggregate individual case studies: the economy, the location, and differing or changing regulations. Using the case study method, it is not possible to hold all the possible variables constant either statistically or experimentally. The study of NOW accounts allowed us to examine implementation without contamination from some of the more significant exogenous variables that might have affected it, though. Therefore we were able to retain the richness of case study while incorporating some of the advantages of survey and experimental methods.

Our preoccupation was to discover clues to successful implementation— to find what characteristics of the organization as a whole and what interpersonal processes have positive or negative influences on implementing an innovation. We used the cases to probe into every area we could think of to gain that understanding. We came away with some new directions in the study of implementation.

2
Methodology

In this chapter we describe our research design, the methodology we used to implement it, and major research questions. It is important that this design be read in the context of the conceptual and empirical literature we explored in chapter 1, because the questions we asked about each organization were grounded in that literature. In order to provide as close a linkage as possible between the research design and the material from chapter 1, this chapter is divided into five parts. First, we define our terms and review our placement of the NOW account in the conceptual framework of Pelz and Munson (1980). Second, we describe the NOW account itself and its status at the time these organizations first introduced it. Third, we describe our research design and our approaches to data collection and analysis. Fourth, we present the major questions we sought to answer. Finally, we outline some of the major limitations of approach that should be kept in mind when reading the case descriptions and our inferences from them.

Innovation—Definitions and Concepts

Innovation is defined as the process of introducing a technology, product, or service that is perceived by members of a particular organization to be new to their organization. However, it is often convenient to talk about the technology, product, or service being introduced as an innovation. To avoid confusion, we usually refer to the NOW account by name; as much as possible, we reserve the word *innovation* to refer to the process.

Second, we use Pelz and Munson's (1980) concepts of diagnosis, design, implementation, and stabilization (as defined in chapter 1) to delineate the four stages of innovation. In the case analyses, we have grouped diagnosis and design together as the design stage, and implementation and stabilization together as the implementation stage. Also, as we stated in chapter 1, often the effort to implement may force organizations to rediagnose and redesign. Thus, sometimes the implementation stage may include diagnosis and design activities. However, although the lines cannot be drawn unambiguously, once the embedding process has begun, we consider these activities to be part of implementation.

Third, we define routine innovation as the process of introducing "something" that can be implemented with only minor adaptations of existing organizational routines and that fits within the existing norms and values of organization members. Radical innovation is the process of introducing something that is new to the organization and that requires the development of completely new routines, usually with modifications in the normative beliefs and value systems of organization members. Although it would be best to consider routine–radical as a continuum, this book treats the variable as if it were a dichotomy. We decided to accept this deficiency because we knew of no measure that would allow us to determine the degree of radicalness that the NOW account represented for each of our organizations, and we did not have the time to develop such a measure prior to collecting our data.

The NOW Account as a Radical–Routine Innovation

The Depository Institutions Deregulation and Monetary Control Act of 1980 made it legal for banks and savings and loan associations to offer NOW accounts to their customers for the first time. The law was passed on March 28, 1980, and went into effect January 1, 1981. In simplest terms, the NOW account is a checking account on which the holder of the account receives interest. Although banks had provided checking accounts for many years, they were not allowed to pay interest on demand deposits. However, for a year or two, many banks had circumvented this prohibition by "zero-balance" checking accounts. This procedure required a customer to have both savings and checking accounts with the bank. The balance in the checking account was kept at zero; when the customer wrote a check, the amount of the check was transferred automatically from the savings account.

Given this history, we expected that the NOW account represented a routine innovation for a bank; the bank was introducing a new product but, because the product was similar to ones that had existed in this organization in the past, little in the way of new routines and patterns of thinking would be needed to implement the innovation. On the other hand, savings and loan associations could not offer checking accounts prior to January 1, 1981. We reasoned that since checking accounts involved many new tasks, from data processing to physical facilities to treatment of customers, the adoption and implementation of NOW accounts represented radical innovations.

This situation provided the conditions to study a natural experiment. There was no difference in the general service the two types of organizations could provide. By law, each organization choosing to offer a NOW account operated within very narrow constraints (such as interest rates that could be offered). Thus, different organizations were introducing virtually the same new product, in the same geographic area, at the same time. However, for some organizations (banks), it was expected to be a routine innovation; for other organizations (S & Ls), it was expected to be a radical innovation.

Because several years earlier, NOW accounts had become legal in New England, a great deal of information was available on the experience of financial institutions with NOW accounts. (See, for example, Crane and Riley, 1978; Basch, 1976). Following the Munson and Pelz (1980) typology, the organizations in the midwestern state we sampled from were not initiating and were not developing a new product for the first time. Thus, our design focused mainly on firms that were innovating by borrowing. As we will see, however, some adapting took place; consequently, in several cases the process of innovation could not be classified in only one row of the Munson and Pelz framework. (See figure 1–1.)

Details of the New England experience were well known in 1979–80. At least one book on the subject (Crane and Riley, 1978) had been published. Numerous articles had appeared in publications such as the *American Banker, Magazine of Bank Administration, Bank News, Forbes,* and the *New England Economic Review.* Data on customer response, alternative strategies, costs, and problems were well known. For example, Basch (1976) provided a convenient summary of the adoption rates and outcomes of these experiences. Guides to break-even analysis (such as Simonson and Marks, 1980; Whittle, 1979) were readily available.

The published literature gave clear direction for strategy—in a phrase, "Be careful!" For example, Whittle (1979) noted that the national S & L associations were encouraging a slow approach in order to avoid the problems experienced in New Hampshire. There the strategy was to offer the NOW account free, "hoping to lose money on every account and make it up in volume" (p. 4). Whittle advised bankers to keep his article and even send it to the S & L down the street to help the industry try to avoid the catastrophe that would result by underpricing. Weberman (1980) reported on the problems that S & Ls were apt to encounter from not knowing how to calculate the costs of running checking accounts and from the increased competition in the industry. In addition, some published information on the likely behavior of competitors in the Midwest was available and it too was consistent with adopting a conservative approach. Smith (1980) reported on results of a survey of banks indicating that in September 1980, almost all banks surveyed intended to offer a NOW account and pay the maximum rate of interest. However, in most other respects, she reported that many planned a fairly conservative strategy: 67 percent planned charges in addition to a minimum balance; only 7 percent planned to automatically convert current accounts to NOWs; 9 percent planned truncation (nonreturn of cancelled checks to customers); and 74 percent planned to sell it only to the current customer base. On the other hand, it was expected that the S & Ls would be much more aggressive in seeking new accounts.

Private sources of information were also available. For example, several firms in our sample contacted banks and savings organizations in New England. They collected data about such issues as costs and customer responses from firms that had been offering these accounts for several years. Such information played a central role in strategy formulation and planning.

Overall, the NOW account was a well-known entity to organizations in our sample. The nature of the product was clearly specified. The problems earlier innovators had faced were well documented. Moreover, it was fairly easy to predict what one's competitors were apt to do. Clearly, the innovation process we studied took place in an environment that appeared reasonably predictable. The one unpredictable element that was important for NOW accounts was the change in interest rates during a period in which the cost of funds was in rapid flux. When the cost of funds was high for instruments such as the certificate of deposit, the interest paid on NOW accounts at 5¼ percent or 5½ percent looked relatively low. At this point in time, it was difficult to predict the cost of funds.

Several features of the context limit the generalizability of our finds to other innovations. First, as we have suggested, substantial borrowing was possible. Our findings may not reflect the processes of innovating a completely new product. Second, the NOW acount was an early step in deregulation of the banking industry. The industry was expected to become much more competitive and turmoil was predicted. Brokerage houses and firms from industries other than finance were beginning to enter into the banking industry. Thus, the NOW account was one of the first of a series of changes that managers would soon face in what had been a very stable environment. Finally, there was at least one important contingency that was confounded with the routine–radical component of our study. The NOW account for the banks involved an important cost as current customers switched from their traditional checking accounts. The bank needed to pay over 5 percent interest on money that previously was "free" to them. On the other hand, the S & Ls did not have to worry about such "free money," because previously they did not have checking accounts. Moreover, S & Ls now had a chance to compete with banks in a way they could not have before. Thus, the NOW account had much more to offer S & Ls than banks. As a result, the routine–radical aspect of our study is confounded with several aspects that we summarize by the phrase "relative attractiveness."

Finally, the general state of the economy and the economic conditions of the banking industry must be noted. Government deregulation had and was expected to continue to increase competition and to threaten the survival of many organizations, particularly smaller banks and savings and loan associations of all sizes. Although it is not clear what influence these events had on the processes we studied, several points should be kept in mind. First, bankers were rethinking many of their services. In particular, they were beginning to examine the prices they were charging for the products and services they provided. The general trend was toward charging customers fees for each service they used (such as credit cards, safe-deposit boxes, and overdrafts) so that no one service subsidized others. Second, the extremely high interest rates seemed to encourage greater consciousness of the prices for services. It was commonly agreed among the bankers that the NOW account would increase costs and, because of this, interest rates would in the long run be at least a bit higher than before. Third, the expectation that many organizations would fold or be forced to merge was clearly a concern to many managers we interviewed. (One of two S & Ls that declined to participate was bought shortly after we approached them.) Fourth, there was an expectation that the savings and loan associations that did not survive would become much more like retail banks. This appeared to be a major factor motivating the S & Ls to be aggressive in using the NOW account to attract customers, and influencing the large commercially oriented banks to be less concerned with small customer accounts.

Research Design and Methodology

Pilot Study

Prior to designing our instruments and sampling, we conducted a small exploratory effort in a medium-sized bank. This study accomplished several objectives. First, we learned that while some adjustments were required of the banks, these were minor compared to those at the S & Ls. Consequently, we were assured that in fact the NOW account was likely to have been experienced as a routine innovation by banks and a radical one by S & Ls. Second, we were introduced to some of the literature on NOW accounts. Third, we became aware of the nature of probable problems and how they were apt to have been dealt with. This information helped us design our questionnaires to be sensitive to these matters. Finally, we became conversant with the terminology of checking accounts marketing and operations.

Based on this information, we decided to employ open-ended structured interviews. These schedules were pretested for clarity and general sensitivity through interviews with people who had recently been part of an unrelated innovation in an academic setting. This procedure assured that the questions we were asking would be clear to our respondents and allow us to answer our research questions.

Sampling

Because the NOW account was expected to be a relatively routine innovation for banks and a relatively radical one for S & Ls, variance in the routine–radical dimension could be operationalized by selection. Accordingly, lists of all the banks and S & Ls headquartered in the midwestern metropolitan area we call River City were compiled from *Polk's Word Bank Directory* (1980) and the *Membership Directory of Members of the Federal Home Loan Bank System* (1980). The firms were ranked on total assets.[1] Examination of the rankings of assets of the banks indicated three rather distinct groups: nearly $1 billion and over, $298 million to $750 million, and under $171 million. These groups were labeled large (4 banks), medium (6 banks), and small (15 banks), respectively. Since there were large gaps between these categories and no banks fell in the gaps, these three classes were treated as discrete sets. A similar procedure for classifying the savings and loans also yielded three rather discrete categories: $600 million to nearly $2 billion (3 S & Ls), $200 to 500 million (11 S & Ls), and less than $75 million (12 S & Ls). Again, no S & Ls fell between these categories. This procedure resulted in a six-cell matrix—two types of firms (banks and S & Ls) and three levels of size (small, medium, and large). The design called for two organizations to be selected from each cell. Two organizations and alternates were chosen randomly from each cell. The results of this sampling are shown in table 2–1.

In implementing this design, several unanticipated problems resulted in some additional confounding of the independent variables and misclassification of one bank on the dimension of size.

The first difficulty stemmed from differences in the average size of banks and S & Ls. The asset size of organizations in all three S & L categories was smaller than the corresponding bank category. Given this difference, random selection among the large organizations yielded banks that were on average larger than the S & Ls. However, as shown in table 2–1, there was overlap. First Commercial Bank[2] had approxiamately 50 percent more assets than First National S & L, but First National S & L had almost twice the assets of Second Commercial Bank. Second Commercial Bank was larger than Second National S & L, but the magnitude of the difference was comparatively small. Thus, although size was somewhat confounded with type of organization (and hence with the routine–radical dimension), there was considerable overlap in size between the large banks and large S & Ls.

Second, a structural variable was confounded with the routine–radical dimension. The banks were holding companies that owned individual banks throughout the state. Each of these individual banks had its own president who, despite an apparent independent status, was constrained both formally

Table 2–1
Approximate Asset Size of Organizations Sampled
(millions of dollars)

	Size Classification	Asset Size
First Commercial Bank	Large	$3,000
Second Commercial Bank	Large	980
Third Commercial Bank	Large	1,200[a]
First National S & L	Large	1,800
Second National S & L	Large	827
First Regional Bank	Medium	298
First Capitol S & L	Medium	300
Second Capitol S & L	Medium	330
First City Bank	Small	115
Second City Bank	Small	105
First Neighborhood S & L	Small	60
Second Neighborhood S & L	Small	65

[a]Assets originally recorded as $750, which were only the in-state assets of an interstate bank holding company.

and informally by the wishes of executives of the holding company. Nevertheless, the holding company executives did seek to obtain the support of the presidents on issues of policy and strategy that impacted directly on the individual banks. In contrast to the banks, the heads of the branches of the S & Ls were less apt to be consulted on matters of strategy and policy; they were viewed more as branch managers than were the presidents of the individual banks. In short, although in both cases executives at headquarters exercised considerable influence over the branches or member banks, the process was different; holding company executives at the banks tended to try to convince the presidents of the individual banks; the S & L's executives were more apt to direct the work of the branch heads. The result for introducing the NOW account, however, was that executives from headquarters played the dominant role in major decisions in all organizations in the study.

Third, the use of total assets caused a misclassification of one organization. The list used for sampling reported only assets held within the state. Because we were informed that banks headquartered in the state could not hold assets outside of the state, we assumed that the list provided an accurate ranking of asset size. However, after collecting the data, we discovered that one bank originally classified as medium-sized had substantial assets out of state. As a result, our data include three large and only one medium-size bank. This sampling problem means our design was not fully implemented as intended and thus our comparisons of medium-sized organizations involve only one bank.

This problem complicates the interpretation of our findings about size, but we believe it hindered our search for clues about implementation only slightly, if at all.We believe the impact was minor primarily because of two characteristics of the one true medium-sized bank we studied. First, this bank was the smallest of the medium banks in the population. Second, despite this fact, it approached the NOW account in a way similar to the larger banks but very differently from the smaller banks. Thus, we concluded that within the range of banks we studied, the level at which size made the qualitative difference suggested by Tornatzky et al. (1983) (see the discussion of size in chapter 1) was between the smallest medium-sized bank and the largest small bank.

Data Collection

A letter stating the purpose of the study and requesting access to the organizations selected was sent to each firm's chairman of the board and, where necessary, followed up by phone. All of the large and medium-sized banks contacted initially agreed to participate; two small banks declined to participate and were replaced by alternates. One large and one small S & L also declined to participate and were replaced by alternates. Typically, the chairman referred us to the vice president who had primary responsibility for introducing the NOW account. This person became the key informant and was the first person interviewed; these interviews usually lasted from 2 ½ to 3 ½ hours. After the interview, key informants had a clear idea of what type of information we were seeking. We asked them to provide us relevant documents from the archives and introduce us to other people who had played critical roles in the process. In addition, key informants were asked to suggest a location that was apt to give us a representative picture of how things went at the level of the individual banks and/or branches and to introduce us to the head of each unit.

All people the key informant said had played an important role in implementation who were still with the organization were interviewed. (Unfortunately, in a few cases a person who had played a key role had left the organization and we were not able to get permission from the organization to contact him or her). Additional people were interviewed based on the suggestions of other respondents. Also, in two cases, external consulting firms had played a critical role in the process; the head of the relevant consulting team was then interviewed. Finally, the head of one individual bank or branch, other managers who had played a key role in implementing the NOW account at that unit, and two or three customer service representatives were interviewed. All interviews were conducted between ten and seventeen months after the opening of the first NOW accounts in January 1981. This procedure was expected to have the two advantages of multiple respondents reported by Jick (1979)—greater confidence when reports converge, and new insights and more complex models when they diverge.

Two patterned interview schedules were used. The one for managers appears as appendix A and the one for customer service personnel appears as appendix B. Interviews with the managers consisted of two major parts: the first dealt with the initiation phases and focused on the decision to introduce the NOW account; the second treated implementation—personnel and organizational matters and outcomes. A brief third section dealt with the overall posture of the organization and future plans. Interviews took between 1 and 3 ½ hours. The interviews of customer service personnel centered on implementation— including how they were informed about the NOW account, the role they had played in its introduction, and their perceptions about changes in their jobs and how well implementation had gone. These interviews usually lasted one-half to three-quarters of an hour. Typically, all the interviews were conducted using the appropriate patterned interview; the only exceptions were when someone outside the organization was interviewed or when we interviewed someone higher in the organization hierarchy than our key informant. In these cases, schedules were designed to fit the objective of the particular interview.

Data Analysis

This procedure yielded voluminous data which had to be distilled. The headings shown in table 2–2 were sensitizing concepts that we used to focus our analysis of each organization. The schema was developed to provide a complete description of the main themes of every respondent, with the formation and labeling of the sensitizing concepts informed by the organizational and innovation literatures and developed inductively from reading of the interview responses.

The categories listed in table 2–2 enabled us to classify all our interview responses and most material contained in the archives. Moreover, these categories reflect most of the topics in our review of the organizational innovation and change literatures presented in the previous chapter. There are, however, a few notable divergencies. First, certain new variables appear such as technological readiness and some matters related specifically to the NOW account (promotion effort and pricing, for example.) Second, we observe a much richer set of outcomes for assessing success. Third, although the categories reflect both formal structure and social processes, not all of these categories are isomorphic with variables treated in chapter 1. For example, organic and mechanistic structures do not appear in table 2–2.

Table 2–2
Sensitizing Concepts Used in Focusing the Data Analysis

Variables related to design of NOW account

Strategy of organization and goals for NOW account
Decision to offer the account
Pricing
Promotion effort
Relationship between pricing and promotion
History (of organization and NOW account)
Routine versus nonroutine aspects
Relationship with environment
Constraints on decision

Implementation variables

Technological readiness
Changes in standard operating procedures
Monitoring
Constraints on decision making
Learning how to implement contingency planning

Variables related to both design and implementation

Power tactics
Structural factors
Decision-making process
Group dynamics
Centralization (number of people involved and level at which power was concentrated)

Success or failure (outcomes)

Organizational learning
Time invested
Profitability
Readiness to implement
Impact on other organizational goals
Impact on personnel
Ease of data processing

However, topics such as centralization, decision-making process, and standard operating procedures do. Therefore, to relate the findings to the previous literature, we will have to make some inferences about the relationship of the variables listed in the table and the concepts in the existing literature.

These inferences will be aided by the detailed descriptions of the twelve innovating firms reported in the following chapters. These summaries are organized by using the sensitizing concepts presented in table 2–2. When we were preparing them, if respondents commenting on a particular matter were judged to agree, the consistency was interpreted as indicating the event or process had actually occurred in the way described. In a few cases where there was disagreement or when the response was unique to one individual, the conflict or uniqueness was noted in the write-up. In addition, material

from the archives was used to help describe the process and interpret unique comments or disagreements.

The detailed summaries provide a rich description of the events and perceptions of the processes that took place in the twelve organizations. They represent our efforts to reconstruct as complete a picture as possible of what took place. Undoubtedly, occasional errors of interpretation occurred in this process. We attempted to reduce these by using the actual words of the respondents. The significant errors are most apt to occur in our classification of these statements. By presenting the actual words, however, readers can make their own judgments. One other error could have resulted from what we omitted from the write-ups. Most omissions resulted from many respondents saying much the same thing or respondents being judged to have little relevant information pertaining to the questions we asked. Clearly, this approach limits the replicability of the study. However, given our objective of finding clues, the major impact of the limitation is likely to be reflected in clues that we missed rather than in reported clues that had no impact.

The decision to provide detailed qualitative summaries rather than code the data and develop a more quantitative presentation was based on several factors. First, the objective of the study was to find clues to what made a difference in implementation. These are qualitative dimensions. Second, the literature indicated the need for knowledge that such a case approach is best equipped to provide—"in-depth and organizationally dependent analyses of implementation situations" (Schultz and Slevin, 1975, p. 8). Third, as it turned out, in many organizations much of the relevant information was possessed by only one or two people; consequently, following Berelson (1954), *frequency* of mention seemed to be less important then *whether* something was mentioned. Fourth, the organizations were different from each other in ways that made uniform coding, in the absence of a clearly articulated theory, very difficult. In some cases decision making was extremely centralized; in others it was very decentralized.

Moreover, the level in the hierarchy where centralization occurred also varied. In addition, some firms had substantial archives; others had virtually none. Some had used outsiders and others had not. In short, the sources of data were not fully comparable. Consequently, we treated each organization on its own terms. Some topics that were important in some firms were not mentioned by respondents in other firms. Consequently, the narratives do not all have the same topical headlines. Also, because we tried to present a description of each case that captured the flow of information in that system, we did not treat the major topics in exactly the same order in every case. In the chapters that follow, an attempt is made to present the full data (organized by us through our categories). We search for clues concerning implementation by treating innovation as a process and studying each organization engaging in the process as fully as possible, using the words of the participants.

The rationale for this approach to study innovation—especially implementation—has been advanced by many including Yin (1977). It was perhaps best stated by Gibson (1975), who observed that if implementation is viewed as a complex multivariate process of influence, then the case-by-case method to understand it is the most appropriate approach.

Research Questions

While the primary purpose of this research was to discover clues to successful innovation by examining the postadoption phase of implementation, because implementation is rooted in the preadoption phases, we were concerned with them as well. Informed by the innovation, organization theory, and organization change literatures, our search was guided by the following general questions:

1. What types of structural arrangements facilitated implementation of innovation? (Of particular interest were organic versus mechanistic structures.)

    a. Did these differ for radical versus routine innovation?

    b. Did these differ as a function of organization size?

    c. Did these differ at various stages in the process?

2. What types of interpersonal transactions were more or less conducive to effective implementation?

    a. Did these differ for radical versus routine innovations?

    b. Did these differ as a function of organization size?

    c. Did these differ at different stages of the process?

3. What types of personal and political actions were more or less conducive to effective implementation?

    a. Did these differ for radical versus routine innovations?

    b. Did these differ as a function of organization size?

    c. Did these differ at different stages of the process?

4. What import did various factors such as the organization's history, culture, environment, and strategy have on the process of implementation?

Because we assumed that the answers to these questions required an understanding of the history of the NOW account in the context of each organization, we collected information on the organization generally, but centered our focus on the NOW account, from preadoption through implementation. The findings of this search in the twelve organizations are reported in the next section.

Documentation of the process that occurred in the larger organizations required considerably more space than was needed for the smaller organizations. As a result, we devoted entire chapters to the larger organizations and grouped the smaller ones together. In every case, however, we attempt to present a complete picture of how innovation was perceived by the members of the organization and those who advised them. First National S & L is presented in a somewhat different format. The stresses of implementing a major radical innovation in a large organization resulted in an unusually informative case, full of many stories about what happened. We have presented those many stories as chronologically as possible to communicate all the subtleties and complexities of implementation for this association. In developing our summaries we refer to the organizations, to the people we interviewed, and to the geographic units involved by fictitious names.

Limitations of the Study

Two sets of factors limit the generalizability of our findings. First are deficiencies in the design and execution. Second, the innovation we studied had a number of unique attributes. Consequently, generalization to other innovations is problematic.

Deficiencies in Design and Execution

Although we are convinced that the general comparative case study method was the only feasible one, inherent in such studies are problems of reliability, validity, and replicability in both data collection and interpretation. We tried to deal with these problems in several ways. First, we obtained multiple respondents within each organization. This permitted us to obtain a range of perspectives on most matters and helped to guard against idiosyncratic views coming to appear as representative at the entire organization. Second, we present full scenarios for each organization in our data chapters. Although we do not present everything, we attempt to present every theme from our interview notes that was relevant in the general research questions. These detailed accounts allow readers to draw their own conclusions and to critically evaluate ours. Obviously, personal judgment was required and the interrater reliability of these judgments is unknown.

Again, this shortcoming seemed to be unavoidable. Our study was guided by some general orientations and concepts rather than a well-articulated theory. Our approach was inductive; preserving the richness of each perception and action in its full context seemed preferable. Another design problem involved what we had intended to be a major dependent variable. We had expected to use the number and profitability of NOW accounts as the major outcome variable, but as we have seen, such a measure would have misrepresented the goals of numerous organizations. Under these conditions and given the conclusions from previous research concerning the importance of elements that are idiosyncratic to individual organizations, we did not attempt to develop a more refined set of categories than those presented in table 2–2, and the interrater reliability of the interpretation of the interview data is not substantiated.

In addition, there were certain deficiencies in our data collection. For one, our sampling procedure resulted in having only one medium-sized bank. Second, at two firms people who had played a key role in the NOW account were no longer with the organization and managers discouraged us from attempting to interview them. We suspect that these people would have had quite different perceptions than the people with whom we spoke. As a result, our scenarios may overstate the degree of agreement among members of several firms and omit some important perspectives. Third, the major sources of data were after-the-fact interviews. Such "after-only" designs have many serious flaws. Quite probably our respondents had forgotten much. Moreover, what they said was influenced by things that had occurred after the NOW account was in place, including a socially constructed view of the introduction of the NOW account itself and rationalizing of their own behavior. Also, as Schwenk (1985) observed, models derived from participant recollection are apt to differ in two important ways from those based on more direct sources; the former are apt to make the decision process appear to have involved a series of distinct phases and to appear more purposeful than the latter. Our use of archival data only partially protected us against this possibility.

Fourth, our method of selecting respondents within a firm may have led to systematic exclusion of people who had played important but not highly visible or distinguishable roles. Also, it is possible that the criteria used by those who referred us to respondents introduced certain systematic biases. Finally, the NOW account was not the only change taking place or being anticipated; therefore, what we learned was a function of other changes. As in much field research, control over many confounding events was not possible. One of these contemporaneous events is the fact that the environment of the firms we were studying was becoming turbulent after a long period of stability. The industry was on the verge of becoming very different than it had been for a long time; in Miller and Friesen's (1984) terms, this was an early step in changing from a quite conservative to a more entrepreneurial industry. Things might have been very different in a continuously turbulent environment.

The final set of design problems is reflected in the confounding among our conceptually independent variables. Size and routineness/radicalness were confounded because the banks (routine innovators) were larger than the S & Ls (radical innovators), although our organizations did match up reasonably well. More seriously, the routine/radical variable was confounded with other things including the expected value of the innovation itself—the S & Ls felt they had much to gain, the banks felt they had little to gain and something (the shift of money to interest-bearing from noninterest-bearing checking accounts) to lose. More generally, it could be argued that there are important qualitative differences between the banks and S & Ls. At least in River City, the banks are perceived by many to be more sophisticated than the S & Ls. Moreover, the banks offered a larger array of services and serve different clients than the S & Ls. Corporations and large organizations are major clients for the banks whereas the S & Ls traditionally focused on home loans as their major source of revenue. In short, a good argument could be made that radical/routine innovation was confounded with different segments of the financial service industry.

Nature of the Innovation Itself

A second set of constraints on generalizability stems from the nature of the particular innovation and the context in which it occurred. Our findings will reveal a number of dimensions on which this innovation was different from many others, including the facts that it was borrowed, that it involved a core function, and that it was a combined product and service rather than a technology. In addition, it was a foregone conclusion that the NOW account would be introduced in almost all of the firms we studied. As a result, the adoption decision was undoubtedly closer to a nonevent than it is for many innovations.

Despite these limitations, the twelve case studies that follow reveal some important insights about innovation. These insights, we believe, are of both theoretical and practical importance.

Notes

1. Although total assets is but one of a variety of indices of size, it provided the most expedient way to classify the firms from published data. There was a strong,

positive association between assets and other possible measures such as number of locations and number of employees. In short, had we used other indicators of size, we would have achieved a similar classification. Still, it is important to recognize that we had no theoretical reasons for the classification we employed.

2. First Commercial Bank is a fictitious name, as are the other names of banks and savings and loan associations in this book.

II
Case Studies

3
Consultation and Project Management

The holding company that we refer to as First Commercial Bank was cofounded in 1969 by a major bank and a major trust company in the River City area. At the time of the introduction of the NOW account, the holding company had acquired 19 banks in key markets throughout the state and had consolidated assets of over $3 billion. It employed approximately 3,600 people. In addition to affiliates in River City and Prairie City (a second large city in the state), First Commercial had affiliates in a number of smaller cities. The combination of rural and urban facilities meant that First Commercial served diverse markets.

The introduction of the NOW account came at a time when managers were making a number of major changes. The annual report described these changes as "part of a total strategy to become a preeminent banking organization in Mid-America." These changes included the construction of a palatial new office building and a change in company name (effective in 1982). The new name was chosen to reflect the explicit strategy designed to make First Commercial a preeminent regional bank and, by giving its affiliates a common name, to increase the effectiveness of its marketing function. As part of this strategy, a major reorganization of the administration of the out-of-state banking affiliates had taken place late in 1979. At this time the state was partitioned into four administrative regions; in each region a president of one of the banks was appointed regional president and charged with overall responsibility for the affiliates in that region. While this change had been announced earlier, it had not been implemented fully. The early steps in this reorganization and the analysis and design of the NOW account took place simultaneously.

The new structure was designed to make it possible for each bank to operate independently, but also to operate under common direction on a regional basis. A major objective of the reorganization was to maintain autonomy while helping the local bank presidents to utilize the expertise and corporate resources of the entire company more effectively. The regional presidents became "linking pins" between banks in their regions and the holding company.

Also, early in 1981, other changes were made. As described in the annual report, "New banking groups were formed, and existing groups were realigned consistent with the target markets where the company is concentrating its efforts." Operational and investment banking activities were restructured. Key staff members, who were best qualified to service newly designated markets and products, were assigned new responsibilities. Separate planning units were established for each market; planning was decentralized to ensure effective implementation. By year-end, the reorganization was completed. One feature of these changes was the introduction of the "personal banker" in the retail area. As a result of this change, the banks' larger customers were assigned to one individual who was responsible for many services the bank offered to each customer.

The introduction of the NOW account at First Commercial just happened to occur simultaneously with these sweeping changes in the organization. These changes were being discussed and implemented while the NOW account was being investigated and designed, and continued during the time when the NOW account first became operational. The organization restructing was initiated in anticipation of a number of changes in banking, of which the NOW account was only one. The changes reflected an awareness of the possibilities for achieving greater synergy among the individual banks, while simultaneously preserving the diversity and autonomy that management desired for responding to diverse markets.

The reorganization affected the process for introducing the NOW account and altered how future innovations would be implemented. Respondents indicated that once the reorganization had taken a firmer hold, the company approached innovation differently than before; had the structure been in place sooner, the NOW account would have been dealt with differently than it was at the time. In fact, the NOW account itself was a vehicle through which managers shaped and learned about the realities of the new structure; the NOW account helped to legitimate the new structure.

Our first contact with First Commercial was through a letter to the chairman of the board, who referred us to Mr. Mueser, vice president in the retailing division at the lead bank. Mueser provided us with many details about the overall process and specifics of the NOW account. He also referred us to other managers in marketing and operations and to the regional presidents. In addition, we interviewed new-accounts representatives at the lead bank. Since the regional presidents were also presidents of individual banks, these interviews centered around both their roles as regional presidents and their experiences as presidents of individual banks.

Routineness

Every respondent interviewed supported our expectation that the NOW account was a very routine innovation for First Commercial Bank. Besides having offered checking accounts for many years, the bank had previously installed a product called "Interestcheck."[1] Under Interestcheck, a customer had two accounts: a savings account and a checking account. The checking account was kept at a zero balance; when the customer wrote a check, money was transferred from the person's savings account to the checking account. Respondents from all levels and departments commented that the NOW account was simpler than Interestcheck, primarily because it required only one account for each customer.

The perception of routineness was shared throughout all the departments we interviewed. Mr. Wayman (currently vice president of operations), who had been in charge of the data processing side of the NOW account, observed, "This wasn't too controversial a project. There are only so many ways you can pay interest on a NOW account. We got the parameters down and put in the options that were identified. There were really not too many options and we already had some experience from Interestcheck." In assessing the way he handled the project, Mr. Wayman indicated that if he made a serious mistake, it was assigning too many of his most talented people to the NOW account. "In fact, I even considered removing some of the people from the NOW project to work on other projects which were in trouble. It was a mistake that I did not move them. In fact, one other major project failed." He noted that there was nothing unique or special about the process of implementing the NOW account; for the most part, existing forms and procedures were adequate.

The perception of routineness existed throughout the organization. A regional president commented that the NOW account was much like Interestcheck and as a result, there were no problems with the computer or elsewhere. Moreover, he noted that the statements that the customer received were much simpler than those with Interestcheck. "Nothing new was done here. The NOW account is very similar to passbook savings. There were no operational problems." In comparison with Interestcheck, the procedure was much simpler to explain to the customer. Because Interestcheck was somewhat complex, "It was hard to explain to the customer what the statement really was. On the NOW accounts it was just routine. The statement is easy. The customer understands it. It's really a very simple product. The NOW account was very straightfoward and continues to be." Another regional president observed that whereas in the past, it had often been necessary to send people to River City to learn the detail of complex changes, no one needed to be sent there for the NOW account. Similarly, Mr. Mueser indicated that First Commercial's experience with checking gave them a major advantage over the savings and loan associations. "Opening accounts was quite simple. All that the personal bankers needed to do was change the codes on previous accounts." This perception was shared by the new-accounts people. They commented that it was simpler than Interestcheck and had no effect on their job. They observed that it was merely an addition to their package of services and all they had to do to open an account was to enter a new number on the computer.

Interestingly, it appeared that the introduction of Interestcheck at First Commercial had also been routine. A major reason for the routiness of both products appears to have been environmental analysis, planning, and staffing that had taken place several years ago. As Mr. Wayman put it, "In 1976, we began systems development. In fact, this is what I was hired to do. We designed it for the NOW account back then. Thus we could implement it for NOW accounts pretty easily. The NOWs were on the East Coast and we knew they were coming. We had a place to put the system."

Design of the Innovation

Each of the financial institutions in the study was faced with choosing a particular design of the NOW account that would be consistent with its overall strategy. Most of those design decisions were in the realm of pricing and promotions and were made on the basis of assumptions about the profitability of the NOW account. However, there were many potential goals in adopting the NOW account in addition to making a profit.

Goals and Strategy

Analysis of what First Commercial hoped to achieve with the NOW account can be best summarized by treating the reasons for introducing it separately from the specific objectives that the managers considered in designing the NOW account. The former can be dealt with quite briefly; the latter are more complex because they are related to the overall strategy of the bank.

Strategy. Most high-level managers indicated that once NOW accounts were legal, First Commercial had no choice but to introduce them. A regional president commented, "We had to do it even if there was a drop in earnings. We did not do a full analysis. We simply felt that we had to do the NOW account." Similarly, Mr. Mueser observed that the NOW account, like the automatic transfer account, had to be offered for competitive reasons to avoid the loss of customers to other institutions. Mr. Mueser commented, "At first, we were defensive. Our major objective was to tell the customer that we had it too." In short, they innovated defensively.

However, the defensive posture, arising out of a need to pay interest on money that was previously free, was less intense than it might have been had the automatic transfer account not come first, because the automatic transfer also required the payment of interest on money that previously would have been held in interest-free demand deposits. Most respondents agreed that attitudes toward the NOW account were more positive as a result of Interestcheck and clearly were more positive than the attitudes about the automatic transfer account had been.

The automatic transfer account had also been introduced primarily as a defensive measure. It was developed to protect the customer base, especially the bank's largest customers. Likewise, the design of the NOW account, particularly the marketing strategy, sought to hold on to this important group of customers. The defensive approach had been successful with Interestcheck and the NOW account merely extended it. With Interestcheck in existence, the introduction of the NOW account resulted in little increased cost in terms of interest payments.

Comments by Mr. Stone, vice president and division head of retail banking and vice president of the holding corporation, suggested that the NOW account was a defensive measure for banking generally. He commented that the entire banking industry had lobbied very hard for NOW accounts in order to enable banks to compete with parallel financial institutions, such as Merrill Lynch, which were not under the same type of regulations. The NOW account enabled the banking industry to hold some of its good customers who would otherwise have been attracted to interest-bearing checking accounts outside the banking industry. Thus, at the industry level, the reasons for wanting to provide NOW accounts were also defensive, although in this case, the defense was that of a large segment of the financial industry against some other segment.

As we will see, the decision to introduce the NOW account at First Commerical Bank was virtually identical to that of the other banks in our study in two major ways. First, the thought of not introducing the NOW account once it was legal was never seriously considered. Second, the major motive was defensive. However, the particulars of the defensive strategies varied across organizations. The particular variations introduced by First Commercial reflected a set of goals and concerns that were somewhat unique.

Operationalizing the Strategy. It was clear that the major goal for the NOW account was to hold the best customers; attracting new accounts was not an operating goal. As Mr. Stone indicated, 80 percent of their deposits come from 20 percent of their customers. It was this 20 percent that they sought to keep from moving their accounts. Thus, while the general strategy was defensive, the posture with respect to these individuals called for aggressive promotion. Each of these customers (approximately 3,500 at the lead bank) was called by his or her personal banker. Customers were informed that the NOW account would soon become available and advised to sign up if they wished. In Mr. Stone's words, "The day that the accounts were legal, we had many accounts open. This protected us greatly from the savings and loans. When they began to promote, our customers looked around and said to themselves they already had this service."

First Commercial (and the eleven other organizations) offered the maximum allowable interest—5¼ percent.[2] It set a minimum balance for a free account at $1000.

However, there were variations in this strategy elsewhere in the organization. For example, a regional president from a rural area indicated that a much more aggressive promotion policy had been implemented in his bank and others in his region. He had been aggressive in introducing Interestcheck and followed this same procedure for the NOW account. While the bank did not have any targets in mind, he observed, "It was my decision to go ahead with it aggressively. It was a good product and our customers would like it. We had no choice about offering it either and we agreed that we should offer it in a noncomplaining manner." He followed his normal marketing procedures, emphasizing the typical 13-mile radius. He started with his own customer base and then moved to attract additional accounts. He also reported there were differences among his company's banks in his region. "The banks in my region went in different directions on the NOW account and I permitted this. We are results and earnings oriented. If the results are satisfactory, we let them go in different ways."

In contrast, in the Prairie City area, as in River City, the approach was much less aggressive. The regional manager commented:

> The marketing approach was to slide into it. We said the NOW accounts are here; we have to have them. We weren't sophisticated about our marketing effort. The NOW accounts were marketed by having the customer having to activate the change themselves. Some customers have not done it. Our marketing effort,—the profile was low, because of the cost fears, and because of the horror stories [from New England]—led us to move cautiously. We all agreed it's part of the evolution—its's coming—but let's do it slowly.

Thus, First Commercial was able to achieve variation in implementation between regions. The banks in the large cities tended to be more defensive than banks in the rural regions. In some cases, this defensive strategy involved aggressive tactics to hold on to their best customers.

The basic defensive posture was implemented through pricing as well as marketing; the costs of running checking accounts played an important role in setting the price. In Mr. Stone's words,

> We found that the cost of servicing checking accounts was about 3 to 3 ½ percent of our outstanding. You use outstanding for such calculations. When you add the interest of 15 percent (at that time), then the total cost is about 8 ½ percent of outstanding. It is a matter of mathematics. We were looking for about a 10 percent spread, which yielded a 1 percent profit after tax. The price was decided on the basis of these costs and an effort to

position the account for the person who wanted to leave $2,000 to $3,000 and have no service charge. We felt we might lose customers. However, we did not expect anyone to gain customers. The inertia of bank customers is very great if they are receiving satisfactory service. We still kept the checking account in place for those who wanted a plain checking account. However, we advertised the NOW account and told our customers about it. Only a small amount of media advertising was used.

In Mr. Mueser's words:

> Our total advertising budget for the whole NOW account was $50,000. This is very small for us. It included our statement stuffers, and our internal costs. When you consider advertising rates in the major newspapers and the enormous cost of producing any type of television commercial, this was a very small amount.

As indicated, the major marketing effort was through the calls of the personal banker to the top customers. A major part of the strategy was to give the customers good advice with respect to their break-even point in switching from the Interestcheck or their old checking account to the NOW account. People at all levels of the organization emphasized the importance placed on giving the customer accurate advice. Mr. Stone observed:

> Our personal bankers told the customers that the break-even point for them would be a deposit of approximatley $750. Customers were told that if they had Interestcheck, the NOW account would be good for them if their deposits were above this amount; but if they were lower, we did not suggest they you switch over.

For the most part, the initial decisions held up throughout the process. The only exception we discovered was in one rural bank where the price was lowered to meet the competition.

Overall, the promotion efforts appeared to closely parallel the intended approach. In large metropolitan areas, the strategy was basically aimed at preventing losses of major accounts. Efforts to attract new accounts were minimal, and uniformity was maintained within the relevant region so that customers from one bank in the region were not getting different services from those offered by other banks in that region. On the other hand, diversity was permitted between regions, and within one region local banks were free to become more aggressive to meet local competition.

Markets and the Environment. The NOW account strategy was influenced by First Commercial's goal to achieve preeminence in the region and by their already large size. The size and self-perceived position as a leader in the region influenced the deliberations on the NOW account in several ways.

First, executives believed that other banks in the area would follow their lead on pricing. Consequently, they felt it was extremely important that their pricing strategy be sound. As Mr. Stone put it, "It is amazing how organizations follow the first organization to announce. However, this is a problem. If you screw up, you are leading everyone else off." Second, given the expectation that others would follow, managers felt that it was important for them to announce their price early. Mr. Stone continued, "We announced what we were doing price-wise pretty early. We wanted to avoid having to change either up or down. If you set the trend and it's a good trend, it is positive that you can get everyone else to think the same way. We have banks that follow us pretty well; thus we think it is wise to be up-front." Thus, managers at First Commercial realized they would influence what a number of other organizations did and when they did it.

A correlate of First Commercial's size was its regional diversity. There was a difference in markets across the various regions. The emerging structure was designed to grant the local banks enough autonomy to be responsive to the different customer needs while at the same time achieving advantages of scale, such as synergistic advertising within the regions. Thus, although not really a goal, it was important to be sure that the member banks had a consensus and the consensus allowed enough autonomy for the individual banks to respond to their particular environments.

Another change in the environment associated with the NOW account was the entrance of the savings and loan associations into the checking business. The standing objective of First Commercial was always to be competitive pricewise. However, now they were confronted with a number of aggressive competitors who were willing to offer checking accounts inexpensively. The entry of the S & Ls into this business caused a great deal of apprehension, careful analysis, and close monitoring of the customer accounts.

Another issue affecting the banking community at the time was the move toward pricing for particular services. Managers at First Commercial Bank emphasized that the future would require that individual customers pay the cost for the particular services that they used. As one of the regional presidents put it: "It was about this time that the banks were going more into pricing for services in such a way that every party paid fairly and equally for the services they used but also in a way to be competitive. This was the way it was at this bank for sure." This new approach influenced pricing of the NOW account; the managers wanted to be sure that the NOW account paid its way. As a regional president observed, "We did not want to convert all our demand accounts in a way to have all the 'junk' accounts going for free." As a result, an important part of the decision process became the analysis of cost to define competitive and profitable prices.

Finally, the analysis of costs, the growing competition on the retail side from the savings and loan associations, the desire to price for services used, and other changes that were emerging all encouraged First Commercial to, in Mr. Mueser's words, "look at our customers' total relationship with the bank. We looked at the complete deposit relationship. This also necessitated looking at the service charge on other checking accounts. We repriced some of our other DDAs [demand deposit accounts] so that if the balance never came below $200, it was free. We needed to look at our overall pricing so as not to force money from one account into the other." As we shall see, this analysis became an important factor in selling the approach to the NOW account in the organization.

Strategic Decision Process

Mr. Stone was given overall responsibility for the NOW accounts. For the most part, the actual decision process used to design the NOW account was more typical of the older organization than of the newer one. Most of the respondents indicated that managers in the holding company did much of the initial work and made the decisions. They also reported that had the new structure been in place, much more input from the regional presidents would have been sought. As one regional president noted, with respect to the NOW accounts, the regional managers really got involved about three-quarters of the way through. "At that point, it was a reality."

Mr. Stone indicated that he faced competing objectives—to permit autonomy, yet, at the same time, to create a product common enough to obtain the advantages of scale, particularly common advertising for the whole geographical area. He described his approach as a combination of persuasion and participation.

> You have a difference in markets. The holding company banks have great autonomy. We want them to be responsive to different customer needs. We find that we have to be competitive in different areas. For example, Prairie City and the rural areas differ. My job is to get the banks to agree on a common product so we can have synergistic advertising within regions.
>
> The NOW account provided a vehicle which clearly displayed our needs for commonality. We used some salesmanship. If something made sense to us, we assumed it would make sense to them. But we do not mandate something, we sell it. There is always give and take. If our banks can convince me that any particular change would be negative for them, I will give in. If they can't convince me, I say to them, "Look, you are being stubborn."

In the "selling" process, managers relied heavily on the collection of information and analysis at the holding company offices. While a wide variety of sources were used, a great deal of emphasis was placed upon interviews with managers from individual banks to test ideas and to encourage these managers to test ideas at lower levels in their own banks. In Mr. Stone's words:

> The key is that we have a very compatible group who cooperates. We stress a theme. We have good communications. We have not had to come down hard. We in the holding company have greater capabilities to design and price products. The banks like for us to do it. They trust us. We also have a guy who is pretty much the boss of the retail and affiliated divisions. He is well liked. Basically, the retail banks in River City and affiliated banks have a great deal in common. It is easy to iron things out.

In short, the product was designed centrally, although as we shall see, information came from many sources. As a regional president observed, the NOW account was designed by marketing at the holding company and communicated by memo.

The actual design was based on extensive analysis *inside* the organization. Mr. Mueser summarized the process:

> We had bankwide input. It was companywide. Each bank is in a different market area, but we were striving for a common product. Finding common pricing required much research. We used our employees in retail divisions, rank and file, officers, marketing people, retail managers, and CEOs of all the banks for direct input. They all signed off on the final package. We visited other banks in our system; we got input from all areas. The operational people offered input too. We did market research and tried to anticipate customer needs. What we could offer all needed to be correlated with our software capabilities. This required some changes; for example, operational changes were necessary to enable us to provide form 1099 for tax purposes. We also got input from our customer base.

Mr. Stone's observations were similar:

> The retail and marketing arm of the lead bank tried to determine the customer needs. We used the limited experience of the New England banks. We got the advice and counsel of our operations people. From that point, we talked to our field representatives. When they were in agreement we went out and talked to the CEOs of all the banks for their input. We were looking for areas to achieve commonality of the product, which we achieved. We did this by looking at the whole depositing relationship. This was unique to our bank at the time. Numerous levels of management were involved. The marketing people and I went out to the various banks. We also had regional meetings. We also had many trade groups presenting different sessions on this topic.

Mr. Stone observed that part of the success stemmed from a high level of trust within a relatively compatible group, regular meetings, the testing of ideas on managers, and in turn the testing of these ideas by these managers on lower-level participants. Mr. Mueser reported one additional factor that played a major role. While there was common ground from the start, there were many different market areas and different points of view. However, "using the total savings as a pricing mechanism helped." In other words, an important part of the process was the calculation of profitability on the basis of customers' total relationships with the bank. This perspective provided the framework out of which an agreement could be achieved.

Committees played a major role throughout. A coherent focus was achieved formally through submitting their recommendations on major items to top management for approval. Less formally, however, the common focus on total relationship of the customer to the bank seemed to help operationalize the defensive strategy in a way that was understood and accepted throughout First Commercial Bank. Mr. Mueser noted that although imitators had followed, the focus on the total relationship with the customer was unique to First Commercial at the time. Thus, one aspect that helped First Commercial innovate was a conceptual approach that itself was an innovation. Also, the emphasis on the "total relationship" was paired with a more aggressive strategy of cross-selling, trying to be sure that customers used First Commercial for all their banking needs. This undoubtedly helped to show the overall strategy more clearly to the personal bankers.

The strategic emphasis on diversity and participation was greatly aided by the competence levels of First Commercial's members. In fact, the technical competence of First Commercial allowed them to treat different policy alternatives as variables in their data processing system. In other words, in addition to finding out what the different preferences were, de facto consensus required the technical capacity to develop programs building the various preferences in as options. In the words of one manager, "We do everything possible to achieve consensus here. We build in variables, but there has to be agreement that it is a variable. We got the parameters down and put in the options that were identified." The result of this capability can be seen at the regional level. A bank president reported, "First Commercial designs a model and offers it to the regional banks as a model. They then can adjust up and down based on their own situation. My banks are isolated. My banks can do very different things." In short, wide acceptance for the plan was achieved by a combination of persuasive and consultative leadership, granting autonomy on certain issues, developing a framework or rationale that made sense to most of the key participants, collecting data from many different people, and having the technical capacity to build in options.

Several factors constrained the decision process at First Commercial.

First, as has been suggested before, managers were concerned with holding major depositors. In addition, they were concerned with maintaining reasonable local autonomy of the branches but at the same time achieving synergy, particularly through common advertising. Third, because this was the first product that was being introduced through the new organization structure, people were apparently learning how the procedures would operate under the new structure; they also were learning some of the advantages that the new structure might provide.

One additional constraint was First Commercial's tradition of always being competitive in price. However, the entrance of savings and loans meant that the competitive price might be lower than desired to maintain profitability. This constraint seemed to have little effect on the actual price, but it did cause First Commercial to monitor customer accounts very closely.

Search. The decision-making process was informed by a very extensive external and internal search for information. To gather the data needed to decide the form that the NOW account would take, First Comemrcial did considerable research in New England. Mr. Stone reported: "We were very fortunate that we had the Boston experience. We did a lot of research in Boston. They held seminars. Two of the banks there are correspondent banks of ours. Thus we had little trial and error. We had two years of experience to key back on. It is amazing how similarly the patterns that existed there held up here. Their experience was the key in the planning process."

The information from New England seemed to be particularly important in supporting the defensive strategy. As one of the regional managers commented, "All of us individually knew that NOW accounts were coming and we were trying to understand these ahead of time. We knew of the horror stories from New England. We did not want to make the same mistakes. That was our biggest concern early on."

In addition, a great deal of in-house research was done. Besides the extensive consultation with employees, data were collected from customers. Surveys of current customers were conducted by the personal bankers. Customers were asked how they would like certain types of services; prices were tested on them. "Personal bankers invited customers into the bank. They were given the assignment of talking to ten people of a certain demographic pattern. We then met with the personal bankers and pooled the information. The marketing people also called in people for interviews."

To determine what would be an appropriate price, managers responsible for the NOW account analyzed the total relationship customers had with the bank. They also extensively analyzed customer demographics. In addition, a great deal of internal analysis was done on the cost side. Some consulting firms were used in this part of the process. They also used trade groups, magazines, and Federal Reserve publications. Finally, possible competitors, especially the savings and loan associations were examined. It was known throughout the industry, as Mr. Mueser put it, "that one savings and loan [in River City] was giving away 30,000 or 32,000 free check orders." Finally, once the NOW accounts were introduced, people who closed their accounts with First Commercial were contacted and asked why they closed their accounts.

In short, First Commercial searched extensively in New England, throughout its own organization, and in the local marketplace—including its competitors and customers—to decide on an appropriate price and to keep abreast of ongoing developments. Thus, arriving at the defensive strategy required a great deal of time and effort. Similarly, keeping in touch with the environment to be sure the approach was working as planned during implementation required continuing work.

Implementation of the Innovation

The processes necessary for implementing the NOW account were not complex because the change was routine. In addition, management had anticipated the coming of the NOW account five years before it was legislated and had purchased demand deposit software that included a NOW account package. At that point, they had hired staff and developed the necessary routines. Thus, while there were some concerns about technology, for the most part there was confidence throughout the organization that there would be few technical problems.

Complexity

First Commercial Bank was a highly complex organization. It provided a wide variety of services to large and medium-sized businesses, certain specialized businesses, individuals, and other banks. It also had extensive trust assets.

Branch banking was legally prohibited in the state. First Commercial was a holding company; each separate bank had its own board of directors, bank president, and staff. Consequently, there was more diversity at the level of the separate facilities than might be found among branches of banks in states where branch banking was permitted.

The overall complexity was measured by the number of occupational specialties mentioned as participating in design and implementation. Respondents identified five different job positions at the upper levels of the holding company—including vice president of operations, vice president of retail, new products manager, regional presidents (group presidents), and field representatives in retail—as having been involved in the NOW account. In addition, six different job positions at middle or lower levels of the holding company were also noted as having been involved. These included programmers, middle-level people in the retail division, middle-level people in marketing, the deposit group in operations that actually implemented the NOW system, and the project manager for the NOW account. In addition, clerical staff at the holding company participated in implementing the NOW account. Finally, there were nine positions at the individual bank level involved in implementing NOW accounts. These ranged from the bank presidents, who played a major role in the policy-making, to the executive vice president, cashier (head of bank operations), customer service people, account officers, personal bankers, teller supervisors, tellers, and clerical staff. In all, twenty different positions, many of which were filled by several people in the organization, were involved in implementing NOW accounts. First Commercial was highly differentiated and complex; so was its approach to innovation.

Decision Process

Mr. Wayman, vice president of operations, was responsible for the operational side of things. He reported that he managed the NOW account by delegating it to a project team, in the same way he managed other projects. The project proceeded from a written action plan that had the target dates and the "business issues" stated up front. Business issues involved elements that were important to managers who were concerned with customer relations, timeliness of output, and ease of use by bank staff. In Mr. Wayman's words:

> In our plans we have the business issues stated up front. Every plan has certain policy and timing issues that must be addressed. The page may be blank initially but these things are considered up front.
>
> The project was managed under the standing operating procedures of the company in much the same way as we managed all systems projects. I assigned it to one of the groups that reports to me. I assigned it to the deposit group. This was the obvious choice because it involved deposits. The project manager included it in her plan. Our guesstimate was 100 man days. This was truly a guesstimate. On these projects you can only make some very very rough estimates. In August 1979, the planning process to convert to the NOW accounts was begun. We targeted for completion for January 1, 1981. In assigning the project, I put two constraints on it. First, get rid of the automatic transfer system. Second, be ready by January 1, 1981. It was a well-run project. It was operational by January 1, 1981. In fact, it was ready in November 1980.

The project was monitored by Mr. Wayman using a timetable established as a basis for comparison with progress as reported at weekly staff meetings and in monthly status reports.

The project committee was chaired initially by the woman who headed the deposit systems. Included on the committee were a member of her staff, a computer operations person, and members from the reatil area and user banks. Specific action plans were developed; they began with two features—the planning dates and a clear statement of the business issues. However, the plans were kept flexible. In Mr. Wayman's words:

> The plans are good for about a minute and a half after they have been written. Keeping them up to date and keeping the distribution list current is very hard. People say, "Oh you changed the target date. Why didn't you tell me?" These problems always occur. There is nothing unique to this plan. It is probably much better thought out than most other plans.
>
> The particular group [the one on the NOW accounts] does higher-quality work than other groups. Perhaps it's not higher in quality in terms of how it looks. They may handwrite it, spend less time on fancy covers, and so on.

Thus, it appeared that a somewhat informal, but nevertheless well–thought-out process was developed. The technical people involved were perceived to be highly competent by others in the organization. Potential users were included early in the planning group, which operated flexibly within known parameters. This group played a key role in getting decisions made quickly and effectively. The fact that the chairperson of this committee left the bank during the process without any problems was seen by Mr. Wayman as attesting to the competence of this group. In his words "The project practically ran itself."

There were a number of different groups that needed to be consulted and have their interests represented. A major theme of Mr. Wayman's approach, just as it had been with Mr. Stone and Mr. Mueser, was to achieve consensus throughout. In his words, "We do everything possible to achieve consensus here. We build in variables, but there has to be agreement that it is a variable." While the NOW account was not too controversial, the project commmittee tended to grow as issues arose that involved other people or departments that were not represented on the original project team. As Mr. Wayman put it, "People would say, 'Well, Bill is affected by that; let's get Bill in.' There is always the problem that someone is not consulted." Often what happened was that issues on which there might be different preferences among different banks were termed variables and these variables were built into the system in such a way that local autonomy could be exercised.

There were issues on which priorities conflicted; political skills seemed to be important in their resolution. One major issue was whether to do away with the automatic transfer option when the NOW account was introduced or to maintain both types of systems. There were two basic options, one of which was to combine the two accounts and the other to add the interest to the demand deposit account. The second was preferable from an operations point of view and made no difference to the customer. Mr. Wayman said, "We did not counsel with the marketing side on this. It was an operations decision only." On the other hand, there were decisions where consultation had to occur.

The most controversial of these issues was whether or not to back-date NOW account transactions. Back-dating involves the crediting of interest for transactions made on one day but for some reason not reported until some later date. Of course, customer-oriented departments would prefer high precision on this dimension. Operationally, however, back-dating causes considerable problems for what is a very small amount of money on most accounts for one day. As Mr. Wayman put it:

> You are basically talking pennies at most. Very few people keep close enough track of their checking account to even know the difference. From the operations point of view, we felt it was not worth the expense for the precision which would involve recording deposits on the actual day on which the transaction was made. This was discussed for some time and we have memos about it still going on in April and May of 1981. The issue was still being debated then.

Basically, there were three sets of parties involved: retail administration, the operations people, and the banks and S & Ls that First Commercial contracted with to process their accounts. Resolution of the issue was achieved through negotiation but with a proactive stance by the operations people. In Mr. Wayman's words, "I felt that back-dating was not warranted for all transactions. You could always use manual procedures for the particularly large transactions. I lobbied with the other interested parties. I got the bank representatives to say that it wasn't that important. Then it was two against one and River City (i.e., members of the holding company) backed off."

Another tactic used to reach agreement was to offer trade-offs on other priorities. In this particular case, there was another major project that interested the retail arm. Mr. Wayman argued, "If we did the back-dating, we just could not get the other project done." He observed that the systems people have rather absolute power on such matters because other managers do not have the knowledge to dispute the systems viewpoint. However, he indicated that this only works if the systems people have the perspective of the whole. When there is a conflict between business issues and technical issues, the technical people must be willing to accommodate the business issues. Where it makes little difference to the business managers, he noted, most managers are willing to go along. Again, it appeared that trust and a large degree of mutual respect were the major factors allowing these conflicts to be resolved. All interests outside data processing were represented where it was important that they be represented, but where interests outside data processing were less critical, data processing was willing to go ahead without long delays.

Overall, conflict was managed by consulting other parties where their interests might be important. Obviously, this required some a prior knowledge of what their interests might be. The other side of this was the confidence to proceed when their interests were not affected, or, to paraphrase Mr. Wayman, not making consultation a fetish where it was less important. Mr. Wayman's comments reveal the critical elements: a willingness to represent the requirements of his part of the operation effectively, yet in a manner that did not sacrifice the interests of other departments. The importance of stating the business issues "up front" probably cannot be stressed enough. This step appeared to provide an orientation that prevented the technical issues from dominating. Thus, when the operations people did move ahead they were—and were perceived to be—responsive to the interests of other groups. In short, effective differentiation and integration were achieved simultaneously by following normal procedures.

A similar process seemed to be followed on another source of conflict, one concerning service charges. Some customers were allowed to keep their old automatic transfer accounts; this meant that their checking balance was always zero and therefore interest could not be calculated on their accounts in the same way as on NOW accounts. Mr. Wayman commented, "The problem was sent to me with five possible alternatives. From the operations point of view, two of these were viable. I preferred one and I did some lobbying to sell this issue. I used the lack of response to my recommendation as an indication to charge ahead." Again, decisions seemed to be made by transmission of information, the definition and communication of acceptable alternatives, and a willingness to move ahead without unnecessary delay, guided by knowledge of what would and would not be important to others.

The managers we interviewed consulted widely throughout the organization with people at all levels as needed. The people that we interviewed at customer-contact levels indicated how far this approach was carried. Supervisors were involved in the design of the training they were expected to administer. Moreover, the new-accounts people had a good perspective on their roles as participants even though the ones we interviewed had not been consulted. As one of them indicated, "We never gave any input. We do give input when we know more about something; that is, when we've handled it in the past, like the certificates. In this case, no one knew how to set up the accounts and yet we had to be competitive so it was not something that we were asked about." Although undoubtedly there was variation among the local banks, the two bank presidents we interviewed reported similar procedures for implementation within their bank. They delegated the matter to an employee who typically handled new services. The guides from the holding company were contained in written materials and the manager to whom responsibility for the NOW account had been given distributed the materials and discussed matters thoroughly with all concerned. In both cases, the person given responsibilities had a position that permitted him or her to act as liaison between the major units involved.

The picture that emerged was of an organization that delegated implementation to lower-management levels situated so as to handle cross-functional relationships and predisposed to thorough communication with all involved. Thorough communication included not only the procedures but an understandable strategy. While the customer-contact people in the banks did not have input into implementation decisions, middle- and lower-level people in the holding company were essentially responsible for implementation, within very broad guidelines and understandable rationales determined and communicated by upper managers.

Flexibility

Apparently, only a few modifications needed to be made during orientation. There were basically two sources of problems. First, the requirement of calling all their individual customers became too time-consuming, at least for some of the personal bankers. As a result, statement stuffers were used with brochures, but some of these brochures were put into corporation statements sent to business accounts which were, at the time, not eligible to open NOW accounts. The result was a lot of calls that needed to be handled to explain the fact that these accounts were not eligible. Also, there were apparently a few problems for the first day or two in getting accounts onto the computer system. A personal banker reported having to do a large amount of paperwork that normally would have been processed by the computer. However, by the third day the accounts could be converted directly to the computer system. Thus, she reported an initial "mess" that was resolved quite quickly.

Some of the potential difficulties had been anticipated by extra staffing. Mr. Mueser reported, at least at the lead bank, that while no additional staff was added, there was an anticipated increase in phone inquiries. To handle this, some additional clerical people were trained to handle the inquiries that would normally go to the personal banker. In Mr. Mueser's words:

The girls are truly junior personal bankers. It is hard to back up personnel in retail. There were no new hires; the learning curve is too long. We had to use our own skilled retail people. The personal banking concept takes a long time to develop in a personal banker. They need to know many different areas which prior to the personal banker were divided into six different departments.

A few new standard operating procedures were needed, primarily in response to new rules issued by the government, such as those making nonprofit organizations eligible to open NOW accounts. Also, the more complex pricing required that more information be transmitted throughout the bank in order to respond to different types of customers. For the most part, these changes were communicated by the bulletins, interoffice mailers, and weekly training sessions. The new regulations were sent out to people as they came into the bank. In addition, certain minor revisions in software input forms and signature cards were introduced.

No special motivation devices or new leadership patterns seem to have been introduced. The only motivational device specifically connected with the NOW accounts was giving each employee a free NOW account with no minimum balance. The one person who spoke to this point indicated that she thought that this was a big benefit to morale.

Readiness

In all respects—strategically, technologically, and organizationally—First Commercial was well preapred to deal with the NOW account. We have seen that they had a well-researched, clearly articulated strategy.

Also, as we have indicated, technologically they had been ready for some time. The work of Mr. Wayman beginning in 1976 had resulted in a well-documented system for managing the demand deposit accounts. The major changes had already been made. As Mr. Wayman said, "The preparation on the demand deposit side was extremely important because some banks wound up buying totally new DDA systems just for the NOW accounts." Moreover, Mr. Wayman's comments revealed how great the potential for problems was because the checking function is so central to banks. "The DDA systems are unique to each bank. This is the way the bank organizations evolved; they are built around that system. When we changed the demand deposit system here, we removed the spinal cord of the organization." However, as we have already indicated, First Commercial had for some time possessed a new system designed to handle the NOW account. In fact, the system was better designed to handle the NOW account than the previous Interestcheck account.

Still some changes were needed. The NOW account required that interest and tax information previously required only for time deposits be entered into the system designed for demand deposits. Most changes in forms seemed to go smoothly. One bank president observed that the only real changes involved adding a few columns and/or rows to old reports. For the most part, these revisions were made by data processing and it was simple to add these items. Another president observed that probably the only change in forms had to do with the format of the customer statement— a very routine matter. Technically, First Commercial was well prepared.

Somewhat paradoxically, a major element of this technical readiness seemed to be a tolerance for ambiguity that allowed the managers to avoid being immobilized by forcing themselves to answer questions they were not ready to answer at a particular time. For example, earlier we noted Mr. Wayman's observations about estimates and about the rapid obsolescence of plans for implementing the NOW account. He also commented on the readiness to leave pages blank in planning documents until decisions could be made on these. In short, part of the technological readiness may be recognizing where it is unrealistic to be prepared at any given time and moving ahead without getting bogged down in what is presently "unknowable."

In addition, they were well prepared to meet organization requirements. The introduction of the personal banker concept and the parallel move toward organization redesign had put the organization in the position to implement a strategy that could vary between market areas and could be targeted to specific groups of customers. The organization was changing in ways that permitted it to deal with each individual customer across all services it provided, to have the information and technical capabilities to analyze the costs effectively, to avoid forcing money from one account to another, and to collect information from its customers as a basis for the design of the strategy.

Finally, not only was the technical staff in place, but the emphasis given to achieving consensus throughout the organization appeared to make First Commercial ready in human and social terms. A climate of knowledge, trust, and mutual respect allowed efforts to be coordinated readily without interference in the individual routines. In addition, according to Mr. Mueser, "First Commercial puts a great deal of resources, and in my judgment very effectively, into the training and development of people." Historically, First Commercial was concerned with people and process issues. In fact, one theme in our data suggested that managers may have viewed this focus as a source of competitive advantage. Several times during our interview, Mr. Mueser was hesitant to discuss how they were structured for fear of revealing their secrets to other banks in the area.

In short, on almost every relevant dimension, First Commercial was well prepared to introduce the NOW accounts effectively. In the minds of the individuals in the system, the two factors that contributed most importantly to this level of readiness were the high levels of trust that characterized their working relationships and the high level of development of the computer software.

It was also clear that First Commercial had a clear picture of how all the parts fit together and how to operationalize this understanding. They had a written action plan and project budgets. An idea of how complete these plans were can be obtained from Mr. Mueser's answer to our question: "Did you have a written action plan?"

> Yes. We knew the day we would be allowed to open them [NOW accounts]. The timing of advertising was critical. The coordination with agencies is critical. You need to have good graphics.
>
> In house we had a budget and wanted to include deposit growth as part of the budget. We operated under budget constraints. An advantage we have is the personal banking concept. This can be more important in marketing a new product than media advertising.
>
> We had to put new people on phones to meet the anticipated demand. We did not let people schedule their vacations at this time and we prearranged lunch hours. This foresight led us to train people ahead of time to staff the phones. Normally the personal banker would have handled all these, but we needed some backup for anticipated volume. On day one, the team was ready. They knew the answers to the questions then.

Training

Training for the NOW account cannot be separated easily from the normal stress given to training. Managers and personnel of all levels indicated that First Commercial Bank had a tradition of investing in training and development of people. For example, a regional president commented:

> Our bank always has been a teaching bank. We routinely have Wednesday morning, Wednesday afternoon, and Thursday morning meetings and also have monthly staff meetings. So we have continuous contact with our people. We use these sessions for training. We also emphasize clear written instructions. We write it, test it on a few people, rewrite it, and pass it out and discuss it.

As noted earlier, Mr. Mueser made similiar observations about the emphasis that has always been given to training. Also, a teller supervisor commented, "We always have teller meetings and we are always retraining."

The development and implementation of training for the NOW account followed a process that paralleled the general strategy of development of basic guidelines and procedures in River City. River City materials were made available to the individual banks, who used them as they saw fit. Emphasis was placed on giving people at all levels a rather holistic view of the overall strategy. Mr. Mueser commented, "We train everyone. Account officers, officers at all levels had the NOW account reviewed with them. To maintain a defensive strategy, it had to be communicated to the front-line people." The training efforts for the staff, according to Mr. Mueser, made heavy use of professionally developed visual aids and handouts.

> We had a staff training room. We walked people [the front-line people, supervision, and personal bankers] through the concept. We went over the history of the NOWs. We discussed the New England experience, the laws, the forms, and procedures; we provided handouts of all of this. We even did some role playing in techniques on sales. We gave the employees desk materials for examples and charts so that they could show particular customers what they should have in the way of minimum deposits and so on for it to be advantageous for them to switch.

The individual banks followed their own approach to training their personnel. A president of an affiliate bank commented:

> We had a basic plan come to us. The first thing we did was to instruct our own line people to get acquainted with them. Our approach is to pinpoint the product, in that we orient one person as an in-house expert who trains all the others. This person then trains all the line people and the officers. They have operational meetings to instruct the others. Also, the marketing people came in and talked about the marketing concept with the people in our bank.

He added that with every product the holding company sent information containing basic product guidelines, such as a description of the type of product and information to help to introduce it. "We supplemented a bit and made it more specific. This tells people how to input things into the computer, who it affects, who is involved, and so on. The holding company also sent out pamphlets about the information for the customer. The individual banks may develop some descriptions for their own personnel."

Another bank president observed, "With the NOW account the cashier would be responsible for the system. Our customer service department had responsibility to develop the forms, techniques, and advertising. We tried to anticipate the questions the customers would ask. The information from the holding company is helpful here also. We asked them to work it into their conversations with customers."

The extensive training meant personnel were prepared to serve customers. Training of the customer-contact people and the design of charts and graphs were geared to help the accounts people to help the customer make the right decision. Several managers noted First Commercial's practice of giving the customers good advice. Again, this was part of the overall strategy which, as Mr. Mueser put it, was First Commercial's response to the fact that "our competitors were giving it away. Our key was to sharpen our skills and train our people." However, this approach (which relied heavily on the skills of lower-level personnel) was built on a long history of personnel development. As Mr. Mueser observed, "We do a lot of training of people. They play the key role. We meet one hour per week with all of our personal bankers. Maybe little banks could not do that; a large bank is more sophisticated. For example, as part of the training, we have our legal staff come in and talk. These are the advantages of being big."

Specific preparation of the new accounts people began approximately two weeks before the accounts were to be opened, through a series of meetings, which used visual aids and handouts. A supervisor commented:

> The first meeting was on what the product was, what it would offer, how to sell it, and what the charges were on what accounts. We had pamphlets that we gave people. Then, we had meetings on opening the account, on what numbers we needed to enter to inform the system on the account that we were opening. Then we had to consider how to close the NOW account. For these we had written instructions with a sample to tell how to do each operation. We made up instructions so that each person could refer to them.

The success of this overall approach can be seen in the comments of a personal banker. She observed:

> I called my customers with large balances and told them that NOW accounts would be available within a month or so. After we knew the bank policy, I personally solicited my customers, sent them a brochure, and advised. Of course, these accounts don't pay for some people but I tried to advise them anyway. I would refer to our policy but I would also tell them that different things change between institutions. I tried to be honest, thinking that if people are loyal, they will stay even if there are different conditions on minimum balances between institutions. Then again, the savings and loans didn't know what was involved in the change, so they might be at a disadvantage, too.

Thus, with respect to training, it is clear that First Commercial Bank designed a set of procedures and introduced them in a manner consistent with their overall traditions of handling products, developing understanding at the lowest levels, and allowing local autonomy. Expertise of managers at the holding company was used to develop procedures that became effective guides for introducing the change in a manner allowing active participation at the lower levels. There was a set of clear procedures and a high level of information throughout the system that allowed the overall strategy to be implemented successfully.

Monitoring

The procedure for monitoring paralleled the approach of delegation used for introduction. This is clear from the posture taken by Mr. Wayman on technical issues, statements from the new-accounts people at the bank, and statements of the regional presidents about how their bank handled the training and implementation. In addition, at least for the two presidents we interviewed, the monitoring of the accounts seemed to be delegated by the presidents to someone within their bank. In one case, it was an executive vice president; in the other, it was the cashier of the individual bank. These people monitored their daily reports on new accounts, cash movements, and so forth.

One president commented that his monitoring relied on the normal monthly financial reports, which contained the number of new accounts and the amount of money in each type of account. From this information it was possible to see if new accounts represented new money or resulted from switches of accounts within the bank.

At the level of the holding company, Mr. Stone indicated that progress was monitored closely. Four elements were observed. First, the accounts were tracked. In Mr. Stone's words, "We got a report on every customer who left and we tried to call them to find out why they left. We watched how big an effect pricing was having on exits. We were concerned with exits. We looked at this very closely for nine months and then dropped it. We were not losing enough customers to worry about it." Second, normal monthly reports were used. Third, input from the personal bankers was used. "They are a great source of information. We meet at least twice a month with them. They have much information." Finally, the general monthly financial reports were used to look for trends. NOW accounts were looked at closely for about six months and then basically forgotten. In looking at the particular reports, Mr. Mueser commented that deposit balances, the flows of funds within the banks, and the flows of funds in and out of the bank were followed closely. Although there were no definite criteria established ahead of time, some projections were made of how the mix of accounts would change during the year and budgets were based on this. Since the reviews indicated that the projections were reasonably accurate, no intervening steps were taken.

Internal Outcomes

As we have indicated, there were only a few minor problems, and these were experienced mainly by the customer service people in the first few days of operation. One supervisor indicated that a problem occurred with the tellers who found it difficult to understand differences between NOW accounts and other accounts when closing an account. With the NOW account, as opposed to the demand deposit account, interest needed to be added when an account was closed. She also indicated that there was some resistance to change from the older tellers. "They wanted to know, why do we have to change.?" She tried to explain in terms of how quickly they could balance and what the new system provided the customers in terms of speed and efficiency. She added, "Now when the system is down, they panic because they are so used to it." She also noted that one outcome of the new procedures was improvement in the work and reduction in work load.

One new-accounts person indicated that there was some problem with the negative opinion of the people selling the product. "It was a question of accepting change. Then again, it was annoying to accept the change when the computer was not set to go. It was hard to be enthusiastic when you knew how much work it was going to cost you." She attributed the failure to causes outside the system. She felt that it was impossible to forecast all these things and that all the necessary capabilities just cannot be built in. Again, all the problems appear to have been minor, well confined, and dealt with quickly. These problems were reported only by respondents in the new-accounts area. No one in management mentioned them. Managers from the lead bank, the holding company, and the out-of-state affiliates consistently reported that the process went smoothly from the first day and that the only changes needed were in response to new or altered regulations. We do not know whether those problems were never known by the managers, had even been defined as problems by them, or had been forgotten. Clearly though, the problems were fleeting, even for the customer-contact people.

With these exceptions, all respondents felt that the new procedures worked extremely well. Mr. Wayman reported, "It was one of the better systems that we have. It runs smoothly, it doesn't break, and it gives good reports." Mr. Mueser indicated, "It has always been as smooth as silk. Anticipations of costs, new accounts, and money flows were right on target." He said that such excellent results are not always the case. A regional president indicated that there were no problems in his bank concerning the NOW account. Another regional president indicated that he experienced no problems, although some changes were made in pricing at one bank in his region to meet competition. Overall, the changes that First Commercial made after January 1, 1981, were minimal. Most of them were in response to changes that could not have been anticipated prior to the introduction of the accounts, and these changes themselves caused no serious disruption. Their effects were confined to the lowest levels in the organization and the problems were handled quickly. Obviously, the autonomy granted to the divisions and the flexibility that had been built into the process were the primary reasons that the modifications made by an individual bank involved little disruption.

Perhaps the most significant major internal outcome was the role of the NOW account in helping to institutionalize the new structure. Recall that the introduction of the NOW account overlapped the creation of a new organizational structure. As a result, in working on the NOW account, organization participants learned about the new structure. As Mr. Stone put it:

> We are finding pretty much of a common market, but there is some diversity between regions as to product. The only restriction is that if you advertise commonly, you have to have a common price. The NOW account led into the whole process. We needed to get common prices for our services. We had to act together. The NOW account proved the vehicle that truly displayed our needs for commonality.

Similarly, Mr. Wayman commented that, prior to NOW accounts, it was often difficult to get the downtown River City bank and the affiliate banks to agree on what was needed. The NOW account was part of a process that led to a loosening of the connections between River City and the various banks. He observed, "The NOW account contributed to decentralization but did not do so alone. Basically, we evaluated our productivity and we are finding we spend too much time talking to banks. The banks outside River City are too different to do things the same way as the River City banks." From an operation's point of view, it was so successful that "we have tried to model the development of other processes after this system." The NOW account, in combination with the automatic transfer account, indicated the importance of being prepared. "Many things will occur like the NOW account experience in the future as deregulation continues. We will be better prepared."

The regional managers also commented on the learning that had taken place during this process. They indicated that the NOW account was one factor that improved communication about new products internally and led to the development of procedures with which they were quite comfortable. Both presidents we interviewed indicated that they were now familiar with the new structure and that the new structure gave them greater input into decisions of this sort than they had had during the introduction of the NOW account. One regional president in particular felt that he would now be in a position to argue much more strongly for his view that they should have been more aggressive in his region.

External Outcomes

The product outcomes of the NOW account were consistent with expectations. Overall, First Commercial's defensive strategy was successful. Approximately 80 percent of the dollar amounts had switched to the NOW accounts, but only about 50 percent of the customers had changed. Approximately fifteen months after initial introduction, there was still a gradual increase in the number of NOW accounts. Most important, however, few customers went elsewhere. Mr. Mueser commented, "Our accounts lost to competitors were negligible." Commenting on the experience at the lead bank, he indicated that they had lost only a handful of accounts out of many thousand that they had and discovered that the ones they lost had not been profitable. The concern over the shift of funds to the savings and loan associations was unnecessary. "We were aware that they were giving away thousands of check orders. But the accounts didn't move. Our loyal customers stayed with us. People don't change banking relationships easily. If the customers are satisfied and are getting good service, they don't leave; they remain loyal." In addition, he felt that the NOW account had attracted a considerable amount of new money to the bank—well over $1 million in the lead bank, and these accounts have continued to grow. Also, it was clear that the initial calls from the personal banker were successful. According to Mr. Mueser, "Many of the customers said, 'Do it on the first day you can.' It was very simple to change codes, which was all that was required to open the account. Consequently, we opened many accounts right away." Mr. Mueser summarized their outcomes: "We have experienced nothing but consistent growth and attracted some new deposits. We accomplished our basic purpose of retaining our depositors." He indicated that they would do nothing differently if they had to do it over again.

Mr. Stone indicated that while they were generally successful in maintaining their accounts, he wished they had priced their accounts higher. "We could have charged much more for the low-balance accounts. Customers wouldn't have gone into it; we would have fewer shifts. However, at the time we were afraid that if they did not have a NOW account they would feel like a poor relation. We were afraid we would lose them, but we lost so few. We could have priced it at $6 or $7 per month."

The experiences of the regional presidents varied. The regional president of the Prairie City area reported a similar experience to what had occurred in River City. It basically was a low-volume activity; approximately one year after the NOW accounts were introduced, of a total of about 9,000 accounts, only about 1,500 were NOW accounts. He indicated that they had required the customer to take the initiative to open the account and that many of them did not.

> We found that most of our customers are passive; they sit there with money in a checking account. We ask them why and they say, "I know I should change it. I'll do it when I get around to it." Many of them just don't get around to it.
>
> Thank God for the passive ones; it has kept the money cost down. It is not high-cost money. It has been an acceptable item. We are not paying market rates for this money. It did take some of our demand deposit accounts and thus raised our money cost, but not drastically. To the degree that it raises money cost, you have to pick it up on the other side. The NOWs are not a big cost due to the high interest rates, but they have had some impact. They do not have a heavy impact on profit.

The other regional president ranked the NOW account approach as only a moderate success. He indicated that the industry was a little guarded because this was the first major change in a long time. Also, there was great concern about cost, which led to people not pushing it hard and also designing the accounts so that the customer had to activate them. However, it was an acceptable item in terms of cost. It has been successful, with success being defined as "when money doesn't move into six-month certificates." It must be noted, however, that banks in his region had been very aggressive in promoting the Interestcheck account. This aggressive approach continued into the NOW account. He observed:

> It was my decision to go ahead with it aggressively. It was a good product and our customers would like it. It did increase cost, but we could recoup that. It worked out well. We kept money from moving into more expensive forms. This was hidden initially and appeared more than we expected. We felt that money would move from the NOW accounts at the same rate as it did from the demand deposit accounts, but it moved more slowly. People tend to leave more money in the NOW accounts than they should because they are getting something on it. In rural banks such as ours, people who have passbook savings don't combine it with their checking. They think of the checking account as something to pay bills with while passbook savings is for longer term. This may be peculiar to country people, but they keep separate accounts.

With respect to specific figures at his bank, roughly 60 percent of dollar assets were in time deposits and NOW accounts and roughly 10 percent were in demand deposits. Approximately one year after the introduction of the NOW accounts, the demand deposits stabilized and stopped going down.

Overall, "We are seeing a nice growth in our 5 ¼ percent money. That's what I see as success." (This was at a time when the prime rate was 18 to 19 percent.)

Overall, he evaluated the account as successful, but it could have been much more successful had the approach been more aggressive at the start:

> I would have gone for a wider market. Our normal radius is 13 miles for marketing. I would have gone to 26 miles. I would have doubled our advertising budget. I would have made a concentrated effort to get new business. We were just using it defensively. When you have a good product, you should go more aggressively. I was too easy on my competition. We did not take full advantage of it. I would do more offense, not just defense.

Summary and Interpretation

Radical versus Routine Innovation

First Commercial Bank provides an example of a routine innovation elegantly implemented. For this bank, implementing NOW accounts was seen as something so simple that it was actually easier than the combination savings and checking accounts they had offered prior to the legislation permitting NOW accounts. The organization's size did mean that they had to engage in many activities to get the new product off the ground, even though it was routine. Nonetheless, everyone in the organization believed this to be a routine innovation.

History/Unique Characteristics

The major reason the innovation was perceived as routine was the bank's history with checking. Introduction of the NOW account followed the introduction of Interestcheck. Most people felt that the NOW account was much easier to handle than Interestcheck. A NOW account was just a variation on a product that was already central to the bank's mission. Moreover, it had anticipated the new product and developed itself accordingly. It should be recalled that other changes were being made concurrently. Thus, the results we obtained might have been different if we studied the next innovation First Commercial attempted or if this innovation had occurred a few months earlier or later.

The culture and values of the organization aided implementation. Over and over again, people described a culture of trust and respect for the requirements of other functional areas. There was almost no competition reported among the interdependent functions; instead, there was a deliberate effort to make decisions that would account for the interests of other functions in addition to one's own. At the same time, there was a willingness to disagree and to move ahead swiftly without going through due process if it appeared that no significant disagreements existed. In other words, people did not spend time waiting for a consensus to emerge if they believed that there was no major opposition to a particular plan. As a result, managers at First Commercial were able to move ahead quickly, with good integration among functions, effective use of information in different units and at different levels, and positive relations throughout the organization.

Goals and Strategy

To First Commercial managers, the NOW account was another checking account, but it would cost them more than regular checking. They therefore wanted to limit the costs associated with the product. However, they feared competition, they wanted to not lose accounts to the savings and loan associations which were expected to market NOW accounts very aggressively. Their strategy reflected these two goals. They priced the account at a high level to cover the costs and discourage expensive low-balance accounts, but they marketed it aggressively to their high-balance customers through telephone calls from personal bankers. Their strategy was thus defensive in the sense that they had no desire to bring in new business with the product but simply to retain their current good customers, as they made great efforts to do. Also, their approach to the NOW was affected by their general desire to create a common product for all the banks.

Search

Their choice of a defensive strategy was based on large amounts of information gathered from many different sources, particularly Boston banks with prior experience with NOW accounts. The external search process involved many levels and functional specialties and was dispersed. They were also informed by their own employees, market surveys of their customers, consultants, and publications.

Complexity

For a number of reasons, implementing this defensive strategy was easy for them, despite their size and the considerable complexity of twenty positions being directly involved in the NOW account. Moreover, a number of different positions had to be integrated just to make the NOW account systems operational. They managed their complexity well.

Flexibility

One strength in managing complexity was First Commercial's flexibility. While they had written action plans, they expected the plans would change. They tolerated gaps in planning because they knew the gaps had to be there. Their orientation to planning allowed them to plan under conditions of uncertainty. In addition, their vertical and horizontal communication gave the organization flexibility in adapting to unforeseen events. Much of the horizontal communication was built in through their use of project teams composed of representatives from different functional areas. People knew enough about the requirements of others to take action that would satisfy the interests of others without lengthy delays. Their practice of consulting with employees at different levels kept them informed so that they could make changes as necessary. Finally, where possible, on issues where there were a variety of opinions, the technology available was used to allow the contentious issues to be treated as variables; consequently different preferences could be satisfied by allowing choices on these variables within the context of the overall framework.

Power Arrangements for Decisions

The structure of power relationships contributed to the smoothness of implementation. Various mechanisms encouraged everyone from regional presidents to personal bankers to contribute to the decision-making process. The basic decision of whether or not to offer the account was almost taken for granted. Major decisions, especially the defensive stance, were made centrally but only after extensive internal participation and external search. Prior to implementation, many people were consulted. Later, the process became even more participative, at least for upper-level managers, particularly bank presidents. In addition, the project teams were autonomous as long as they stayed within certain business constraints. All had clearly structured action plans. Their ability to do what they were charged to do without constantly seeking approval resulted in a timely implementation; in fact, they were ready early.

One reason for the project team's success was its autonomy; another equally important reason was integration of the different interdependent functions whose input was necessary for implementing the NOW account. The project team provided a structure and accountability for accomplishing the task, while getting each necessary functional area involved. It was a vehicle for managing conflicting interests, because differences could be ironed out there. The project team was effective at ironing out these differences, first because the culture supported conflict resolution and second because upper management had a clear expectation that the team get the job done with no excuses about who had not been cooperative or contributed fairly. In sum, the task was delegated to the team with very little supervision, with the understanding that the team would resolve differences and get the job done on time.

This style of delegating and trusting employees to do what needed to be done was accompanied by a method of monitoring progress that was not personal. That is, careful monitoring was done by looking at the numbers of accounts and average balances, not by looking over the shoulders of individuals. Individual mistakes that were caught in this process were treated as issues requiring further information for the employee, consistent with the trust the organization placed in the employee. Thus, the project team in particular and other members of the organization as well had the trust of upper management that made it possible for them to actually exercise their autonomy to make rapid decisions and resolve differences quickly, resulting in readiness to implement the NOW account.

Readiness

Part of this early readiness went beyond the effectiveness of the organization structure, though. Unlike almost all the other organizations in the study, First Commercial Bank had purchased a NOW account software package five years prior to the date NOW account became legal. While they still had to test the program, they were far ahead of those banks and S & Ls that had to begin with searching for a program. In addition, since the NOW account was in no way radical, First Commercial Bank had all the organizational routines in place for swiftly implementing this new kind of checking account. This included having had project teams for various tasks for some time, something that no other institution in the study had.

Internal Outcomes

The results of their high level of readiness were positive. They had a few problems in providing accurate balances for a couple of days, but the number of problems was almost negligible for an organization of this size. From the beginning, statements came out on time, because staff was ready so early. There was no reported overtime and almost no employee stress, with the exception of the first couple of days after the accounts were legal. In addition, the NOW account provided a laboratory for experimenting with their new decentralized structure, so it led to considerable organizational learning about how to function in that structure.

Product/External Outcomes

The NOW account also met First Commercial Bank's goal of retaining its good customers. They lost very few customers. Their high price kept the low-balance customers in regular checking, while their sales efforts through the personal bankers moved high-balance customers into NOW accounts. Moreover, the cost of funds was high enough that NOW accounts were easily profitable. Overall, then, First Commercial Bank engaged in an unusually successful implementation of a routine innovation. The organization's process, structure, and culture easily accommodated the change, resulting in a tranquil and in no way traumatic implementation of a product that contributed exactly what managers hoped it would to the organization's mission.

Notes

1. Interestcheck is a fictitious name for the product.
2. Since all organizations paid the maximum interest, we give little attention to it in discussing the various strategies.

4
Learning from the Past

Second Commercial Bank, a holding company headquartered in River City, operated multiple banks in eleven regions throughout the state. It also served several hundred correspondent banks. The senior management emphasized that it is managed on a decentralized basis.

Our initial contact in the organization was with the chairman, who directed us to Mr. Jones, the senior vice president who had been project manager for the introduction of the NOW account. He provided considerable background information in a lengthy interview and made his personal files on the NOW account available to us. He suggested that we talk to the vice president responsible for marketing (Mr. Mann) and the vice president in charge of operations (Mr. Ellis). Occupants of these two positions had been heavily involved in the planning of the NOW account, although Mr. Ellis had not been vice president of operations during the introduction of the automatic transfer that preceded the NOW account. Mr. Ellis's predecessor was no longer with the organization, and we were unable to interview him. (Apparently his departure was in large measure due to his ineffectiveness in the introduction of the automatic transfer account.) We also interviewed the president of one of the individual banks, one of his assistants who had been involved in the introduction of the NOW account at his own bank as well as in the preparation of materials by the holding company for other banks, and two new-accounts persons at the individual bank.

Routineness

There is clear evidence that the introduction of the NOW account itself was a routine operation. Comments from individuals from the senior vice president down through the new-accounts people were uniform in emphasizing that there were no major changes in their work and no problems with any aspect of the technology or preparedness; in fact, no difficult problems were encountered. The most typical statement was that the NOW account simplified things because it transformed two accounts into one. Top executives labeled it a nonevent. New-accounts people said that all they did differently was to use a new form. However, all of these statements need to be put into the context of a major change that had taken place earlier when the automatic transfer account was introduced.

Fourteen months prior to the introduction of the NOW account, Second Commercial had had a rather traumatic experience in introducing the automatic transfer or option account. Most statements about how easily introduction of the NOW account had gone compared it with the experience of the automatic transfer account. Moreover, in the minds of most respondents, the introduction of the NOW account was anticipated and planned in the design of the automatic transfer. Thus, while pricing, promotion, and other strategic decisions about the NOW account can be separated from the automatic transfer experience, its introduction here must be understood in the context of the automatic transfer experience. In fact, when asked to talk about the NOW accounts, respondents would often say something like "I remember the option account better." In short, understanding the introduction of the NOW account in Second Commercial requires adopting a different time frame than we used in examining the other institutions. While these circumstances complicate interorganizational comparisons, they also must be viewed as data that indicate the need for longitudinal studies.

Design of the Innovation

Goals and Strategy

The major decisions on promoting and pricing the NOW account centered on profitability. The service was priced to be consistent with the overall objective of 1 percent return on assets and a 15 percent return on equity. It was assumed that competition would dictate the need to pay the maximum interest rate allowable and that there really was little choice as to whether or not to offer the NOW account. They believed they had to do it or else lose market share.

Several considerations acted as goals and/or constraints. One goal was that the service be profitable on its own terms. In other words, although it was recognized that the NOW account might influence the demand for other bank services, they did not consider added revenues from cross-selling when calculating the price. Second, a major concern that appeared to run throughout these deliberations was the desire to "not tamper with the big-balance customers." Thus, the effort was geared to maintaining the customer base, with the large customers being of particular concern. In fact, the possible loss of certain problematic small accounts seemed to be a possible positive side effect of pricing the account at a level where it was profitable in its own terms.

Two other factors acted as constraints on the process. First, as one vice president observed, "We are an extremely decentralized bank relative to others our size in the city." Consequently, the strategy and means of implementation were influenced by the organizational structure. Second, managers believed that it was important to have a common approach across the member banks, and that without the common approach certain advantages to scale (such as promotions, systems design, and training materials) would be lost.

The objective of requiring a common approach in a decentralized structure played an important role in all phases of the process. All of the individual banks were analyzed to determine what price would be best for that bank. However, in Mr. Jones's words: "There was so much commonality that we could use a common strategy." A few of the banks with many lower-income customers and several of the rural banks that had little competition were the least enthusiastic about the NOW account. Presidents of these banks were willing to go along with defensive strategy on the condition that, as Mr. Jones paraphrased them, "You don't go crazy on advertising." From the analysis Mr. Jones did, it was clear that the small banks were placed in a more difficult situation than the larger ones, because the small banks would be under the most pressure to offer the account, yet had the most to lose by it due to the large percentage of their funds that came from individual accounts which previously were interest-free.

Operationalizing the Strategy. The goal for NOW accounts was simply not to lose market share. As a result, the posture chosen was defensive; aggressive promotion was rejected and a fairly high price was chosen. Mr. Jones had concluded from his research that the NOW account would become a national generic product. Thus he chose to stay with "NOW" as the name. Also, he had concluded that a major concern would be the high transaction volume on such accounts. Interest on checking needed to be computed monthly as opposed to quarterly or semiannually as before. The average number of transactions per month was expected to be fifteeen to seventeen for a checking account in comparison with three to four for a savings account. The high volume for such a large system dictated that the process would have to automated. Second Commercial had developed capability to handle this volume when it introduced the automatic transfer.

A number of strategic questions were addressed. One question concerned how the account would be treated internally. Was it a checking routine or was it a savings routine? It was decided early in the process, based on the research in New England, that the account should be treated as a checking routine. Another strategic issue centered on whether or not to require one policy for all the banks. The decision was for a uniform policy, the exception being that banks in one or two regions were permitted to set a lower price to meet competition in their particular areas.

One of the most important strategic decisions was to follow a defensive posture on the NOW account. This stance was reflected in the pricing and promotion of the accounts, and in the design of internal procedures. In considering pricing, managers focused on profitability of the account. When they looked at the total scope of their operations, they concluded that they had a number of small-balance accounts averaging $500 to $600 that were expensive to service due to frequent overdrawing and other problems that required special attention. Thus, it was concluded that it was not profitable to price the NOW account in order to maintain these accounts. A large inflow of funds was not expected; the strategy was to price to get a $3,000 average balance. Via mathematical models they determined that a $1,500 minimum balance was needed to achieve the $3,000 average balance. Thus, $1,500 became the minimum balance a customer needed to maintain for a "free" account. The account was defined for the customer in terms of the minimum rather than the average daily balance, because they reasoned that the customer was used to thinking more in terms of the minimum balance.

The pricing decision was made exclusively in terms of the profitability of the NOW account. Although there was an awareness that cross-functional analysis was required to measure the full effects of the NOW account on the profitability of the bank's services, these calculations were not done at the time.

Also, a major consideration was avoiding any inconvenience to customers who currently had large-balance accounts. To this end, the defensive strategy involved a proactive step. Automatic transfer accounts were converted into NOW accounts internally; Second Commercial bore these special costs. One other feature was also directed to protect the large accounts. Mr. Mann commented, "You need to keep current large accounts. The customer service people were prepared to negotiate. If it was an age-old customer, you might make some concessions on a particular rate." One final step taken to avoid disturbing the customers was to buy them their first set of checks. The new-accounts people were explicitly instructed to avoid telling customers that they could not use their old checks. Reliance was placed upon the customer to inform the bank as to what checks were outstanding when the new account was opened, but then an internal system was used to send the old checks to the new account. Again, they made every effort to avoid disturbing large customers.

On the other hand, in some instances, customers were discouraged from opening a NOW. As one vice president put it, "We wanted to be in the market but not to make it easy for customers to open up NOW accounts. We made it necessary to fill out a new-account form. We did this deliberately to make it difficult to open one up. We came up with this approach by profiling account size and activity." In other words, part of the defensive strategy was designed to slow down the rate of movement of smaller accounts into NOW accounts.

The advertising was also defensive and designed to prevent the loss of the customer base. Mr. Mann (vice president of marketing) described how the defensive advertising was implemented.

> We needed to be sure the customers knew that we had the product. However, informing customers required different ads than we would use to attract customers. Basically, the emphasis of this kind of ad is product information rather than emotional appeal. We were definitely interested in keeping customers but not attracting new ones. Thus we did not use TV. We used radio; we directed it at intelligence and not at emotional appeals. We did not use a sales promotion or pitch. Then we let it run down. We wrote a letter from the CEO to our customers; we did not include it with the bank statement because many people might not open their bank statement in the first place. We also ran a newspaper ad or two. That's it. Then we just listed it as a service. We did not give any premiums or anything else to attract business.

It was recognized that there would be some transfer of funds to the NOW accounts, but as one officer put it, "We wanted it to be slow." (He contrasted this with the fact that the savings and loan associations were already paying interest on their balances and thus the NOW account did not increase their costs as much.)

Markets and the Environment. Second Commercial Bank was clearly one of the leaders in the regional banking community. Smaller banks and savings and loan associations frequently said Second Commercial Bank decisions influenced their own policies. However, in comparison with those of other large organizations we studied, Second Commercial Bank's managers appeared to be less concerned with its ledership role in the local financial community. At least, no one mentioned it as respondents at First Commercial Bank had. Nevertheless, being one of the largest banks in the area, Second Commercial Bank did influence the way other banks in the area responded to the NOW account. Mr. Jones gave lectures to correspondent banks. He was often asked what price his bank would charge and what would be its general approach. His response was, "I cannot say what we are doing; that would be price fixing. However, we are leaning toward . . ."

Strategic Decision Process

Strategy emerged from a centralized decision process, although the presidents of the individual banks were given the opportunity to make comments. In his role as project director, Mr. Jones played the most important part in the decision process. In addition to being the primary source of information from New England, he oversaw and coordinated the planning and design of the entire process. He relied heavily on the vice president of marketing and the vice president of operations of the holding company. Mr. Jones, as senior vice president, was also liaison with the bank presidents. His perception that he had good rapport with the bank presidents was confirmed by our interviews in a member bank.

Based on his analysis of the New England situation and the profit goals of Second Commercial, Mr. Jones defined his major task as that of being sure that the NOW account was priced high enough to generate profits. His planning assumptions included the belief that banks should offer this service at a price that would be profitable for the bank but still competitive for the largest customers. He also believed that most funds in NOW accounts would come from current customers, that advertising and promotion were apt to be of limited value, and that the NOW accounts were much more of a threat to profit deterioration for small retail banks than for larger wholesale banks. These views he summarized in a letter: "An approach that stresses proper pricing as a much more important factor than market share can generally be expected to yield better results." Based on his research, Mr. Jones was convinced that adopting a defensive posture was essential. Given this view and the decentralized nature of Second Commercial, Mr. Jones's major task became one of establishing a common product across all the banks, without forcing it on the banks, and at the same time not having them price the account at an unprofitably low level. To accomplish these ends, the regularly scheduled meetings of the bank presidents were orchestrated by Mr. Jones and Mr. Mann.

The basic approach was to present data in a form that Mr. Jones hoped would lead the presidents to arrive at the same conclusion he had. He began the first meeting with an example of what appeared to be a highly desirable outcome from the introduction of a low-priced NOW account in a typical bank. The projections showed large increases in the number of accounts and total bank balances. He then showed that, in fact, such an outcome would be extremely costly, particularly to the small banks. As a result, most of the presidents agreed on the merits of a defensive stance. While there were some disagreements among the presidents as to the appropriateness of this strategy, Mr. Jones did not perceive these to be strong objections. There is some evidence, however, that there was residual disagreement. A bank president reported that at a meeting several months later, one of the presidents began pushing for lowering the price of NOW accounts. The chairman of the holding company angrily terminated the effort. " 'You can discuss anything you want at these meetings, but we are not going to discuss the price of NOW accounts.' "

Mr. Mann's comments generally confirmed the description of a centralized process for formulating strategy and the importance of logical argument in the decison of the bank presidents. He observed, "Some presidents saw it as an opportunity for a new market share, so we had a few people to illustrate our thinking to. These people quickly fell in because the trends were so obvious that the way we did it was the right way; that is, with a nonaggressive posture." He continued that the posture of Second Commercial and the reasoning for it was spelled out in the preliminary meetings with the bank presidents during which time everyone had a chance for input.

> By the second meeting the facts said no, you don't do this. We had tremendous data from New England. The patterns were convincing for every single month. Pure logic dictated our posture. We knew we had to have the product, we knew its nature, and we knew how every change would impact earnings, but we needed to monitor it. It was all laid out objectively for them before the meeting.

The information from the president of the individual bank we interviewed supported this perspective.

> The presidents of the individual banks were asked for their opinion, but I'm not sure how much difference that it made. The project had been researched. The holding company had made up their mind. They wanted to have regional commonality. In a previous case I had been opposed to free checking, but I was prevailed upon. We had a series of pricing meetings. There was general consensus that a thousand dollars minimum made sense. Some banks wanted to go lower.

Discussing the format of the meetings, he continued,

> Typically the CEO of each bank is there. The format is usually very open with lots of dialog. The plan is laid out. It is not all that democratic; it is not a plurality of votes. That would not be a good way to run the organization. In the main, they say to you, "you are part of the process; therefore we ask you to make the decision in this way." Uniformity is needed in regional services.

In short, consensus was achieved though acceptance of the regional concept by the presidents, heavy reliance on information presented by Mr. Jones, and the pattern of reliance on the holding company that the individual banks presidents had established in the past. As the bank president put it, "The individual bank presidents see the holding company as an important resource."

This is not to suggest that there were not substantial disagreements during the meetings at which the approach was decided. However, several forces made the holding company's view prevail and be generally accepted. The meetings ended with the presidents agreeing to the general defensive approach and requesting the holding company to go forward with that approach.

Mr. Jones's words best summarize the strategic decision process:

> Nobody on the clerical staff was consulted. The decision was made by eight to twelve people. About one-third of the people in the entire organization were ultimately affected by it. I presented my data to the bank presidents. I am the liaison with them. We have a good flow of communication with them. Having done this type of thing, we have a natural dialog. We get together to discuss common issues. There is a great amount of information we had. They said, "why don't you go forward and do it. Whatever you say is okay. However, keep us informed and don't go crazy advertising it.

Search. This strong conviction about the best strategy for NOW accounts came from a thorough search for useful information. Early in 1977, Mr. Jones visited twelve financial organizations in New England. He sought answers to such questions as: Where does the money come from? What is the transaction volume? Can you market price? What are operational issues? What do you need to look out for? What is the cost of funds? What are the regulatory requirements? What tax forms are required for customers? How do you pay interest? What agreements, documentation, and advertising is recommended? Are there urban and rural differences? Are there legal problems? Who opens interest-bearing accounts? How do you link savings accounts with checking accounts?

In addition, in his role as project director, he provided for a continuing flow of information from 1978 to 1980 with the organizations he had visited in 1977. He kept abreast of their experiences by letters and telephone calls, maintaining a continuous file of their financial experiences with the NOW accounts. In addition, the archives contained numerous articles and reports on the NOW accounts and reports on seminars that he had attended. One of the most important seminars was led by a nationally known consultant on these accounts. This man was used as a sounding board in late 1979 to check out the assumptions that Second Commercial Bank was using in designing the NOW account. Although the search was broadly based, there was a general agreement throughout the organization that the New England experience had played a major role in the strategy formulation.

To summarize, Second Commercial Bank had relied heavily on information from New England banks in determining its defensive strategy. The information was collected primarily by one high-ranking executive. The data he collected from New England were extremely convincing to others in the holding company responsible for the NOW account; they in turn sought to convince the bank presidents to accept the wisdom of previous experience. They did not attempt to solicit differing views either from bank presidents or from those lower in the organization, although they used the existing structure to persuade and to allow discussion.

Implementation of the Innovation

Complexity

Second Commercial Bank was also highly complex, though slightly less so than First Commercial Bank. At the upper levels of the holding company, four people worked on the NOW account. They were the chairman and CEO, whose role was minor; the senior vice president, who had the primary responsibility for designing and implementing the product; and the vice presidents of operations and marketing. At the middle and lower levels of the holding company, six positions were involved with the NOW accounts. Programmers, systems people, and data processing services staff provided user support; trust staff, correspondent banking staff, and internal audit staff were also included. Finally, at the banks, eight positions participated in designing and/or implementing the product. They were the bank president; senior vice president; vice president of operations; assistant vice president of operations; vice president of advertising, PR, and marketing; personal bankers; new accounts representatives; and tellers. In all, eighteen positions participated in NOW accounts at Second Commercial Bank, two less than at First Commercial Bank. Still, this was high differentiation for participation in one new product, particularly one so similar to products already offered.

Readiness

The strategic considerations and the specific procedures for the introduction of the NOW account at Second Commercial bank can, as we have done, be treated separately from the automatic transfer. However, in discussing the readiness of the system to introduce the NOW account, the experiences of the organization with the automatic transfer approximately a year earlier must be considered part of the process. In fact, the strategy for introducing the automatic transfer was influenced by anticipation of the NOW account; many participants, when asked about the problems of introducing the NOW account, saw experiences with the automatic transfer as part of that process. Respondents from all levels of the organization reported that all the necessary preparation for the NOW account had been achieved in implementing the automatic transfer; as a result, the NOW account was perceived as "a piece of cake." However, the automatic transfer had been anything but.

Therefore, our analysis of the system's readiness must begin with what we could reconstruct of the history of the automatic transfer. The first automatic (or option) transfer account was opened in November 1978. The option transfer required new software and hardware in the computer area. The systems introduced did not work and resulted in major problems throughout the organization.

Initial planning for the automatic transfer in the spring of 1978 indicated that a complete revision in the demand deposit account system would be needed. However, according to the vice president of operations, Mr. Ellis, documentation was not received until September and the system had to be up by November.

> The documentation did not work and the vendor didn't know why. Basically, we got rid of the management group who did it. This was going on at the same time as the revision in the front-end process of checking— ten million transactions per month. This is an incredible load. All the other systems have three quarters of a million transactions per month. So you can see just how large a system was being affected. Someone just did not do their homework.

Some of the difficulties also stemmed from the time-driven nature of the innovation. The organization was responding to a date given externally as to when the service could be provided; it interpreted this date as a deadline. Consequently, it made mistakes. In Mr. Mann's words:

> The operations division needed to be brought up to par so they were ready for D-Day. Basically they were ready. Unfortunately we bought a bad system; we had to reprogram it and debug it. It took a tremendous amount of work and stress. The reason for this crunch was that we didn't have adequate time to prepare and then the government made changes while we were part way into the process. Basically it was not a normal product change environment. If we had time we would have developed our own system.

People at all levels of Second Commercial recalled the problems well. Mr. Jones remembered vividly the stress that he and other people experienced.

> What happened was that what normally should have been a 1 ½ year project had to be condensed into much less time due to the timing of the change in regulation. There were times during this process where some programming and systems people worked thirty-nine days in a row. There was tremendous stress. Basically, we told the individuals, "Let us know when the pressure is too much." Many nights I was here until 3:00 or 4:00 A.M.

Mr. Ellis observed:

> It was most traumatic for the systems and the programming people. There were seven or eight key people in the conversion, and now all but two have

left as a direct result of working on this project. Also, some clerical and bookkeeping people have left, but we didn't lose any of the supervising or management people that we didn't want to lose.

Two of the people who have not left are very long-term people. Those who left were in many ways typical of turnover among programmers. They have born the brunt of the problems, working around the clock for three months. That's how I got my job; others screwed up. The previous manager just didn't know any better. There are basic rules to follow in project management. First, there are front-end objectives, to find the problem. Second, you set reasonable implementation guidelines. Third, you get the people to execute. These were not done. The automatic transfer system problem was a management problem.

Several major reasons for the difficulties stemmed from the time pressure to be ready when the regulations permitted the automatic transfer and the inadequacy of the past system. Mr. Ellis commented:

> The evaluation of our system indicated that our software was not able to do what we foresaw. The timing was such that we could not design our own so we acquired a new package. There were not many choices for small banks at the time. We went to the vendor of the then existing software and bought from them. The demand deposit system is one of the most complex in the bank. It is a high-transaction volume. This leads to all kinds of problems. We were talking about a number of systems that have to be interfaced. Reconciliations, inputs, central information system, payroll system, and tax system changes are all involved. Every regulatory change leads to four or five systems that need to be changed. It impacts everybody.

The process used to implement the automatic transfer was centrally directed and formal in nature although some input was solicited from lower ranks. The information about the automatic transfer system itself was sent out in a manual to relevant personnel. The manual was a guide containing information that the user would need for daily processing. It explained what the demand deposit and automatic transfer system was and what options were available. It included samples and instructions for opening an account and for using the input forms. The guide was designed to aid the bank in training tellers, new-accounts personnel, and other personnel about the automatic transfer systems. The individual bank was allowed to use its own discretion to segment the guide in order to facilitate any specific training needs. Available in November 1978, it was developed with the consultation of individuals from the various banks. As it turned out, this consultation was thought to be so successful that it became a standard procedure for later changes, such as the NOW account.

Another major source of problems was attributed to the processes used to introduce the automatic transfer. Mr. Ellis noted:

The management of operations at that time gave a deadline and stuck to it. We wound up having five or six key programming people working twenty-four–hour days, seven day a week. It took a long time to undo mistakes in documentation, training materials, and profit edits. Every measure and principle you could violate was violated.

Mr. Ellis observed that from this experience, they learned to take data processing people more seriously when they said they could not meet a deadline.

To cope with the difficulties, the organization went into a crisis mode. Many people worked long hours. It became necessary to do many of the calculations by hand for a couple of months. Lists of things to be done were made and the items assigned priority. Mr. Jones told us that individuals who came forward with complaints or problems were told, " 'That is number x on our priority list. We are going to deal with the most important problems first. We'll get to it when we get a chance.' " The entire situation was compounded by the fact that the severest crisis was experienced around the Christmas holidays. The process did not operate completely smoothly until the next April, four months after automatic transfers were legal.

In setting priorities for coping with the difficulties of the automatic transfer, mistakes that would be visible to the customer were considered first. A detailed listing of the problems encountered with the option account was started on November 1, 1978. Bank personnel listed and collated problems and sent out a completed list of the operational problems on a weekly basis to the people in charge of the account at the various branches. They asked those people to go over the list of problems and send back a reaction to the list. Major problems included the calculation of service charges, operations documentation, the use of control numbers, missing information on microfiche, and confusion over account numbers. Similar technical problems continued to appear for over a month. By December 18, items needing attention were numbered, assigned priority level, and described as being work in process, work to do, or completed work. Priorities were periodically reordered at the holding company and communicated to the individuals involved. In March 1979, a meeting at the holding company was held to set priorities for enhancement of the demand deposit accounts (DDA) system. People were asked before the meeting to send their particular requirements. By April, the system seemed to be functioning effectively.

As a result of these events, several other things happened. First, when it was all over, the bank gave a party for everyone involved. In addition, Mr. Jones gave out cash bonuses ranging from $200 to $3,000 to individuals who had been part of the process. He observed, "This was the first time such a thing had ever been done here and it was appreciated. Basically, they saved our butt, and we owed it to them." Second, changes were made in the operations area. Mr. Ellis replaced the previous vice president of operations; new staff personnel replaced the data processing people who left. Third, people remembered the process as one they would never want again.

However, some outcomes were positive, especially what the organization learned. The automatic transfer experience resulted in Second Commercial Bank being ready—both technologically and organizationally—for the NOW account. At the time the NOW account was introduced, Mr. Jones reported receiving calls from the individual banks asking about how much typing of forms would have to be done again. He was confident that this time they were prepared—so confident that "I told them if there was any typing of forms to be done, I would personally come out and type them myself. I never got any calls." Mr. Ellis observed that the bank developed a whole new approach to project management (to be covered in the section *internal outcomes*). When it came time for the NOW account, Second Commercial had both the hardware and the software to proceed and had learned a great deal through the process of introducing the automatic transfer, which improved their ability to manage projects. In marked contrast to the reports about the automatic transfer, everyone we interviewed indicated that the introduction of the NOW account was easy. Technically, all the NOW account really involved was making two accounts into one. Still, a number of things needed to be done, requiring further internal changes to implement the new type of account.

Decision Process

Many of the concerns of the presidents, as a result of the trauma from the automatic transfer, centered more on technical than strategic issues. But even here, the presidents were willing to rely heavily on the holding company. Mr. Ellis observed, "The big problem would have to be the systems one; that is best done centrally for economies of scale. We had already regionalized data processing. Basically, they told us to go with that and keep us informed."

Within the holding company, the system decisions were made by a project team headed by Mr. Jones, although Jones delegated a good deal to Mr. Ellis. The use of the project team was a direct result of the experience with the automatic transfer. As Mr. Jones put it, "Since the introduction of the automatic transfer, we have changed how we do these things. Now we get a lot more people involved and do a much better job of processing. People at the bottom get a chance to speak. If a programmer says he can't do it in two weeks, we don't assume that he can, which is what we did on the automatic transfer account."

The project approach used for the NOW account, however, worked much better. Mr. Ellis described their approach to project management:

We did front-end analysis through discussion with members of the holding
company as to what they wanted to do. Then we programmed guidelines
and set prime programs. We decided external help was needed. Then we
documented and asked who was affected, who needed to get involved.
Basically, we set a Gannt chart—marketing, accounting, systems—everyone
who was a part of the project was consulted.

In describing their process in general, Ellis said the top management team
consults with the head of data processing and others who will be involved
on an as-relevant basis. "We are sure we get all the input, then we schedule.
We let them know what to expect. We fill in people, places, things, and
dates. We get feedback on time and requirements to meet the deadlines. We
have periodic meetings to check out where we are. We have reports
periodically for management to review." Thus, a team approach was used;
the process was structured by top-level executives and primarily involved
individuals at the holding company in River City.

In contrast to the process by which the systems decisions were made,
the process used to determine the procedures for operationalizing the NOW
account drew much more heavily on input from the individual banks. People
were selected from the individual banks on a voluntary basis. As Mr. Jones
put it, they wanted people involved "who would do the training and who
would ask tough questions." These people brought the forms and systems
from individual banks into meetings at the holding company held to design
the procedures. Mr. Jones indicated, "All the key details which they needed
to anticipate would be in the minds of the people who ran the checking
services daily. It was from these ideas that they built the detailed training
material." These materials were then made available to the individual banks.
Mr. Ellis confirmed this pattern. "We have to tell the other banks what we
are doing. We have the data processing services group which does this. They
provide booklets, manuals training materials, and so on. We tried to keep
people involved and then trickle-down to their banks. We train the key
people and then they take the training back to their banks and train as
needed." As he noted, this approach contrasted sharply with the strategic
decisions.

A basis for the more decentralized approach used to determine the design
of the implementation procedures also arose in part from the earlier experience
with the automatic transfer account. People were selected from the individual
banks on a voluntary basis. As Mr. Jones put it, "From our earlier training
efforts, we had pooled personnel systems from banks, and built on it." The
process as experienced by a participant was: "I had written a manual on the
option account earlier." While this pattern led to input from the individual
banks, this procedure did not mean that a general pattern of participation
existed. In the individual bank where we interviewed, one manager had been

among the representatives from the individual banks who had been heavily involved in the work at the holding company, so of course he reported a great deal of involvement. At the level of the customer service people, however, no participation was reported. On the other hand, their observations did reveal that an informal process at their bank operated effectively in providing them with information and helped them cope with any problems. They reported that the things affecting their particular jobs were explained to them, typically in an informal, often one-on-one fashion. As one put it, "When there was anything new, Mr. Park, who is in charge of operations, would come over and tell us everything—just informally during open hours. We didn't have a meeting room. He just would come over to where we sit, gather us around a little bit, and tell us."

Training

Once these procedures had been devised, the people who had designed them participated in training at the holding company. Mr. Jones acted as training coordinator and proceeded on the assumption that every person that had contact with the customer needed to be able to explain the account to the customer. It required the tellers to learn to uncompound interest; new-accounts people had to learn to walk through the agreement with customers. In addition, the mechanisms had to be developed to record the deposits and to provide information to the customers.

Mr. Jones played a major role in training. His primary methods were four-day sessions, which he led for people who came from the individual banks. These people than went back and trained their own people within their own banks. For the most part, training focused heavily on the mechanics of opening the NOW account, although Mr. Jones noted, "We covered everything that we had uncovered from our research." Thus, the general rationale was also included. (Since the new-accounts people had already been trained in cross-selling and marketing, the training could focus primarily on mechanics of the NOW account and filling out the forms.) The training also incorporated a two-way process. Participants were asked to send in their questions and problems that could not be answered in the training "so that everyone could benefit from this information."

Other steps to prepare the system included the development and dissemination of manuals and related forms prepared in consultation with individuals from the member banks. The standard materials were distributed at the four-day training sessions to be taken back to the individual banks. It is useful to note that this formal process was supplemented by an informal one introduced by the participants. Mr. Jones observed: "One of the things people did was to bring their secretaries with them to the training sessions.

It is the secretaries that often answer the phone and have to answer the questions."

One other aspect of preparing people for the new product was the role of lower-level managers in motivating and reducing the fears of tellers and new-accounts people. One manager reported that these people were like any sales people—always nervous about a new product. A supervisor reported, "The tellers don't like change. People like to do the same thing." When asked how she handled that difficulty, she responded, "Why, you just have a good attitude."

Monitoring

Monitoring was done at two levels. At the holding company, the market shares of each bank were reviewed on a continuous basis. At the local bank level, monitoring appeared to be done informally by the bank president scanning the daily ledger. The new-accounts people reported that once they were informed of their new duties, only occasionally would they be asked by management, "How many [NOW accounts] have you had?"

Other monitoring was also done informally at the local bank. As a new-accounts supervisor reported, "There were only a few problems. The accounts were not going into the computer correctly. You just correct this by sending in the difference sheet. We checked the computer and it was okay. Sometimes programs are goofed up when they are new. We were afraid of errors with a new system like this. It's good to check by doing calculations by hand." Thus, it appeared that much of the monitoring was done more or less at the initiative of lower-level managers rather than by formally mandated procedures.

Internal Outcomes

As we have suggested, the consequences inside the organization differed dramatically from the automatic transfer to the NOW account. One positive outcome resulting from the introduction of the automatic transfer system was that Second Commercial anticipated and built in routines for handling the NOW account. As a result, there were virtually no difficulties internally in implementing the NOW account. Second, the process used to introduce the automatic transfer had resulted in considerable organizational learning, which enabled the organization to implement the NOW account and other new services much more readily. Third, the introduction of the automatic transfer resulted in restaffing in the operations area of the bank. The previous manager had left the organization. There was a clear consensus among all the managers we interviewed that the operations side—particularly computer capability—was now more competently staffed and managed than before. In sum, the automatic transfer had resulted in the organization being in a much better position technically, managerially, and in its processes to innovate in the future.

Participants at all levels of the organization confirmed that there were no problems of any magnitude with respect to the NOW account process. In addition, Second Commercial was completely ready on January 1, when others were not. No manual backup work was required and only minimal stress was reported by the participants. Mr. Jones's comments that no one called with problems is an indication of how smoothly it went.

While overall the process of the new-accounts level seemed to work well, one source of dissatisfaction existed. The customer accounts people felt that the price that Second Commercial charged for the NOW accounts was much too high for their customers, particularly in view of the competition from the savings and loan association next door, which had set a $100 minimum. As with several of the other banks and S & Ls we studied, there seeemd to be some tendency for the new-accounts people to sympathize with the interests of their customers when these interests conflicted with the pricing of the accounts. These concerns had some impact on implementation because they seemed to influence how the new-accounts people communicated with customers. As one manager observed, "They were a bit squeamish about telling the customer the high minimum. Also, we had two ways to avoid the service charges. One was with a $2,000 minimum balance. The girls would not explain this to the customers. We asked them why they didn't and they said 'the customer wouldn't understand.' " There was one other complaint. The new-accounts personnel did not want to have the customers fill out a new card—"the new-accounts screener"—which they felt was unnecessary.

Overall, the internal processes involved in the NOW were very different from those used two years earlier for a similar new product, the automatic transfer. Whereas the automatic transfer was a source of stress and a tremendous burden on the system at all levels, the NOW account was viewed almost as a nonevent. The implementation and routinization of the NOW account was a straightforward procedure. The computer systems were in place; the major training tasks centered on preparing local banks to be able to respond to customers and on providing the banks with necessary information for processing accounts by filling out the forms correctly. The process worked smoothly.

With respect to the NOW account itself, the search process was highly centralized and resulted in the generation of information used to achieve consensus. While the form of the decision process in achieving consent of the bank presidents was one of open discussion and give-and-take, de facto, given the tremendous inequalities of information and expertise, the decision was centralized. In contrast, the actual implementation of data processing systems was given to a project team, while procedural decision making was decentralized. Local banks played a role in the design of materials for dissemination to all banks in the holding company; then each individual bank was responsible for implementing the procedures itself.

One specific question we asked about the process was whether or not it was a typical one for the introduction of new services in this bank. This question yielded three useful findings in Second Commercial Bank. First, it was suggested that the automatic transfer experience was important in learning how new services should be introduced, and that the procedure used for the NOW account was one that had been learned fairly recently and was now much more typical of what was done. Second, because the change was related to the demand deposit function, decisions were much more complex than others might be. Third, as we noted earlier, both changes were responses to deregulation. Consequently, the time frame was determined externally and the organization was forced to do things (such as buy programs rather than write them in the case of the option account) that it would not have done had it been able to determine its own time schedule. However, Mr. Jones speculated that this time-driven process was probably going to be more and more typically as new or altered services were spawned by deregulation of the banking industry. Nevertheless, since some of the special problems introduced here and in several other organizations in our sample were a function of the pressure caused by efforts to meet an externally imposed deadline, such time-driven innovations might deserve more special empirical and theoretical treatment than they have received to date.

Product/External Outcomes

With respect to the success of the product, the objectives of the managers who designed the NOW account were met. Almost all of their accounts came from current customers. In addition, the rate at which customers switched from their old demand deposit accounts to NOW accounts was slow. As late as a year after their introduction, one vice president noted that out of twelve thousand accounts at the downtown bank, there were only three hundred NOW accounts. The defensive strategy appeared to be successful in slowing down the rate that customers switched to NOWs. Clearly, it was slower than the 11 percent to 15 percent shift per year that Second Commercial had expected from the New England experience. Also, a number of the smaller $500–$600 accounts were closed. Follow-ups on these closings indicated that they had gone to other savings institutions. From Second Commercial's point of view, most of these accounts were the costly problem accounts. Thus, their "loss" is probably best considered a successful outcome.

There was some evidence that not everyone throughout the entire organization saw the process as a success. Managers at the local bank we studied saw the number of new accounts as being the criterion of success. As one of them noted, he would rate the success of the NOW account as 3 on a 10-point scale with 10 being high. He said informed customers went elsewhere. "Success to me revolves around whether they're flocking in or not." Clearly they were not.

Others at that bank recounted that there were not that many new accounts, that it should have advertised more, that it only attracted established accounts, and that it had mainly the same customers as before. Still they felt that no good customers were lost as a result. (At this particular bank, approximately one year after the introduction of the NOW account, $1 million were in NOW accounts, which was $500,000 less than in checking accounts.) The management of this bank felt that this was not particularly successful. There was also some feeling that while the dispute over pricing had been heated at the time, that it had mainly been forgotten.

Summary and Interpretation

Radical versus Routine Innovation

The implementation of NOW accounts at Second Commercial Bank was smooth and relatively uncomplicated, largely because it had learned from previous mistakes in implementing another innovation. Everyone saw the NOW account as routine in the extreme—a nonevent. It was just another new product, just another kind of checking account.

History/Unique Characteristics

The perception of the NOW account as just another checking account can be attributed largely to the bank's very difficult experience implementing the automatic transfer account. While in many ways it would seem that the automatic transfer was no more than a merging of two already existing products—checking and savings—in fact, the technical requirements of designing such an account in a short time were very demanding. As a result, there was tremendous strain put on the organization as it tried to develop a data processing system that would handle the automatic transfer. People worked extremely long hours and many people in data processing were replaced. Out of this stressful process came an examination of their systems for implementing new products. They concluded that they needed to get more information from those closest to the critical problems. When they were ready to implement NOW accounts, they moved to a project team structure rather than the more hierarchical structure used during the automatic transfer implementation.

Our data do not permit us to arrive at as clear a picture of the culture of Second Commercial Bank as was possible with many of our other organizations. People in this company simply talked little about values and norms. However, the facilities and the executives at the holding company yield the impression of professionalism and sophistication. Clearly holding company executives wanted to centralize major policy decisons and convince the presidents of the individual banks on the basis of data and logic.

On the other hand, there was a desire to decentralize. Second Commercial Bank was the first large bank holding company in the region to decentralize structurally, a fact that was one of the first mentioned by the senior vice president who had designed and implemented NOW accounts. The decentralization meant that banks had their own structures and did their own hiring. It did not mean that the banks managed their facilities in any way they wished.

The tone of professionalism and the efforts to centralize key decisions seemed to be associated with a more formal orientation than we observed at many other organizations. For example, in contrast to First Commercial Bank, there was little mention of a team orientation or team spirit.

Goals and Strategy

Second Commercial Bank's strategy for the NOW account was simply to retain their best customers and make a profit on each account. They emphasized that they did not mind losing small-balance customers and in fact would like to use the NOW account as a way of getting small-balance customers (whose accounts were relatively expensive to maintain) to move their business elsewhere. As a result of their profit orientation, they chose a very defensive strategy, one of the most defensive of any organization in the study. They had a high minimum balance of $1,500; they promoted mainly through radio announcements intended to inform rather than appeal to emotions. They even required current customers to fill out new forms to open a NOW account, unless the customer's balance was very high. So, they not only priced the account at a high level to be sure they made a profit on it, but they did little promotion and for some customers actually made it difficult for them to open an account.

Search

The decision to use such a defensive strategy was based on an extensive search outside the organization for information on the NOW account. The primary source of information was New England banks, whose experience led them to the defensive strategy operationalized particularly as a high price for the account. They also used numerous other sources of information which all led them to the conclusion that the defensive strategy was the most profitable.

Complexity

Like the other large and medium institutions in this study, Second Commercial Bank was very complex, making the implementation of the NOW account somewhat more challenging. Eighteen different positions were associated with designing and implementing NOW accounts. This complexity was one of the factors contributing to the problems with implementing automatic transfer accounts. No integrating mechanisms existed for managing that complexity, except through management by a common supervisor at a high level of the organization. The result seemed to be a sluggish response when rapid reaction was necessary. Project teams were introduced to manage the complexity for the NOW accounts. People from different functional areas were brought together to solve implementation problems, allowing people from different specialties to talk together as necessary to accomplish the task.

Flexibility

The project team provided a flexibility the organization had not had before. Although the organization still had many formalized procedures and required a common approach to the NOW account, the project team could work together to solve problems without going through an awkward process of communicating only through functional lines. It also gained flexibility by allowing individual banks to use the procedures manual in whatever way fit their facility.

We found very little evidence that adjustments were made during the process. Since things went so smoothly, probably few were needed. Alternatively, the needed flexibility may have been effectively incorporated in the plans and procedures. In any case, Second Commercial Bank was as flexible as it needed to be for this particular innovation.

Power Arrangements for Decisions

Although Second Commercial Bank was structurally decentralized, in fact most of the decisions were made at the top of the holding company, leaving employees below that level with only modest input into the decisions made. Top-level managers were sensitive to the need for employee acceptance of their decisions; but their approach to that problem was selling rather than true consultation, let alone employee participation in the process. Strategic decisions were also made at this level. The result was that employees did accept the decisions, but upward communication of ideas and problems was limited. The problem of upward communication was mitigated somewhat by the project team established for the operations implementation of NOW accounts. But while they had instituted the project team, the team for NOW accounts remained closely supervised by the senior vice president of the holding company. This meant that final operational decisions were still being made at the very top of the organization, even though communication channels had been opened up among the functional areas. The only exception to this pattern of control from the top of the holding company was in devising forms and basic procedures for tellers and new-accounts people that were not tied to data processing. Those decisions were given to a committee of bank employees, and training in the use of those procedures was left to the individual bank. For the most part, though, both strategic and implementation decisions were made at high levels of the holding company.

There were few negative feelings associated with the holding company control. Monitoring was impersonal and not punitive. Conflicting interests were usually resolved through the process of influence or selling rather than coercion. As a result, employees from bank presidents through tellers accepted the process of decision making by a few people at the top of the holding company.

Readiness

Second Commercial Bank's previous experience with automatic transfer accounts made them so well prepared for the NOW account it seemed to be no challenge at all. They had learned some management techniques, had developed the concept of project teams, and had already formed a committee of bank representatives for drawing up the routine procedures for handling NOW accounts. When they began to implement NOW accounts, most of the necessary organizational routines were in place. Furthermore, the software package they had purchased for the automatic transfer included a NOW account program. As a result, they had relatively little work to do in getting the NOW account program up and running. Their technical readiness combined with the use of a project team that included all those whose input was necessary for implementation made the organization very ready to integrate NOW accounts into the product line.

Internal Outcomes

Internal outcomes were all positive. The processing of accounts and statements was accurate and timely; there was almost no employee stress or overtime. There was little new organizational learning, but this was primarily because the organization had undergone significant changes based on learning from the automatic transfer.

Product/External Outcomes

Second Commercial Bank got very few NOW accounts, just as it had intended. While the small number of accounts pleased the holding company personnel, it was less pleasing to bank personnel who would have liked more money in NOW accounts. Some of them believed they had lost good business to competitors and that they could have made money on NOW accounts given the cost of funds at the time. In all, the holding company accomplished exactly what it had hoped, keeping most of its large-balance customers, losing many smallest-balance customers, and attracting few NOW accounts from people who did not already bank at Second Commercial Bank.

5
Centralized Direction and Decentralized Adaptation

At the time of the introduction of the NOW account, Third Commercial Bank owned all or substantially all of the stock of 12 banks: 7 in the metropolitan area, 1 in another area of the state, and 4 in other states. Collectively these banks operated in 32 locations.

Our initial intent was to study Third Commercial Bank as a medium-sized bank. With assets of roughly $750 million in the state, it was smaller than any of the other large banks or S & Ls. However, after we began interviewing, we discovered that Third Commercial Bank also had holdings in other states. Its combined assets were over $1.1 billion, approximately the same as Second Commercial Bank's. We therefore classified it as a large bank, with a resulting loss of one medium-sized bank in the study.

As with the other large bank holding companies, Third Commercial Bank's lead bank was located downtown. Our data collection focused on this bank and an affiliate bank also located in the city. Despite their geographical proximity, these banks served two quite different clienteles. One bank, located in the heart of the business center of the city, according to the annual report, derived "a growing percentage of its income from commercial banking." It served businesses of all sizes but specialized in middle-market companies. The other bank, although located only a few blocks from the lead bank, was on the fringe of the commercial area, near lower income neighborhoods. Respondents reported great differences in the sophistication of these two banks' customers.

A major feature of the lead bank was the provision of services to banks owned by the holding company and other banks and savings and loan associations. These services were provided by a service company headed by its own president. Through the service company, the bank for some time had been at the forefront in the computer area. As the president of the service company put it, "We tend to be innovative in the computer areas. We have had an ongoing system ever since 1965. We get into a lot of new things early; our users come to us on many of these things."

We initially wrote to the president of the holding company. He referred us to the president of the lead bank in River City, Mr. Meyers, who was also executive vice president of the holding company. Following our interview, Mr. Meyers referred us to Mr. Conrad, who was vice president of the holding company and president of the service company. Based on the recommendations of these two men, we spoke with Mr. Olin (senior vice president for operations of the bank), Ms. Rollins (an assistant cashier who headed up new accounts in the lead bank), Mr. Madison (an assistant cashier who was responsible for the checking area and deposits for all accounts in the second downtown bank), and several new-accounts people. In addition, we interviewed Ms. Elton, head of a public relations firm that had served as a consultant on the marketing aspects of the NOW account.

Routineness

Comments from almost all respondents indicated that the innovation was routine and that the procedures the organization had followed were similar to the ones normally followed for changes of this size. As one manager put it, when asked if the procedure had been typical, "Yes. For anything of this magnitude. On many less major things we would see what we needed to do and if we could make the changes with fewer meetings, and so on. Yes, generally this was similar overall. Heavy reliance on informal contacts." Mr. Conrad, president of the service company, stated, "The procedures and forms were set. It wasn't a big deal." Mr. Olin, vice president of operations, observed, "We had no problem. We made our checking account look like a savings account to the computer. It allowed us to do what we need to do."

Responses from the new-accounts personnel were similar. They noticed only minor differences in their work, mainly new forms and a few new things to check on in opening a new account. One said, "The NOW account just breezed right in here and ran smoothly with very few things that were new to us." Another said that she and her coworkers did not see anything very different in their work. "You just signed authorization forms. Basically, it is just like opening a regular checking account. We had to explain the rules and regulations. Everybody was freaking out at first, but it was easy."

Part of the routine nature of the innovation stemmed from the data processing capabilities that the organization had developed. Although substantial data processing requirements in implementing NOW accounts were not taken lightly, the organization was so advanced in data processing that it was able to handle these requirements in a fairly routine way.

Support for routineness of the innovation was also found in archival records. The operations for the NOW account were outlined in a September 1980 memo. "Third Commercial Bank's method of handling NOW accounts is basically the same as demand deposit [checking] accounts and, therefore, is parallel to the standard checking accounts operational and computer systems, but it provides for an interest-earned calculation." A later section read, "The day an account is opened, all standard procedures will apply, unchanged. All NOW accounts should be created according to demand deposit new-account preparation instruction in the SPI (SPI refers to the standard practice instructions for the demand deposit accounts.) This memo also included exact codes for opening new accounts, samples of customer statements, and a description of specific requirements for using these materials (such as the size of the envelope needed for this larger statement).

Not all aspects, however, were as routine. One change that the NOW account called for affected the demand deposit department. Ways had to be found to put in interest and other charges that were new to them. Moreover, a parallel change was introduced to cycle all accounts to get them out on the same day. This required special routines for certain accounts but they all worked out well.

Several other aspects of the NOW account necessitated procedural changes. In some areas, disclosures and descriptive statements were required; one statement involved printing out additional information. These required extensive programming but nothing more. One of these required calculating a daily balance. This was a new accrual problem. Also, tax laws required that they issue new 1099 statements that put all of a customer's accounts on one statement. Finally, the bank had to arrange procedures to close old accounts and introduce new ones with a minimum of confusion. As will be seen, the service company under Mr. Conrad's leadership played an important role in these matters.

Design of the Innovation

Goals and Strategy

Third Commercial Bank was primarily a commercial bank. Managers viewed the other major commercial banks in the area as their major competition, although managers in other banks and S & Ls did not refer to it as a leader as they had First and Second Commercial Banks. Third Commercial Bank wanted to use the NOW account to enhance its image as a commercial bank by advertising the NOW account to potential business customers. This was a very different goal than any of the other banks' and shaped its particular NOW account strategy.

In addition to outcome goals, the organization's culture shaped the process goals for the introduction of the NOW account. It had to be done in a certain way. The marketing consultants sensed that top management (Mr. Meyers) had a strong belief in personal selling; Mrs. Elton felt it was important to be consistent with this basic orientation of the organization. Ms. Elton noted:

We tried to personalize it as much as possible. He wanted to tell us to be personal with the customers. However, there was a conflict of interest here in that you didn't want everyone to change over from their noninterest checking account at once. I could see his style was to emphasize the personalized aspects; we tried to enhance his efforts. Organizations are geared in certain ways. We picked up the signals and acted accordingly.

Third Commercial Bank had anticipated that the NOW account was coming for some time. Accordingly, management had investigated the possibilities and had decided that it needed to offer the NOW account if it was to establish its presence among its commercial customers and avoid losing its individual customers.

Operationalizing the Strategy. Third Commercial Bank's strategy is best described as moderately defensive. It was not looking for large numbers of accounts, but it aggressively pursued a strategy of increasing its visibility in the business community. The interest rate was the maximum at the time (5.25 percent) and was compounded daily. The required minimum balance for a cost-free checking account was $1,000. However, the account was graduated in such a way that a $5 service charge was assessed if the account ever dropped below $1,000 and an $8 monthly service charge was added if the balance dropped below $750. Similarly, if the customer kept a minimum of $1,500 in the regular savings account, the NOW account was free, no matter what the checking balance. All banks in the metropolitan area had the same policy.

The marketing strategy was also moderately aggressive, given the generally defensive posture. Brochures were sent to all customers with their statements, phone calls were made to all the customers, and a letter from each bank president was sent to the customer announcing and explaining the service. Also, the lead bank typically sponsored a business program on a major radio station; part of this time was devoted to introduction of the NOW account.[1] However, major newspaper and media advertising was limited and the telephoning was defensively motivated. Ms. Elton noted that the radio advertising was on a business show and the decision was made to not be really aggressive in the media. She observed, "They didn't want to go all out. Initially they were concerned with presence but once they got that, that's all they wanted. They wanted to be sure that commercial customers saw them as mainstream." The president reported, "We called all of our customers to let them know it was available. We didn't want them to go to a thrift institution. It was very successful. Our customers were appreciative. The telephone did not involve cold calls; we called only our own customers."

In this sense, the strategy was defensive, but the actual process of operationalizing this defensive strategy was more aggressive than that of most other banks, as shown by the use of media, telephone calls to customers, and a marketing consultant, in addition to the normal mailing and posters in the lobby. However, this stance was not directed primarily at opening NOW accounts. It was to let people know that this bank was in the mainstream—as one of our respondents indicated: "To show them that we were a big bank too."

Markets and the Environment. As with the other large banks, managers did not want to compete with the savings and loan associations for new accounts. However, they did want to avoid losing customers to them. Their approach emerged out of the fundamental views of top management and the position the bank wished to have with its commercial customers. According to the consultant, a major objective of the campaign appeared to be establishing presence in the business community. Ms. Elton noted, "We did a bit more marketing to business customers, particularly the follow-up on our promotion materials."

Unlike the other large banks, no mention was made of a leadership role for other banks in the area. They did, however, express some concern for helping their correspondent banks make decisions that would be profitable and compatible with Third Commercial Bank's processing routines.

Strategic Decision Process

The decision process with respect to strategy appeared to be based on information collected from a diverse sources. The bank presidents had input but nevertheless most decisions were made by Mr. Meyers. Ms. Elton mentioned: "Mr. Meyers is a strong individual; he is a majority of one. For example, the pricing decision was made in meetings of the bank presidents. The diversity of the banks was associated with the different preferences with respect to pricing. However, Mr. Meyers made it very clear that pricing and marketing were going to be uniform in the area. In fact, the result of the first meeting to discuss the price did not yield a decision on price but rather a further analysis of costs from which an ultimate decision was thrashed out at a future meeting. Thus, there was give-and-take, but Mr. Meyers was the dominant force.

Information Flows. Major information flows concerning strategy formulation also centered around Mr. Meyers. Both Ms. Elton and Mr. Conrad reported working with him almost exclusively.

In describing her work with the president, Ms. Elton commented, "We presented him a list of ideas and discussed them with him. We worked together. We would write some things; he changed and commented. We would rewrite." However, she also indicated effective reciprocal relationships with other members of the organization. For example, she indicated that a major problem had been the rapid change in government regulations and the slow rate at which important policies were revised and then announced. "This drove you nuts. We had to change and rechange our copy. We would get information from lawyers. We would submit copy to them, and they would make changes."

Mr. Conrad also reported that he frequently worked directly with the president on major issues. At the same time, the service company played a major role in developing a framework for shaping the NOW account both internally and with external clients. The president of the service company, Mr. Conrad, described his extensive work to get the individual banks to consider costs and operations. He observed that often bank presidents are sales oriented and do not understand the operations side. However, when things become tight, they do become concerned with operations. The service company played a major role in demonstrating what the true costs were. Mr. Conrad noted that two years earlier they had given seminars for their own bank presidents and for the presidents of other banks and savings and loan associations they served. He observed:

> Many users didn't know what the NOW account was or how to sell it. They had no idea what to charge. We consulted with them, saying "Don't give it away; you'll go broke." We went through pricing with them. They had a problem of determining break-even on it. We showed them they had to have a $1,000 minimum balance. We spent a lot of time trying to show them what the costs were. In banking, many times we compete and give our shirts away. We spent time with our own banks—three-hour seminars at our expense—to educate first our own banks and then our users as to cost.

At the strategic level, operations capacity was also considered important, although it received relatively little specific mention when respondents were asked about strategy. The consultant, Ms. Elton, did mention that Mr. Meyers was very concerned with the operations and data processing aspects, but he said, "If you have the right hardware, these take care of themselves." Clearly the heavy role that Mr. Conrad played in the process and the discussion he reported having with the president indicated that operations was a critical area but also one for which the organization felt it was prepared. While operations did receive much attention with respect to implementation, the absence of concern with it in our data on these strategic questions perhaps indicates that management quite accurately felt it was prepared in this area.

No one else indicated that they had had any significant input into the actual strategic decisions. Ms. Elton did report that the president of the holding company had attended one of the meetings and had participated in selecting the name of the account.

Mr. Meyers corroborated his central role in the decision process. For example, he noted that on the plans for dealing with the operations component, the operations people made their recommendations and he made the final decisions. It appears that most of the major strategic decisions were made by one person, who based his decisons on input from many sources.

Decisions on the NOW account took place under several constraints. Top management had indicated that the banks within the area must adopt a common product. Second, the product needed to be offered in a way that would cover costs. Third, there was some emphasis on using the account for cross-selling, but new-accounts people reported that they were always required to do this anyway. The major cross-selling objectives were more general: demonstration to the commercial customers that Third Commercial was a major financial institution in the city. Fourth, the emphasis of top management on personal selling was a major factor in the actual marketing procedures that were developed. Finally, the heavy emphasis that the organization had previously placed on its data processing capacity and the role that this technical branch had played in shaping the thinking of the presidents about the NOW account undoubtedly predisposed the executives to a greater concern with costs than might otherwise have been the case. Certainly, the influence of the technical branch increased the chances that the technical aspects would not be overwhelmed by "business" issues.

Search. The search process that provided the basis for Third Commercial's strategy was led by Mr. Meyers and Mr. Conrad. It included information from the New England experience, ideas from seminars conducted by professional banking and savings and loan associations, advice from a marketing consultant, and cost data and other information from individual banks. The service company conducted extensive data collection concerning the needs of the various member banks and the other banks and S & Ls that they served.

Information on costs, prices, and operations was gathered from a variety of external and internal sources and pooled under the leadership of Mr. Meyers. Two constraints guided the decisions. One of the constraints had to do with the diversity of the banks who were members of the holding company. In the end, all the banks in the metropolitan area had the same prices, but the out-of-state banks varied their prices to meet local competition. Second, costs were a major consideration in pricing, and these were well known. Information on costs was obtained through study by each bank president of his own bank.

The service company conducted extensive studies of the programming requirements and the design of statements, attended various seminars, and through questionnaires collected information about the needs of their customers approximately two years ahead of time. Internally, pricing was geared to meet costs based on internal calculations. As Mr. Meyers put it:

> We knew that the introduction of the NOW account means increased cost to the consumer. The cost of demand deposit accounts now required interest. It made sense for passbook savings customers to convert to it. We did an analysis of demand deposits and savings to determine the level of conversion and cost, and then we set our price. We knew the cost of opening, closing, and check clearing. We introduced a graduated account for those individuals who wanted to keep their savings accounts separate from their checking account. We looked at competition in the market. Our chief competition here is [names of three large banks in the area]. We knew we had to have a plan that would not put us out in left field.

In addition, the marketing consultant researched the pricing and other procedures of competitors, and observed what they were doing with respect to media advertising and promotional materials.

Overall the search activities were quite centralized at high levels, in the hands of the president and Mr. Conrad. At the lower levels, the search process appeared to be less formal. As we will see, considerable emphasis was placed on meetings at which participants were encouraged to anticipate problems with what was being planned.

In sum, the president of the lead bank, with considerable influence by the head of the data processing group, designed a product to enhance the bank's image as a leading commercial bank and maintain current retail customers without attracting new customers to the more expensive NOW account.

Implementation of the Innovation

Complexity

Third Commerical Bank was the most complex of any of the banks or savings and loan associations we studied, being slightly more differentiated than First Commercial Bank and First National S & L. As with other banks, much of that differentiation showed up at the bank level. However, they were also complex at the holding company, where six different upper-level positions were involved with NOW accounts. Those were the chairman, president, vice president, service company president (data processing), lawyers, and financial people. The top people participated in a major way in designing and implementing the NOW account. At the middle and lower levels, six more positions were involved, just as at First and Second

Commercial Banks. Those positions were the marketing manager (who left midstream and whose function was replaced by a consultant), marketing staff, operations staff, personnel staff, data processing staff, and part-time student workers in data processing. At the holding company's banks, ten different positions were cited as participating in the NOW account: the bank president, vice president of operations (cashier), assistant cashier, bookkeeping staff, savings department staff, the head of customer service, customer service staff, the head teller, tellers, and clerks in demand deposit. In all, twenty-two positions participated in the NOW account, making this organization highly complex with respect to this innovation.

Decision Process

Analysis of implementation decisions can best be treated by looking at the role played by Mr. Conrad and the service company separately from the actual operating decisions.

Technical decisions were closely linked to the policy decisions made by the bank presidents, as was evident from earlier comments of Mr. Conrad and Mr. Olin, particularly those on the important role played by the technical side led by Mr. Conrad in stimulating the presidents to consider the costs involved in NOW accounts. However, it was also clear that the operations side of the organization played a large role in getting the individual bank presidents to understand the cost side.

Obviously, in order to do this, the technical people had to have a strong business orientation. Mr. Conrad's earlier comments voiced a stronger concern with costs than he attributed to the bank presidents. In his view, the presidents of banks were often sales oriented and did not understand the operations/cost side of issues. However, it is also important to recognize that the operations people focused on providing the diversity required by the various bank presidents, including those using different strategies outside the area. For example, Mr. Conrad observed:

> We really tried to lay it out for them. We sent questionnaires out to see what they wanted so that we could go ahead. In working with customers, we need to know their needs, then design procedures, and get their okay; then they can go their own way. For example, as long as I build "minimum balance" into the program, they can set the minimum at whatever level they want. Basically, people really were ready to help you. It was a joint effort.

Mr. Conrad also commented on the "business" side of things at a number of other points in the interview. His orientation was reflected in the following statement: "We had to discover the needs of our customers. We have to think ahead in programming about two years. The banks relate to account numbers, not to the total customer. The customers call the bank and the first question they're asked is, 'What is your account number?' We want staff to relate to the customer as a total customer."

In other words, the operations side of the organization took the lead in developing a reciprocal process in which they could provide what the various banks needed to meet customer needs. They influenced the process heavily, but their influence was grounded in the type of thinking that the more business-oriented side of the organization was likely to require. They anticipated the needs of the business side of the organization and attempted to solicit information from the business side of the organization with substantial lead time. They also developed a system flexible enough to meet special needs of particular banks. Said Mr. Olin, "All the banks can change to their own needs within the constraints of the computer. Actually, there was little variation in what the banks did."

The operations side was proactive in one other way that helped reduce problems to the business side. They designed a process allowing customers to open new accounts while using their old checks. In Mr. Conrad's words,

> It would have been a big problem if customers all had to open new accounts. Some had a large enough account to maintain the account without additional costs. Closing and opening an account is expensive. A problem also occurred when customers used old checks and their account had been closed. We arranged to let them use the old checks. The new-accounts department allowed us time for doing this.

This system allowed accounts to be merged without entering all new information.

Despite the involvement of the operations and data processing people in the decision process, Ms. Elton, the market consultant, saw them as hesitant to assert their views.

> I kept saying that we needed to get the operations people involved. They seemed to hold back and wait to see what he [Mr. Meyers] would say. I played the role of sensing problems. I would say, "I see problems down the road on this one." For example, at one time it appeared that the computer people were not ready but they were quiet.

Ms. Elton mentioned that she talked to the president about this, and he accepted her observations and asked her to bring it up from time to time.

Mr. Conrad indicated that the implementation work with the operations people had been handled mainly by his assistant, Mr. Olin. The design of the operations procedures involved a highly interactive process between Mr. Olin and operations personnel. While Mr. Meyers took responsibility for the major operations decisions, his recommendations were based on opinions and information from a number of different sources. Mr. Olin, senior vice president of operations, reported getting together with the bank president at their normal monthly meetings and then transmitting their decisions to the operations people. In his words:

> They give guidelines; you put them into effect by meeting with the operations people at the banks. We got together with the operations people and said "This is what we anticipate" and asked "How are your programs set up to do it?" They went to their people and came back and said what needed to done or what could not be done. Then maybe we had to revamp our situation. We tried to see what is now in their programs and what we want to do.
>
> We all had the same problem and had to arrive at the same solution. All the banks can change things according to their own needs within the constraints of the computer. We got together and decided on the best way and then went to the program.

In sum, the process which occurred seemed to be a mixture: decisions about certain parameters influenced by the presidents, communication of these decisions to the technical people through one individual (Mr. Olin), the technical people developing procedures that were given in the form of recommendations to Mr. Meyers, who made the final decisions. This whole process of mutual adaptation took place within the policy limits set by Mr. Meyers and Mr. Conrad.

Customer contact people had almost no influence over implementation decisions, as seen in the process of meetings held to discuss NOW accounts. Ms. Elton described the content of these meetings:

> We began by organizing breakfast meetings with all the people who would have customer contact. We had coffee and doughnuts and about fifty people attended four separate meetings where we kicked around what should be done. Basically, these meetings focused on internal communications—a lot of issues other than the new accounts were discussed. We provided fact sheets. We had an employee contest with a $50 prize to name the new account. This was to get employee involvement.
>
> At these meetings, Mr. Meyers said a few words and then asked for questions. Most of the questions came from the tellers about the mechanics of banking such as handling good customers if they overdraw and other nuts and bolts things. They wanted to know the parameters and the rules of the accounts. This and the telephone campaign to current customers were the best things that we did.

She felt that these meetings had had an important residual effect.

The involvement carried over beyond the NOW account. The employees didn't really get the sense that the focus of these meetings was on the NOW accounts. For example, they raised bank-robbing concerns. Mr. Meyers responded to these questions at the time. The phone campaign had the same kind of effect—a great deal of camaraderie. We were all working together. Mr. Meyers got pizza—all the people relaxed. It was a picnic-like atmosphere, which is unusual in banks. Banks tend to be quite structured. Often the rank and file do not see the personal side of top management.

Flexibility

Third Commerical Bank achieved flexibility by allowing people to modify the decisions of upper-level managers. It was clear from comments made by Mr. Madison, assistant cashier in the smaller bank, that there were opportunities for people to participate, primarily by discussing problems they foresaw. In essence, participation was not especially encouraged in the creation of ideas; rather it consisted of finding problems in what had been proposed. Some revisions needed to be made in procedures as problems were discovered. Many of these problems were due to changes in regulations. The process was a continuous one; individuals discovered problems while they were working with the NOW accounts and these were communicated and rectified either on a case-by-case basis or through Mr. Olin in data processing. People were asked to think about what problems they could foresee with the system. Mr. Olin initiated meetings of bank staff to try to be sure that all the things that could occur had been taken into account. After a few days, the group would meet again to, in Mr. Olin's words, "talk over the problem until it is resolved. If you can prove to them the solution will work, it's okay. If you cannot prove it to them, then maybe you have to go back and make changes. It often requires more than one meeting." In Mr. Olin's view, there were difficult problems in making proper disclosures and descriptive statements, but these were "not decisions; you just needed to be sure you were conforming."

One middle-level manager commented:

As things got going, we discovered where certain problems arose over details we had overlooked. We got them ironed out quickly. I would see a problem, or get a call from a customer. I'd go to the person in charge of the department involved and explain the situation and it would get ironed out. Large problems I would discuss with Mr. Olin. Nine out of ten problems were small ones. These would all be handled by contacting someone in the other department—often just through a telephone conversation.

Mr. Madison felt that he had contributed important ideas; it is interesting to observe that his only complaint was that he did not know ahead of time what issues would be discussed at the inital meeting. "Oftentimes you first learn about the change at a meeting and then you don't have time to think about the questions. Perhaps a second, more in-depth meeting could be useful." In essence, the structure of the meetings presented solutions which people were to react to, rather than participate in their creation. Whether planned or not, the lack of preannounced agenda contributed to this "reactive" participation.

While some of Mr. Olin's meetings with his employees were for problem detection, others, especially those with the new-accounts people, appeared to have a different emphasis. From Mr. Olin's point of view, these meetings were designed to communicate to all people who had even a remote connection with NOW accounts:

> We had meetings ahead of time. We told new-accounts people what to expect, what to look for, what we were going to do. Basically we write procedures for customer service people. You have to sit down with people and inform them about how something is going to affect their department. It is a matter of communication. If it is done well with the departments, there are no problems. If not, the first day is crazy.

Some subordinates felt that these meetings were highly repetitious and that they were being told what to do over and over again. This type of meeting did not particularly enhance the ability of the organization to adapt to unforeseen events, at least in their view.

This same communication process was followed downward in the organization with people such as Mr. Madison and Ms. Rollins, the assistant cashier, having similar meetings with their employees. Heavy emphasis was placed on ad hoc communication. While few of these meetings resulted in any change in formal procedures, people were encouraged to anticipate problems. Basically, these meetings served as training sessions. Again, these meetings did not contribute to flexibility.

The flexibility came mainly from interdepartmental exchanges fostered by informal lateral relationships among lower-level participants. As a result, immediate adjustments could be made in response to the problems particular customers were having. Accounts personnel reported calling members of other departments in response to customer complaints or other problems and getting them taken care of right away. It was difficult to determine how these relationships came into being. In some ways, it appeared that they were developed by people for self-defense. As one person put it, "You never want your customers to go upstairs. They're our responsibility. We do a lot of pacifying cusotmers, even if the errors were somewhere else, like in demand deposit."

Regardless of their source, these relationships at lower levels were important. The first-line supervisors commented on the ease with which needed adjustments could be made and relations maintained with other departments. For example, Mr. Madison said that he would be contacted about errors that had been made in the customer's account. "In those cases I'd figure out what the interest was and make the adjustment. We do not hassle data processing." He estimated overall there had been at most fifteen errors during the first year.

In sum, even though the implementation decisions tended to be centralized, the use of frequent meetings and discussions helped to anticipate problems at lower levels where the decisions were implemented. Flexibility was introduced by strong lateral relations at lower levels. The degree of problem solving versus communication varied between departments. Overall, people knew what to expect and how to cope with problems as they occurred, including referring them to an appropriate person or department elsewhere in the organization.

Readiness

In almost every respect, Third Commercial Bank was well prepared to handle the NOW account. The bank had been a leader in computerization; its operations staff not only appeared very able to do the technical aspects but also had a strong sense of the particular business interests involved. In addition, the service company was in the business of providing computer and related services for a large number of banks in the region. Consequently, they were customer oriented and in a good position not only to serve the outside customers, but to relate well to internal customers—the banks owned by the holding company. Reports throughout the organizaition indicated that all the major functions were performed well.

Perhaps the only area where the organization was not fully prepared was marketing. The woman who had been in charge of the marketing department had left the organization prior to the consideration of the NOW account. Ms. Elton, the external public relations consultant, indicated that the marketing head worked primarily in the employee relations area on such things as morale and employee communication, and had not really done marketing. In essence, the bank had no internal marketing function.

Third Commercial had established a working relationship with Ms. Elton's firm in the preparation of the annual report. Thus, Ms. Elton already had some feel for the organization and was prepared to develop a marketing approach consistent with the basic fabric of the organization. Consequently, she was able to step in easily, so the one possible gap in readiness was not a problem.

Not only was the organization technologically prepared, but it appeared to be organizationally prepared as well. First, at the level of top management, the technical aspects had strong representation which was expressed with a clear understanding of the major business issues. Second, it appeared that culture at the lower levels was quite conducive to implementing a new product. People knew each other across the departments and were able to deal with any problems that arose with a phone call or two in a short period of time. Moreover, middle-level managers appeared to be committed to contributing ideas and to developing their own expertise.

This feeling was most clear in the comments of the two assistant cashiers. Both exhibited a strong desire to be on top of things, a strong customer service orientation, and a proactive stance to be sure that information was disseminated. Mr. Madison observed, "A decision was made from really higher management to go with the NOW account. I tried to look at all the effects in my department. We had some problems with the EDP program, some adjustments were made on their part, but most of the time they could explain it to our satisfaction." Ms. Rollins commented on her efforts to get information when top management failed to let her know what was being planned soon enough that she and her staff could answer customers' questions. Basically, she had conducted her own information search by following closely what other banks in the area were doing. For example, she had a file containing information from newspapers and related sources on what the competition was doing. Often she learned details of what NOW accounts were to be from customers, newspapers, and other external sources rather than through communication from management. She often had to push management to be sure that she was informed. "We have to be a nuisance sometimes to management. We have to ask questions, we have to be more aggressive to upper management to find out what we need to know. If you are not aggressive, you have problems. They can't guess what you need to know."

Training

In a strict sense, there was little mention of training. However, there was strong encouragement for people to prepare themselves, and resources were provided to help them at numerous meetings.

To some degree, lower-level managers became prepared because the individuals were anticipating what would be needed and what the effects of offering NOW accounts would be in their department. They were aggressive in seeking information and had developed relationships across departments that allowed day-to-day problems to be handled. At the lower levels of the organization, such commitment and informal interdepartmental relationships, along with the heavy reliance on the ability of people to develop their own understanding of what they needed to know, played key roles in successful implementation, particularly in permitting ad hoc responses to problems as they occurred.

Ms. Rollins commented on the support that she got from a variety of departments to answer her queries. "The legal department and management were extremely helpful in answering our questions. They are very supportive. We feel secure in what we are doing. We support them too."

The new-accounts people had similar perceptions. "We went to the meeting where they informed us. We received memos from our attorney. We knew it was coming; we just had to be patient. We have little meetings in our department all the time." One commented that her supervisor was careful to keep her informed. "If she gets a memo, she passes it around and lets us read it. If it's something we will need daily, she'll make us a copy. But I understood it better from her than from the memos." Said another new-accounts person, "Mr. Olin would explain the procedures and get any ideas to make it easier—if there was any way to make it easier [laughter]— which in the long run we did. They cut down on the EDP forms. That gave us a break, made it easier on us." Said another, "We had meetings about it. We, together with people from bookkeeping, central file, the savings department, and teller supervisors. We get these memos from these guys upstairs that FDIC was changing the regulations. Our supervisor would come over and explain it to us." One respondent commented, "We were saturated. We were told things over and over like in school at various meetings. This is an organized way to make people aware. We were ready to go on the first day." She also noted that people knew a large percentage of the information ahead of time.

> We knew how interest was paid on savings. In conversations we'd pick up things. We knew the system would be similar to what we had. Tellers were called into the meetings—even though they were not involved in opening these accounts. Basically, we realized the customers would be asking some questions, and the tellers would need to know the answers. Persons with even the most remote responsibilities were called into these meetings.

Obviously, Mr. Olin's belief that you needed to tell people what was going to happen was operationalized in extensive communication. People were prepared primarily through meetings conducted by line managers as well as through formal memos and statements on procedures handed out ahead of time. Redundancy was high. People understood what was coming and that they were responsible for their own knowledge. Supervisory personnel took responsibility to coordinate communication. Few problems were reported. Individuals felt confident in what they were doing. People understood the process and felt able to communicate about possible problems. Lower-level participants were committed to keeping themselves abreast of what was happening.

These meetings constituted the training made available to the staff. Mr. Olin said:

> Basically there was no special training. It's just a matter of communicating face-to-face in meetings with departments. During the meetings I tried to write up an outline and give it to them and tell them to think about it for a few days with their departments. Then we'd get back together again and talk over the problems until they were resolved.

This same process seemed to be followed at the next level down. An assistant cashier commented that he conducted meetings with his own staff and with "anyone affected by my department. We tried to tell them, 'This is what you have to watch out for.' We went to a new descriptive statement with the NOW account. They had to familiarize themselves with it." In addition to the numerous meetings, Ms. Rollins reported:

> We were given sheets even though we didn't understand them. We were given information on paper to alert us and let us know what some of the problems would be down the line. We get everything that is published since we deal with the customers. We get reams of paperwork—much of it not critical to us, but it makes us aware of what the problems are internally.
>
> Later on we were given things we are going to work with, such as a copy of how the customer statement would look.

In other words, they received a great deal of background information about all aspects of the account prior to the actual meetings where matters particularly relevant to them were discussed. Supervisors made decisions about what was necessary and filtered the information accordingly.

With respect to the informal training, Ms. Rollins noted:

> We have to rely on people knowing what is going on. We have to rely on the new-accounts clerks to do the work that the bank officers used to do. The clerks have to know what the requirements are. We would have to have a book of operating procedures. It's better the way it is done. They tell you what you think you need to know and then they ask for questions. Each person writes down what he needs to know. Then you rely on memory and experience. Things are not put in writing. If you need to know, ask us. It's counterproductive to put it in writing. You make your own notes.

In sum, what training there was took place through meetings and the informal communication process. The amount of repetition apparently left little to chance.

As a result, evidence from the interviews with people at the lower-management and new-accounts levels indicated that for the most part the system was ready on the first day. A new-accounts person reported that they were quite ready early on, and that any problems could be taken care of quickly. "We even took forms and signature cards early. We got everything ready to go. Customers had already signed the agreement form so what we converted to on the day we began offering them was ready to go." There was, however, some feeling at the actual levels of implementation that management had been slightly slow to respond. Ms. Elton reported, "The other banks were a bit ahead timewise." Mr. Olin commented that they had run out of time and could not do the test runs he would have liked. Ms. Rollins indicated that management was slow in letting the accounts people know what the bank was planning with respect to NOW accounts and that her people were unable to answer questions from customers in the months before January 1, when other organizations were actively promoting their accounts. However, they were processing accounts on the day they became legal and had very few problems in doing so.

Monitoring

Monitoring was performed in both formal and informal ways. Formally, new accounts supervisors were required to fill out a weekly form reporting the number of new accounts, the amounts in the accounts, and other information. Top management followed this information closely. Second, with respect to operations, tests were run on the statements during the first month. Mr. Olin observed:

> We pulled some sample statements and corrected them before the next ones came out. Basically, what this involved is printing out statements as of a particular day some time during the month and checking them out like you would a test account. We planned test accounts but ran out of time. Normally, we would have run test accounts.

Other monitoring of the process was done much less formally, mainly through managers and supervisors finding problems and making ad hoc corrections where they could and reporting any major problems upward for correction.

Overview

Attempting to weave the various strands of the implementation process into an overall picture reveals a somewhat complex mixture. While emphasis was placed on personalizing the process for customers and getting understanding and committment at lower levels of the organization, the president was a very strong figure in the process and, at least in the view of one respondent, appeared to inhibit upward communication. Moreover, the communication flows appeared to be open enough for most of the important matters to be attended to ahead of time and the informal communication system was well enough developed for people to get problems resolved themselves, usually without raising matters in formal meetings.

At the same time, there was some emphasis among the individuals we talked with on being sure that things were settled without having matters go to higher management. Whether this was out of fear, a sense of professionalism, or something else cannot be determined from our data. It did appear, however, that there was a rich flow of communication at the lower levels of the organization that made the change go smoothly, and top management had made specific efforts to break down barriers with informal meetings and encouragement during the phone campaign. At the risk of going well beyond our data, we speculate that the informal process that developed among lower-level participants was a response to some reluctance to report actual problems upward. If so, we suggest that some mutual adjustment systems may develop, to contain problems. These might help integration across departments and thereby help innovation. Of course, potentially they could slow management's ability to make needed systematic adjustments because an underworld exists that protects itself from upper management by censoring the flow of upward information. Nevertheless, despite the appearance of a somewhat truncated flow to the very top of the organization, the internal processes were quite effective for this particular innovation.

Internal Outcomes

The introduction of the NOW account was successful in both its direct and indirect results. Although a bit more time would have been useful for testing the systems for customer statements, the organization was well prepared to offer NOW accounts on January 1, 1981. While lower-level particpants experienced some anxiety, this was at a manageable level and was dissipated rapidly when things went smoothly and people became aware that they had been adequately prepared.

In the beginning, people expected the NOW account to be difficult to implement. Although the new-accounts people anticipated a hassle, the early meetings and the ease with which ad hoc adjustments could be made had been helpful in reducing their concerns. Mr. Madison observed that the women in central file had difficulty getting new accounts set up on time when volume was great. As a result, there were some small errors, but the adjustments were readily made on the computer. As one woman put it:

> I thought it was a good idea. Then I thought it was a hassle. I really did not understand it in the beginning. Oh, no! Lots of new forms. As things went on, it was like any other change, first you see the forms, then you think it's going to be a lot of work. The more I found out, the easier it

got. After you got into it, found out what you were going to do, it got easier. We had a lot of problems with statements in the beginning. Customers thought they weren't getting the right amount of interest in some cases.

However, she also indicated that there was a lot of anxiety early in the process. Comments from another new-accounts person indicated the close relationship between their readiness and the routineness of the innovation. "The departments we contact normally were the same. The NOW account just breezed right in here and went very smoothly with very few things that were new to us. It doesn't really change the job. It just gives you more to do. More responsibility. You have to make sure that you are thorough and that everything gets followed through."

Thus, while there were some minor problems with interest payments to customers and the discovery that a new process was needed to handle certain tax forms, the organization was extremely well prepared to cope with them. Initial anxiety appeared to dissipate quickly as people realized that they understood what was happening. Problems could easily be handled by phone calls. As one new-accounts person mentioned, "I get a few calls from the customers about not getting the interest. I put the customer on hold and call over to Mr. Madison in the demand deposits department. We do not correct the mistake, but we find out what caused it." She then would tell the customer what had happened and that the demand deposit people would straighten it out. She added, "There are no delays." Such responses of the customer contact people to customer problems seemed to reflect that the personal selling approach Mr. Meyers had emphasized has been institution-alized at the lower levels.

Customer service personnel and their support departments were in close contact with an important part of the organization's environment, its customers. Although this part of the environment was not complex, it did present a number of unique events that required rapid responses. The personnel who were required to deal with this variable environment had the awareness, the flexibility, and the authority to get a quick response. In short, they were able to respond to the changing environment quite well, even though the organization overall seemed to be highly centralized. Although other interpretations of this capability are certainly possible, Mr. Meyer's emphasis on personal contact with customers appeared to be part of the fabric of the organization which permitted such responsiveness.

There was minor dissatisfaction with the slowness of top management to communicate exactly what was going to be done about the NOW account. Those experiencing it seemed comfortable in pushing for more information. In fact, the individual who reported it most strongly indicated that it became the responsibility of the managers to push to get the information that they needed.

The outside consultant reported that the process of introducing NOW accounts had spread positive effects elsewhere in the organization as a result of the camaraderie generated during the phone campaign. Our internal respondents provided no information that would either confirm of disconfirm her observation.

The few errors and problems that did occur were readily handled, with no one reporting any great difficulties. The major mechanism responsible for this appeared to be that the systems were competently designed so that little in the way of serious error occurred. In addition, people received ready support when they contacted specific staff departments or other departments to be sure that problems were addressed. Issues were addressed quickly and people believed that the customer was served well.

Another outcome was the satisfaction of individuals who discovered problems or solutions that upper managers acknowledged. One individual in particular indicated a great deal of personal satisfaction for a particular problem that he had anticipated.

There was one source of dissatisfaction with the product itself at the very lowest levels. New-accounts people indicated some disappointment with the high minimum balance, which they felt many customers could not afford.

Some reported problems stemmed from the frequent changes in regulations. While these changes seemed to be inconvenient and costly to the organization, no one indicated that the organization was unable to cope with them successfully. At the very top level, Mr. Conrad reported, "Basically there were no problems I was aware of. If you talk to the people downstairs, I think they would say it went smoothly too." The president related: "This transition was smooth. There were no problems. With the proper hardware, it is automatic."

For the most part, these perceptions were shared at the lower organizational levels as well, but the few errors on such things as interest payments were perceived as more significant to the lower-level personnel than to top management. Ms. Rollins reported that some problems did occur with customers, but these were easily handled on a case-by-case basis. For example, sometimes a customer's statement indicated inappropriate charges. "We were caught in the middle. We were told nothing would go wrong and promised the customers that nothing would go wrong. Then something went wrong. We had to be very ingratiating with the customer. We told them it was a computer error. If demand deposit [in the data processing department] could not handle it that day, we would do it so as not to lose the customer." In other words, they would make changes for the customer before demand deposit could get to it. "We didn't lose a customer." She also noted that sometimes the statement effective time (the time for computing interest) did not go as planned. "We told the customers it was just a little error and we would straighten it out. If we didn't pay interest for whatever reasons, we had to go in and compound it manually. But overall, except for an occasional service charge, there were no real problems for one and one half months. Now there is no problem at all. We don't think about it."

A few other minor internal problems were indicated by Ms. Elton. She felt there had been some inefficiency in the phone campaign because they did not have enough information about the types of customers. "We could have targeted better if we had known the high-balance checking account people or if we had known the people who had checking and commercial accounts. We would have saved a lot of phone time." Also, she noted that the regulations changed so quickly that they probably wrote the copy too early. "Legal questions kept forcing changes. However, perhaps this could not have been avoided since interpretations of this sort always change."

Product/External Outcomes

Overall, Third Commercial Bank appeared to achieve what it had intended through the introduction of the NOW account. There was an initial flurry of activity as people opened NOW accounts, but this subsided quickly. With respect to volume, the president reported that it had been successful. When asked to be specific about what "successful" meant, he observed, "We had a figure in mind that we should achieve at each particular day."

Other people also indicated the product was successful. Ms. Rollins commented that they were as successful as any other bank. "The people who use it, do it in the beginning. There was very little new money, mostly switching." Ms. Rollins also reported that case-by-case adjustments were made promptly for customers' problems; as a result, no customers were lost due to any of the errors that did occur.

Mr. Olin indicated that they had no complaints from customers. He said they experienced a big demand early on, but later there was no big demand for NOWs. The new-accounts people reported that many customers changed to NOWs and were enthusiastic about it, although other people just said, "It's not for me."

Success was clear from the marketing perspective as well. As Ms. Elton stated, "The major focus of the bank was commercial rather than retail." Consequently, the focus was to some degree on establishing a commercial presence. From Ms. Elton's perspective, the result was that she would rate her work on the project as successful at the level of 6 on a 1-to-10 scale. "We did not attract enough dollars in customers. Part of this was due to the decision not to be aggressive in the media. They didn't go all out. They didn't want to. Initially, they were concerned with presence, but once they got that, that's all they wanted. They wanted to be sure commercial customers saw them as in the mainstream." Thus, from one perspective the organization did not achieve growth in terms of accounts. However, this was not really the objective at all. The bank felt that it had established its commercial presence early on, and then became less aggressive.

Summary and Interpretation

Radical versus Routine Innovation

The NOW account was a routine innovation as perceived by nearly everyone in Third Commercial Bank. As with other banks, it was just a variation on a checking account. In addition, it was even more routine because Third Commercial did a sizeable data processing business for other banks and S & Ls and therefore had experience and expertise in data processing, including handling changes.

History/Unique Characteristics

Three background features were critical to the successful implementation of the NOW account. First, the executive vice president was a strong leader. Second, the data processing function was influential. The computer services component played a major role in preparing the organization for the innovation. Third, in contrast, to the centralized decision procedures, the organization had a strong tradition of informal communications at lower levels and placed great stress on people knowing what to do without being heavily bureaucratized or oriented toward standard operating procedures.

Goals and Strategy

The particular strategy chosen was a direct outcropping of the general objectives and position of the organization as well as its previous management style. The NOW account was a retail product, but the major emphasis of the bank was commercial. Although the bank was a major one in the area, it probably ranked lower in public awareness than several of its major competitors. Consequently, even though the product was for its retail customers, managers wanted to use it to enhance the bank's position with its commercial customers. They wanted to be percieved as being in the same league as other large banks (such as First and Second Commercial Banks) and they believed they could use the NOW account to help shape that image. The second goal was similar to the other banks': to retain current customers without adding too many NOW accounts. Since the NOW account would make checking more expensive than it had been in the past, they wanted to incur as little of that expense as possible.

These twin goals resulted in a moderately defensive strategy, one in which they were aggressively trying to create an image and retain customers while limiting the number of NOW accounts they got. In particular, they required a high minimum balance to discourage low-balance accounts and make the product profitable. At the same time, they called all their current customers and advertised on a radio business program.

Search

They determined their strategy based on a wide search for information via numerous outside contacts. However, they relied most on their own internal calculations of the cost of checking in determining their minimum balance and fees.

Complexity

With respect to the NOW account, Third Commercial was the most complex in the study. In all, twenty-two different positions, many at high levels in the holding company, participated in designing and implementing the NOW account. This complexity could have posed problems in coordination, particularly given the power structure and the lack of project teams. However, the bank was able to manage it effectively through an excellent communication system.

Flexibility

Lateral communication and communication from the lowest levels to be middle levels were open and uninhibited, allowing the organization to adapt its policies to the individual banks and to respond to unforeseen outcomes of the policy. First, a middle-level operations officer worked with bank operations people to uncover constraints in their procedures that might interfere with implementing the data processing plan. Based on this information, the service company modified its planned procedures. Second, once the account was offered, people in different functional areas in the banks worked together to solve customer problems. They did not tell a customer to call someone else but rather the customer contact person worked it out with the other departments involved. This all occurred at lower levels without use of the hierarchy, making response to the customer rapid and satisfactory.

Power Arrangements for Decisions

Major strategic decisions were centralized. All of the policy decisions and nearly all of the implementation decisions were made by the executive vice president of the holding company. He was heavily influenced by the president of the service company. While the bank presidents had an opportunity to discuss the policy, their views also were strongly shaped by the president of the service company. Despite all this influence and potential influence, the shared view was that the executive vice president was in charge and made the decisions. Lower-level managers and staff were given an opportunity to modify the decisions related to operational matters, though they often felt unprepared and lacking information and therefore had very little influence. Given the strong top-down directives, a real danger existed that the top would be out of touch with the nitty-gritty requirements of implementation and would make costly mistakes. A good communication network at a much lower level kept that from happening.

Readiness

For many reasons, then, the organization was ready when NOW accounts became legal. First, the innovation was routine and did not require much change in order to become ready. Second, they had planned well in advance for their data processing needs and were technically ready. Third, they already had organizational routines in place and they incorporated these routines into their plans rather than forcing an incompatible plan on the existing routines. As a result, all agreed that they were ready with the exception of not doing test runs on their data processing program. They were also somewhat slow in preparing their customer-contact people to answer questions before the January 1 date, but by January 1, they were ready to process the accounts.

Internal Outcomes

In general, the implementation process proceeded smoothly, though there were a few problems. Due to a well-designed data processing system, statements were out on time. There were a few problems with statement accuracy during the first three months, but the number of inaccurate statements was small and problems were easily managed. There were no reports of employee overtime. While some of the new-accounts people were a bit anxious about NOW accounts at first, that anxiety dissipated quickly as they acquired experience with them. Employees expressed neither satisfaction nor dissatisfaction with the implementation process. No one described learning anything new about their organization or about implementing new products as a result of this experience.

Product/External Outcomes

Managers at Third Commercial did not reveal the number of accounts they had targeted or actually opened. They reported that they did not lose any customers and that they had no customer complaints. They believed that the NOW account had helped to increase their visibility as a commercial bank. The NOW account did not attract new retail customers, but that was not the bank's goal. The managers perceived the product as successful.

Note

1. In this industry, the use of mass media (radio, TV, and newspapers) is considered aggressive marketing. Less aggressive marketing involves contact with current customers by including pamphlets with account statements and doing other routine mailings.

6
Aggressive Radical Innovation

irst National S & L was a multibranch savings and loan association, having twelve branches in the metropolitan area and in rural areas of the state. Its total assets at the time of sampling were $1.8 billion, making it the largest thrift in the state and one of the largest in the country.

Our initial entry into the organization was through a letter to the chairman and a subsequent telephone conversation in which he referred us immediately to one of the vice presidents, Ms. Smith. Our first interview with Ms. Smith revealed that the introduction of the NOW account had been a traumatic and complex process. As a result, to capture what happened, we needed to interview a wide variety of individuals in the organization and one outsider. In addition to Ms. Smith, we interviewed:

1. The current senior vice president in charge of data processing. He had been hired after the NOW account had been introduced. (Unfortunately, we were not able to interview the previous head of data processing, who had been in charge at the time the NOW accounts were introduced; he had left the organization.)
2. Two individuals who had played key roles in the data processing part of the NOW account process.
3. Mr. Brennan (president of one of the main branches) and several new-accounts people at his branch.
4. The president of the association.
5. Mr. Warner, a senior vice president and head of the group that had primary responsibility for implementing the NOW account.
6. Mr. Donaldson, a member of a "Big Eight" accounting firm, who had headed a team of consultants who worked with First National on the NOW accounts.

We were unable to interview the man who had headed up the marketing effort, because he had left the organization before our study began and managers of First National did not want us to contact him.

Routineness

All these respondents indicated that the NOW account was a radical innovation for this organization and that it affected many areas of the association. For example, one stated, "We had never done anything like this before; we could only go on projections." Another said, "It was the biggest thing we had ever done." A third respondent described it as a whole new world requiring new expertise. Mr. Warner summed the situation up well:

> There are key things in checking accounts which are not present in savings accounts. Checking accounts are time-critical. You have twenty-four hours to refuse to pay a check. You must process every day and have the records that you need to do this. Also, our system had no way to process statements. You need to see the history of accounts in new ways, ways that are not the same for a normal savings account.

Senior managers found themselves in the positions of rookies. One commented:

> We were babes in the woods when it came to checking. We had never passed a piece of paper; we had no relationship with the fit. This is why our banking competitors predicted that we would never make it. But I'm a born and bred savings and loaner. Give me a savings account and I can make a buck. There have been great changes. We are on the puberty side of banking.

Several people observed that the completely new routines required the development of a new language; in fact, one of the first steps taken was to develop a glossary of terms. One manager observed, "We did not know the verbiage linked with checking. We hired people with the experience in checking, proofing, and check processing. They used all these terms, and we did not know what they were saying. All types of things about clearing checks, dealing with printers, and types of checks available needed to be learned." In addition, the move to checking caused changes throughout the organization including the need to renovate and expand the lobbies and drive-up windows of many branches in order to accommodate the new volume; adjustments in work scheduling to accommodate changes in customer volume; increases in cash requirements and deliveries; and the development of a more guarded attitude toward customers.

The NOW account was also perceived to be the first of a series of radical innovations that would result in savings and loan associations becoming similar to retail banks. Most respondents recognized that, because savings and loan associations were relatively unsophisticated in many aspects of banking, much learning was required. Several observed that an entirely new way of thinking was needed. As one manager noted, "It was very hard for some people to accept. Some people had been here for ten to fifteen years and had experienced very little change. They were set in their ways. Some resisted the change; they wanted to do things like before. They didn't want to think like a bank thinks."

Design of the Innovation

Goals and Strategy

Several aspects of First National's history and position in the community appeared to influence its overall strategy for the NOW account and/or affect the processes involved in implementation. First, it was one of the most aggressive and innovative S & Ls in the area. Managers had typically used the media heavily for advertising and promotions. They had pioneered in locating services in supermarkets, placing tellers on line, and promoting services aggressively. Second, they recently moved from their original headquarters to a much larger, modern ten-floor office building. The NOW account was their first major project after the move. Third, they were well known throughout the metropolitan area for down-to-earth relationships with customers. The phrase "that short-sleeved feeling," used in their promotions, described the climate. As one of our respondents observed, "You must understand First National. It is a shirt-sleeve organization. When I first came to town, I saw on TV the chairman of the board celebrating the achievement of a billion dollar in assets. Five years later, they had two billion." He described how they had done this in their old headquarters, continuing to operate with rather unsophisticated, primitive systems. He added that, to some degree, this type of climate continued throughout the branches.

Our observations corroborated those impressions. A customer accounts representative indicated that she was continuing to balance personal checkbooks for a couple of customers. The office of the branch president that we interviewed was separated from the lobby by glass walls. He moved our interview to another room because "if customers see me in the office, they will just walk in; it doesn't make any difference who is there." As shall be seen, this low-key tone of the organization appeared to be a factor that both helped and hindered the introduction of the NOW account. Another indicator of the informality came in our initial efforts to establish contact with First National. As was our standard procedure, we followed up our letter to the chairman of the organization with a phone call. The chairman was not in at the time of our first two calls and these calls were not returned. However, on our third call, the chairman answered his own phone directly from the switchboard operator.

It was clear that First National was committed to an aggressive approach to introducing the NOW account. Archival materials entitled *Management*

Direction and Scope contained the following statement: "Full commitment of First National to 'NOW.' Bring to the marketplace a program that will retain existing customers and permit us to acquire new customers in at least the share of the market we now enjoy and expand our present savings and loan market." Interviews also indicated that no one ever doubted that they would go after the NOW account aggressively.

This aggressive approach was consistent with First National's tradition. As one vice president observed, "we have always been a heavy marketing-oriented organization." With respect to the NOW, he added that whereas the banks said they could not make money on them, what they were really saying is that they can't make enough money out of it. I can make money on 9 to 10 percent cost of money. We have to be smart enough to see where the banks are screwed up."

The aggressive strategy also meshed with the expectation that in the future, successful S & Ls would be more like banks than they had been in the past. First National clearly intended the NOW account to be a major step in becoming a transaction-oriented institution, much more like a bank that it had been in the past. Managers were anxious to have a transaction account; they set their sights on twenty to twenty-five thousand accounts initially. In order to increase the chances of getting the market share they sought, they felt it was critical to be the "first out of the starting gate." The importance of being first was based on the assumption that customers do not switch their checking accounts easily. Thus, in order to get the desired large market share, First National decided to try to be first in the marketplace and to do it in a big way. Based on their analysis of the New England experience, they anticipated a 10 percent positive response to their initial mailing to the current customers and projected the need to achieve a $500 average balance.

In addition to the general goals described in the archives, managers were pursuing several objectives simultaneously. First, there was a desire to build a customer profile data base. Second, their tellers had been on-line since 1965; they wanted to continue this arrangement as they introduced checking. These objectives added to the difficulties First National was to encounter. In addition to embarking on a complex, radical innovation, they were attempting it in concert with objectives that compounded the complexity.

In sum, when the normal aggressive approach was combined with the perceived short-and long-term benefits of the NOW account, the choice of strategy was almost a foregone conclusion. First National would be aggressive.

Operationalizing the Strategy. The aggressive stance was operationalized by making the account extremely attractive to customers. The interest rate was set at the legal maximum; minimum balance was $200. Moreover, current customers who opened their accounts early would not have to pay service charges during the first year, even if their accounts fell below the minimum balance.

Promotion was also to be aggressive, but ultimately was moderated due to the success of the early part of the campaign. As a first step, information about the offer was sent to 280,000 customers out of about 400,000 accounts that were current at the time. Opening a NOW account prior to January 1 entitled the customer to *all* of a set of premiums including steak knives, a one-year subscription to a magazine from First National, a no-bounce privilege attached to the savings account, free travelers checks, free check cashing at local supermarkets, fifty free personalized checks, and use of the automatic teller machines located around the city. The offer was described in a letter dated November 1980, and signed by the chairman of the association. It was anticipated, based on the New England experience, that approximately 10 percent of the letters would result in NOW accounts. The actual response was about 26,000 the first month or so. This response (which was actually a bit lower than the 10 percent projection) put such a great strain on the organization's resources that a planned media campaign was terminated, although a few television, radio, and local newspaper ads could not be withdrawn. Thus, the aggressive strategy was implemented primarily through notices about the product and premiums to current customers. The success caused a curtailment in other planned parts of the promotion.

Markets, Size, and the Environment. First National's large size and its leadership position in the community contributed a number of additional pressures and problems. First, managers believed they were highly visible and could not afford to make mistakes. As one noted: "When you are large, the public expects you to perform. They would tolerate errors from smaller organizations, but they would not tolerate one from First National. Thus, you spend more time to get things right. But, you also have more resources to do it." Managers observed that if they made significant mistakes, it would certainly be noticed and it would be embarrassing to the organization. (This perception was justified by our interviews in the banks. Several bankers pointed to First National as having had a disastrous experience with the NOW account. A typical comment was, "I'll bet they wouldn't talk to you.") Moreover, like other savings and loan associations, First National needed to buy certain services from the large wholesale banks in the area. However, because First National was so large, it was also a potential competitor. Thus, the managers indicated they needed to be cautious about the advice that they were accepting from the banks.

In the eyes of its managers, First National's size put three additional pressures on the organization. The first was inertia. As one manager commented, "It's difficult to change an organization this size rapidly. "It's like stopping a locomotive." Second, as one respondent put it, savings and loan associations are relatively unsophisticated relative to banks. However, the larger ones need to be much more sophisticated; the need to be more like a bank was stronger for the large S & Ls than for the smaller ones. Third, managers commented that trade associations such as the U.S. League of Savings Associations were geared to providing information and services that were relevant to the majority of their members, which were average and small savings and loan associations. As a result, managers at First National felt that the information available from the trade associations was of little use to them in introducing the NOW account. One vice president summarized the sources of some difficulties.

> This all comes back to bigness. We are so big and we are doing everything for the first time and others are following. We have made some contacts with other large associations nationally. We are $1.8 billion size, but the trade group has never expanded to the segment above $500 million. They assume that if you are larger than $500 million, you have all the problems you can have. As a result, informal peer groups have formed in such areas as marketing and data processing. These are informal associations of the very large savings and loans in the country. They are not highly organized. They have meetings, largely round table, informal sessions. They do have programs sometimes with outside speakers, but they are not formal either. You can talk at these meetings much more openly than you can talk to local people. The local people are also competitors.

Ms. Smith observed:

> Basically the seminars [on NOW accounts] sponsored by the savings and loan trade groups were unfair to large S & Ls. The seminars assumed that we were low volume and had excess tellers. However, we are not that way. We have big volume. They made assumptions that did not apply to us. Our branches were very busy; the idea of looking at more volume at the teller window was a big problem for us.

The impact of size might not have been as great had management adopted a less aggressive strategy. Taken together, however, First National's size and the aggressive marketing meant that a large initial volume of work, both in opening new accounts and in processing checks, was expected.

Size put constraints on certain decisions. As Mr. Donaldson observed, First National had to deal with huge volume, integrating new and existing systems, and knowing where to put the NOW account organizationally. "On the other hand, it was a nonevent for smaller banks and savings and loans." As the president observed, "When you are as large as we are, if you have even slight success with something like this, you have a great deal of business. Hence, you must develop the internal systems. If we got only a few accounts, we could have done it by hand, but we got many accounts." Because a high volume was anticipated, an emphasis on internal processing was assumed to be required almost from the start. It was ultimately concluded that the routines needed to process the NOW accounts were available and had already been debugged by previous users, and, with some modification, a package from outside would be adequate. As we shall see, though, these decisions were neither arrived at nor implemented easily.

One additional problem stemmed from First National's position of leadership in its environment. The major technology needed for checking had to be either developed *de nouveau* or adapted from that used by banks. Clearly, it would seem that the latter made the most sense. However, because its teller system was on real time, in one respect First National was more advanced than most banks. As a result, their computing needs were different than those of typical banks and, because most checking account packages were designed for typical banks, they were not easily adaptable to First National's needs. Consequently, the normal computer packages did not fit their current system. In essence, they had special needs because they were behind the banks in their knowledge of checking, more advanced in their teller technology than the average banks, and larger than the normal savings and loan association. They were technologically different from most financial organizations, so that there was a paucity of external technical resources from which they could choose.

On the other hand, First National's size and leadership position did give it some advantages. First, it made them potentially a major customer for vendors as well as a showcase for vendors seeking to market their services to other savings and loan associations in the area. Second, managers felt that their size was associated with the availability of resources, both physical and human, which enabled them to do what was needed. Ultimately, the availability of financial resources enabled them to resolve their problems in a way smaller firms could not have.

Strategic Decision Process

First National began planning for the NOW account in November 1979, fourteen months prior to the January 1, 1981, opening date. Part of the reason for the early start was the expectation that the NOW account might be made legal prior to January 1981, and their aggressive strategy called for them to be "first out of the gate." The early work was perceived as going smoothly; it was reported that "Many of the key issues had been identified as early as January 1, 1980." The president observed, "We thought we had a very good game plan."

Three or four years earlier, First National had begun what was called the Electronic Funds Transfer Committee (EFTC). It had been created to deal with the automatic tellers and was composed of the heads of major areas of the association—marketing, operations, data processing, and the controller. It was chaired by a senior vice president, Mr. Warner. In June 1979, Ms. Smith joined First National as a vice president. A major reason for her appointment was her banking background; First National was anticipating the need for such expertise. She joined the EFTC. Because this committee was the major interdepartmental entity and the NOW account required integration of many functions, it was assigned to the EFTC. (When the NOW account was assigned to it, the word *Electronic* was removed from the committee's title). The decisions regarding strategy were made spontaneously by this group, almost without discussion, because the organization's culture and history precluded alternatives to their aggressive strategy. These decisions, however, were informed by an extensive base of information.

Search. First National anticipated that with deregulation of the financial industry, savings and loan associations would become more like banks. Their investigation into the NOW account was explicitly seen to be related to the need to educate members of the organization that important changes were coming. The president observed:

> We learned from the trade organizations that kept us informed of the legislative process. We then needed to develop an awareness level in the organization that we were entering an entirely new business. We sent a number of people to get an overview of what it means to be transaction oriented. At first we sent primarily the technical people. They would brief us. We needed to develop an awareness among the senior-level people as well. We sent them around to trade conferences and other banks, primarily in the Northeast. We had them study performances and the published results in the various journals. Then it became obvious that we did not have the in-house experience to manage it. We hired Ms. Smith and gradually have added to her staff.

Much of the early investigation into NOW accounts was led by Ms. Smith. Her search involved a number of paths. Meetings were conducted with some of the larger commercial banks in town. Data obtained directly from the financial organizations on the East Coast and from the U.S. League of Savings Associations were analyzed. In addition, software vendors, consultants, journals such as the *American Banker,* and a number of direct contacts that Ms. Smith had with East Coast organizations were utilized. With respect to marketing, they relied heavily upon the advice of the vice president of marketing. With respect to data processing, they attended seminars conducted by the U.S. League and gathered information about what other S & Ls were doing. Also, a manual was purchased from the

Newport Group in California to serve as a guide for communicating back-room procedures. Overall, First National gathered large amounts of information from a wide variety of sources.

Implementation of Innovation

Complexity

Unlike the banks, savings and loan associations were permitted by law to have branches managed by the home office. The result was that the large and medium S & Ls and banks had similar numbers of positions involved with the NOW accounts, but much of the differentiation at the S & Ls occurred at the home office rather than at the branches. In fact, the structure of the branches tended to be very simple indeed.

First National was a prototype of the pattern. At the upper level of the home office, there were five positions involved in the NOW account: president, senior vice president of operations and data processing, vice president of marketing, and controller. While the exact makeup of this group was unique, as it was for each organization, the numbers of upper-level people involved are comparable to the large and medium banks. However, there are many people involved at the middle and lower levels of the home office. Instead of the usual six or so positions involved in the banks, eleven positions participated in planning and implementing NOW accounts: the vice president of NOW accounts, members of the back-room staff that worked for her, the data processing project manager in charge of NOW accounts, systems people, data base programmers, checking programmers, a procedures group which wrote user manuals, accounting people, audit staff, microfilm people, and couriers. At the branch level, there were five positions participating in the innovation: branch president, new-accounts supervisors, new-accounts representatives, teller supervisors, and tellers. While they did not participate very much in policy, they played an important role during the operational phase.

Altogether, twenty-one positions were reported to have some significant participation in the implementation of NOW accounts. In sum, First National was highly complex with respect to NOW accounts, though the complexity was greater at the home office than at the branches.

Decision Process

From the start, the funds transfer committee thought of the NOWs as interest-bearing checking accounts as opposed to savings accounts on which one could write checks. After devising an initial statement of the status and the goals at a retreat, the committee met on a regular basis. An early project was to develop a glossary of terms because so much of the jargon was new to them. As projects emerged, they were assigned to individual members who consulted with branch managers, various operating groups, and people inside and outside the association. Periodic reports were made to the committee.

In January 1980, the assumption was made that the NOW account would be approved in the very near future, so planning activity intensified. Somewhat paradoxically, this early start was a cause of some of the problems encountered down the line. A vice president observed:

> Data processing people and others did not want to spend their resources until they knew exactly what the regulators would require and what type of product they would have. They did not want to spend something like $40,000 on software or make commitments to check suppliers without knowing exactly what the product would be. Historically, regulators tend to underestimate the time it takes to introduce a new product.

The nonroutine nature of the project complicated the decision process. Top managers described the process as one of "learning as we went." As one of them said, "Most things tended to feed off themselves. You discover new problems while you are solving other ones. As you go through, you find there are sources needed and that people would be affected on a project-by-project basis." Another manager commented, "It was a totally new operation. We went down a number of erroneous paths; occasionally we had to turn around." The "learning by doing" created some stress, but more than that, it took a great deal of time which interfered with actual implementation. One of the managers stated:

> It was a good process, but it took much time. It took so much time because the people involved didn't really understand checking accounts. There was much learning involved. This took a long time to work out the details. Once people understood processing, they could figure out what was required in their areas. Some problems were worked out over the next six months. We are still refining the process to make it easier for the working departments.

Most of the managers agreed that, although the process was mainly ad hoc, ultimately everyone who would be affected was consulted as their interests and expertise became relevant. Our data seemed consistent on this point, except for the new-accounts people who felt that they had not been consulted when they should have been. All of the managers also agreed that this general process, which relied heavily on the use of committees, was typical of the decision-making process at First National until that time.

Size also influenced the decision process. Some of its effects were positive ones; others were negative. As Mr. Warner put it, "We have been very successful in everything that we have done. As a result, we have a wealth of resources, people, and management of people."

On the negative side, because of its large size, First National needed to make a lot more decisions than other firms did. Mr. Warner noted:

> Smaller associations buy services from various service groups. They can purchase a service directly from a bureau by phone. It takes little in the way of skills; they are just buying a packaged service. However, our size dictated that we do much of this in-house. Thus we had many decisions in deciding how to go about this. One of the key ones was whether to build our own system or get ready-made software. We decided to go outside and this turned out to be the right decision. The size influenced us in terms of the number of clearings, the number of accounts, and so on. In some areas it is geometric.

He added that bigness affects the timing of decisions as well.

> Size impacts on everything. The check supplier, for example, says 'I need to know your marketing plan and due dates as soon as possible,' because it will mean a sizeable bubble has to pass through his system because we are big. Things like segmenting of the accounts and lead time are influenced by size. A printer can probably give you a thousand forms off the shelf, but if you need a much larger bundle, then he needs lead time.

The radicalness of the change introduced another question that had to be decided early on: Where did the NOW account belong organizationally? Was it a savings account? Did it belong in operations? Was it a completely new area? They chose to put it under operations, making the senior vice president in charge of operations head of the project committee.

These general factors influenced the decision process throughout what appeared to be three somewhat distinct yet clearly interrelated phases of the decision-making process at First National. During the first phase, an approximately eight- to ten-month period following the initial meeting, the committee met regularly and subprojects were discussed and moved forward. A second phase emerged in the late summer and fall of 1980. During this period, there was a growing recognition of an impending crisis, ending with awareness that a full-blown crisis existed. Phase three began in mid-December 1980, with the entry of a team of outside consultants. It ended in late January 1981, with preparations for the departure of the consultants and incorporation of the completed project into the organization.

It should be noted that from the beginning until the entrance of the consultants, managers at First National followed their normal procedures to reach decisions. Committees played a major role. Responsibility was centered in the FTC. It met weekly; as pressure became more intense, it began meeting daily. As one vice president said, "The project was approached as a team effort. This is the key to our success. We created a team atmosphere."

Phase I: Initial Efforts

This period was one of search, frequent meetings, definition of issues and problems, and delineation of the key decisions that needed to be made. It was a time when a whole new perspective needed to be added to the organization. As Ms. Smith observed, they needed to learn how "to approach it from a processing point of view. Was it a savings account or was it a checking account? Our savings accounts have less volume than checking. I approached it as a commercial banker, but our savings officer approached it more as a savings account."

Other managers agreed that a whole new way of thinking had to be established. They observed that checking accounts are different than savings accounts in key ways. They are time critical and high volume; they involve large paper-processing operations. Although some decisions could be made easily, a great deal needed to be learned before others could be made. During this period, the specific marketing approach was defined, procedures for operation were developed, and members of the organization became familiar with much of the vocabulary and demands of checking. Most managers viewed this period as one of discovering one problem and, while working on its solution, discovering some others. Each new problem required marshalling resources, consulting individuals from different parts of the organization as they were affected, and coming up with a workable procedure. For the most part, managers described the time as one of discovering problems as they went and making many nitty-gritty decisions.

Some decisions were easily made; others proved difficult. Marketing decisions seemed to be the easiest. The vice president of marketing made his proposal and it was accepted with apparently little debate. Marketing was a strength of First National and its spokesman had considerable influence. As one of the other vice presidents put it, the vice president of marketing really knew the River City market and no one would consider challenging his judgment. Similarly, decisions such as the check supplier and accounting matters appeared to be resolved after consultation with a number of different people in and outside the organization but involved little extraordinary difficulty.

One issue that caused considerable research and debate was whether to proof checks at the teller window (on-line) or to do it off-line in the back room. Even though it was more time-consuming, the committee decided to proof at the window, because the procedure's newness made them cautious.

As one vice president put it, the major factor in this decision appeared to be that it was the "supersafe" way. Managers were concerned that First National would be the target of "every paperhanger [bad check passer] in town" because it would be seen as an easy target due to the NOW's newness.

While the proofing decision was a hard one, the most difficult decisions involved data processing. Although many aspects were considered, the core issue about data processing came down to whether programs would be purchased on the outside or written on the inside. Some of the difficulties stemmed from people's fear that they were not competent to make the right decision on this issue. As one DP manager put it, "We had no one in DP who knew enough to make that decision. The funds transfer committee could not make the decision, because they didn't know enough either."

Other problems resulted from some characteristics of Mr. Southworth, the DP head, and his informal relationships with the rest of the organization. The issue of whether to buy a package was debated but not resolved for several months. At one meeting, in spring 1980, committee members agreed that they would made the decision before leaving the room. The issue was put to a hand vote and everyone except Mr. Southworth voted to go with outside programs. However, Mr. Southworth did not do what was needed to implement this decision. The association president reported that on one occasion when the the vendors came to discuss the programs they had sent in advance, Mr. Southworth had not opened the programs and neither he nor any of his people attended the scheduled meeting. This episode was an omen of the crisis that the organization was to experience, a crisis that it would be slow to address.

Almost all aspects of the NOW account were reciprocally interdependent with data processing. When the DP area failed to deliver, many other subprojects could not be brought to completion and were put on hold. One manager noted that a firm order could not be placed with the check supplier until certain data processing information was available. Another commented on the delays in establishing the proofing and other back-room operations caused by problems in data processing. On the other hand, problems elsewhere made things more difficult for data processing. A member of the DP department observed that since decisions elsewhere in the organization took so much time, the time available for programming was too short.

Since the functioning of the data processing department was such a key matter, detailed discussion of its role in the decision process is required. The data processing manager, Mr. Southworth, appears to have been an extremely loyal, competent, and respected individual up until this point. The president of the association commented, "He had been here more than twenty years. He had an M.B.A. degree, was very bright, and had his admirers. He could do a great deal with the machine; he just did not attend to the management side. He would come in on Monday and discover a problem, stay in the building until Thursday, taking twenty-minute naps here and there. When he would leave on Thursday, he would throw the switch and it would work. The organization had gotten to the point where things needed to be managed and planned, and he just did not do this." Many others in the organization shared the view that Mr. Southworth was extremely good technically, even to the point of physically working on the machines himself. For the savings account transactions prior to the NOW accounts, his centralized, hands-on approach was extremely effective. However, the introduction of checking routines was too complex for this style of management. Moreover, several respondents noted that he approached the entire project from a savings and loan perspective. As one manager commented, "He seemed to feel if you treated it as a savings account, it would become a savings account." Most agreed that his approach was not suitable for the issues that checking accounts presented.

Several people discussed Mr. Southworth's management style and a failure to develop his staff. As one vice president related:

> It was the beginning of the end of his career here. He had been here for about fifteen years. His department's performance was not up to our needs. After he left, the manager who came in indicated that the department had not been well organized. Apparently, he was unable to delegate. He was a brilliant man; most of his employees could not match his abilities. He wanted to check out each program that they wrote. He would usually come up with a more efficient program than they had written. For example, he would assign someone a project that took a week of their time. He would review their work and basically throw it out. Thus a week's work was lost. He worked extremely hard, but he did not have enough fingers to keep in all pies. He came on board when our data processing department was reasonably small. It grew; he didn't grow with it. He viewed himself as a data processing person, not a manager. He liked to play with the machines. When a computer broke down, people would wait for him to go to the computer room and fix it. Our current manager never goes to the computer room.

Although only one respondent explicitly used the word *resistance* to describe Mr. Southworth's behavior, the picture that emerged suggested the aptness of this word. One manager commented, "The data processing manager just did not want another system in his operation. He had been there for some time." Another respondent suggested Mr. Southworth had "created divisiveness," but would not elaborate further. A manager commented, "Many things in data processing were just not done. In particular, projects had not been assigned to the programmers concerning how the various parts would be integrated. The data processing man was not going to do that; but once the decision was made to use outside programs, he had to do it." However, these things did not get done. A member of the data processing department indicated that although he would report problems upward, there was a block somewhere, and the key problems were not getting reported to upper management. He did not explicitly identify the data processing manager as the block, but others did. The blockage continued unattended for a long time. The president commented:

> Things just were not happening that should have. The data processing guy had not opened the package [the program that had been purchased outside]. The firm who wrote it came out to explain the package to us. He did not attend the briefing and did not send any of his people either. That was the biggest clue. Once I knew of the difficulty, then a lot of people came forward, such as the vendor.

We asked why no one had come forward before. "We had many people in different segments. Maybe no one had the perspective of the whole. Also, no one wants to be an organizational snitch."

The proclivities of the data processing manager caused others in the organization to greatly underestimate what was needed to implement the NOW account, because information was not being communicated upward in the organization. The data do not clearly answer the question of whether this was due to the DP manager underestimating the magnitude of the project, not communicating its magnitude upward, or both. However, it appears that both factors were operating. We have already commented extensively on the communication blockage. In addition, however, most people acknowledged that the DP manager and First National underestimated the magnitude of the task. For example, one of the members of the DP department noted that at first it seemed possible with existing resources, "but there were unexpected technical things that arose, such as interfacing the hardware and installing the data base and the software. It was just an underestimate of the possible problems that could arise." Moreover, it should be remembered that First National was intending to do the NOW account simultaneously with the development of a central information file on its customers. This later project was not abandoned until October 1980. Thus, it seems that in addition to any "resistance" that might have been involved, underestimation of the technical difficulties was at the root of the later problems. It is clear that the data processing department did not have adequate staff to do what was required. For a long time, the organization was going forward without having these inadequacies confronted.

Whether it was only for lack of communication or for other reasons, everyone agreed that First National had greatly underestimated the magnitude of the project, particularly on the data processing side. The data processing area was thinly staffed relative to the demands of the project; the DP manager apparently made no effort to get additional staff. One member of the DP department reported how much difficulty he had getting through to top management that additional people were needed. At that time, he was working by himself on several special projects. Approximately a year and a half later, at the time of the interview, he had seven people working for him on these types of projects. He observed:

> Management did not realize the magnitude of what we're doing. It had never gotten up to them. It was a communications problem. They had not been informed. So why hadn't management gotten the message? Let's put it this way. That communications channel is now open. There was a block; but once management realized it, they removed it. Everything that goes on now does get reported to them.

Clearly, two of the outcomes of the NOW account were a growth in the resources devoted to data processing and a substantial increase in data processing's centrality in the communication structure.

However, this change seemed to require a crisis and an outside agent as a catalyst. Left on its own, First National did not appear capable of removing this barrier or of working around it. A major role in opening up the channels, according to the data processing staff member, was played by the external consultant who did not enter the scene until the crisis phase in mid-December. In the meantime, there was a period of growing awareness of the severity of the problems.

Phase II: Impending Crisis

It appears clear that the data processing manager was able to delay both the decision to purchase software and implementation once the purchase decision had been made, as well as to delay the flow of information about the severity of problems to top management. Yet, the absence of information flowing upward was not, per se, an adequate explanation for the failure of top management to react. Information of an impending crisis was apparently available to top management several months before action was actually taken. For example, Ms. Smith, who described herself as a "memo writer," had sent a series of notes to various members of management beginning in September 1980, warning of problems with implementation and outlining what needed to be done. She also reported writing a memo directly to the president early in the fall describing the crisis she saw coming. From her perspective, no action was taken.

Exactly why Ms. Smith had so little impact at this point is not clear. Mr. Donaldson, the head of the Big Eight consulting team, said that Ms. Smith knew what was needed but did not have "enough clout." Ms. Smith attributed the problem partly to her newness but also to the inability of the organization to comprehend the demands of the new process.

> I had been concerned about the progress in software, as to whether we would be ready. I always thought that the NOW account would go big, and if it happened, that we would be in trouble. It is difficult to make those who have never dealt with checking accounts understand how much they require. I felt like Chicken Little crying, "The sky is falling!" Many of the people had known each other for twenty years or more and had a strong family type feeling about each other. Under these conditions, it was very difficult to make the thorny decisions.

Other managers speculated that her newness to the organization and the failure of others to give appropriate weight to her banking knowledge were factors. One observed that people in the organization reacted to Ms. Smith "as you would to a foreigner." He also noted that Ms. Smith was the only one with a banking background, but that "she had many hurdles to overcome. For example, banks do check processing off-line and savings and loans have always done it on-line. Also, we had different opinions on other things involving the bank and the savings and loan philosophies. We only had one check-processing–oriented person." In short, it appears that Ms. Smith lacked influence because her messages could not be decoded easily by other members, who had a different understanding of the situation, and because she was new and not influential in the existing informal patterns. Her competence was "unknown" in the organization. On the other hand, Mr. Southworth's considerable influence came from the consistency of his views with that of others, his informal standing, and his known competence.

In contrast, in an area new to First National, the back-room operations, Ms. Smith had rather complete control. Preparation here seemed to be timely and effective. This was accomplished primarily by her hiring people from banks. She reported never having any doubts about the readiness of this component. In short, where there was not a previous pattern of relations to be rearranged, expertise and power seemed to work in concert to produce "readiness."

From the perspective of the president, although he did not comment specifically on Ms. Smith's memo, he began to realize things that should have been done were not getting done. This led him to become involved in the process, initially by contacting individuals outside the association. After several weeks of study, he concluded that the data processing head was a major source of the problems, but that he could not be removed until the project was completed because of the information that he had.

A full explanation of the timing of the president's actions cannot be developed from our data. Why did he not act sooner? One respondent speculated, "Perhaps he did not realize the severity of the problem. If only one of your people is complaining that things are not running right, what are you to do?" Also, he had been in office only a year or so, and there was so much else going on in the industry that he did not have time to pursue the information he received. Piecing together comments from the president, the latency of his response seemed to stem from two factors. First, when he pushed people he had confidence in, he received assurances. "Many times people would say that something was not done, but they would always say that it would be done next week. However, things were just not getting done." Second, he was slow to recognize the weaknesses of a very competent employee to do the new tasks. In the president's words:

> I recognized that there was a serious problem in data processing, and I did not address it soon enough. It involved a long-standing employee, a very effective guy with more than his share of idiosyncrasies. He just did not grow in the organization. He was into questions of operating the computer but not the overall management. I concluded that the real block was in data processing.

As will become even more clear, the failure to remove someone viewed as an indispensable resource contributed to the problem. However, when an alternative was discovered, progress was possible. The president continued:

> I realized that I could not recruit and replace him quickly enough. Essentially, I slid him aside and let him handle the normal routine part. I tried to fill the gap. Due to our relationship with the consulting firm, I was able to get in contact with really senior people in New York and in the Washington office. When we got the people we did, I was convinced that I could not afford a false start. I wanted to be sure that the people we brought in would take hold. After a few rejects, I finally worked with a local man from the firm who formerly was a banker and had a great deal of experience with internal operations.

The data processing problem resulted in considerable delays in the entire decision process. People could not decide how the customer statement should be constructed, how the back-room operations should function, and how the whole project would run. The president observed, "The proofing operations and the back-room things were delayed because the data processing work was not done. Ms. Smith did not get the information she needed and was counting upon as a result of the problems in data processing." For many reasons, including the outmoded ways of thinking, the newness of Ms. Smith, the influence of Mr. Southworth, and the president's delayed response, First National was very slow to rid itself of its past routines and introduce the needed new ones.

As a result, the stage was set for the crisis that began to take full force in late fall 1980. Decisions concerning many aspects new to the organization needed to be made; but few of them could be made firmly until certain information about the data processing function was made available. Of course, a major exception to this was the marketing strategy, which was aggressive and put into operation in mid-November 1980. As we have suggested, First National knew how to market—the great success of the aggressive promotion strategy had resulted in approximately 26,000 accounts being established between mid-November and mid-December. It was apparent to Ms. Smith that a backup system was needed. In late November 1980, she wrote a four-page memo detailing the need to develop an alternative, temporary system to deal with the crisis. Also, about this time, pressure was alleviated by a decision to delay implementation of the customer information file, which up until then First National had been trying to develop simultaneously with the NOW account.

As late as September 1980, it was not known whether the computer system could be made to work. A letter from IBM during that month warned:

> The IBM 3624 can operate as a 3614 under the COLTS Extended FDP, when installed as shipped. This is not the version of the FDP that First National has installed; and further, your installed version of the older FDP has been modified heavily by you. For these two reasons, we cannot tell you whether the 3624 will operate under your installed software. It may; it may not. It is not advisable for you to assume that it will.

The lack of technical expertise made it difficult to get the knowledge that was needed. For example, Mr. Donaldson observed that when the consultants entered, they tried to get the software vendor to come up and work with them. The vendor said, "We don't travel during winter." Mr. Donaldson observed, "Probably what happened is that they felt that they were wasting their time when they came up, because the people at First National did not understand enough to use the vendor effectively." Moreover, since First National had automatic teller machines and their tellers used an on-line system, horrendous problems were created in introducing the software. Their needs could not be met by normal vendors.

The most complete assessment about First National's readiness came from Mr. Donaldson's observations. He had had experience with internal systems of many banks and could assess what was in place in comparison with what was needed. For the most part, Mr. Donaldson described the state of affairs as one where lack of knowledge was a key factor. He indicated that it was not so much that unlearning was required or that resistance had to be overcome as it was that there were just a lot of inexperienced people when it came to managing checking accounts. Mr. Donaldson commented that the lack of people with banking backgrounds, the inability of members of First National to use the vendor effectively, the fact that it was the first savings and loan association to use the vendor's program, and the fact that the vendor's program had not been piloted all contributed to the difficulties. Moreover, the computing staff was very thin.

Mr. Donaldson also observed that savings and loan associations such as First National did not understand many aspects of the NOW accounts.

> They were not sure of the effects it would have on their own accounts as well as how important the source of new funds would be. They didn't have the technical know-how to deal with the problems it raised. There were tremendous problems with volume and integrating existing systems with new ones. They now needed to know how to service the accounts, how to manage float, proofing, and so on.

This lack of readiness was reflected at many points during implementation. Teller manuals were rewritten several times and were still being rewritten as late as January 1981. Back-room procedures were also being revised after January 1, 1981. One manager indicated that people did not know who was responsible for what and did not know whom to go to if they were unable to make a decision.

Major problems arose from the magnitude and complexity of the project. The NOW account required that many different departments integrate their services. As one of the data processing managers said, "It was the biggest project we ever tackled. Data processing has done big projects, but this one had so many different departments involved. In this project many other departments had to do things with us. In the other projects the data processing could do it more alone."

Because the delays introduced by the data processing problems were so pervasive, it is difficult to assess how much other factors contributed to gaps in the organization's readiness. As we have indicated, several managers said that the complexity of the problem was such that it required a much more interdependent, holistic perspective than the organization had needed before. Moreover, in the past, First National appeared to have been able to handle crises by ad hoc measures. As one manager observed, "The big bubble of paperwork [crisis measures introduced between November 15 and mid-December to process the new accounts] was not new here." He observed that frequently during sales promotions, people were moved into new positions temporarily to handle the backlog. Thus, it seems reasonable to hypothesize that even if things had gone smoothly, many problems might have been handled by the use of slack and ad hoc arrangements in any case.

However, those ad hoc arrangements failed for a radical innovation of the broad magnitude of the NOW accounts. The organization had just never managed a project of this magnitude and complexity. The knowledge and process difficulties together amplified each other. Being unable to reach decisions because of technical deficiencies, they could not even prepare to implement their plans. On the other hand, since they could not make decisions and monitor and enforce deadlines, necessary information was not only unavailable but *not known to be necessary*.

Paralleling the evolving crisis at headquarters were events at the branches. Generally speaking, the branches seemed to have been informed of what was happening, but were not heavily involved in the process. For example, Mr. Brennan, the branch president whom we interviewed, noted that the presidents had discussed the matter with headquarters management in casual conversation for well over a year before the NOW accounts were to go into effect. Information was distributed at weekly meetings with the senior vice president, Mr. Warner. As the date came closer, requests from headquarters for information became more focused. Mr. Brennan observed, "About six months before the NOW accounts were opened, Mr. Warner began feeling us out on them." Information from the individual branch managers about their particular needs was sought. "He talked with each branch's president individually and gave input from the New England experience on such things as increases in lobby traffic [more customers coming into the bank]. We had no input in the decision strategy of the company concerning how to draw our people in. They did ask our opinions."

Mr. Brennan observed that the branch presidents' lack of knowledge played a role in the process. He noted that whereas on other issues the presidents might have argued more, there was no disagreement among them as to how the NOW account should be designed, because they had so little knowledge of what was involved. "Today there probably would be disagreement because we know what we are doing. At that time we had no idea. We knew what checks were but the whole theory of checking in banking was unknown to us." He added that he had no specific issues in mind on which there could be disagreement, just that typically their meetings are wide open and "the fur really flies." In this sense, the radical nature of the innovation may have provided one advantage.

In addition, there was a feeling throughout the organization that not enough training was done; this was attributed by the managers to a lack of time. Ms. Smith observed, "We had planned to do more training than we did, but we were not able to do all the training because the software was not ready. Basically they learned [what to do] by some of the training and by the procedures manual that we developed; then they telephoned in problems as they occurred. We did do some follow-up training later on." New-accounts people also commented on the lack of training. As one observed, "They should have trained us so we would know a little bit more about them, so we would know how to handle them. We were trained, but it should have been more extensive. One week we trained and the next week we were opening them. We had to learn as we went along." However, the same person noted that her supervisor and members of management were good at answering questions. This was particularly important because changes were continually being made during the operational phase of the project. Thus, as shall be seen in more detail, the severity of the problems that might have been caused by the absence of training were compensated for by flexibility and informal communication. Though the system was not ready technically, the participants were able to function, albeit under considerable stress, through ad hoc communications. Using Ouchi's (1980) term, we might conclude that the clan relationship became an important resource at the time of crisis. Moreover, the way the crisis was handled, at least to a degree, strengthened social relationships among the organization's participants.

Overall, the organization attempted to prepare itself in a number of different ways during the precrisis phase. It had educated key personnel through a formal process but much was left to "learning by doing." It had wanted to do more training, but even without the training, it was able to get by because it had hired people with backgrounds in banking to play key roles. It attempted to inform its branches on matters of direct relevance to their operations, but did little formal training. Finally it relied upon flexible, open relationships to compensate for the absence of formal procedures. On the other hand, its personal, open culture seemed to inhibit the confrontation of critical issues. It appeared that the organization's informal, decentralized mode made designing procedures difficult. The crisis might have been alleviated by more systematic procedures in the design process.

The nature of the process through which the impending crisis became a full-blown crisis can be best described by archival data. First, on October 14, a memo from Ms. Smith indicated that she had just purchased a manual that could be used as a guide for developing procedures. More important, she expressed concern over the failure to assign responsibility for tasks and provide information on the status of all parts of the project. She was also concerned about the data entry and audit procedures, staffing, general facilities, supervision at the branches, the savings service and funds transfer parts of the system, and the need to have tests of the systems and procedures. Her numerous concerns reveal how much needed to be done in two and a half months.

One week later, in a status report on the progress of the procedures department, a number of potential problems became evident. While the first drafts of several important manuals and sets of procedures had been completed, key modules were not yet started; completion dates of other key components were listed as unknown. A memo dated November 14 in Ms. Smith's files indicated that such key issues as the transaction codes, the printing and mailing of certain account information, and procedures for making corrections and related operational matters were ambiguous. One particularly sharp question, "Does our data processing department understand how essential it is that the system be run on the proper dates?" indicated that she had not been successful in sensitizing key actors to the time-critical nature of checking as opposed to savings accounts.

On November 15, Ms. Smith wrote a memo to the funds transfer committee. Among other things, she observed the need to plan a backup system because it did not appear First National would be ready by January 1.

> We are less than forty days away from opening our first NOW accounts and I think we have all agreed that the FSA system with CIF and TCS interface will not be available to the users 11/15. (In fact, it will take a total, dedicated effort to have the system and all necessary interfaces tested and operational 12/31/80.) We must, therefore, devise a viable alternative immediately.
>
> Any alternative will require extra effort on the part of the user and will require strict auditing controls to keep everything in sync. In my opinion, there is no question that any type of stop gap measure (alternative) increases our cost, reduces our productivity, and most importantly, increases our vulnerability to error and customer dissatisfaction. I would oppose any type of interim plan if I were not convinced that there is no other way. I am insistent that any alternative plan that we accept require minimal programming, duplication of effort, manipulation of data, and conversion effort while providing adequate audit history and balancing controls.

She went on to propose a complete interim system for handling the opening of accounts and account processing. Near the end of the memo she added:

> I want to reemphasize that I am agreeing to this interim processing only because I see no other choice if we want to continue as a financial leader in River City. I am also agreeing to this alternative with the understanding that it will *only* be used through 12/31/80. If data processing feels that there is *any* chance that the NOW account system will not be available as requested following adequate test time, I recommend that we immediately reevaluate our NOW account marketing and implementation plans.

She concluded:

> I cannot make the program a success, nor can marketing, nor can branch operations *unless* we have the tools to work with. That includes sound data processing systems, adequate hardware, and efficient data processing

operation. Again, if we do not feel that this is possible, now is the time to reevaluate our position.

On December 1, a letter from the assistant internal auditor added another dimension to the impending crisis.

A potentially dangerous situation exists. First National will be processing with no "back-room–proof" operation. As a result, the on-line data processing system takes on greater importance. However, in recent weeks, our data processing system has experienced a large amount of down time. This has caused problems in balancing both tellers and working funds.

On January 1, 1981, matters will be further complicated with NOW accounts and the resulting increasing transaction volume. Since the NOW account drafts are time-sensitive, they must be processed with as little delay as possible. With continued computer problems, First National will be left vulnerable to possible monetary losses such as those resulting from drafts paid on insufficient funds, as well as customer losses.

In discussing the computer problems with the data processing department, it was learned that the recent difficulties were "IBM problems" rather than First National problems. Nonetheless, we *must* minimize our data processing down time to help maintain control over our NOW and savings accounts.

Finally, on December 16, 1980, Ms. Smith wrote a memo on unresolved questions regarding checking accounts. She indicated that she had no answers to over twenty vital questions, including calculation and collection of balances, handling of special accounts, information, storage and availability, transaction codes, and possible errors such as the accidental deletion of names and addresses of customers. It was at this time that the consultants from the Big Eight accounting firm entered the picture.

In sum, until the entrance of the consultants, the radical nature of the innovation for First National made it nearly impossible to make the necessary decisions for several interrelated reasons. Some reasons were technical. The required knowledge did not exist in the organization, which did not have the expertise to access it. Other reasons were more organizational in nature: the informal power of the DP manager, the failure of the FTC to win the DP manager's commitment, Ms. Smith's lack of power, and the failure of the organization to have a process that permitted deadlines to be established and met on this project. Moreover, complexity and the high degree of reciprocal interdependency were new to First National. It appeared the decision making prior to the entrance of the consultant was stymied by the radical aspects of the innovation.

The magnitude of the crisis was created in part by First National's ability to do well a task that was now routine for them—aggressive promotion. By December 15, the day the promotion ended, they were ten days behind in processing the mail concerning the new accounts. By that time, 26,000 NOW accounts had been opened. Thus, the day the consultant first visited the site, three days before their work began and seventeen days before the first check needed to be processed, it appeared highly probable that First National would not be able to process the checks written by these 26,000 customers.

Phase III: Crisis and Response at Headquarters

The inability to make sufficient progress in implementation put members of the organization under great stress as the January 1 deadline approached. A number of people during this time were putting in long hours. One individual in data processing was working fourteen to eighteen hours per day, seven days a week. Yet, things that needed to be done were not done, and people were not clear on what to do or how to get other people to do what needed to be done. As one of the data processing people put it, "You never really felt comfortable. We lacked the education to know for sure whether we had done something right. We were never sure what to do and when to have it done."

The data processing people were not the only ones under tremendous pressure; so were other departments. Ms. Smith reported that the whole thing was a major crisis for her department because of its newness. "My department was not here before the checking accounts were here. This was a big crisis for our department." Moreover, throughout the association there was a general fear of potential embarrassment. As Mr. Donaldson put it, "First National knew that everyone in the community was watching. We would be the laughing stock of the industry if we were not ready. There was tremendous pressure." Another concern among the managers at this time was that they would be tested by the community. People might attempt to pass bad checks; their own long-standing customers might be wary about First National's competence at handling checking. No one provided any evidence that they actually were tested, but this was an explicit, pervasive concern that many managers voiced.

In short, all the conditions for a high degree of stress were present. Stakes were high; the motivation was great, but they were unsure about their competence and ability to cope; and they lacked the resources with which to cope. This was the situation when the consulting team began work less than two weeks before 26,000 checking customers would be expecting to write checks. It should also be noted that this was the Christmas season— employees at all levels of First National and those of the consulting firm had personal obligations they were expected to meet.

On December 10, 1980, the consulting arm of the Big Eight accounting firm that had served as First National's auditor for some time was called in to help deal with the crisis. The consultants first visited the organization on December 15, studied the situation, and made a proposal. The proposal included an organizational chart on which the consulting team was placed directly below the president with authority over the employees (of First National) involved in this particular project. The consultant team agreed to attempt to develop a "Band-Aid" effort but was unable to guarantee whether the system could be up in time for the January 1 deadline. In view of the number of unknowns at the time, the consulting firm was unable to give a total cost estimate prior to starting the project. Their contract with First National indicated billing would be using an hourly rate.

Decision Process under the Consultant. Mr. Donaldson observed that upon entry, the consultant team discovered that many key decisions had not been made. "Data processing and policy decisions had not been finalized; the service delivery system was not in place." The first step was to bring in some technical expertise. "I got on the phone to marshal resources. I begged for a data processing manager who had considerable experience in large projects. I got our DP manager here who had worked on the First National account before. I also got someone who had run a large data processing department before. He had recently joined our firm." Thus, the consultants added substantial technical resources.

In addition, with the entry of the consultants, the decision process changed markedly. According to Mr. Donaldson, "The president of the association called a meeting of all the key people in the organization and said, 'This is [name of consulting firm]. They speak for me.' We took over the project." As soon as the consulting team entered, the nature of the internal process at the corporate level changed dramatically. They adopted what Mr. Donaldson called "an aggressive project management style. We literally took control. We set up a task force." Since no flowchart had been developed, one was. They took over a room and named it "the war room." The consultants designed a task force, made assignments, established priorities, and crossed things off as they were done. Mr. Donaldson observed:

> We tried to analyze all areas and to be the catalyst and devil's advocate. For a long time we had two project meetings a day with ten to twelve people. We had one in the morning and one in the afternoon. At each meeting we asked, "What have you done since we last met? What are the problems? What are the priorities?" Later on we went to a meeting only once a day. Every day we set priorities. We found out the tasks that were not getting crossed off; we went after them and asked why they weren't getting done. What are the problems? Our people got involved in every part. Pretty soon, ten or so of our people were there.

At the meetings we used peer pressure and kicked butts. We'd say "What do you mean you're not done? This is what you have to do!" We went to the pressure points where we found them and attacked them. We set priorities and accomplished them by short-interval planning. We took the highest priority and the shortest time ones first. The project was so massive. We monitored closely. We got constant feedback. There was a great deal of stroking and yelling.

Our team also met three times a day: at lunch, after work, and different times during the day to discuss what was happening. We used a critical path method to identify our remaining tasks, the time requirements, and the personnel requirements. The major objective was to develop a Band-Aid system that would not be transparent to the customer. We set up a testing group with people from other parts of the organization that had not been involved prior to this. They were a testing team. They tested everything, made suggestions, and did it. They took over an office, too.

Priorities included having the NOW account system ready by January 1 and getting the customers' statements out on January 30. In addition, the consultants requested a new temporary head of the data processing part of the project. The data processing manager was a key person because he had all the information, "but we could not control him. He would make changes and not document them. Then he would make changes on the changes and not document them. We wanted to throw him out the window, but we couldn't." He was basically given other things to do in order to meet other year-end demands. Ultimately, he resigned during the project.

The consultants also forced issues to be confronted. People who had previously been willing to forget deadlines and continue to debate issues now faced demands to change. Mr. Donaldson gave an example of a person who had previously been content to ignore deadlines. "One of the things that had to be worked out was the no-balance arrangement for overdrafts. One of the guys on my staff, at one meeting, got up and said, 'I want to finalize this now. Goddammit, I don't want to hear anything about this again.' "

In sum, under the consultants, the decision process became much more routinized. They used a project team approach, assigned priority to issues, and forced decisions. They replaced the committee approach with a project mannagement process. As shall be seen, the process was accompanied by tremendous stress, but for present purposes it is enough to show that the decision process changed markedly on December 18. In addition to routinizing the process and forcing confrontation, the consultants realigned the power relationships. At their request, the president moved the data processing manager out of the process. From the perspectives of the managers we interviewed, a major role of the consultants was to unfreeze the decision-making procedure, in terms of both the personnel involved and the processes used. The managers reported that the project approach brought in by the consultants was far better organized than anything the organization had experienced until that time. Moreover, the consultants' ability to have Mr. Southworth reassigned away from the NOW removed blockages that previous relationships had institutionalized, while bypassing the normal committee process used in the past. Ms. Smith described the change by recounting how the consultants had the influence to move the project along:

> Previously, monitoring was always a problem. We had status meetings. I found this unsatisfactory. Everyone would say at the meeting, "Fine," but the real problems were not taken care of. The consultants came in because organizationally it was difficult to have the control we needed. Organizationally, I was new and I did not have enough clout. The consultants came in and took power. There is no question that they had clout and they ultimately transferred it back us.

This last sentence is extremely important. The consultants acted as catalysts for a permanent change in control.

Managers at several levels agreed that part of the success of the consulting team was a function of their ability to operate outside the existing social fabric of the organization. One said:

> The reason they were so successful is the total autonomy that they were given. It is not just here, but in other organizations as well that you never have this autonomy to do what needs to be done. When you bring in a consulting firm, they can do what they want to do without fear of compromising because once they left that would be it [i.e., there would be no long-term consequences for them]. They don't have to answer to anyone. They don't have to worry about the guys in here that might be mad as hell.

Ms. Smith commented, "The consultant could come in, make the tough decisions, and leave. It didn't make much difference whose feelings would be ruffled or hurt.

The president of the association observed:

> We needed to bring in someone who could be hard-nosed and who could then disappear. Decisions needed to be made. I was looking for effectiveness. At this point I could not afford someone who would be sidetracked by someone saying, "Well, Martha is ill today." Generally, I believe that business needs to accommodate people in a normal business environment.

In essence, the consultants were able, at least temporarily, to institute a new process for moving information, forcing decisions, and realigning the distribution of power to fit the demands of the present task. The consultants were able to develop an entirely new decision process. As the president put it, "The consultants had an absolutely necessary role. They could bring together internally fragmented groups."

Under the crisis, with the aid of the consultants, First National moved from a state of very low readiness to successfully implementing the NOW account within only a few weeks. However, the process, particularly that of decision making, required considerable learning, stress, conflict, and the extensive use of outside consultants. The reports of the participants about this ordeal provide significant insights into the implementation of nonroutine innovation. The entrance of the consultants made the radical innovation possible. They contributed needed technical resources and managerial skills, changed the dysfunctional internal power alignments, and helped manage environmental components, especially the vendors. The entrance of the consulting team provided ten or so knowledgeable people to add to First National's staff. These people helped compensate for the lack of a strong DP staff.

The consulting firm provided more than vital technical resources; it provided important help in managing work and work-related informal relationships. Among other things, the consultants introduced project management to the organization. This style was recognized by nearly all our respondents as an important benefit. In addition, the consulting team helped the organization deal with key aspects of the environment, particularly the software vendor and IBM. Mr. Donaldson observed that the vendor had become unwilling to travel to First National. The consultants' prestige and potential power in interorganizational relationships apparently helped to persuade the vendor to come work with them. Moreover, they used their working relationships with IBM to get IBM to label the project "code red," a very high priority operation. In short, the consulting firm played an important boundary-spanning role.

In addition, the consulting firm was able to free up decision and communication processes that had inhibited First National from coping with its new product. Mr. Donaldson observed that the firms culture was one where past loyalty of an employee or unfortunate personal events often interfered with needed personnel and organization shifts. In his words, there is "a story behind every person" who needs to be moved. The consulting firm was able to remain outside this culture and make necessary personnel changes.

To fully appreciate the role of the consultants, recall the context starting in mid-November 1980, when the initial promotion materials were sent to current customers; recall Ms. Smith's memo of December 16, 1980. Then consider that by the end of January 1981, most people agreed that the system had been designed and was working.

The combination of project management skills, access to external help, and technical competence resulted in a growth in confidence within First National. As one data processing manager observed: "Within the first week they were in here, they had set up a framework that would work—if anything could. They set up a framework of pieces that fit. The first week they were in here, I felt good. You knew that they knew what they were doing, and that they had done it many times before." Another added, "They set up things to find out what the users needed; they saw that the hardware was available and that enough programmers were available."

The consulting team was also a force for focusing attention on the high-priority items. Once they began their work on one, they froze work on a number of other projects. Whether this change was a function of their project management skills, their ability to make unpopular decisions, their recognition of the technical problems, or the crisis nature of the situation cannot be determined from our data. Nevertheless, some things that First National had been attempting to achieve simultaneously with the NOW accounts were deferred.

The differences were obvious to First National's managers. Some of the changes reduced stress. The resources were available, people knew what needed to be done, the priorities were set, and a clear project flow was established. However, some of the actions of the consultants also introduced stress. Mr. Donaldson commented, "Things got very testy. We had grown men crying in meetings because they could not do what needed to be done. I would never want to be involved like this for another five years."

The consultants introduced the hard-nosed approach that First National appeared unable to do on its own. When the head of data processing was removed from the project, the flow of information to top management about the need for data processing resources improved. One result was a great increase in the size of the data processing staff. As one member of the data processing staff indicated, "we now got the resources that we needed." In a sense, the consultants enabled First National, at least in the short run, to free itself from the remnants of its traditional processes and to establish new ones.

Still, certain characteristics of First National had contributed to the effort. The previous struggle of the organization to come to terms with the NOW account had produced enough learning so as to make it possible for the consultants to succeed.

Several people suggested that the preliminary efforts that resulted in the development of vocabulary and some of the decisions prior to the entry of the consultants were necessary for the eventual success of the project. For example, the president observed, "However, without all the work we had done before, they would not have been able to do it." Moreover, the open communication and the high commitment to the organization of people at all levels seemed to create a resource that permitted the tapping of the tremendous amount of human effort required to process checks by January 1. A vice president commented on how the use of humor and the general feeling of harmony in the organization made it possible for the organization to draw on the high levels of commitment of its employees that were needed during the crisis. Mr. Donaldson commented on how important the previous culture was.

> You have to understand the nature of First National. Loyalty, that shirt-sleeve feeling, and making a good place to work are all important. They are down-to-earth people; there is personality in that association. They have a paternal attitude, but it is not limited to aspects of benefits or compensation. It is a feeling, an attitude; you have to be around every day to pick up the atmosphere. It was an incredible event. Their people really responded well.

There was also evidence that the open and supportive climate continued through the critical time following December 18. Several people commented on the supportive role the president played. He attended project meetings frequently; his appearances on Saturdays and Sundays gave morale a boost. Mr. Donaldson noted that the president "would ask what he could do to help. He ensured interest, involvement, and concern." One manager commented, "You knew it was important to him because you saw him around." Also, during the process, salary changes were made and bonuses were given. At the end of the process, a party was given by the president for all those who had played key roles.

On the other hand, Mr. Donaldson indicated that the firm's type of culture made if difficult for First National to change. Personal feelings and relationships seemed to make it difficult to fire anyone or change positions.

The behavior of the consultants, although hard-nosed, appeared to bring out the best in everyone. People reported that they now knew what to do, that they got the resources they needed, that communication channels were open, and that the necessary structure was provided. The consultants also motivated through their own dedication to the project. As Ms. Smith commented, "We worked twenty hours per day and the consultant team worked with us. The only time off was Christmas Day. We worked Christmas Eve, New Years' Eve, and New Year's Day. Some people weathered it well; some people did not. But you did not feel that the consultants were being dictatorial. They worked with us."

Another manager said:

> There was no change in my life. I was still working fourteen to eighteen hours a day. But there was a big change in life-style for some other people;

they were working these hours too. It was a hard pressure situation. Others responded well too, better that I had anticipated. They realized how important to the association it was. We all knew that the first people out there would get the new accounts. Most people were very positive as a result. Also, the association paid recognition to the people involved. I would not have considered it necessary, but they did. They were very appreciative. They had a nice banquet for all who were involved after it was up and running.

Overall, however, the key to implementation at headquarters was the recognition by the president that a crisis was at hand—it could not be business as usual. Though he still maintained his view that a firm needs to accommodate people in the normal course of business, he realized that this was not a normal situation. Consequently, he was willing to delegate tremendous authority—he let the consultant team run the project. Underscoring the consultants' autonomy, the president took a previously scheduled vacation during part of the crisis. He communicated by phone with the consultants, but it was obvious that the consultants were running this segment of the show. This autonnomy undoubtedly helped them to uproot the old patterns and to develop and implement new routines.

One unforeseen event complicated things momentarily. Savings and loan associations did not have the authority to operate checking accounts before January 1, 1981; the Federal Reserve Bank would not accept the checks before January 2. Consequently, there was concern that if the checks got to the customers too early, they would write checks that would be rejected prior to January 2. The checks were to be mailed third class on December 27 to avoid the problem. As it turned out, this was the same date that the state government mailed out its income tax forms. Consequently, the post office ignored third class mail and customers who were expecting their checks did not get them. Several backup procedures were devised. First, the check supplier made a small number of special trips to mail the checks to people who really needed them and mailed them first class. Second, some customers went to the post office and were allowed to sort through the relevant bags of mail to get their checks.

Implementation. Implementation at the branches was less complex but often produced considerable stress. The stress at this level stemmed from two primary sources: from the heavy promotion during the mid-November to mid-December period, and from the lack of knowledge about what to do during the period immediately following January 1. However, most reports seemed to center on the period before January 1.

During the fall, in order to prepare employees at the branches for the NOW account, people were sent to checking classes and given in-house teller training. All the branch managers, tellers, and new-accounts people were brought to headquarters. These sessions, labeled "rah-rah" sessions by the managers, were a typical procedure for new products. They involved lunch and presentation of information through slide shows and other media. These meetings were to be motivational as well as informational. As one officer put it, they were to "get the troops turned on to checking." These meetings were followed by some training of people in the branches who would in turn train other people in their branch. As indicated earlier, more formal training was planned than time permitted. Also, new standard operating procedures were introduced. The procedures groups wrote new teller and balancing procedures, plus new procedures for opening accounts and handling customer inquiries. However, the newness of these procedures, the need for changes in procedures early on, and the lack of adequate training time combined to produce a great deal of stress and anxiety among lower-level participants. This can best be seen through our interviews of participants at the branch level.

A branch president observed:

> We had a lot of meetings. We would have one meeting and then a little while later have another meeting to change what we had announced at the previous meeting. We would announce one thing at an 8:30 meeting and change it at a 1:00 P.M. meeting. There was much use of the hotline providing instant communication among all branch presidents and officers at headquarters. It was hectic. It was the nonexperience factor. We finally had it together on the first day, but even one week later we were still changing things. We said we were set, but we weren't. Most of the changes made once things were in operation were with respect to internal processing. Changes were made in where the information was sent in some of the forms.

Overall, however, more of the stress at the branch level seemed to result from the promotion than from processing procedures. The initial response to the aggressive promotion was overwhelming. Headquarters was interested in how many new accounts were being opened and how many people were waiting in line. The branch president commented:

> We could not handle all these accounts here, so we sent them up to headquarters. We were working weekends. The response to the offer was mind-boggling. We got hotline calls. (The hotline is a system that people such as vice presidents, data processing, and advertising have access to. They can dial a number on the phone that makes all the managers' phones ring in a certain way so they know it's the hotline.) The hotline was in constant use. They wanted us to tell them what was going on now with respect to receipts, number of accounts opened, and so on. We were in touch every day during the first week or two.

The whole process was done with little documentation. The major monitoring was counting the number of premium items (such as steak knives) that had been given away. As the lines increased, the new accounts were not fully processed while the customer was there; instead new-accounts representatives and tellers took the customer's name and address, and the necessary paperwork was done by backup people at headquarters. A vice president pointed out:

> That bulk of paperwork was not new for us. We are used to having special project groups doing things like this. Basically, we used the back office system with special couriers to the people at the branches; the couriers would bring the paperwork in to be processed here. People here would have no customer-contact responsibilities. At the branches they just handed out receipts. The big bubble took about sixty days to get through. We wound down gradually returning a couple of people to the branches periodically. Basically, this approach "deskills" the job—you just need to have someone to type. They do not need to know the whole process. You can use lower skills and less-trained people to do this. This approach is not new. We have used this special approach before. It has a long history— years ago, when we used to give dividends twice a year, we used this approach.

Considerable stress was experienced by customer-contact personnel. Again, the response to problems was often ad hoc. Significant problems were fed up the line and responses fed down. For the most part, this system worked successfully as far as all participants were concerned. However, there were problems and mistakes. As one new-accounts person observed:

> It was the most stress I ever had. When the doors opened at 9:00 A.M., people would line up at the receptionist's desk and on out the door. They were just given the receipt for the money and their gift, and out the door they would go. We worked till 9 or 10 every night and on Saturdays and Sundays. We had to actually do the work twice. We first put it in on a ledger; then we went back and redid it. We had to be quick at the time. It made it rougher, but we had to do it all that way to keep up with the volume.

Part of the stress that new-accounts people experienced was due to their perception of the way the procedures had been dumped on them. One reported, "I called the central office about a problem and was told, 'We think you do it this way, but if it doesn't work don't call us.' "

For the most part, the initial fears and actual stress experienced were managed through the ad hoc process. As one new-accounts supervisor said, "I thought it was going to be a mess. I didn't feel confident in my knowledge; and I projected that to my tellers in my training. But it didn't seem to faze them. There were not enough machines to train the people on, but somehow they managed. They got enough of the information and they got through it." Mr. Brennan, a branch president, reported playing a supportive role to show his thanks to his employees.

> During the crisis, no one got coffee breaks; we shortened lunch hours and started earlier in the day. We ran as fast and as hard as they could keep up. To keep the troops up, there was lots of give-and-take. You can't whip only, you have to give sugar cubes and apples sometimes. If they missed their breaks, they would understand what we were doing and why. We would say to them, "Later on we will give you a one half-hour break instead of the fifteen-minute break, to make up for the loss. Thanks a lot for your help." We would also talk about what to bring in for dinner that night— deluxe pizzas, Chinese, whatever.

In short, while people at the lower levels resented not being consulted ahead of time, there seemed to be considerable personal communication that facilitated resolution of problems. The close contact among supervisors and workers and among supervisors and branch presidents seemed critical. As Mr. Brennan put it, "At the point of such hyper activity, you can tell when the troops are running out of gas. At first it was exciting; then you started to wonder when they would stop coming in. I just kept my eyes and ears open and tried to be as accessible to them as I always am. I would buy meals for them at the end of a hard day and try to keep their spirits up."

A new-accounts supervisor observed, "For me, the biggest challenge was keeping the morale up and keeping the people informed." She also observed how the new-accounts people were so excited and motivated— simultaneously with being tired. Again, the open, flexible, supportive relationships that characterized the organization continued through implementation. These relationships seemed typical of River City and appeared to have contributed to a culture that helped people be committed to the effort needed during a crisis. These relationships enabled them to solicit necessary information and help from their superiors to cope successfully.

Two types of criticism from the branch level were directed toward headquarters. The first was that adequate incentives for good work were not possible. As one respondent observed, "The 'rah-rah' sessions were not enough. You need to give people rewards and incentives for good work." Second, the customer-contact people felt that managers did not understand what the new-accounts people did and hence did not know what they needed. However, although there was considerable frustration, the new result, at least several months after the event, was positive feelings about the incident itself and the organization.

Internal Outcomes

In the final analysis, despite mishandling of the NOW account at earlier stages, First National was able to process checks well, with few mistakes or problems. In addition, it had learned much about managing an innovation of that magnitude. Mr. Donaldson observed that the association did not miss any date with the Federal Reserve Bank and, in fact, by January 2, people were confident that the situation would be all right. This confidence grew every night when they met a new deadline. Paperwork gradually got caught up, and by February 1, people were relatively confident that it was running smoothly. Ms. Smith commented, "Given all the problems, it went incredibly well on day one. We never missed a date. People knew what to do. We never felt we were in trouble. On the other hand, I never quit worrying about it. However, once we went through the first cycle, once the system was up and statements had been sent out on January 31, I felt we had the problems licked."

The NOW account resulted in First National becoming different as an organization, in the functions it performed, in the way it was managed, and in the work people did. While these changes were most visible at the management levels, the changes affected the work of people throughout the organizational hierarchy.

In some ways, they became a different organization. As Mr. Donaldson said, "In retrospect it was very successful. They startled the financial community, including themselves, with their great success. They became a hybrid; they were not a bank, but they were not a savings and loan either. All of this caused great internal adjustment." A senior vice president observed, "The banks have looked down on savings and loans for a long time as being unsophisticated—in many cases rightly so. Many savings and loans are very small. However, those of us who are of larger size have found the need to be more sophisticated." He emphasized that most of the major changes had taken place at the management level, rather than in the branches. Many new things had been involved, especially the emphasis on speed, such as rapid processing of checks. Another vice president commented that the NOW account enabled First National to realize the need to be transaction-oriented. "The NOW account was a catalyst that made us realize that we were customer-transaction–oriented, a retail bank. This spilled over into many other areas." Again, a major part of the change involved changes in orientation toward speed and volume. As a vice president commented, "You needed to have the entire staff recognize that we now had a fluid, high-volume account. It needed to be dealt with instantaneously."

As we have indicated, most everyone in the organization felt that the introduction of the NOW account was the largest and most complex undertaking First National had ever attempted. The traditional patterns of operation proved inadequate and changes were made for this particular project. Significantly, most managers indicated that many of these changes became relatively permanent features of the organization. In addition, a number indicated that a great deal of learning had taken place, which made the organization better able to handle change in the future.

Learning had occurred from the top to the bottom of First National. For example, we asked the president, "In retrospect, what would you do differently if it were November 1979?" He responded:

> It's easy to say I shouldn't have underestimated the size of the problem; but more seriously, at first I should have thought out a more hard-nosed definition of the problem and development of the planning process. I should have asked for key bench marks and time frames. Second, as we entered new areas, I needed to hire the appropriate talents into the organization. We did some of this but needed to be more far-reaching and not only hire people at the top but also at the lower levels. We needed to watch closely and if we had made a bad decision, we needed to take appropriate action quickly.

Learning also was reported at the next level. Project management was a particularly important adaptation within the organization. For example, a vice president observed, "People were not used to the formal way of managing a project where they were required to work for someone other than their boss, such as a project manager." The willingness of people to play these roles and the ability of others to manage projects was a major outcome of the NOW account process. This vice president continued that among the things they learned from the consultants were the use of flowcharts and project management. "We learned their techniques by working with them. Now all of our projects are formalized. For example, we are now working this way to handle check processing. We are following their ideas in doing this project." Mr. Donaldson observed, "There were also many green people involved. When they got done, they were tired, wiser, better people. They are now project managers." The data processing manager observed, "The type of crisis that existed could not happen today because of what the organization has learned. Today the resources are dedicated and the dates are set on the basis of the resources you have available. The dates are moved accordingly. Back then we had limited resources and the date was set ahead of time." Looking back on the process, most managers agreed that while it was a most trying time, they learned a great deal and now felt better about their skills. Ms. Smith's comments seemed to summarize the views of many others. "Personally, it was a tremendous experience. There is no way I could learn that much. Of course, there is no way I could go through this again. Also it was a great success, and this is a source of personal satisfaction. It was fun."

Other changes were made, particularly in data processing, which greatly strengthened First National's position for the future. A data processing manager observed:

> The organization in the company has changed a bit as a result of this project. In the past some departments reported to different areas. This was changed to get department groups functioning. In fact, data processing was totally reorganized. At that time we did not have data processing groups who were responsible to particular functional areas in the organization. Now we have this. They are responsible for certain applications, such as mortgage loans, savings and checking. We have a team leader whom members from each of these functions can contact and say, "This is what I want to do, but I don't know how to do it. What can I do?" This shows that the organization is beginning to realize that customers may use different services. They crossed departments. The departments need to have information about the customer from other departments with whom the customer is dealing. The people in the department and the branches are now aware of the need to cross-sell. This is all part of learning how to be a full-service financial institution.

In replacing the head of the data processing department, a new vice president with banking experience was brought in with help from the consultants. His style was recognized as different than that of the previous head. He emphasized building the commitment and responsibility of department members through increased delegation. Whereas the previous data processing head was highly involved in the computer technology, one manager reported that the new data processing manager had probably never been in the computer room. While gradual refinements were still being made at the time of our interviews (approximately sixteen months after the system was up and running), everyone in the organization felt competent to make these changes. Improvements in monitoring, measuring the effect of interrelated accounts, elimination of mistakes, and reduction of customer time at the window were all intended; but these were viewed by almost everyone as very tractable tasks at this point.

Branch-level personnel described a similar pattern of stress followed by satisfaction with the outcome and with the personal learning. They also perceived that the organization was now much more like a bank than it had been in the past. They noted an increase in volume of customers in the lobby, as well as a change in the timing of transactions throughout the day. Particularly later in the afternoon, the volume was much greater than it had been in the past.

Perhaps the most noteworthy change reported by personnel at the branches was in the relationships with customers. The rather informal relationship that had characterized First National in the past had also characterized relationships of employees with customers. This was changed by the NOW accounts. One contributing factor was a feeling that customers were different. A manager observed:

> People were more used to the savings customer whom they had served in the past. These were steady customers with passbook accounts. At this time, it was not only that the checking account was introduced, but there were many new types of accounts and services such as the certificates. The people didn't understand these. They resisted them; they were complacent. Also, the customers seemed to become more conscious, more involved; they were asking more questions. The people were asking themselves, what am I going to do? How can I answer these questions? It became clear that we had to learn new things, especially in the branch areas for the customer-contact people. How were we going to handle these customers? The advent of checking accounts created more questions and complaints from customers than the normal passbook savings account did—it is a more volatile account. Some people were just not used to this. They needed to learn how to respond.

One branch president expressed the change in this way: "In the savings business we always bent over backward for the customer; we assumed he was a good guy. In checking it is different. You have some customers that are just a pain in the backside. You cannot afford to be as gentle with them. Some of them you just do not want to keep as customers, those who are habitual writers of bad checks." He observed that this was a major change for an organization that had been so highly customer-oriented. The whole experience had altered feelings about customers, particularly the response to the free items. He said, "At the time we were offering the inducement of free items. Some times you had to grit your teeth when people wanted extras of these. People get greedy for free goods. That is just human nature. You have to stand back and look at the whole scope of things. It is not money, but I felt we had overdone it on the goodies. I surprised myself thinking that way." At least some of his concern was due to the fact that so much had been given to the customers, but so little had been given to the employees as incentives or rewards for the hard work that they put in.

Also, at the branch level, there was a feeling that while confidence was lost initially in the process, over time the branches grew more familiar with their new roles and began to handle customers much more effectively. Moreover, some people felt they had become better supervisors as a result of the process. Others felt that people had become more mobile and could be transferred to the higher paying jobs if they wanted. Mr. Brennan, a branch president, said, "It also helped them to know more about accounts by having them help the customers. They enjoyed it. They feel more comfortable with checking. It is just another service we offer."

Overall, the organizational change was exhilarating as people looked back on it, having become comfortable with their new tasks. One supervisor observed that they needed something like that now to keep people from becoming bored.

The mixture of stress and exhilaration found at upper levels could also be found at lower levels. As one new-accounts person commented, "There were long hours. It was kind of frustrating. Yet, it was neat. We were comparable to a bank. It was something so new." She also reported positive feelings from new duties that she took on as a result of more responsibilities with checking accounts. However, the fact that these pressures came during the holidays and that there was so much learning by doing increased the reported stress. Another new-accounts person reported similar feelings. "I never came so close to quitting in my life. I did not know whom to trust; one hand did not seem to know what the other was doing. Looking back on it, though, it was a big jumbled mess. I didn't know what we were doing, but we must have known what we were doing because it worked."

Under these conditions, people were exhausted and mistakes were made. However, she also observed, "Actually it was fun. We worked hard together as a team. We could use a couple of those days now to boost morale."

In summary, people at all levels and locales of First National felt extreme stress during implementation. This stress did not cause internal disintegration, however, because supervisors took care to support and praise employees, reinforcing a strong bond of commitment to the organization.

Product/External Outcomes

There was a clear consensus throughout the organization and from Mr. Donaldson that the overall strategy had been a very successful one. At the time of our interviews, approximately 40,000 NOW accounts had been opened. Since interest rates had risen greatly, NOW accounts were one of the cheapest sources of funds for many financial institutions. First National was the leader in the state in the number of checking accounts. According to their analysis, they had taken accounts from neighboring banks, held their own customers, and had low losses in funds. From all reports, customer reaction to the NOW account was good. It was believed that customers did not actively use their accounts at first, for fear that First National could not handle them, but gradually the transaction volume was increasing and was closer to initial expectations. New accounts continued to be opened at a rate of roughly one-hundred per day through March 1981. At certain points, when more accounts were desired, rather moderate promotions were effective in bringing in new accounts.

The average daily balance had grown from the initial level of $800 to approximately $1,000 over time. First National more than achieved its calculated breakeven level of $400 to $500 average balance. Managers saw the overall impact of the NOW on the financial status as highly positive. They estimated that roughly 50 percent of their NOW accounts came from accounts that had initially been passbook accounts. In contrast to the banks, which were now having to pay on money that was transferred into NOW accounts, the savings and loan associations were paying .25 percent less interest than they had on the initial passbook account. Ms. Smith commented that it had a very positive impact on their investable funds. Mr. Donaldson observed that they basically had captured the retail market and it was now their cheapest source of funds. In his words:

> They beat the pants off everyone else in the Midwest. All the bankers were scoffing at them. However, they made a good strategic plan. It is their second cheapest source of funds. Their strategy was to capture the retail market; it worked. It has put them in the same category with the largest banks in the city. They did this without losing too much of their own funds. They did well.

Of course, the financial costs of employing the consultants so intensively to resolve the crisis were also large. Although we were not able to get the exact figure, Mr. Donaldson observed that it was expensive, "although the half million dollars that [First National] is rumored to have paid to the consultants is an overestimate." However, it must be emphasized that First National's financial resources enabled them to extricate themselves from a terrible situation in a way that less well endowed organizations could not.

Summary and Interpretation

Radical versus Routine Innovation

The innovation of NOW accounts at First National S & L was extremely radical. Many parts of the organization were changed by the demands of implementing checking. They required a whole new organization structure which included the use of project team rather than committees and linked data processing functions more tightly to other units. They had to install a data processing package that was more complicated than anything they had previously used. New personnel were needed in DP and elsewhere. They required a new language plus a new vocabulary for handling checking. Their time orientation, a subtle but fundamental variable of the organization's culture, had to change in order to accommodate the time pressures of checking. For this they needed new standard operating procedures. Their orientation toward customers had to change from one of almost complete trust and high levels of service to one of wariness and efficiency. In addition to these basic changes, they had simpler changes to make in the forms they used, the data processing codes entered for transactions, and methods of selling and opening checking accounts. Moreover, these changes were the first stage of a series of changes in moving the institution from a traditional S & L to something more akin to a retail bank. In short, the NOW account shook the organization to its roots, causing changes as small as the type of forms it used and as large as its fundamental culture and long-term organizational strategy. It was indeed a radical innovation.

History/Unique Characteristics

Design and implementation of the NOW account were influenced by First National's history. While First National had been an unusually aggressive marketer and a leader in the products offered by thrift institutions, it had no experience whatsoever with checking. It had no previous knowledge of any of the internal requirements of checking, from back-room operations to data processing to the space requirements high-volume demand deposit accounts would impose. A banker from First Commercial said that demand deposits were the backbone of any bank. First National had absolutely no experience with demand deposits, the product that was soon to become its backbone. Moreover, it had a tradition of aggressive marketing which made an aggressive approach almost automatic.

Its culture and its value system had a mixed impact on the organization's attempt to implement this radical innovation. On the one hand, the culture was described as a "shirt-sleeve feeling." People perceived themselves to be a family. Their value system was associated with low social distance across strata. Employees at all levels felt they were respected. They were motivated by stroking and a sense of commitment to their work "family" rather than threats of punishment and close monitoring. All these elements of the culture seemed to contribute to an unusually high level of willing participation even under conditions of extreme stress. They also led to the open communication channels which were very important in giving the organization the flexibility it needed to adapt to the many new problems it encountered during the final weeks of implementation.

On the other hand, the culture also meant that the organization had difficulty mobilizing the power necessary for making decisions when new modes of operations were needed, especially when there were competing interests, as in the case of the vice president of data processing and the vice president of NOW accounts. There was a hesitation to use power or force a resolution of the disagreements so that deadlines could be met. There may even have been a hesitation to use less extreme means to resolve the differences, because the friendly environment meant that confrontation was uncomfortable. The president was clearly uncomfortable in removing the vice president of data processing, because the man had been a loyal employee and the organization's norms required giving him loyalty in return. Moreover, the "shirt-sleeve" culture was associated with a heavy reliance on committees of equals for integrating across functions. Given the size of the organization, the funds transfer committee was quite large. Yet there was no mechanism for deciding among equals and no mechanism for steering this committee to integrate the many different tasks that needed to be performed by the different functional areas. Finally, the culture was so strong that it was difficult for outsiders to receive a hearing, even when they had necessary data the organization did not possess internally and their advice was crucial to the organization's success in implementing NOW accounts. For example, Ms. Smith was responded to "as you would to a foreigner." So while the friendly, family culture led to the flexibility necessary for implementing so radical a change, it also led to an unwillingness to listen to outsiders and a lack of structure and direction for integrating and accomplishing the many tasks required to implement on time.

Goals and Strategy

The goals and strategy of First National further contributed to the organization's difficulties in implementing the NOW account. They intended to use the NOW account to catapult them into the retail banking business. This goal required them to capture as much banking business as they could as quickly as they could. Their aggressive marketing strategy was dictated by this goal; they opened more checking accounts than any other bank or savings and loan association in the state. The tremendous number of accounts, however, was beyond the capacity of their underdeveloped checking systems.

Search and Size

First National's relationships with components of its environment were affected by its size. On the negative side, their size made them highly visible to the rest of the local community and increased the pressure on them to perform competently. On the positive side, they were able to hire expert consultants and a banker with significant checking background; they were able to persuade vendors to work with them, both because of the size of their orders and because their size made vendors' products visible to a larger market; and they were able to seek out information from a wide variety of sources. Unfortunately, they were not always able to use the information they gathered, because their historical lack of experience with checking made some of the information unintelligible to them.

Complexity

The structure of the organization changed during the effort to implement NOW accounts. It started by being complex, only slightly formalized for an organization its size, and polycentric with power delegated to committees at the holding company level with respect to the NOW account. No one from the branches was heavily involved in policy decisions, not even implementation policy. Still, it was a complex process with twenty-one different positions directly involved in implementing NOW accounts.

Flexibility

The process was only slightly formalized, with policy manuals developed but regularly superseded by telephone or face-to-face conversations; and polycentric with power delegated to project teams. Prior to the entrance of the consulting team, there had been no accountability for completing tasks toward implementation. The consulting team brought more order to the process, although their temporary attachment cannot really be said to have formalized relationships. What the consulting team did was introduce a process of setting goals and deadlines, and make people accountable to a project manager appointed by the consulting team. The project teams gave the different functional areas the autonomy to determine what needed to be done in their domains, aided communication with other functional areas through team meetings, and provided a structure for accomplishment that the committees lacked. Also, they moved resources to the places they were needed.

Power Arrangements for Decisions

The early committee structure and the low influence of Ms. Smith did not allow necessary decisions to be made and implemented. The consultants introduced new patterns of relationships. They were able to install a new temporary structure because the president gave the consulting team complete authority over the NOW account project. As a result, the consultants could overrule any parochial interests that interfered with the project's success. There was little internal revolt against the outside consultants. Their authority was clear; their power was aided by the perceptions of them as being objective when it came to parochial interests, and as being knowledgeable about banking and data processing. The combination of their neutrality, technical expertise, and unusual authority allowed them to quickly uproot existing organizational routines and move to the new structure rather efficiently. The movement was not without pain—grown people crying in meetings—but it was efficient given how different it was from current styles of functioning at that time.

Readiness

The organization was clearly not ready to implement until the consultants came in with their expertise, outside contracts, and new structure. In fact, First National was facing a crisis of disastrous proportions. Conflicts with data processing had not been resolved despite months of meetings. As a result, programs were not ready two weeks before they were to start processing checks. Since data processing and NOW accounts staffs were not working together, many simple decisions requiring integration had not been made.

The consultants made the organization ready in three ways. First, they implemented a new project team structure. Second, they used their own expertise to get the software up and to interface the software with other organizational systems necessary for implementing the NOW account. Third, they used their own contacts to get special treatment for First National. In particular, they got IBM to treat First National as a special crisis case and they got the software vendor to consult with the association. These actions made First National organizationally and technically ready to process checks on January 2, only two weeks after the consultants had entered the organization. The association was not completely ready at that time; there were still policies to be worked out and minor bugs in the program. But they were basically ready. They were not hand processing large numbers of statements, and the number of errors was minimal. So after revamping their structure and many of the processes they had used before, First National was ready to process over 26,000 accounts.

Internal Outcomes

The outcomes were generally positive, though such a difficult implementation process was not without human and financial costs. One important positive outcome was the tremendous amount of learning. First National went from a traditional (albeit innovative) savings and loan association to a hybrid bank and S & L, with project teams, a new efficient data processing manager, and a sophisticated data processing function which was better integrated with the rest of the organization then its predecessor. These changes taught them how to make the future changes they would have to make in response to continued deregulation in the financial services industry.

This organizational learning had come at the price of extreme employee stress, including unusually large amounts of overtime for people from vice presidents to the tellers. Almost everyone involved reported having been anxious, fatigued, and irritable with those in other functions or at other levels. At the same time, in retrospect they felt exhilarated at having become closer as a working unit and having accomplished the "impossible." When they were done, they had a system that worked well, a product that customers liked, and a new organizational mission.

Product/External Outcomes

The product was also a financial success. As the leader of the consulting team said, they startled themselves and the rest of the financial community with the extent of their success, a success that cost them several hundreds of thousands of dollars in consulting fees. They had gotten the number of accounts they had hoped for—40,000 by the time we interviewed them— and were making more money on them than they had expected, because their average balances were higher than expected, they had almost no losses due to fraud, and they benefitted from abnormally high interest rates. The huge number of accounts had indeed catapulted them into retail banking, and their customers were satisfied.

7
Rigid Top-Down Direction

With assets of $827 million, Second National S & L was less than one-half the size of First National S & L, but it was nearly as big as Second Commercial Bank. Second National S & L had been very successful until rising interest rates began to squeeze mortgage lenders. In 1981, they had expanded beyond their available space in their downtown offices and were in the process of building a luxurious new building in an exclusive suburban area, but the high cost of funds, the relatively low income on fixed rate mortgages, and the expenditures on their new building had depleted their cash reserves. These were the financial conditions surrounding the introduction of the NOW account.

Managers at Second National had a history of being aggressive and innovative in the products they offered. For example, they were the only financial institution in the area to offer telephone bill payment, which made them the only S & L to have some prior experience with transaction accounts. Their innovative orientation could also be seen in the marketing division's anticipation of national networks using automatic tellers and debit cards. Similarly, they had anticipated the NOW account for over two years. On the other hand, they were conservative in adopting innovations that had significant costs. They wanted to be sure that they would recover their investment before moving ahead with any change. As the manager of the savings division said of their decision to innovate:

> It's a real opportunity. The difficult thing is to prioritize, to do a bottom-line analysis on which to implement. The only thing that tends to mitigate the enthusiasm is current earnings pressures that have affected the S & L industry for the past two years and probably will for the next year. The bad side is that these pressures may inhibit our ability to implement things rapidly, but on the good side they cause us to be more tough minded in our analysis.

The study of Second National began with an interview with the manager of the savings division. The NOW account had been placed in the savings division, which was essentially responsible for all operations except data processing. We then interviewed a regional manager in the savings division, the person directly in charge of NOW accounts (called the transaction accounts manager), two branch managers, one new-accounts representative, and the manager of the marketing division.

Routineness

As expected, Second National experienced the NOW account as being very different from the products they offered prior to 1981. It required new standard operating procedures both for opening and processing checks, new data processing capabilities, increased staff, and extensive training of personnel. The decision to offer NOW accounts thus demanded considerable problem-solving capability. They clearly were attempting radical innovation.

Many comments indicated how much the NOW account departed from the organization's normal routine. For example, one manager stated that they had had no idea how difficult and time consuming data processing would be. The marketing division manager said they had not known how many accounts to expect; they greatly underestimated the volume of accounts they would have. Branch managers and new-accounts representatives described numerous fundamental modifications in standard operating procedures, including decreased time spent with each customer and the way the customer was perceived. Finally, the NOW account was so new and different that the manager of the savings division found it necessary to estimate changes in the need for desks, file cabinets, and other basic equipment. Second National found the product extremely different from anything they had offered before. The attempt at radical innovation created problems in fitting the NOW account into their structure and existing routines.

Design of the Innovation

Goals and Strategy

The general strategy at Second National was to become much like a retail bank. They wanted both to keep the customers they had and to increase their market share by offering people all the services they could get at a bank. The NOW account was the first step in accomplishing those goals.

The managers agreed that the primary goal for the NOW account was to increase market share. Said one, "Our intent was to have it be a loss leader." According to the savings division manager Martin Wiley, "We came away with an elementary design to increase market share." Similarly the manager of the marketing division, Mark Johnson, offered, "I had already concluded it was a necessary service, a lead service in a package of services if we wanted to talk about the industry becoming a family financial center." In addition to increasing market share, it was an opportunity to reach a new market segment. Again, Mr. Johnson said, "The target market was a little different from the traditional customer base. It was the best opportunity we had to begin to serve a younger market." In other words Second National wanted to offer the services usually offered by a retail bank and thereby reach new market segments and increase their market share.

While market share was a primary goal, profitability was also an expressed goal. The expectation was that the accounts would initially lose money but after a number of months become profitable. The emphasis on long-run profits was expressed primarily by Mr. Wiley, the savings division manager:

> The cost of funds along with the system already being in place assisted in meeting our profit objective. Our research showed that in New England a high minimum balance requirement would increase the average balance but decrease the number of accounts. Low or no minimum fee would increase the number of accounts, but the average balance would fall rather significantly. Studies showed that a $100 minimum balance would produce an average balance of $900. Our break-even point showed that we would be profitable at $900.

Thus, they were concerned to find that point at which they could attract significant new business and still be profitable.

Operationalizing the Strategy. In fact, Second National was extremely aggressive in their NOW account strategy. They had two criteria for evaluating the outcome of the NOW account. One was the number of accounts they got. The second criterion was an average balance of $900— the break-even point.

Both the pricing and marketing strategies were very aggressive. They tried to do everything possible to get as many accounts as they could. They required a very low minimum balance, $100, specifically to increase market share. At the same time, they believed that the minimum balance that they set would attract high enough average balances that they could be profitable. Mr. Johnson, the marketing manager, said, "If you require a $100 minimum, the banks are getting a $700 to $800 average balance. S & Ls were running higher; ours has never been less than $1,000. If you go to $200, $400, or $500, you get a 5 percent higher balance which reduces market penetration by 20, 30, or 40 percent. So you get a substantially smaller percentage of the market plus a great deal less money."

Another indication of their aggressive stance was the large marketing budget. They budgeted $117,000 for NOW accounts, $60,000 of which was used for mass media. Advertising began in the fourth quarter of 1980. All of the telephone-bill-payment account holders were contacted by mail to let them know that they were going to receive packets of checks in December but that they would not be legal for use until January 1. A major advertising campaign in the fourth quarter encouraged people to come in to open accounts early. All that they had to do then was deposit $25, which made the account very attractive and easy to open.

Together these steps—pricing the NOW accounts lower than any of their competitors, automatically opening checking accounts for all of their telephone-bill-payment customers, advertising via mass media, and setting a large promotion budget—indicate a very aggressive strategy. While there was clear concern with profits throughout, they were willing to sacrifice short-run profit in order to get market share. This was their general strategy in becoming more like a bank and luring away customers that in the past had been bank customers.

Markets and the Environment. Second National's goals for NOW accounts did not appear to be related to any kind of image they were trying to project. Some banks and savings and loan associations made decisions based on an image they had in the community. This association was not oriented toward an image. Their concerns were related almost entirely to increasing market share and making money. They did not perceive of themselves as the leading innovators in the area, but they did see themselves as being relatively early adopters of profitable innovations. The services administration manager, John Carter, commented, "As an organization we tend to be prudent but also on the leading edge." With respect to the NOW account, that meant adopting a strategy which would change their market position but simultaneously contribute to profit.

Strategic Decision Process

Decision-making authority at Second National was clearly located with the division heads. People at lower levels had little information about what had transpired. However, among the top group of people, there was apparently a process of decision making by consensus. Mr. Wiley described the process.

> A lot of the implementation proceeded by committee. We formed a committee that involved the division heads, and as we got more and more into details, we involved more and more lower-level individuals, department heads, subdepartment heads—people actually responsible for running it. Various segments were developed by the specific division responsible; then the financial department would analyze it. The committee would then meet and vote for recommendation that would be forwarded to the chief operating officer for approval. The committee in terms of operating decisions made most decisions by itself.
>
> We did have differences of opinion. Generally, it was not an overriding problem. We worked it out through discussion and interaction. There were no serious problems.

Consistent with this description of discussion until consensus was reached was the viewpoint of the marketing division manager, Mr. Johnson, who reported that on one occasion his views prevailed over the views of the chairman of the board, but on another occasion he was overruled on two issues having to do with service charges and payment of interest. At the upper levels, managers negotiated until they had resolved their disagreements, with little use of the hierarchy to settle matters and no one person obviously dominant over the others.

While people at the level of division manager made decisions by consensus, few lower-level people were involved. Mr. Wiley indicated that they had a process for getting input from people in the branches, but the process did not always work the way they intended.

> We hold bimonthly branch managers meetings, but it rarely turns out to be bimonthly. It's a forum to address issues that need to be addressed. We attempt to have the regional maangers get a feel for the nature of the problems, and then to have the people who can deal with these problems at their meetings. We have two regional managers who are troubleshooters; it's their job to communicate, to be accessible to the branches.

He indicated that the system seldom works the way they would like. In talking about what he would do differently on NOW accounts, Mr. Wiley said, "There may have been a desire to involve branch people, but by and large, I don't think things would have changed much."

The savings administration manager, John Carter, who reported to the savings division manager, concurred that branch people were not involved in the decision making. "As a branch manager, my own experience was that I harped on that nobody asked us. Sometimes what is desirable is not always feasible. Practicality came into play." The transaction accounts administrator, Bill Wizewski, who reported to the savings administration manager, also agreed that it was an upper-management decision. Finally, branch managers said that they had no participation in making the decisions about NOW account strategies. "All decisions were made downtown. I don't recall having any input."

Even though there was very little involvement of people below the division heads in the decision-making process, there were no data indicating dissatisfaction with the process. People apparently did not expect to be consulted and did not express any irritation because their opinions were not taken into account. No one really evaluated the process, for except Mr. Wiley, who indicated that it may have been desirable to have more involvement at the branch level.

In sum, Second National cannot easily be categorized with respect to its decision-making process on NOW accounts. It was not highly centralized because, like most savings and loans, it used a committee structure, and those who were involved in the committee made decisions by consensus. Furthermore, the chairman of the board did not make decisions by fiat, but rather allowed the group process to take priority over his own point of view. In these discussions there seems to have been a lively exchange of ideas and a fair balance of power between marketing and the savings division. On some issues the savings division prevailed; on other issues the marketing division prevailed. However, few were involved in this committee and critical decisions were made at the top with only a little input from those immediately below division managers and no input from people at the branch level.

Search. In order to meet their goals, top managers engaged in a search process that culminated in their particular strategy for using the NOW account. They began to gather information on the product as early as 1977, though concrete planning began in fall 1979. The early quest for knowledge was consistent with their desire to be prudent but on the leading edge.

Unlike some firms studied, Second National did not send anyone to New England banks to study their experiences with NOW accounts, although they did communicate with one New England bank in 1979. Information about New England NOW accounts came primarily from the U.S. League of Savings Associations. They also attended several data processing seminars. Moreover, they were active in creating data about their own market by doing a market survey.

The search process was primarily one of attending seminars and reading relevant materials from the U.S. League. Said Mr. Wiley, "We actually began attending seminars as early as 1977 or 1978, and began collecting data, information, and literature." In addition, there was some communication with a New England bank in 1979.

Implementation of the Innovation

Despite a history of innovation, early planning for the NOW account, and a strong commitment to the product, Second National had difficulties implementing their strategic decisions. One source of problems was their internal process. Another was their technological readiness, which was affected by a lack of funds to support their technical needs.

Complexity

Second National was highly differentiated, again with the greatest complexity at the middle and lower levels of the home office. At the upper levels, six different positions participated in the planning and implementation of the innovation. They were the CEO, president, manager of savings administration, manager of marketing, manager of systems, and an upper-level manager from the financial group. At the middle and lower levels, eleven different positions were involved. These were regional managers who oversaw the branches, the manager of Bank from Home (the unit that housed checking), three Bank from Home clerks with different functions, accounting staff, the manager of data processing, programmers, computer operators, training staff, and a marketing staff person. In the branches, only two positions were mentioned: branch managers and teller counselors. Second National was a very complex organization with nineteen different positions designing and implementing the NOW account.

Decision Process

The structure at Second National was neither completely mechanistic nor organic, but it tended toward the mechanistic. That is, it had formalized communication primarily down the hierarchy, with decision making concentrated at the level of division manager; there were no project groups. There was a mechanism for upward communication, though Mr. Wiley perceived it to be less effective than he would like.

The organization was highly formalized. There were strong tendencies to use written communication and to develop rules and guidelines in the form of written manuals and memos. For example, there was an extensive savings procedures manual as well as a NOW accounts procedures manual. There were so many memos written about the NOW account that Mr. Carter (who had not been in his position as service administration manager when the decisions about NOW accounts were made) could give us a reasonably detailed description of what went on. However, they also used face-to-face communication, primarily in their regional meetings to train people in NOW accounts. These meetings were relatively infrequent, though, indicating that the organization could be considered more formalized than not.

People made very few comments about the decision-making process after the policy was determined. It appears that the most important people were still those at the top of the organization. For example, Bill Wizewski, who was two levels below the savings division manager, had no knowledge of the written action plan. This could be explained by the fact that he came in after policy decisions had been made. On the other hand, he was the main person in charge of implementation. One would expect him to be involved in making decisions related to implementation; but he expressed no such involvement. In addition, branch employees all indicated that they did not participate in the decision-making. Asked how much she participated in the planning of the NOW account, one branch manager said, "Very little. We have the services department from the home office do all the planning. They may come to the line to get feedback." Then she said they had not come to her for feedback on the NOW account. "The downtown branch manager seems to get more requests for feedback." Similarly, another branch manager said, "I participated very little. All the decisions were made downtown. I don't recall having any input." The entire process from early planning through implementation, then, seems to have been characterized by decision making by a group of people near the top but not at the very top of the organization. The main decision-makers were the vice presidents of the divisions, though people at the level just below them were brought in to present information and ideas, according to Mr. Wiley and Mr. Carter. However, only upper-level managers actually made the decisions. People at lower levels had very little input either into the strategy or into the implementation.

Along with formalized communication and decision making by a small group of high-level managers, Second National frequently used assertion to influence strategy and high control to monitor subordinates' performance. That is, managers tended to expect their subordinates to do something simply because they were told to do it, and they carefully monitored subordinates' performances to make sure that subordinates were in compliance. While decisions were often communicated by memo, monitoring was often personal. One manager joked that he used fear to monitor his subordinates. He also said that he used a "cover-your-ass strategy" in getting information from his subordinates about what was going on with the NOW accounts. He indicated that written reports for monitoring were not readily available, so it was necessary to have face-to-face meetings with subordinates to discuss what they had been doing. One branch manager indicated that her function was the constant monitoring of her staff and that checking has meant more reminders from her to her staff. Likewise, the other branch manager said, "My role is to insure compliance. Time constraints mean managers have become brow beaters." She said that her staff members now have to get more approvals from her.

There were some exceptions to this style of management. For example, one division manager was oriented toward persuading employees to accept his decisions, rather than simply using his authority. He said he tried to convince people of the need to do various sorts of things: gathering data that would support his point of view, indoctrinating people to agree with him, letting his employees conduct their own meetings, and so on. In addition, another manager at a lower level said that he allowed his staff autonomy because they knew what they were doing. However, top-level managers in the savings division and the branch managers did not talk about persuading and convincing. They used terms such as "cover your ass" and "brow beating," indicating that people were expected to do what they were told without a great deal of explanation of why they should do it and without participation in the decision; and once the decision had been made, employees' compliance with the decision was monitored closely. Implicit in the language they used is the notion that punishment and the threat of punishment were used as methods of controlling employees.

Flexibility

All of these internal processes made it difficult for Second National to be flexible enough to modify its NOW account strategy as needed. As shown, interaction between bottom and top was infrequent, indicating that little feedback reached the top about the problems that lower-level people were running into as a result of the policy that had been set. Mr. Wizewski also reported problems in communication across departments, particularly between his group (which processed checks) and the data processing department. When problems occurred in implementation at lower levels, there were no routines or informal expectations that allowed modification of those problems quickly. Changes such as the need for more staff in the NOW accounts department required memos, jutifications, and approvals up the hierarchy. Mr. Carter, to whom Mr. Wizewski reported, explained, "Reports were available for staff support and for promotion recommendations. Reports take the form of crisis reporting, [information that] would document our problems. It's done out of a defensive posture. That department [transaction accounts] racks up a tremendous amount of overtime. We need to be able to explain what is happening to senior management."

To summarize, the organization (at least below the very high levels of management) was characterized by top-down, formalized communication and decision making. This made it difficult for the lower levels of departments to communicate with each other and contributed to a serious problem in coordinating data processing and the checking department. Moreover, the time it took for information from the front line to reach top management was considerable. One would expect an organization with these characteristics to respond slowly to any problems that might arise, including data processing and staffing inadequacies. This was in fact the case at Second National.

Readiness

In general, compared to other organizations, Second National planned in great detail and trained extensively well in advance. However, they delayed implementing critical elements of the plan. In addition, they lacked the resources to fully staff and provide adequate data processing. As a result, many people experienced NOW accounts as a major burden initially and at the time of the interviews still considered them problematic operationally. Despite great planning, Second National was not technically ready.

Managers at Second National began planning some time in 1977 by attending seminars and collecting information on NOW accounts. Mr. Johnson said that he forecasted authorization of NOW accounts by the Congress a year before they were actually approved. He had already determined in his own mind that they were necessary for the association. During the year prior to the approval of NOW accounts, managers planned everything from the number of desks and account numbers, to confidentiality of information, to the computer system. An initial decision on pricing was made as early as September 1980, according to a memo in the files of the marketing division manager.

This extensive information gathering, planning, and training should have made the system fairly ready to introduce the new product. However, it did not. There were four problem areas: technology, the high level of service that they provided, failure to anticipate the volume of paperwork, and understaffing and other resource constraints.

Technology. First, and most significant in the eyes of managers, their data processing capabilities were severely inadequate to allow them to do many of the things they needed and/or wanted to do. For example, according to Martin Wiley, they had first thought that their service bureau could provide a software package that would do what they needed. The service bureau had a program used in New England, but it was inadequate for what Second National wanted to do; and a more sophisticated version that was promised never materialized. Moreover, from the beginning, they wanted to control their data processing internally, but they felt they were not ready. They had a minicomputer used for telephone bill payment, and they originally planned to use the mini for checking; but they discovered that there were no demand deposit account programs available for a mini, and there were none that they could adapt. So they decided to contract out for service.

In addition, they were concerned about flexibility. Could a program be modified to do what they wanted and needed? Also, unexpected events occurred. The most important was that their service bureau was bought by an out-of-state bank, leaving Second National's managers feeling even less in control of their data processing. As a result of these technical problems, over a year after the implementation of NOW accounts there were still data processing problems. To cope with these and future concerns, they bought their own computer and began the process of converting to in-house data processing. Again, lack of technical strength prevented them from doing this successfully. Mr. Johnson said, "We still can't promote NOW accounts because data processing is not ready, but we hope to do so in the next three or four months." According to Mr. Carter:

The service bureau was totally incapable of providing us with systems support. To list all of the problems would take the rest of the day. It's still not smooth. We've managed to be persistent with systems failures. In hindsight, we should have converted to our own data processing system five years in advance of NOW accounts. There was nothing to do at this point.

Mr. Wizewski also saw their systems problems as being the most difficult. "The biggest problem was systems constraints which led to our problem of generating statements." Technical readiness was more difficult to achieve here than at other savings and loan associations because the unique service of telephone bill payments offered by Second National made statements harder to balance.

Level of Service. Second, the system was not ready to manage the increased volume of business because they continued to follow their previous routines in handling customers. This policy of continuing high levels of service was doomed to failure because of the amount of customer service associated with NOW accounts. More specifically, Second National continued to use the savings paradigm for the account. That paradigm implied rather extensive contacts with customers—high intimacy and high levels of service. This problem was felt primarily by people from the transaction accounts administrator down through the branches. Mr. Wizewski explained:

We are doing statement balances, answering inquiries, and processing the checks all in one department. We've never been staffed to handle it. We have become direct support to both the branches and the customers. Savings and loans tend to be friendly and customer oriented. Still, service is not as personal as it was before checking. We do one thing that banks don't do. We give the customer a balance; we tell them if their checks have cleared. It's a highly service-oriented account; we're always talking to customers.

Similary, branch managers said, "We've tried to keep personal touch with the customers, but it's hard on people." A new-accounts person indicated, "People don't balance their accounts, so then they come in expecting the tellers to do it. We would like to see them not offer free balancing services to everyone. We don't always have time to sit down and help them."

Paperwork Volume. The third factor that operated to overload the system regarding NOW accounts was failure to anticipate how great the volume of paperwork would be. Eighteen months after initial implementation, top-level savings division people saw volume overload as a minor problem, while lower-level people perceived it as still one of the critical problems. Both Mr. Wiley and Mr. Johnson acknowledged that people in the understaffed transaction accounts department felt harried due to the high level of activity for the NOW account. According to the transaction accounts administrator, they had many more accounts than they had anticipated, and at the same time they were surprised in the beginning by the volume of paperwork and the pressure of meeting banking deadlines associated with checking accounts. Likewise, a branch manager indicated that people working in the branches did not foresee the huge increase in activity.

Staffing. However, if there had been adequate staffing resources, the paperwork could have been done and the services provided. Such was not the case at Second National, but it was more than an issue of planning. Even after it was clear at the top level that more people were needed, they were not hired. Most people felt that the transactions accounts department was still understaffed a year and a half after the first NOW accounts were opened. According to Mr. Wiley, "Earnings pressures inhibit our ability to implement rapidly." Even 18 months after implementation, Mr. Wizewski said, "The staff still averages fifty to fifty-five hours a week just to keep our heads above water. Staffing is important to the people in this department. They see themselves as overwhelmed." He said that he would prefer to offer only truncation (not returning cancelled checks) and to staff accordingly. A branch manager said, "We still don't have enough employees to handle the traffic adequately. We have to work more Saturdays than before. We should have built up staff levels prior to offering the account rather than waiting two to three months afterward. The check processing department needs more people." Similarly, a second branch manager said, "Staff levels haven't increased in proportion with the transactions."

Training

The training provided was both formal and informal and more extensive and intensive than in many other organizations that we studied. People who were not in a position of selling NOW accounts had a one-hour orientation to the new product. For those people who actually sold the accounts, there was a series of seminars held in each of the two regions. Although there is conflicting information in the different interviews, it appears that there was a total of eight hours of training, part of it done by their check vendor. Despite the fact that this training was more extensive than some organizations provided, all of the people interviewed in the branches felt the need for even more training prior to opening their first NOW accounts. In addition, there was no time for training in the department that processed checks. Instead, they hired people from banking and counted on them do it correctly.

Internal and Product/External Outcomes

On the one hand, Second National had anticipated NOW accounts and planned to promote them aggressively to gain market share. On the other hand, internal inflexibility, inadequate data processing facilities, and inadequate resources constrained their ability to implement the innovation. As might be expected, there were mixed results. More than in the other organizations, the internal and product (external) outcomes were diffficult to separate, so they are treated together here.

There were both very positive and very negative outcomes of Second National's implementation of NOW accounts. On the positive side, they got a large number of accounts with high average balances. Since their goal was both to increase market share and to be profitable, they clearly met their goals for the NOW account. At the time of the interviews, they reported having twelve thousand accounts with an average balance between $900 and $1,200. At that time, this volume was still so large relative to their capacity that the marketing department could not advertise NOW accounts for fear of overwhelming the operations people. Moreover, they achieved their first year's goals for volume in six weeks. So from this perspective, they did exactly what they had attempted to do.

There were high and largely unanticipated costs for this achievement. Most of the problems arose from the fact that the system was extremely overburdened. According to everyone interviewed, statements generally ran late at first and they were sometimes out of balance. Mr. Wizewski said that at one time they were one-thousand accounts behind in getting accounts into the system. Early on, it took six weeks to generate a statement. While many of those problems were alleviated somewhat, the introduction of their own computer system had perpetuated some of these problems. A second result of their overloaded system was poorer service to customers. They lacked enough staff to adequately handle the lines in their branches. Consequently, customers had to wait much longer to be served after the introduction of NOW accounts. Of course, poorly served customers increased the demands on the system.

One critical outcome of NOW accounts that was related to the overloaded system was that customers were often unhappy. Almost everybody interviewed mentioned unhappy customers. According to Mr. Wizewski they were closing NOW accounts at a high rate, although they were simultaneously opening new ones. One of the reasons that the system was overloaded was that Second National tried to provide personal service. At the same time, the fact that the system was overloaded resulted in a reduction of the personal service; one branch manager said that customers felt that Second National had lost the personal touch. Several people reported negative customer reactions to the long lines.

A related cost of NOW accounts that resulted from the overloaded system was considerable stress on the employees. This was particularly true for people who worked in the branches and people who worked in the NOW account department. By the time of the interviews, some of that strain had been reduced for the branch people. For example, one branch manager reported that NOW accounts had become routine and that the staff had worked out procedures. However, all of the people interviewed in the branches indicated that they were still overworked, that there was still not enough staff, and that they were under a great deal of strain. Turnover in the NOW account department had been great; the head of that department felt he was unable to adequately train staff because they were always behind in getting their work done.

In sum, NOW accounts accomplished exactly what managers of Second National hoped they would accomplish. They increased their market share and they were profitable. At the same time, they resulted in a great deal of internal stress, a certain amount of turnover, and reduced service to customers, which resulted in a negative customer reaction and a loss of some customers. Clearly, NOW accounts would have been more successful if the goals for profit and market share had been achieved without the internal cost and the loss of customers.

It is also interesting to note what was not reported at Second National. No one spoke of improved capability or personal or organizational learning, as respondents did at other organizations. Similarly, no one said it was fun or stimulating as some had elsewhere. The impact on the goodwill and capacity of the organization and its relationships with clients was almost exclusively negative.

Summary and Interpretation

Second National S & L had serious problems implementing NOW accounts, problems that ranged from inadequate staffing to inaccurate statements. Despite serious efforts to plan the implementation effort in detail, managers had many surprises.

Radical versus Routine Innovation

One of the reasons that Second National had difficulty in implementing the NOW account was that the product was radical, being unlike anything they had done before. While they had some experience with transaction accounts through telephone bill payment, checking accounts were much more demanding in terms of technical capacity, amount of paperwork, number of people in the lobbies, and time constraints that could not be ignored. In fact, the NOW account was so radical for managers at Second National, that they had little basis for planning the process.

History/Unique Characteristics

There was nothing in the organization's history to prepare them for the demands of implementing a NOW account. Savings and loan associations had not been permitted to offer many different products in the past, so Second National had little experience with innovation. Moreover, they had a history of aggressively marketing the products they had. In this case, the result was significant marketing without adequate experience in the operations side, leaving them with more demand than they had operations capacity to meet.

The culture at Second National was aggressive and somewhat punitive. People felt "brow beaten" and defensive. There was no team orientation or loyalty to the organization expressed. This culture contributed to the problems in getting information about failures to the top of the organization, because people were careful about what they revealed to those above them in the hierarchy.

Goals and Strategy

Even though there were many obstacles to success with NOW accounts (such as a lack of experience and no routines for implementing them), Second National wanted to offer them in a big way. Managers saw the NOW account as an opportunity to position themselves as a serious competitor of retail banks, taking some of their market share and entering new market segments. At the same time, they had a strong emphasis on long-term profit. To meet these goals, they adopted a very aggressive strategy of offering free NOW accounts with a $100 minimum balance, which they believed would yield high enough average balances to be profitable; they automatically opened checking accounts for all their telephone bill payment customers; and they spent large amounts (relative to their size) on media promotion.

Search

Their choice of strategy was based largely on seminars and printed information from the U.S. League of Savings Associations. While they did have some contact with a New England bank, most of their knowledge came from the U.S. League.

Complexity

Like the other large organizations, Second National was quite complex. Participants in the study mentioned nineteen different positions that were involved in designing and implementing NOW accounts. This complexity required some efforts to integrate the different specialized jobs, since the NOW account required the knowledge and input of different functional specialties.

Flexibility

However, integration of specialties did not come easily, except at the very top of the organization. Communication traveled up and down the hierarchy, not across functional lines. Moreover, top managers were unable to get rapid feedback from lower levels of the association where there was information about customer reaction. They were also unable to get rapid feedback from back-room personnel who had firsthand experience with the statements being generated. As a result, they did not react swiftly when problems arose. Most of the problem with flexibility stemmed from the top-down and formalized communication system supported by the organization's culture. However, even when feedback was received, the organization was not flexible enough to make changes, because managers lacked the resources for taking necessary action.

Power Arrangements for Decisions

Decisions at Second National were made by a high-level committee, with some input from the level below the top vice presidents. Below that level, employee input was insignificant. Not only were employees not included in the decision-making on either strategy or implementation, but managers also made no effort to sell them on the wisdom of decisions made at top levels. Top-level managers just informed those below them of what decisions had been made. No one in the study complained about being left out of the decision process; however, they did report that they had not been involved.

Because all decisions were made at the top, all conflicting interests were ironed out at that level. Division managers resolved their differences by negotiating until they came to an agreement. The chairman did not interfere with this process, and division managers saw the process as fair and amicable.

Monitoring employee performance on the NOW account was somewhat less amicable. Rather than monitoring through reports, which are less personal and direct, managers reviewed the work of each employee personally and let employees know there would be negative consequences if they failed to perform adequately. The emphasis was on punishment rather than reward.

In general, power was held by managers at the top of the organization who used a process of consensus seeking to resolve their own disagreements but who presided over a rather punitive system of controlling employees.

Readiness

Largely because they were implementing a radical innovation in a big way, Second National was unprepared for NOW accounts. They did have in place a transaction accounts unit for telephone bill payment, but that group was unprepared for the demands of checking. They lacked adequate staff to handle the demand; and their savings orientation, which meant more service to customers, resulted in even greater demands on staff time. Technically, they were extremely unprepared, a problem that continued to haunt them for months. They had not anticipated that they would be unable to use their minicomputer, and when they ultimately chose a data processing vendor, they chose one that did not deliver the package they needed. When they finally purchased their own computer, they did not have the internal expertise to do the systems work they needed, so they continued to have difficulties with NOW accounts long after they were first offered. Some of their delay in purchasing their own computer may have been due to their resource constraints.

Internal Outcomes

The internal outcomes were not positive. Second National was plagued by inaccuracies and was late in generating statements. Employees experienced stress and dissatisfaction, while logging large amounts of overtime. The stress in the unit that processed NOW accounts was severe enough to cause turnover problems. Unfortunately, none of this stress was mitigated by excitement or enthusiasm for their accomplishments. There was little exhilaration at becoming more like a retail bank. Instead, there was more of an attitude of grim determination to keep trying to keep their heads above water. In addition, no one reported learning something about what to do next time. The only change was to an in-house computer, which would give them more control. But no one mentioned how they would manage their data processing function in the future or how they might handle lower-level disagreements or get better information from customer-contact people.

Product/External Outcomes

The product outcomes were generally positive, though there were some problems here too. They got a large number of accounts and were successful in getting the average balance they had targeted. Thus, they should have been profitable even the first year. On the other hand, customer dissatisfaction with the long lines, slow service, and inaccurate statements cost them business.

The aggressive pricing and marketing strategy led to an unexpectedly high volume of new accounts—a volume so high that current levels of staffing were inadequate. At the same time, little feedback reached the top of the organization; thus it took some time for top managers to become aware that their staffing levels were inadequate. Similarly, inexperience with the product made it difficult for top managers to predict staffing needs. Even when they were aware of staffing needs, scarce resources led them to continue the practice of skimping on staffing to handle the increased volume generated by aggressive marketing.

The slow feedback in combination with scarce resources and product inexperience also contributed to technological unpreparedness. That is, the organization was not aware of exactly what it would need in a data processing package for NOW accounts. It also had scarce resources and a tendency to be somewhat cautious in adopting new innovations involving large direct costs. These two factors led them to move slowly on the purchase of their own computer system.

Finally, slow feedback internally kept top managers somewhat buffered from the severe impact of their data processing problems, pariculariy in the NOW account department. Not being technologically ready led to problems in statement generation which resulted in staff overwork and tension as well as reduced customer service. The magnitude of the problem that failures in data processing spawned could have been overcome by adding extra staff to handle the work in the short run. Likewise, more upward influence from the branches could have ameliorated the problems of overwork among branch staff and declining customer service.

In a perverse way, the problem was somewhat self-correcting. The reduced customer service led to a negative customer reaction, which then fed back to reduce the number of accounts. However, marketing was so successful that there were enough new customers to compensate for the closed accounts, so that the stress put on the system by the high volume of accounts was not reduced.

Two factors clearly arose as critical in reducing the problem with the implementation of NOW accounts. The first was the need for increased organizational flexibility. Second National needed more information from the bottom of the organization to adjust to whatever problems arose either from the environment (customers) or from internal sources such as the technology. Second, implementation would have been improved by increased resources in both staffing and data processing. This may have been outside the control of the managers who made the decisions, but a greater commitment of resources could have clearly reduced the stress on the staff, probably reduced turnover, and probably resulted in a less negative customer reaction and therefore fewer lost accounts.

The NOW account was still a successful product, at least in the short run. Their problems with implementation were more likely to have long-run impact, though the data were not then available to assess the long-term results.

8
Barriers between Technical and Operational Units

First Regional Bank was a holding company with ten banks and nearly $300 million in assets in 1980. While all of the large and medium bank holding companies involved their bank presidents in decision making in one way or another, First Regional was the only organization that formalized that process in an organization chart. Formal authority was dispersed in two ways. First, there was an office of the chairman under the CEO. This group was composed of the chairman, the holding company president, and the president of banking operations. Under this office was a management committee composed of these three executives plus the vice chairman and a bank president. Under the management committee was the holding company president. Bank presidents and the senior vice president over the staff functions reported to the president.

In addition to sharing power among a group of people at the top, the presidents as a group reported to the president of banking operations through a dotted-line (that is, informal/informational reporting) relationship. The president of banking operations was also the president of one of the banks as well as a member of the office of the chairman and the management committee. He saw his role as representing the nuts-and-bolts needs of the banks to other decision-makers in the firm. While members of this organization did not describe this structure as being designed for decentralizing authority, it clearly opened up lines of communication among the operating units and gave them strong representation at higher levels.

Data at First Regional were collected from seven people. Our contact person was the senior vice president, Bob Friedman, who oversaw various staff functions, including marketing. He had been instrumental in collecting information and proposing policy for the NOW account. From him we got the names of other persons who played central roles in the new product: Kevin Marks, president of banking operations; Steve Cohen, vice president of advertising and marketing; and Jeremy Johnson, data processing liaison. In addition, we interviewed Larry Lewis, head cashier; Sandra Perrot, head teller; and Kathy Finnegan, new-accounts supervisor. These three all worked at one facility.

Routineness

NOW accounts were perceived as a routine innovation, so much so that people were not sure why we had an interest in studying them. One of the reasons NOW accounts were routine was that the bank had offered automatic transfer accounts, which they perceived as more difficult to implement than NOW accounts. Even the liaison for data processing found the transition to the NOW accounts fairly minor. He said that the kinds of changes required were "things like a social security number for interest reporting. A few more flags had to be turned on. That was really the only difference." Similarly, Ms. Finnegan said, "We really didn't change anything. Basically it was remembering who could not have one." To fully understand how this medium-sized bank managed a routine innovation, it is necessary to understand their particular goals for NOW accounts and the resulting organizational strategy.

Design of the Innovation

Goals and Strategy

The organization's general goal for NOW accounts was to hold on to their better customers, though they were quite willing to lose customers with low-balance accounts. Increasing market share was not a goal, while making a profit was important. According to Mr. Friedman, who was responsible for designing their NOW account strategy:

> We decided not to compete with the S & Ls. We couldn't see how they could make money on this. Alex Sheshunoff [a banking analyst] and banks generally are getting more conscious of the rates that banks share for their services. In his study of profitable banks, Sheshunoff found that the ones that were profitable charged for services. It doesn't take much of a genius to figure it out. I agree with him. When it comes to interest accounts like this, we take a position that we have to offer it. Many things we just have to adopt to be sure that people don't move their accounts.

According to Mr. Marks, "We rationalized that we were probably going to lose accounts to savings and loans. We further rationalized that we were better off without those accounts. We wanted to protect the good accounts, and so we reconciled ourselves to the loss of the marginal accounts." As with the other banks in our study, First Regional's goals were not to have a large number of NOW accounts. They wanted first and foremost to insure making a profit.

Operationalizing the Strategy. Having gone through a search for information, Mr. Friedman devised a particular NOW account strategy consistent with the general strategy of profitability. In essence, the strategy was to make the price high enough to exceed costs.

> We priced it high. My philosophy is to try to cover our costs. I thought that we needed about $1,500 to $2,000 minimum balances to break even. I knew from dealing with the bank presidents I wouldn't get this. A number of things were influencing us. First, [names of two large banks] announced. [Name of large bank] had access to the same information we did. Their anouncement of an $800 minimum was basically a reinforcement of the number we had worked back to. We probably would have come to about the same price had we not followed them. We were adamant in not moving too far in the direction of giving it away.

Mr. Marks echoed this sentiment. "When we looked at the financial cost, we thought we needed a $900 balance to break even. Our concern was to break even or make money. So we came in with a $1,000 minimum."

The data on promotion strategy were sparse. The few comments from Mr. Cohen indicated heavy spending and aggressive promotion.

> Our spending was much heavier than we would normally do. We thought it was a viable product; we wanted to be in the marketplace with it. It was a worthwhile investment to promote it. Our first concern was to make certain that existing customers were aware that the product was available to them in our bank. Our second objective was to woo and win customers from other banks.

Mr. Cohen was vague about the specifics of promotion. Other upper-level managers saw promotion as one of their weaknesses. In assessing the product's success, Mr. Marks said he wished they had pursued it more aggressively. "We might have gone after a heavier penetration of accounts, but I think the $1,000 minimum was right." Mr. Friedman remarked, "I felt we really did not get the support out of the marketing area. As an organization, we do not understand marketing. We should have asked, 'Is this a tool that we can get greater penetration with?' We probably could not have, but we need to develop marketing more as an organization." The strategy for NOW accounts was completely uniform across all banks, despite considerable difference in the type of customer served by the different facilities, and in the banks' functioning. One facility was particularly oriented toward commercial loans to middle-market business. Some facilities were retail oriented with higher-balance customers; others were retail oriented with lower-balance customers; still others were a blend. As a result, some presidents expressed an interest in flexible policies to meet their needs.

However, Mr. Marks said, "They all do the same thing. As a part of a holding company, it's rare when one or two banks would be allowed to do something different."

Markets and the Environment. First Regional did not determine its goals based on a corporate image in the community. Some of the firms in our study were keenly aware of their position as an innovator or as a perceived leader. However, First Regional did not see itself as having a particular image and did not develop any goals or policies consonant with such an image. The only exception was Mr. Cohen, who said they decided early to offer NOW accounts because the company is perceived to be an aggressive marketer and innovative. "We pride ourselves on being first in the marketplace. We are leaders. We wanted to maintain that kind of image." No one else expressed that view, though. In fact, managers waited until after the large banks had announced their policies before finalizing their own. They simply wanted to keep their best customers and minimize the expense of offering an interest-bearing checking account. In order to do that, they developed a defensive strategy similar to most of the other large and medium banks.

Strategic Decision Process

The process of decision making on NOW accounts followed normal procedures and is best described as consultative. The managers interviewed, however, reported decision making by consensus. Mr. Friedman said that he determined the pricing and marketing approach that made the most sense to him, based on the information he gathered; then he took it to the management committee (the president of banking operations, chairman, vice chairman, president of the holding company, and another bank president) for approval. While the management committee had the opportunity to influence the decision, they did not do so. Mr. Friedman worked vigorously to have his position approved without modification, and he was successful. In addition, the proposal went to the president's committee. Mr. Friedman said, "I knew that dealing with the bank presidents I wouldn't get as high a minimum balance as I wanted. I started a bit high. After dealing with them for a while, they probably knew this. They knew that I was setting them up." When asked if there was any disagreement, he replied,

> They pretty well accept the recommendations of the staff here. They decided to go along. There was one bank president who called me with his concerns about pricing. The bank presidents do not like to be the highest [priced] on these services. They adopted all of my recommendations on this. Sometimes that's good; sometimes it's bad. When they adopt them and

then later on find out it is not going well, they wonder why they accepted it.

While the agreement of the management committee and the president's committee were most important, others were also consulted. Mr. Friedman worked with a committee of all the bank operations data officers. In addition, Kevin Marks said he kept his people informed throughout the decision-making process. "They didn't participate in the final decision making, but they had input that would have been part of the final decision making."

People below the level of bank president perceived that they had little influence on the decision. The head cashier, Mr. Lewis, said: "I had nothing to do with the planning. I have no idea why they decided [as they did]." At the lower level, one respondent reported being pleased by the fact that the senior vice president had come to talk with them about NOW accounts, although she had no input: "It was an idea that we had to go through. The management group had already decided."

To summarize these findings, the process unfolded as follows: Mr. Friedman designed their NOW account strategy, then went to the management and presidents' committees and convinced them that this was the best strategy. He got their blessing to implement. After that, he met with each bank and described the policy, asking for input. He also met with a group of bank cashiers, who were the operations officers of the banks. Although these people did have the opportunity to criticize and make comments, their actual influence was nil; Mr. Friedman convinced people of the wisdom of his policy rather than changing his policy to reflect their comments. According to Mr. Marks, the process described for NOW accounts was typical for projects for which they had plenty of lead time; however, if they needed to move quickly, very few people were consulted in the decision process.

Much of the influence wielded in this process was based on a combination of formal authority and knowledge. Mr. Friedman had tremendous control over the outcome because he had formal authority, but also because he had the information necessary for making the decision. Formally, the management committee had the authority to veto or modify his policies, but they lacked the knowledge to make an informed decision and Mr. Friedman was very persuasive. Thus, while informed people at all levels had an opportunity to discuss the decisions, in fact they were made by the senior vice president of the holding company.

Search. Prior to starting NOW accounts, First Regional had purchased data processing services outside the corporation; consequently, little additional information was needed in this area. Like the decision process, the search process was rather simple and very centralized. Also, the innovation was routine, so there was little need to search for technical information.

More significant was the search for information on the possible outcome of various strategies. There are no data on the exact time they began their search, but apparently they did it early; several people mentioned having a long lead time. While Mr. Friedman attended seminars and read written materials of various sorts, he relied most heavily on the reports of one particular banking analyst, Alex Sheshunoff. Mr. Marks also did considerable reading on NOW accounts strategy. No one had direct contact with New England banks. Based on their reading and contacts, they devised their defensive strategy. Mr. Friedman and Mr. Marks were the only ones who reported being involved in the search process.

Implementation of the Innovation

For its size, First Regional followed a highly complex process. Two components of those processes had a critical positive impact on implementation of NOW accounts: (1) a concentration of power adequate for coordinating the process and (2) flexibility.

Complexity

Like the other large and medium-sized banks, First National was highly differentiated with respect to the NOW account. It was even more complex at the upper levels of the holding company than the other large and medium banks were, even though it was considerably smaller. Seven positions at the upper levels were involved in NOW accounts, reflecting a complex matrix organization that included an office of the chairman, an office of the president, and a bank presidents committee. At the upper level, the CEO, vice chairman, president, president of bank operations (head of the bank presidents committee), senior vice president-operations, vice president-advertising and marketing, and lawyers participated in making NOW accounts policy. Making up for the large amount of participation at the top, there were only five positions mentioned at middle or lower levels of the holding company. Those were the data processing liaison, data processing staff, advertising director, and two positions in operations. At the bank level, eight positions participated, including the bank president, vice president-operations (cashier), loan department stafff, bookkeepers, new-accounts supervisors, new-accounts representatives, head tellers, and tellers. In all, twenty different positions were involved, again reflecting a highly complex organization.

Decision Process

The process of deciding how to implement NOW accounts was similar to their strategic decision-making process. According to Mr. Marks:

> We asked people for direct feedback. The head cashier has periodic meetings with supervisors. He would ask if there were any questions. If everything was not going smoothly, that information would be coordinated at those meetings. He would then coordinate with me. If it [the problem] was company wide, I would take it to the holding company [as president of banking operations].

Mr. Friedman's meetings with bank personnel were intended to garner feedback about his proposal that might be useful for implementation as well as policy; but as stated before, he did more persuading than seeking modification. While the head teller and new-accounts supervisor felt they had participated, they did not see themselves as changing anything.

This direct communication between upper and lower levels was positively received. Ms. Finnnegan remarked, "Most holding companies don't consult with us. We're fortunate that they do ask us, that they do consult us." Similarly, Mr. Marks said they had no resistance, implying that the staff meetings with Mr. Friedman informed people and lowered resistance. "If there is communication, you get a lot less resistance."

In sum, even implementation decisions were made at the top of the organization, but communication channels were open. This was true even for data processing as described. Overall, though, Mr. Friedman took great care to garner support for his proposals from the top levels all the way down to the lowest levels, so there was little resistance or dissatisfaction. His approach resulted in bank staff being willing to let him take over the task and decide how to implement it.

The biggest problems in implementing the decisions at this stage involved both lateral and upward relations for middle managers. There was a conflict between the bank operations officers and the data processing group that was never resolved.

Mr. Johnson, head of data processing, explained the difficulties. First of all, the firm was in the process of converting from in-house data processing to using an outside vendor.

> New software was planned prior to NOW accounts, and we just pushed it up for the NOWs. The data processing company came on board in July 1980. The conversion was planned for mid-December. Our system was antiquated; with the coming of NOW accounts, all our software was antiquated. We didn't want to invest money to hire someone to write the software packages, [since the outside company would do that].

Thus, NOW accounts were to be offered just two weeks after conversion to a new system. There were significant time pressures put on the internal data processing group. Mr. Johnson said his superiors required him to have the NOW account runninng by December 31. "I told them I didn't think we could do it that quickly, and the people at the holding company told me that it would be done that quickly. So we tried to do it that quickly."

From the operations side, people could see the problems coming but felt helpless to do anything about them. Mr. Lewis felt frustrated in his inability to do anything about problems he anticipated. The inability to manage conflicts is especially interesting given that the computer conversion was managed by a project team composed of operations people from the banks and both internal and external data processing people. Mr. Johnson reported that the team met regularly. Despite this communication, relations were not worked out. At the time of the interviews, Mr. Johnson said the bankers were still angry at him about NOW accounts.

Mr. Friedman, on the other hand, did take action. He had experience in data processing and overruled the objections of the data processing group regarding time needed for developing the NOW account system. Their process was similar to First Commercial's handling of automatic transfer accounts in that protests from data processing were overridden with an ultimatum. The senior vice president may thereby have contributed to the subsequent problems with statements, by using his authority to overrule the judgments of the data processing group. On the other hand, unlike most innovations, NOW accounts had a legal starting date and all firms had to be ready by that date if they wished to obtain a respectable share of the market. Therefore, it is possible that the decision to push data processing may have been the only reasonable solution at the time, though it is likely that alternative methods of becoming ready could have been pursued.

Flexibility

First Regional was fairly flexible in adapting to problems created by the NOW accounts. In general, Mr. Cohen saw the organization as being extremely flexible, citing the fact that they had previously designed and implemented a new product in seven days. At the same time, there was considerable formalization of the policy decisions. For example, the new-account supervisor reported written policies that she was expected to follow. "We had rules and regulations that we had to go over carefully. For example, corporations can't have them [NOW accounts]. As for the legal part, we had to learn how to set them up." The implementation was less formal, though, allowing direct, personal communication in problem-solving efforts. The informality and flexibility was especially clear in data processing. According to Mr. Johnson, "A manual was written. It is in dire need to be updated now." Given that the major problem area for First Regional was data processing, their laxness in following a manual probably had the effect of making them more responsive to feedback from the banks. That is, there really was no formal policy. So when the banks called with problems, it was easy to respond quickly. According to Mr. Lewis, "We'd call and say 'please come out and help us out,' and data processing would come out." Furthermore, there was direct communication between the banks and data processing, further increasing their problem-solving capabilities. Operations people felt no constraints from the formal system. They simply called the person who could solve the problem. Said Mr. Lewis, "We were trying to get whomever we could get hold of." The outcome was that people higher up in the organization felt little pressure from NOW account problems that were handled by middle-level employees.

Readiness

First Regional was not fully ready on several technical matters. Although they were certainly much more prepared than the big savings and loan associations, they were not as prepared as the large banks.

The problems that emerged seemed to be due to time pressure and the inability of data processing people to get their viewpoint across to higher levels of management. Management had decided well in advance of NOW accounts that they were going to purchase data processing outside their own corporation and maintain an internal data processing liaison group to work with the outside firm. However, the NOW account pushed them to convert to external data processing before they were ready. Nevertheless, First Regional had the advantage of working with a routine innovation, so that many of the requirements for managing NOW accounts already existed within its boundaries. Specifically, their data processing service already had the necessary programs, so no decision had to be made about choosing a software package. Their only problem was meeting a deadline. Therefore, despite the pressures of conversion, previous data processing choices meant that they were partially prepared from the beginning.

In looking back, the people at the top thought that the company was ready with their computer technology. To them, data processing was not a serious issue. "We knew we had the software. We just needed to run tests on the system to be sure they worked. Overall, the DP area was not a big concern. There were no computer problems." According to Mr. Marks, because they had to commit resources continuously to updating software, banks that did their own EDP were consistently weak. In contrast, he said their EDP conversion on NOW accounts was smooth.

In contrast, the data processing people perceived themselves as much less technically ready. Due to time constraints, they had to run programs without testing them. As a result, they had numerous problems, particularly with statements.

The head cashier also found the data processing group unprepared for NOW accounts. He believed there was insufficient planning by the bank, the data processing group, and the external data processing company.

> [The data processing liaison group] was not seeing any of the new overdraft statments [from the external data processing service] until the very end. They didn't see any of the new forms until the weekend before they were supposed to implement them. We knew at the time that there would be problems when they couldn't show us the new forms. These problems were compounded by the new computer system, and then there was just not enough time to plan adequately, and there was not enough testing to know what was going to happen ahead of time. There was a lot of frustration.

Had NOW accounts come a year after the conversion, however, the data processing manager believed that implementing NOW accounts would have been very smooth. They had no problems implementing projects that came after the NOW account. Mr. Johnson commented, "It was just an unusual situation. We have done enhancements to this system and the banks didn't even know we did it. In another month we have cash management accounts. We're testing it now. We're getting the jump on it." Though Mr. Lewis was frustrated with data processing on NOW accounts, he acknowledged that subsequent programs were implemented smoothly.

While data processing was problematic with NOW accounts, most of the unpreparedness can be attributed to the coincidental conversion to an outside DP vendor. Mr. Lewis said, "There was a lot of frustration. This was due to the conversion, though, over to the new computer software system, not to the NOW account. It just so happended that when they switched into the NOW account, all the major computer problems emerged." According to the available data, new programs were implemented after NOW accounts were test run and debugged, so there were few data processing problems that negatively affected the bank's operations. Said Lewis: "There are still little quirks, but they're not massive, and we're handling them as they come up. Other things later such as the green machine [the automatic teller] went a lot more smoothly because a bunch of us sat down with Mr. Marks and said 'We're not going to let them do anything until we know what's going on.' " Still, implementation of the NOW account might have been smoother had holding company managers such as Mr. Friedman and Mr. Marks acknowledged the warning signals coming from Mr. Johnson, rather than giving him a strict ultimatum.

Training

The NOW account was routine for First Regional. Consequently, standard operating procedures were not affected and training requirements were minimal. There was only a small amount of formal training on NOW accounts, which came from two sources. First, Mr. Friedman went to the individual banks and explained the rules and regulations regarding NOW accounts. He dealt with such issues as who would be allowed to open them, what the service charges would be, and how interest would be computed. The other training was done by the internal data processing group with the new-accounts people. They went out to each bank and explained what forms would have to be filled out for the interest to be computed. The training was neither extensive nor intensive, but the new-accounts supervisor, Ms. Finnegan, felt well informed and adequately trained.

In sum, along a continuum of preparedness, First Regional was not completely prepared but was prepared enough that they were not thrown into a crisis. Initial data processing problems caused frustration at middle levels, but they managed to get their programs debugged rather quickly. In fact, upper management perceived no problems, though part of this perception arose out of their inability to recognize symptoms of problems in data processing for what they were. Training, though minimal, was probably adequate given the routine nature of the innovation. Overall, they were moderately prepared to implement NOW accounts on January 1.

Internal Outcomes

People at different organizational levels had different views of First Regional's success in implementing NOW accounts. From the perspectives of Mr. Marks and Mr. Friedman, the process was smooth. Mr. Marks related, "We felt we were very well positioned on NOW accounts. In my opinion, NOW accounts were done with plenty of time. [Data processing] worked smoothly; there were minimal problems." In a similar vein, Mr. Friedman said, "It went very smoothly. There were some data processing problems, but they were not really major problems. They were dealt with by the service corporation."

As suggested earlier, middle managers did not share this positive view of implementation. In particular, they felt more frustration and stress over the data processing problems. In discussing the data processing company, Mr. Lewis said, "They would return our report sometimes one, two or three days late so the accounts were old and then we'd have to balance. Customers would not understand. They were irate. Wrong balances were given to them. Fortunately, we had good staff who could smooth it over." Mr. Lewis also had to divert time from other projects to manage the problems with NOW accounts. "I had to spend more time troubleshooting. Other parts of my job just went to the side."

The problems with data processing were also significant to Mr. Johnson. He described problems with statements, particularly combination statements for customers with more than one account or overdraft accounts. "The reason we had so much trouble in defining what problems we would anticipate is that the old software program was not documented. The data processing employees who left took the documentation in their heads. After they left, we hired a couple of guys on a consulting basis to try to remember some of the code." He went on to explain the magnitude of the problem. "The initial order of the number of statements that we got was a half million, and I think between us here we checked and corrected all half million. It was stressful and hectic. There were a lot of people saying they needed a vacation." Furthermore, it took time to get the problems worked out. "It ran smoothly four months after the conversion. Even today we run into problems now and again, but it was probably 3 1/2 to 4 months before I felt comfortable. Usually you figure a month afterwards."

Moreover, bankers continued to have bad feelings toward the internal data processing group long after NOW accounts had been implemented. Mr. Johnson said the duration of their bad feelings surprised him.

Ms. Finnegan and Ms. Perrot experienced some of these problems but seemed to feel less stressed and frustrated. The only problem Ms. Perrot had was in educating customers about the NOW account, and she did not find this a particularly burdensome task. Ms. Finnegan acknowledged the problems with inaccurate statements, but she did not seem bothered.

> We had to do some changing and refiguring interest sometimes. These are typical problems, and they didn't happen a lot. Most people felt the same about the change. They knew at the time we were setting it up that it would require some extra time, some overtime. They were willing to do it because they knew it would last just a little while.

While Ms. Finnegan did not express positive feelings about the NOW account in particular, she clearly tolerated much because she had generally positive feelings about upper-level managers. She said about Mr. Marks, "He's a special person. He's wonderful about passing on information and very good with people."

Organizational learning was probably limited because the pressures caused by NOW accounts were not severe. Consequently, there was little perceived need to change the organization. The one area in which pressure was felt was data processing; this was where some learning occurred. They had felt helpless to do the quality of job they felt they should do, so when other innovative products came up after the NOW account, they tried to develop their systems before they had demands put on them. In that way they could have more control over what the systems would be like, rather than merely respond to the demands of the rest of the organization. Said one person, "In another month we have cash management accounts. We are testing it now. We are getting the jump on it. Then we can tell marketing what we can do, rather than wait for them to tell us what they want us to do." The move toward greater proactive involvement by data processing was the only internal change mentioned by respondents.

Product/External Outcomes

Product success was mixed. While managers had no specific targets for number of accounts or the amount of money in balances, some felt basically satisfied with their 3,800 accounts and $20 million in balances. More significantly, given their initial goals, the number of accounts they lost was not great. Mr. Friedman explained:

> You have to go back to the original reason for doing it. We were not trying to generate new accounts or additional money. We just wanted to keep our existing customers happy. We really did not monitor it. In examining our statements, we have noticed no deposit runoff. It was just one of those unfortunate things that you had to do. However, paying 5 1/4 percent on this money is cheaper than having $20 million in high-yield savings accounts. In this respect, we are way ahead. In fact, we were happy to lose some of the accounts to S & Ls.

High interest rates for long-term instruments made NOW accounts a relatively inexpensive source of funds and therefore profitable for the company. However, their extremely defensive strategy reduced the amount of money they had in NOW accounts. Mr. Marks said, "I wish there could have been more. It was what we thought it would be. We felt we got our share. We could have gotten more if we had had a lower minimum balance. Based on our experience, we will keep pricing the same, but we may pursue them more aggressively because the average balance is such that we were making money." One of the organization's overriding goals was to be profitable. However, in their concern to make a profit they charged a price that prevented possible gains in market share. As it turned out, banks and savings and loan associations with a lower balance also made a profit and their larger market share resulted in greater profits than those made by First Regional Bank. Overall, managers saw the results as more positive than negative, but they had some concerns about their failure to promote aggressively.

Summary and Interpretation

Radical versus Routine Innovation

The NOW account was a routine innovation at First Regional just as it was at most other banks, because it was simply another kind of checking account. No one saw it as being very different than anything they had done before.

History/Unique Characteristics

However, because First Regional was in the process of converting from in-house data processing to an outside service at the time they were implementing NOW accounts, the organization was faced with special problems that introduced some of the same qualities as a radical innovation. The conversion was not routine, and NOW accounts were the first product to be converted to the outside service. In addition, the NOW account had to be up and running in a short time after the conversion, putting serious time pressures on the data processing group.

Goals and Strategy

The goals and strategy of the bank alleviated some of the pressure, because the strategy was defensive and therefore limited the demands on the system. The organization wanted to retain its current customers, but managers did not have a goal of increasing market share with the NOW account. They offered it because they did not want to lose customers to their competitors, and at the same time they were determined to make the product profitable. The resulting strategy was to require a $1,000 minimum balance, a fairly stiff requirement compared to S & Ls, but not high relative to other banks. They also promoted only to their current customers.

Search

They arrived at this defensive strategy largely through their understanding of the recommendations of analyst Alex Sheshunoff. Sheshunoff was strongly in favor of high minimum balances based on the New England experience with NOW accounts.

They also read materials available through trade associations. The senior vice president attended some seminars on NOW accounts. They did not maintain contact with any New England banks. However, they were sensitive to the minimums required by local large banks and used that information to support the decision they had made based on Sheshunoff's recommendations.

Complexity

First Regional was complex with respect to the NOW account. The complexity was especially noticeable at the upper levels of the holding company, where seven positions were involved with designing or implementing the product. There were another five holding company positions and eight positions at the bank level that participated. This complexity required efforts to integrate the different functions involved, particularly those of bank operations and data processing.

Flexibility

Managers in the organization saw themselves as quite flexible. While there is evidence that they had the capacity to be flexible, it is difficult to ascertain how flexible they were with the NOW account. On one hand, the data processing liaison described revising their schedule as needed and changing the data processing procedures as needed without worrying about the written manual. He and the bankers both reported that data processing was quick to respond to the banks' calls for help. On the other hand, data processing was not able to respond with what the bank operations people wanted. So they were flexible and willing to change but unable to change in the desired ways, because they had converted to an outside data processing service and were simultaneously facing severe time pressures.

Power Arrangements for Decisions

The power arrangements appear to have played a role in the difficulties data processing had in pleasing the individual banks. While the senior vice president communicated extensively with lower levels, the design of the NOW account was his and he sold it to others. In addition, the organization's structure gave considerable influence to the banks, whose views were represented well. The position of president of banking operations was at the top level of the organization to represent the banks. The person who filled this position was also a bank president. All bank presidents had a dotted-line relationship with the president of banking operations. Thus, the structure supported the influence of the banks on holding company policy. Furthermore, while the senior vice president essentially sold his proposal to the bank presidents, they had enough power to refuse him and did come in with a somewhat lower minimum balance than he proposed.

On the other hand, data processing reported to the senior vice president and there was no mechanism for giving power to that unit. The structure did include a project team formed for converting to the outside data processing vendor. The team was composed of coleaders from the internal and external data processing groups and representatives from each bank's operations group. However, this project team was ineffective at solving the conflicting interests between the two groups. Data processing was unable to muster the influence to have its problems and constraints heard. Instead, decisions were made by the senior vice president solely on the business issues perceived by the bankers. Data processing was weak relative to bank operations; consequently the technical problems were not treated with great concern.

Readiness

While the routine nature of the innovation meant that the organization was prepared with standard operating procedures that would work with the NOW account, they were only moderately prepared technically. The lack of complete readiness of their technical systems stemmed from the unusual situation of converting to outside data processing at the same time they introduced NOW acounts and the inability of the data processing staff to impress others in the organization with the difficulties of accomplishing both of these tasks at the same time. It is important to point out, though, that the problems that did exist were manageable at middle levels, so much so that upper-level managers never perceived that serious problems existed.

Internal Outcomes

Different levels of the organization had different views of the smoothness with which they implemented NOW accounts. Statements were generally out on time, but many were inaccurate at first. Inaccuracies persisted for four months, a length of time that both the data processing liaison and the bank cashier found unacceptable. Furthermore, the bank cashier was angry that data processing procedures were not worked out completely prior to the date when they first offered NOW accounts. The frustrations of these problems were felt mainly at middle levels in both the banks and data processing. Top managers saw the implementation as smooth. Customer-contact people in the banks recognized the overtime and statement inaccuracies, but they did not feel negative about these problems and knew that they would not last long. Out of these experiences, the data processing group learned and changed. They learned not to promise what they could not deliver, and they learned to keep their eyes open for new developments so they could be prepared even before other parts of the organization approached them. They became more proactive.

Product/External Outcomes

First Regional accomplished its goals for the NOW account. Managers said that they noticed no deposit runoff, indicating that they kept their best customers. They also found the NOW account to be profitable, which was an important goal for them. They regretted not considering the possibility of promoting the product harder, though, because it was profitable and they got fewer accounts than they potentially could have. But they did not think they priced too high. They simply wondered if they should have been more oriented toward using the account to increase market penetration. Overall, they were satisfied with the outcomes.

9
Conservative Design and Concentrated Power

First Capitol S & L had $300 million in assets in 1980. It was unusual as a thrift institution in that its strategy was to engage in real estate development rather than focus on mortgage lending. As a result, it was less retail oriented than all the other S & Ls in the study. It was also more profitable than all the other S & Ls, since it was not strongly affected by the spread between the high cost of funds and the low interest earned on long-term mortgage loans.

The structure and climate were important variables at First Capitol, too. It had no formal organization chart, but Jeff Walters (newly appointed vice president of NOW accounts and data processing), described the structure as flat. "We have a unique organization. There is a chairman at the top, then seven officers below, and then everybody else. There is no other differentiation. It works out well." Along with the flat or simple structure, there was a deliberate informality. According to Gerald Rich (vice president of personnel and branches),"We're a nonstructured environment. The officers are not set up on a pedestal. I'm 'Gerry' to everybody. There's not that kind of formality or structure. We have people thinking that you're working with us, not for us." The flat structure and deliberate informality were important to achieving employee support and adaptability.

The data came from interviews with the following members of the organization: Gerald Rich, Jeff Walters, Ken Rozinski (assistant vice president-research and development), one branch manager, and two NOW accounts representatives.

Routineness

The NOW account was a radical innovation for First Capitol. The newness of the product put heavy demands on the organization, but a relatively small number of accounts made the demand manageable. There were numerous comments from the people interviewed that the innovation was far from routine. It required many new operating procedures and the acquisition of new knowledge. For example, when asked what had to be done to make the NOW account operational, Mr. Rozinski listed ten major organizational adaptations, including changing the data processing system, selecting a processing bank, and designing procedures for the processing. According to the branch manager, Marsha Cox, "It was a horrible yet exciting feeling. There was so much, and it was all so new. A whole new ballgame. We had to learn everything—how to open and cross-sell, what questions to ask, how to set it up. And it doesn't seem like it was that much to do now." Likewise, the new-accounts representatives reported being confused at first because everything was so different. In sum, everyone perceived the introduction of NOW accounts as radical and causing major disruptions to standard operating procedures.

Design of the Innovation

To understand how the innovation was managed, it is critical first to examine what First Capitol was attempting to do with the product and how it fit into their broader strategy for the organization.

Goals and Strategy

There was no consensus of goals for NOW accounts represented in the interviews. There was a fair amount of disagreement on what their advantages were and therefore on how best to position them. In general, there was a commitment to offering them for the purpose of making a profit. However, the chairman was reluctant to approve their implementation because he was unsure that they would in fact be profitable.

Other managers wanted to be more aggressive. Mr. Rich observed: "The chairman didn't want to talk about it. He thought it would be a loser—expensive. He just wanted us to be a savings and loan. We argued that the cost of money was up, that we could farm it out, that it shouldn't increase costs that much. For years, we've been sending customers away because of checking accounts. So we said let us do it." Another manager who shared the chairman's view said the only criterion of success was, "How much does it cost for every dollar we bring in?"

Both Mr. Rich and Mr. Rozinski had the larger goal of being competitive. Mr. Rozinski said, "I wanted to offer it. I didn't want to put ourselves in the position of not being competitive." Mr. Walters talked at length of the NOW account being the first in a number of products that will make savings and loan associations more like banks. "No doubt, we will have to be able to offer the full range of retail banking services: installment loans, innovative home financing, automatic teller units. Savings and loans are five years behind. We have to become a complete financial center."

In sum, there was a conflict between the chairman and the officers about whether to introduce the NOW account. At the same time, it was the chairman's initiative that began the planning process, so people had mixed perceptions of when the decision to do it occurred. On one hand, they expressed fear that all their work might have been in vain because they were not sure the chairman would actually decide to offer them. On the other hand, they presumed that the chairman had made the decision over a year before NOW accounts could legally be offered, since he assigned considerable resources to research and planning for them.

Operationalizing the Strategy. As mentioned, First Capitol's foremost concern was to make a profit; there was little emphasis on market share. Consequently, they decided to go for a modest number of accounts at a price that would be profitable.

Mr. Walters described some of the problems and issues in determining their strategy:

> We had considerations, like two branches generate 75 percent of the transactions. We wondered how NOW accounts would affect line operations there. One of those places was running a store front, so that there was no more space. That one bit of information helped mold the pricing decision. Two branches would have been a catastrophe had they [NOW accounts] been free. We had our hands full at moderate prices.

Managers at First Capitol wanted to attract around 2,000 accounts with an average balance of $1,400, a balance higher than the target of the large S & Ls and the other medium-sized S & L in our study. The chairman preferred a $2,000 minimum balance, though they ended up with $300, again higher than the most aggressive S & Ls. In addition, they did not promote aggressively. Mr. Rich said, "We didn't market at all. It was mentioned in our quarterly newsletter. We didn't advertise until nine months after we opened the first account." They did train customer-contact people in cross-selling, though. Mr. Rozinski emphasized price as the main variable in attracting accounts. "We piggybacked on ads for other services. We got a lot of initial response; it petered out toward the end of January and February. All of this is attributable to the final pricing decision. I can't underscore pricing enough."

Overall, this strategy could be called moderately defensive, though their minimum balance was lower than the banks with defensive strategies. In fact, Mr. Rich said, "We didn't market them; we did it as a defensive thing." Clearly, however, a required minimum of only $300 would have been aggressive pricing for any of the banks. Apparently, managers at First Capitol compared it to other savings and loan associations in determining what strategy constituted defense. For them it meant very little promotion and a minimal balance slightly higher than the large S & Ls.

They modified their strategy after gaining some experience. After they discovered that the NOW account was profitable, the chairman decided that he wanted to market it by advertising and other promotions. However, the belief of many people in the financial industry that checking accounts are rarely moved appeared to be true. By the time First Capitol was ready to increase its market share, most of the money had already been moved, and they received little yield from their later marketing efforts.

Markets and the Environment. While there was no shared view of how NOW accounts fit into the organization's larger goals, it was clear that maintaining an image in the community did not have an impact on the decision to offer NOW accounts. Managers at First Capitol saw the organization as one of the strongest and most profitable savings and loan associations in the area but also a low-visibility organization. Therefore, they did not report any of the concerns about their leadership position in the community that many of the larger organizations reported. Their choices were not related to protecting an image; rather they revolved around whether or not they could make a profit.

Nonetheless, the managers viewed the overall strategy of their firm as an innovative one. According to Mr. Rich, "Fortunately, we haven't been in the S & L business for some years. We have established ourselves as a service corporation in and out of the state, a real estate development business." To Mr. Rich, their ventures into real estate as opposed to mortgage lending was an indication that they were different, and willing to try new things that would give them a competitive edge over the traditional S & L. All the other managers discussed their efforts to offer all the products that were previously offered only by banks. However, these innovations had to pass the test of profitability. Mr. Walters pointed out, "By law, as of January 1, 1981, we can offer consumer loans. But we do not because this is a depressed area; we'd lose money. If the market were right, we'd be likely to go in that direction." Their willingness to innovate, then, was constrained by their estimates of the profitability of the innovation.

In sum, the one shared goal of the organization was profitability, but there was no consensus on whether being competitive and offering what had previously been banking services would contribute to profit. While people seemed willing to innovate, there was dissent about if and how the NOW account fit into the general goal of profitability. However, the chairman was willing to allow the vice presidents to explore the possibilities before making a decision.

Strategic Decision Process

The final decisions about NOW accounts were made solely by the chairman. However, the alternatives were generated by the officers as a group. These people attempted to achieve consensus among themselves but never accomplished the goal. Gerry Rich described the different viewpoints. "Ken [Rozinski] was gung ho. He was disappointed because we didn't have a complete giveaway. Jeff [Walters] was gung ho. I wanted to offer it. Bill [the treasurer] still didn't want it." Mr. Rozinski described his own frustration with the inability to reach an agreement and finalize decisions.

> There was fighting internally. I had ideas, Gerry had his, the chairman had other ideas. We badgered back and forth before implementation was scheduled. There was quite a bit of footwork done. It [the fighting] also precluded not doing it. Getting across my viewpoint to those making the decisions was frustrating. Early decisions were amended when the effects were known later. Pricing we haggled on for months.

The reason a decision was not made was the uncertainty of the chairman, who wanted to make the ultimate decisions. Said one person, "In December 1980, he still didn't want it." When asked how the differences of opinion among the officers were finally resolved, Mr. Rozinski said, "It was on the chairman's shoulders to pick. There were four to six directions. He couldn't wait another day. In that respect, it threw everything that we had done up front out the window." In contrast to the emphasis on innovation that was expressed, the chairman was very cautious in choosing innovations. Said Mr. Rozinski:

> He makes you check and triple check. There is a lot of planning and checking. We scrap projects at the last minute, and it's kind of bittersweet. It's part of the job. It has positive results personally, and I try to learn from it. You get the feeling that it's by design. You have to know what you're talking about and be certain it's right. He treats everybody equally. He will put you through all of this. He has no favorites.

According to another manager, the reason the decision took so long to make was, "The chairman was involved and he didn't delegate. It got to the point of running out of time. There was a lot of study and no implementation."

The catalyst that precipitated the ultimate decision was the employment of a banker. This was Mr. Walters, who had enough banking experience that the chairman trusted his opinions, particularly with respect to implementation. In addition, Mr. Walters's conservative approach fit with the chairman's concerns. According to Mr. Walters, they finally made a decision on NOW accounts after he started with the firm.

> Due to the risks, a slower approach would lead to fewer problems. We got three or four people plus myself and sat around a table; I said, "We won't leave until we agree." We hammered back and forth. The decision was to

attract a small number of accounts—we could grow later. The chairman came back from Europe, and we sat down and finalized pricing—we being the marketing director, Rich, Ken, the treasurer, the controller, and the chairman's son. We basically hammered out the pricing structure.

People in the branches had no influence at all on either strategy or implementation decisions. In fact, while they were surveyed by Mr. Walters, they were deliberately not informed about the decision process because managers were afraid of rumors. Mr. Rozinski explained their reasoning. "We were forty-five days away and we still didn't know what we were going to do. We isolated the line people because we didn't want rumors. It was a very competitive market." Moreover, they had considerable difficulty working through the conflicting views of the officers. "We were juggling six directions, and we didn't need more." Ms. Cox confirmed the lack of branch participation. "There was a time when we were waiting for decisions from management. Customers wanted to know. Questions would come. We didn't even know the questions that were going to be asked, so then we would call and get the answers. Before we knew the specifics, we didn't even know the questions to expect."

To summarize, the final decision was made by the chairman. The officers were charged with the responsibility of making recommendations and thereby had considerable influence on the outcome. However, they saw the chairman as not providing direction even though he wanted to make the decision. He did not make intermediate decisions throughout the planning process. According to one person, he refused to have regular meetings during the planning process. When he did finally meet with them, he negated much of the work that had been done. The decision was ultimately made possible by bringing in an outsider whose expertise was trusted. Because they were slow in making a decision and because the chairman was never fully committed to it, they did not market aggressively and, consequently, got few accounts.

Search. First Capitol used a great many sources of information in their efforts to understand NOW accounts. In 1979, Mr. Rich and the treasurer went to seminars in Chicago. Also in 1979, Mr. Rozinski was sent to New England. Mr. Rich described Mr. Rozinski's mission: "For several weeks, he looked at operations, clearing houses, how they did things, why different plans were used, charges, balances, were they making money and the company profit before starting NOW accounts. If they were profitable and innovative, we paid more attention." Managers also examined written documents including information supplied by the U.S. League of Savings Associations and information from vendors. They hired a consulting firm to perform a market analysis. Finally, two months before NOW accounts became legal, they hired a banker with fifteen years of experience. All of these steps provided them with outside information, some of it well before NOW accounts were legal.

This extensive search was initiated by the chairman. His authorization of the search apparently was based on his concerns about the profitability of the product. According to Mr. Rozinski, "The president took the first step. I received an information-gathering directive from him. He was concerned about how it would affect operations. The cost of money, mechanics, ours not being a volume business. He sent me to New England for a couple of weeks."

The search process into the technical aspects of implementation was limited because Mr. Walters knew the details of check processing. However, they did attempt to gather knowledge in this area also by doing a survey of the situation in the branches. Mr. Walters said, "I was permitted to go to the branches and make a survey. I looked at the location, traffic, customer base, type of people, and type of management."

Overall, the search process at First Capitol was extensive and timely. One can hardly imagine a more serious study of the new and unknown product they were facing. With all this information in hand, they began to implement their strategy.

Implementation of the Innovation

Implementation took place in a brief two weeks, much as it had at First National S & L. The difference, of course, was that First National ultimately had 40,000 accounts, while First Capitol had only 1,400. Still, two weeks is a short period in which to manage all the details of a radical innovation.

Complexity

First Capitol was highly differentiated, even though it was much smaller than many of the other institutions. Much of the complexity appeared at upper levels of the home office.

Seven positions at upper levels participated in implementing NOW accounts. Those who participated were the chairman, chief financial officer, treasurer, vice president-operations, vice president-branches and personnel, vice president-NOW accounts and data processing, and marketing director. At the middle and lower levels, three positions participated: auditors, a NOW accounts clerk, and a bookkeeper. Finally, at the branch level, the branch manager, head teller, tellers, and new-accounts representatives were involved in implementing NOW accounts. With fourteen positions involved altogether, this organization had a relatively complex structure.

Decision Process

As with strategic decisions, the authority to make implementation decisons was concentrated at the very top of the organization. Mr. Walters had the most influence on implementation decisions. According to him, "I said, 'We have to draw up checking account guidelines. How do you want me to do it?' The chairman said, 'You draw it up. If you want any input, get it and go ahead and draw them up.' Rich, the auditor, the chief financial officer, and the treasurer reviewed the procedures I wrote up." While there was considerable debate about strategy among the officers, everyone including the chairman deferred to Mr. Walters on implementation. Only he had the banking background to understand the details of check processing. People in the branches were not consulted or informed about NOW accounts until all policies and procedures had been set.

Flexibility

Communication was generally open and informal. Branch employees felt very comfortable calling the home office with questions or problems which were then resolved. Ms. Cox said that she found out about NOW accounts "through conversation. They [managers] work together with people. Mr. Rich is who I consider my boss, and we talk frequently." She also reported getting information about a book on NOW accounts in the course of a telephone conversation with Mr. Rozinski. New-accounts representative Julia Whittier also described open communications. When asked how they knew what was happening with NOW accounts, she said, "Everybody just mentioned it. Everybody just knew, and later on a memo came out."

This open communication was encouraged by the officers who reported calling and visiting the branches often and soliciting feedback. Mr. Walters said, "I spent a lot of time in the branches. I told them that I was there to answer questions. I encouraged them to call me if they had questions. If I didn't have an answer, I would check with somebody else."

This open and informal communication gave First Capitol the potential to be flexible, to modify policies and procedures as necessary. Both Ms. Cox and Mr. Rich gave other examples of new products that had been implemented just as quickly as the NOW account, which they took as a measure of their own flexibility. Mr. Rich shared his perspective: "Big companies [like First National S & L] change so slowly. My opinion is that the big outfit has bodies [large staff] but they might not be able to do something as quickly." Explaining one of the reasons for their flexibility, he said, "In a large company you have to have powerful middle management to control many people. But we know everybody in the company. They [our employees] have to adapt; that's the way we operate."

No one described any implementation changes that occurred after the original start-up. They were clearly in a position to hear about problems quickly, though. Their top-down decision-making structure makes it less clear what they might have done had they gotten a signal that something at branch levels required modification.

Readiness

As with many of the firms studied, First Capitol's data processing capabilities were not adequate when the first accounts were opened. At the time NOW accounts began, they were purchasing data processing from an outside company. They found that the company was not prepared to provide the variety of programs required for the types of products they wanted to offer. "Working with someone outside is a frustrating situation. They make mistakes and it looks like we made mistakes to the customers. We had problems with data processing, because they couldn't work as quickly as we wanted them to. That's why we're going with our own computer facility."

Only one person discussed data processing problems, though, in marked contrast to other firms where people dwelt at length on data processing. From this we infer that data processing was inadequate but that it did not have a major impact on the organization because of the small number of accounts opened.

The major effort First Capitol made to prepare for NOW accounts was to create a new checking department headed by Mr. Walters. He then brought a teller into the department to do the clerical work and check processing. This structural change was a positive step in preparing for NOW accounts because it allowed them to be seen and managed as checking rather than savings accounts and not forced into existing routines. In addition, despite their slowness in deciding on a strategy, Mr. Walters was able to get forms and procedures ready by the time the firm could legally offer the account. "On January 1, ten weeks after I got here, we were operational. I was drawing up guidelines and procedures, having all types of forms to design, training, handling communications to the customer, and getting everything ordered and disseminated—a lot of work on training and working with people."

Training

While training was valued by First Capitol's managers, the decision on NOW accounts was so late that little formal training could be accomplished before January 1. "By the time the decision was made, we had three weeks to put it together." Therefore, in the early stages most of the training was informal communication about how to proceed with the accounts. Mr. Rich described their process. "We went to each office and explained it. If we had lead time, then they role-played." Mr. Walters said, "I spent a lot of time in the branches."

Once the branch managers understood the NOW account, they took it as their responsibility to train their employees. Ms. Cox said, "From my standpoint, it was up to me that they understood what to do."

After the NOW account was up and running, Mr. Walters went back and provided a formal day-long seminar. The first half of the training session was provided by a check vendor; the second half was a series of role plays that Mr. Walters designed to cover the procedures for opening accounts.

In sum, the delay in making the NOW account decision resulted in branch employees not being trained on time. The tellers felt confused by NOW accounts in the early days and wanted more information. They did eventually get trained, though, because the checking department manager put a strong emphasis on training.

In the areas of data processing and training, First Capitol was only moderately prepared to meet the challenge of the NOW account. Most of their lack of preparedness resulted from the delay in decision-making. However, there were so few accounts generated by their approach that the organization coped with the change well despite not being completely ready.

Internal Outcomes

Overall, people believed the change went quite smoothly. There were some statement inaccuracies mentioned in Mr. Rich's complaints about the outside data processing service. However, neither Mr. Walters nor the branch personnel mentioned these mistakes as causing serious problems with customers or in staff overtime. In fact, no one mentioned staff overtime or stress at all.

Instead, branch people experienced a mixture of anxiety about making mistakes and excitement about offering a completely new kind of product. Ms. Cox described her experience. "Anticipation. A horrible yet exciting feeling. As we talk, I remember more of that feeling. Time was really important. There was so much and it was all so new—a whole new ballgame. We had to learn everything. How to open and cross-sell, questions to ask—it doesn't seem like it was that much to do now." Ms. Whittier echoed those feelings. "It seemed neat but it was confusing. I thought it was a neat idea, but it was so hard to remember everything."

Though branch people felt confusion, and statements were inaccurate, little new learning developed out of this experience. Everyone perceived the implementation as smooth and said they would not change anything except making the policy decisions early. But even late policy decisions were part of their organizational culture, so they were not subject to great pressures to change. According to Ms. Cox, "We're not that prepared for things. It's hectic, but that's how it happens in the business." Even the learnings about data processing came later, after they had had similar problems with a new product that followed NOW accounts. The one major organizational learning that did occur was the addition of checking knowledge by hiring Mr. Walters.

Product/External Outcomes

Eleven months after their implementation, First Capitol had 1,400 NOW accounts with an average balance of $1,500. Mr. Rich was positive about the outcome because the firm had a high balance and had not lost money through forgeries. On the other hand, he said, "There is only $2 million in NOW accounts, so it's not worth it. One person handles $2 million, and the company average is one person for $3.5 million. That's because we didn't market. We're making money because our short-term rates are so high." In a similar vein, Mr. Rozinski said, "Some consider it a total failure because it didn't take off like gangbusters. But it is the cheapest source of funds next to the passbook, and we open very few passbooks now." At least one manager had the goal of using NOW accounts to propel the firm into the retail banking field. According to Mr. Walters, they increased business since the introduction of the NOW account. Furthermore, he believed that if they had had too many accounts, service would have deteriorated and they would have lost business. He thought their service had even improved since checking accounts were introduced. "It has been a successful program. I would have gotten in earlier and been more aggressive up front; but knowing what we did up front, I don't think we took a bad stance."

These comments indicate that the NOW account was profitable, but not as profitable as it could have been with more accounts. Managers were disappointed though they believed they had done reasonably well with the NOW account.

Summary and Interpretation

Radical versus Routine Innovation

The innovation was radical for First Capitol just as it was at the large savings and loan associations. They had no standard operating procedures, no data processing programs, and no history whatsoever that was relevant to check processing. Everything they knew about the NOW account had to be imported from outside the organization.

History/Unique Characteristics

First Capitol had a structure and climate that contributed to its ability to implement such a radical change. Its structure was flat with only three distinguishable levels: chairman, officers, and employees. Within that structure there was differentiation, but it was clear from descriptions of the process that people took on whatever tasks were needed, while at the officer level people often functioned as general managers rather than functional specialists.

Goals and Strategy

Despite the generalist orientation, there was considerable disagreement over the goals and strategy for the NOW account. The chairman and some officers wanted to offer the account defensively, as the banks did, just to avoid loss of customers to other institutions. Some officers wanted to market it aggressively, using it as a tool to increase market share. One officer wanted to use it to propel the organization into the retail banking business. Agreement about the goals was never reached completely; this lack of aggreement was reflected in the strategy—an amalgam of aggressive and defensive. The minimum balance was $300, higher than the most aggressive officer wanted and much lower than the $2,000 the chairman wanted. However, they also decided not to promote the NOW. The only promotion was a description of the account in a mailer with other items. Thus, their pricing was moderately aggressive, but their promotion was extremely defensive. One other aspect of their strategy was their decision to use the NOW account to cross-sell other accounts. In keeping with past policy, they also used other accounts to cross-sell NOW accounts.

Search

Their search process was extensive and they began early. They gathered information from many different sources, starting with a seminar attended by two officers in 1979. Then came a trip to New England to study NOW experience, other seminars, trade publications, and a consultant who surveyed their customers. Their search for information included hiring a banker with fifteen years of experience to help them internalize the operations knowledge they lacked. Few organizations searched as broadly and deeply. The search process was conducted by several different people, though, and did nothing to bring about agreement among the officers.

Complexity

With fourteen different positions involved in deciding and implementing NOW accounts, the organization was quite complex. However, the effects of this complexity were somewhat mitigated by the tendency for people to blur the lines between different functions.

Flexibility

This blurring no doubt contributed to the organization's flexibility. First Capitol prided itself on being flexible enough to decide something on Thursday and implement by Monday. People accepted such rapid change as necessary to remain competitive in a shifting market; they were willing to do it and proud that they could. One of the ways they promoted such flexibility was through an open, informal communication system. People in the branches felt completely free to call the home office and ask questions or give feedback. In addition, they accepted the need to implement changes quickly and did not complain about having short lead time.

Power Arrangements for Decisions

Some of this flexibility was lost, though, through the power arrangements of the organization. Everyone perceived that the chairman made all the policy decisions, though he did not get involved in developing alternatives and proposals. Instead, he asked the officers to work up proposals and then he picked among the proposals he received. This arrangement gave the officers considerable influence, since they had the opportunity to gather information and develop the policies to which the chairman had access. At the same time, this arrangement encouraged competitiveness among the officers, who were not permitted to make a decision but simply to argue their position to the chairman. With many well developed proposals in front of him, the chairman was ambivalent about which direction to take, and consequently, he did not make policy decisions until two to three weeks before the NOW account became legal. This combination of competitive debate at the officer level with no accompanying ability to act reduced the flexibility gained by the open communication system.

Implementation decision making was done largely by the vice president of NOW accounts. He drew up his plans and presented them individually to the other officers. No one described any major debate or disagreement over implementation decisions, and that process went smoothly. No one below the officer level was consulted on any type of decision.

Readiness

First Capitol S & L was ready at minimum levels by the time they were able to process NOW accounts. The vice president of NOW accounts had put together all the procedures necessary for handling checks. However, their data processing service was not ready with programs that would do what they wanted, and branch people had been informed but not trained. Given the relatively small number of accounts that they opened, though, this level of readiness was adequate for managing the new product fairly easily.

Internal Outcomes

As a result of this readiness, implementation went smoothly. Branch people reported some confusion and anxiety which quickly dissipated after they had opened one or two accounts. They also reported excitement at offering such a different product. No one complained about stress or overtime. In addition, while they did have some mistakes in statements, statements were on time and no one reported serious customer complaints about the errors. Despite the time pressures they experienced from deciding the policy so late, no one questioned last-minute decision making and no one suggested that the organization learn from these difficulties and change the way it was doing things.

Product/External Outcomes

First Capitol got somewhat fewer accounts than managers would have liked. They attributed this variously to failure to promote aggressively and failure to price aggressively. The account turned out to be more profitable than the more pessimistic among them had feared; later attempts to get more accounts were unsuccessful. Still, managers said they were satisfied with their strategy, because they could not have known in advance what the outcome would be, and their strategy allowed them to proceed slowly to test the waters.

10
Flexibility and External Expertise

Second Capitol S & L had assets of $330 million in 1980. However, those interviewed perceived the organization as not very complex and small rather than medium. For them, their size allowed easy face-to-face communication and simple coordination. According to Steve Jackson, their vice president of marketing and public relations (who had primary responsibility for initiating NOW accounts), "We are so small, it was a matter of merely dealing with a half-dozen people. It's easy to have informal meetings on a day-to-day basis."

For an organization that saw itself as small, it had an unusually high number of specialized positions that participated in the implementation of the NOW account. We began by interviewing Mr. Jackson. We also interviewed the systems manager, Margaret Wren, who was the operations and data processing liaison; Linda White, training supervisor; Marty Deutsch, branch coordinator; Tom Novak, branch manager; Sara Crane, new-accounts representative; and Julia Marx, teller.

Routineness

Somewhat contrary to our expectation, managers at Second Capitol perceived checking accounts as routine. Our major purpose in comparing banks and savings and loan associations was to examine the effects of a routine innovation (the slight change to interest-bearing checking in banks) with a nonroutine innovation (the major change to checking in S & Ls). But people at Second Capitol made such comments as: "We fit it into a routine we already had." Said Ms. Marx, "There weren't many changes in duties. It was just an extra account we had to know." Ms. Crane in new accounts related, "Nothing much is different. Second Capitol and the tellers didn't think that it was innovative in any sense." These remarks indicate a perception of little change in activities, and little disruption to individuals or the organization as a whole. Compared to other S & Ls of this size or larger that experienced considerably more upheaval, the transition to checking seemed relatively placid and routine. Numerous activities allowed this smooth transition to occur, but from an objective view, as many changes were required at Second Capitol as at First Capitol. People acknowledged the many changes that occurred. For example, Mr. Jackson said, "We were not a bank; the banks had all the experience in handling checks." Despite these acknowledgements of their inexperience, their process yielded a perception that this was "just an additional type of account."

There was one exception to the perception of routineness. Ms. Wren, who was responsible for data processing, found NOW accounts a radical innovation.

> We didn't have anything like NOW accounts. It was a whole new application. It didn't blend in with what we had. It was a completely new procedure. There were differences in the accounting functions on a branch level and in reporting. These were very new and not simply an add-on. They were difficult to grasp. In terms of type of account, the whole program had changed. There were so many things to keep an eye on.

Still, most people perceived these changes as insignificant. As the following data will show, the explanation for the smooth transition is probably a combination of a somewhat conservative strategy early in the implementation phase, a flexible and responsive decision-making process, and upward communication about problems that developed.

Design of the Innovation

Goals and Strategy

The decision to introduce the NOW account at Second Capitol was strictly based on the fear of losing customers. According to Mr. Jackson, the vice president of marketing, "Our philosophy is to wait until (1) our competition has been successful or (2) we're getting enough demands from our customers."

Markets and the Environment. In this case, Second Capitol could not wait for customer demand, because its competitors were set to offer checking as soon as it was legal, and the common wisdom was that people would not move checking accounts once they had opened them. So, like First Capitol and all the banks, Second Capitol felt pushed to offer NOW accounts to retain customers, though it initially feared NOW accounts would be unprofitable. According to branch coordinator Marty Deutsch, "Competition dictated starting NOW accounts. At first, I didn't see this favorably. I wasn't enthusiastic at all. It was something the government decided. We were afraid we'd lose money." Systems manager Ms. Wren indicated the concern for retaining customers. "We needed to compete with other savings and loans and banks. We needed to counter the push of all institutions to offer all areas of service. We want to do anything to satisfy and retain our customers, particularly our mortgage customers." The goal, then, was simply to retain customers and lose as little money as possible.

Operationalizing the Strategy. In keeping with their usual approach to new products, the NOW account strategy was initially defensive. On the one hand, managers were concerned that they would lose money on NOW accounts; on the other hand, they wanted to keep their customers. Out of those conflicting beliefs emerged a middle-of-the-road strategy allowing them to be more attractive than the banks and possibly more profitable than other S & Ls. According to Mr. Jackson, "We did the original research and found that banks would require a $1,000 minimum, while there were a few S & Ls offering it for a $100 minimum. So let's price it at $500 until we get a handle on it and know we are not going to get beat up on it." (One manager indicated that the original minimum balance was $200 rather than $500.) This decision was based on extensive surveys they had obtained and surveys they had conducted themselves including questioning local large banks. Consistent with their concern to retain customers, Mr. Jackson also said that they promoted the NOW fairly aggressively through advertising of various types, even though their price was higher than many S & Ls.

Most institutions that had pursued a defensive strategy realized later that the cost of funds had risen so high that NOW accounts were one of their least expensive sources of money. Only Second Capitol responded to this discovery by lowering its price, though it is not clear how many new accounts were gained after the price was lowered. Mr. Jackson said:

> Originally, it was $500, with anything less than that getting $5 per month service charge. Since then, we've dropped it to a $100 minimum.
>
> Our reason for changing strategy was that it was cheaper to operate than we expected. There was little or no problem in the operation of the accounts. The processing went smoothly, plus interest rates continued to climb. When we first looked at it, the figures said that if we were paying 5¼ percent plus 3 or 4 percent for operating costs, it looked high. Now we're paying 13, 14 or 15 percent for money, and now 9 percent looks cheap. It's easy to handle. The service is being accepted by our customers, and it allowed us to offer more services to a greater number of people.

Strategic Decision Process

According to Mr. Jackson, policy recommendations were made by three officers: the executive vice president, the controller, and him. Those recommendations were approved by the executive committee composed of the treasurer, a board member, and the executive vice president.

"I was primarily responsible. The other two people served as a sounding board as to how it would fit into our organization." Ms. White, training coordinator, also named Mr. Jackson, the controller, and the executive vice president as key, but she included Ms. Wren and Mr. Deutsch as having a significant role in the process. She did not participate herself. Mr. Deutsch described his involvement: "I was in charge of getting outside vendors for the checks. I also attended meetings for six to eight months prior to starting the accounts." At the strategy level, Ms. Wren's participation was giving information on pricing decisions based on her knowledge of costs. She indicated the need on occasion to push her view. "Some of these questions were whether there was going to be a flat charge or a percent rate for services. When it came to interest earning below a certain balance, I was more vocal, because [calculating balances is] easy to do on the system."

Branch workers had no input at all. According to Ms. Marx, "Unless people have worked in a bank before—I hadn't personally—I don't know what could have come from us." Ms. White said, "People didn't have enough information to give input. To explain the system to them so they could give input was too big a task. It's hard enough to explain to them what they will have to do."

In sum, decisions were made largely by senior officers of the firm with some input from two middle managers. Most of the direction came from Mr. Jackson, who used the cost information gathered by Ms. Wren and other information to formulate his position.

Search. In discussing their search strategy, different respondents emphasized different sources of information. From these disparate views, it appears that many sources of information were used but perhaps used or valued differently by different people. For example, Ms. Wren emphasized cost analyses by the Eastern Association of Savings and Loan and research that Second Capitol itself conducted. Ms. White discussed information and training by the check vendor. This wide variety of sources provided a rich data base for making their strategic decisions. The information relevant to strategy was channeled to Mr. Jackson and his committee so they could make strategic decisions. The research from the trade association was conducted largely by Ms. Wren, while the other information was gathered by the top officers themselves. Information from the check vendor was used largely for implementation.

Implementation of the Innovation

The internal processes overall were characterized by considerable flexibility and decision making by an upper-level committee. In addition, Second Capitol was unusually well prepared, especially for an organization with no prior checking experience.

Complexity

Second Capitol had an equal number of positions at upper, middle and lower levels involved in NOW accounts. There were six upper-level participants: the executive vice president, senior vice president-marketing, controller, treasurer, a board member who participated on an executive committee, and the branch coordinator who oversaw the branches. At the middle and lower levels, another six positions participated. These were the systems manager, training instructor, assistant systems manager and systems staff, accounting department manager, and NOW accounts clerks. At the branch levels, those involved were the branch manager, head teller, tellers, and new-accounts representatives. With sixteen positions involved, this organization was differentiated with respect to NOW accounts and so was a moderately complex organization.

Decision Process

Comments from people at all levels suggested a centralized decision process, much like the strategic decision process. Teller Julia Marx said, "We're consulted little. They tell us what they've decided. It all came out in memos. You were to follow step 1, step 2 and step 3." Likewise, the new-accounts representative said, "It was all handed down to me by memo." Even Mr. Novak, the branch manager, said he did not participate in the planning in any way, including the planning of implementation. Mr. Jackson confirmed this perception. "We didn't do any consulting with employees."

Their monitoring of implementation was not particularly well defined, but it appeared to have a sharp edge to it. Ms. Wren reported, "We had weekly and sometimes daily meetings. We finalized the master plan and added to it. We checked up on each other." She monitored employees through the annual performance review. The sharp edge was revealed in her comments about tellers' resistance and anxiety. "Well, we can say, 'There's the door.' But they're still here. They're getting used to it." However, she explained what happened to someone who made a serious mistake. "A manager didn't follow a procedure. He got things recorded wrong. We didn't find out until it didn't balance. Well, we remedied that one—he's no longer here." A branch-level person's comment reinforced the appearance of a somewhat punitive orientation. This person reported that a person's mistakes were put into the personnel file, resulting in a need to cover up rather than discuss problems. However, it is not uncommon for a financial institution to keep a record of tellers' balancing errors. Still, this was not raised as an issue in other organizations, and the comments taken together indicate a certain amount of harshness in monitoring employees' implementation of the NOW accounts.

Flexibility

On the other hand, the organization was very flexible in receiving communication from lower levels and modifying decisions. Ms. Marx said, "The teller manager conveys feedback up the ladder. There were clear communication lines." One middle manager was perceived by some lower-level employees as blocking upward communication and being so critical of them that they avoided contact with this person. However, other middle managers were more open. Recalled Ms. Marx: "I gave the customer's reaction to various procedures to the head teller or to training. It was a natural thing to do, to return with feedback. There is no problem in going to the next supervisor if the immediate supervisor isn't available as long as it's someone who can deal with the problem." Ms. Wren explained how feedback from tellers or other branch personnel was handled. "If there were any problems that needed to be corrected, whether it was brought up by a teller or anyone, we took it to the managers' meeting, talked about it, and tried to come up with some kind of solution." Ms. White commented, "Once we start training, that's when we receive input. Changes are made at this stage. The tellers are expected to make their desires known." The evidence strongly supports the view that upward communication was open and that the organization used information from the bottom to modify its procedures to fit customer needs, even though managers did not solicit employee views in forming their policy or procedures.

The result of this management procedure was that some decisions were postponed until the last minute or changed after they were made. Ms. Wren indicated that pricing decisions were not finalized until November or December so the organization could continue to monitor its environment for any late-breaking developments—such as the major pricing change after they initially offered the account. The changes in policy and procedures were stressful for some, though not for all. Ms. Marx expressed confusion and difficulty in learning the new product resulting from several changes in procedures. "A lot of the decisions weren't very clear. There was a lot of chaos. They said 'This is what we'll do' and then they changed things later on. This is typical. We were constantly getting updated: 'We're going to do this now; we're not going to do that.' It could have gone a lot smoother if management hadn't waited so long to make their decisions." On the other hand, Ms. Crane expressed no confusion or frustration with the changes.

Though there were reports of procedures manuals and many memos to tellers and new-accounts representatives, the organization would not be characterized as highly formalized because face-to-face communication took precedence over written procedures. At the upper levels, formalization was nearly nonexistent. According to Mr. Jackson:

We didn't have any formal written game plan, probably because basically we are a small company. We did have a written guideline set out by the U.S. League. We worked from that, using it as a checklist.

At lower levels, there was more formalization. There were memos for procedures. There were instructional manuals and procedural manuals. There were processes like to stop-payment. There were many memos and procedures incorporated into the training manual for different types of training.

Apparently there was a fair amount of formalization at lower levels, though the procedures were quite modifiable and not written in stone, as one usually sees in a formalized organization. The written procedures were intended to communicate efficiently rather than establish hard and fast rules. According to Ms. Crane, "It all came out in memos. When you have fourteen branches, you can't go word of mouth." In addition, these memos were obviously intended to convey information rather than set down rules. Said Ms. Crane, referring to the memos: "If you don't read a memo then that's your problem. We had meetings with our manager. The memos go through the manager, and we read them and tell them 'We can't possibly do that.' [She laughs.] And you ask, 'Is this what I'm supposed to get out of this? Is this what I'm supposed to be doing?'"

Their informal and open communication gave them the ability to be flexible—they clearly took advantage of it. Ms. Wren described all of the issues they reconsidered after they had already begun offering NOW accounts.

We dropped the minimum to $100 after we were already in the market. Once we saw activity, we wanted to look better to meet the competition. With respect to the service charge, we studied the area banks. There were some disagreements initially about insufficient funds checks, because of getting bank industry rejects. Our attitude was that we would change if our strategy didn't work.

We have little information about the group dynamics, the feelings of the participants involved. No one expressed negative feelings, as they did in some organizations, but neither did anyone express much excitement, enthusiasm, or commitment to the company, as they did in some firms. They simply explained events and situations. Second Capitol sought the commitment of lower-level participants by allowing them to cash their paychecks there, allowing them to open NOW accounts in December, and giving them $1 for every account opened during the introductory period. These facts were explained to us by tellers and new-accounts representatives without much comment about how they felt about those incentives.

In sum, the internal dynamics of implementation had the following characteristics: (1) a relatively centralized decision-making process for implementation, (2) flexibility that was enhanced by open, informal upward communication, (3) a relatively low level of emotion at all levels of the organization.

Readiness

There were differences between managers and customer-contact people in their perceptions of the readiness of the system, though at no level was there a sense of crisis or fear of being unable to process the accounts. Data processing problems were minimal, largely because they used the services of the Federal Home Loan Bank both for clearing checks and for data processing.

The decision to have checks processed for them by the FHLB was an important one. Mr. Jackson explained:

> We thought that the NOW being a new product, we were better off buying and going to an outside processor such as a bank or a data processing center. The way it developed, our own support branch (the Federal Home Loan Bank in Des Moines) decided to set up a processing center here in River City, so we elected to use their service. We knew there would be a lot of unknowns in this account, a lot of intricacies. The banks had all the experience in handling checks. We were not a bank. We knew there would be a lot of pitfalls because of overdrafts and returning checks on time. Not only that, but there was not enough time to develop the proper administrative set-up to our satisfaction.

Thus, data processing demands on the association were few; since the FHLB was reasonably technically ready, Second Capitol was ready. In addition, some of the bugs were worked out by testing experimental accounts in November. By January, everything worked smoothly. Mr. Jackson thought that data processing "couldn't have been any better. It was beyond our expectations. We had just enough lead time for the data processing center to get its act together." The only data processing problem reported came from a teller who said that account histories were erased during early stages of the NOW account. However, there were no reports of inaccurate statements, a problem plaguing many of the organizations we studied.

Training

As in many S & Ls, customer-contact people would have liked a little more training. For example, Ms. Crane described one particular problem. "One thing that was not communicated very well at the beginning was the closing of accounts. People were scrambling around trying to find out what to do."

Ms. Marx complained that there was too much pressure to learn everything quickly. These were minor complaints, though, and the branch manager, Mr. Novak, had no complaints at all.

The main training efforts were a day-long seminar presented by Superior (a check-printing company), a later presentation by Infocheck[1] (a credit check service), and a training manual prepared by Ms. White. She described the training:

> We thought it was best to get everyone together at one time. We did it on a holiday. All savings personnel were required to attend: full- and part-time tellers, managers, savings counselors. This amounted to between eighty and ninety people. We rented a room. People from Superior worked with us and presented what checking accounts were about, clearing procedures, check order forms, and what was needed. I went over new rules and restraints, the forms, signature cards, opening on-line, presignature, giving kits, and duplicates.

The training manual was updated with memos as changes in implementation were made. Ms. Marx further explained, "Along with the seminar, there were lots of memos with regard to how the accounts would work." Ms. Crane added, "Tellers were educated with memos. It was hard to keep all that information in your head." Beside these formal training efforts, there were some reports of follow-up meetings in the branches to discuss issues left over from the major training session. Finally, after implementation had begun, Ms. Marx said, "Recently, we had a refresher at Superior and I think we understand the whole process better. It was good for correcting misunderstandings." The amount of training was similar to First Capitol's. The difference primarily was that training efforts began in October and November, giving front-line people more advance information. From the perspective of training as well as data processing, the system was quite well prepared relative to other organizations studied.

Internal Outcomes

Implementation of the NOW account was very smooth internally, much smoother than people expected. As for employees' feelings about the process, Mr. Jackson said, "I didn't see any particular problem. They have a matter-of-fact attitude. It was just another product, no big deal." Mr. Deutsch and Ms. Wren also said that it went smoothly from the start. Ms. Marx too was positive about the new product, saying, "People were excited. We are excited to have our own checking accounts." Ms. Crane reiterated those sentiments. "People were pleased. It was something new to learn. It added to people's jobs. It made them feel more important. It was a service to our customer.

And if you needed money for lunch, you didn't have to go very far. [She laughs.]" No one reported any major stress, overtime, inaccuracies, or delays. Everything went just as they had hoped.

Perhaps because implementation was so smooth internally, there were few changes. A small NOW accounts department was added to the accounting department, but there appeared to be no major changes in the distribution of authority. Decision making remained the same; there were no new routines or structures devised for managing future innovations. In fact, Mr. Deutsch said the NOW account was fit into existing routines. Overall, even though the NOW account was foreign to Second Capitol they never broke stride in integrating it into their existing processes.

Product/External Outcomes

Second Capitol exceeded its minimum goals for numbers of new checking accounts, so from that perspective it was a success. Managers had hoped for between 1,000 and 5,000 accounts with an average balance of $750. Instead, they got between 2,000 and 3,000 accounts (depending on the source of information) and a $1,200 average balance. In addition, they found NOWs useful for cross-selling. According to Mr. Jackson:

> We have generated additional business as a result of checking accounts. And it costs less than we expected.
>
> Customers were very satisfied. There were relatively few complaints about that particular service—fewer complaints than expected. In any account with a lot of transactions, there is more chance to make a mistake. But there were no customer problems.

Everyone interviewed was pleased with their performance, though one person thought they had lost customers to one competitor.

Their early defensive strategy, using a high price to cover costs, probably did negatively affect the number of accounts they attracted. There is no way to tell how much they recouped as a result of lowering their price. Other banks and S & Ls that tried to become more aggressive found that most of the money moved in the first month or two, and it was difficult to attract customers after that. However, one manager said that after they reduced the price, "We picked up on volume, because we really gave it [the account] away." Second Capitol was successful at implementing, both with respect to the smoothness of their internal processes and the product's success.

Summary and Interpretation

Radical versus Routine Innovation

People at all levels at Second Capitol saw the NOW account as routine. This perception was curious, because they acknowledged how little knowledge they had about checking and described the product as foreign. These are characteristics of a radical innovation that requires much new knowledge not currently existing in the organization. However, Second Capitol used outside sources for much of their implementation of the NOW account, so that much of what was not known to them was handled by someone else. Probably for this reason, everyone except the systems manager saw the NOW account as fitting into existing routines, much as employees at banks did.

History/Unique Characteristics

Second Capitol blended aggressiveness and unwillingness to take risks. They wanted to aggressively pursue market share and were willing to spend money and energy to do this. At the same time, they waited to add products until their competitors had been successful or until customers asked for them. Thus, while they saw themselves as innovative, they were not innovative in the sense of putting out new, untested products. Rather they were fast to adapt innovations that had proved valuable to other organizations.

Goals and Strategy

The initial goal for the NOW account was simply to retain existing customers. Like most of the banks, they were concerned that the account would not be profitable. However, they concluded early on that the accounts were not as expensive as they feared and that they were profitable. Their goal shifted to increasing market share.

The strategy for achieving the first goal was a middle-of-the-road price until they saw how well they were doing on the account. That involved a $500 minimum balance which was indeed right between what banks were charging and what the most aggressive savings and loan associations were charging. From the very beginning, they spent money to promote aggressively. However, it was only after they had seen positive results that they decided also to price aggressively, with a $100 minimum.

Search

They had done a rather extensive search in coming up with their original $500 price. They reported doing their own analysis of surveys from the

Eastern Association of Savings and Loans as well as surveying banks and savings and loan associations themselves. In addition, they talked with local banks, attended seminars, and read articles and reports in trade association publications. This process started approximately six months before NOW accounts became legal. Their search left them with the impression that different institutions were doing widely varying things with the account, leading to their decision to take the middle of the road.

Complexity

With sixteen positions participating in the design and implementation of the NOW account, Second Capitol was moderately complex. While they saw themselves as small and simple, they had nearly as many different positions involved in implementation as the large organizations. Of course, the large organizations had many more people in each of these positions.

Flexibility

Second Capitol was unusually flexible. From the very beginning, they planned to review and revise both policy and implementation decisions. Branch people had come to expect changes, though they did not always like them. In fact, everyone saw it as the customer-contact employee's responsibility to give feedback that would make those revisions possible. They were able to be so flexible partially because they committed little to written policies. In fact, nothing at the policy level was written. While numerous memos were given to the branches for implementation, their purpose was to inform, not to bind people to a clear set of rules. The firm also maintained flexibility by waiting until the last possible moment to make decisions that could be implemented quickly.

Power Arrangements for Decisions

Nearly all decisions were made by a high-level committee of officers with extremely little input from anyone outside that group. People at all levels reported that neither they nor any other employees had input, except through giving feedback on customer reactions. The exceptions were the systems manager and the branch coordinator. The systems coordinator had significant influence through collecting and analyzing the data relevant to costs, while the branch coordinator said he had little influence over the process.

Readiness

Second Capitol was extremely well prepared, even better prepared than they expected to be. This readiness can be attributed almost entirely to the readiness of the services they purchased externally. By using the Federal Home Loan Bank for check clearing and especially data processing, they had little to design or do themselves. As with most of the savings and loan associations, even their training was partially provided externally by their check vendor. Whatever internal changes were required were guided by a checklist from the Federal Home Loan Bank. By purchasing so much service externally, Second Capitol was able to routinize many of the unfamiliar aspects of this very new product.

The centralized decision-making process may well have contributed to the relatively high level of system readiness at Second Capitol. Without the necessity of gaining consensus from large numbers of people, decisions could be made quickly and implementation efforts begun well before the date when the accounts first became legal. They clearly had basic decisions made and processes for implementation started a couple of months before NOW accounts were legal, so there was time for training and testing the computer system. The upward communication allowed adaptability, though perhaps less adaptation would have been required if lower-level input had been gotten earlier in the process. Thus, the internal processes probably contributed to a mobilization of the resources necessary to make and implement the innovation, and to the flexibility to modify the product as necessary, though these procedures may also have allowed more error than necessary by not soliciting lower-level input at earlier stages. The lack of middle- and lower-level participation may also be a factor in the absence of much expression of feelings by employees.

Internal Outcomes

Implementation of NOW accounts was universally perceived as extremely smooth. Statements were accurate and timely. The only problem reported was that some account histories were erased or not available from the data processing center when the teller called them up. While there was some confusion among branch staff resulting from changes in decisions, employees were generally excited and satisfied with the new product, being especially pleased that they were given their own checking accounts. There were no reports of stress or overtime. There were also no reports of organizational learning. This can probably be attributed to the fact that the account was perceived to have so little impact on the organization that there were no stresses or problems that might have motivated them to examine what they were doing and make changes. For this organization, implementation was easy.

Product/External Outcomes

Product outcomes were also generally positive for Second Capitol. The number of accounts they received was right in the middle of what they had estimated. Average balances were higher than expected. Customers were satisfied. The firm found the account to be profitable on its own terms and also to be valuable in cross-selling other products. Because they found the outcomes to be so good, they attempted to market NOW accounts even more aggressively through lowering the price, but it is not clear how many additional accounts they got after the lowering. Overall, the outcome was favorable.

Note

1. Superior and Infocheck are fictitious company names.

11

Simple Structures, Reactive Postures, and Limited Aspirations

The small organizations provide interesting contrasts to the larger ones. The NOW account goals of the small organizations varied, just as those of the larger firms did, but whatever their goals, their size was associated with several critical factors that seemed to make implementation easy. First, there were so few accounts opened that the problems caused were never very serious or threatening. Also, when problems did occur, it was easy to handle them. In addition, communication was relatively effortless. Decisions were more readily made because there were fewer people to press their ideas and fewer variables to consider. Finally, they had neither reason nor the capability to do anything but accept the constraints imposed by their technical environment. Most importantly, they limited the design of their products to the data processing capabilities available to them. There was no thought of making their data processing programs fit the product. For all these reasons, implementing innovation in the small organization was a rather simple process.

The simplicity of these organizations means that we can summarize their implementation processes quickly. Therefore, we have grouped the four small organizations into one chapter. However, as with the larger organizations, some elements that were unique to individual organizations produced some differences in strategy and implementation.

The Small Banks

The small banks, like their larger counterparts, defined the NOW account as a defensive product. Their size and the defensive strategy combined to produce easy implementation.

First City Bank

First City Bank defined and used the NOW account quite differently than did the other firms we examined. This institution's mission emphasized two areas. The first was commercial lending, and the second was a special billing service, using their data processing facilities, that they provided to firms in the transportation industry. Clearly, this specialized mission made First City quite different from other small banks, even though, with only 184 employees, two facilities, and $115 million in assets, it was similar to other small banks demographically.

The banking side of First City's business was geared to lending to small businesses. Their history and location had in part determined this mission. According to the chairman:

> We were not in a good location. We were just east of [a major urban housing project with a high crime rate]. Any business that came in had to be brought in.
>
> We didn't believe in what was being written about retail being the future of the banking industry; that warned us not to make a significant commitment to the retail market.

In addition, consumer lending was ethically objectionable to the chairman, which may also have influenced his decision to take the bank toward commercial rather than retail banking. Using a general strategy of commercial lending and service provision, First City had been very profitable, enjoying a 2 percent return on assets year after year, the highest in the metropolitan area.

First City also was innovative historically. For example, the billing service they provided to transportation firms was something that only a few banks in the country offered, and the others were all large banks. In addition, the chairman talked about experimenting with free services for a time, and he had also radically changed their transportation service at one point. "I sensed in 1974 that we needed a different approach to transportation. So we made a significant commitment, a decision to build a whole new system. If we hadn't done that, we wouldn't have any business today, because the market changed markedly."

While the bank had been innovative, it appeared that most of the freedom to innovate lay with the chairman. No one else mentioned an innovative orientation in the bank. In fact, one person said the bank was behind in some areas.

The data from this bank came from four executives. We first met with the president, who oversaw the lending side of the bank's operation. He gave us an overview of the bank's mission and its introduction of NOW accounts. We then spoke with the chairman, who had guided the decision-making process; an assistant vice president of operations, who had initially been responsible for NOW accounts; and the director of operations for banking, who directed data processing for NOW accounts. The chairman indicated that they had opened so few NOW accounts that we would not learn much from new-accounts representatives. Based on that, we did not interview tellers or new-accounts representatives.

Routineness

People clearly agreed that the NOW account was an extremely routine innovation. In part, it was routine because so few accounts were opened that it put little stress on the system. Paul Cohen, director of operations for banking, said that the bank had opened only twenty to thirty accounts after offering them for two months. According to him, "NOW accounts have zero impact on data processing. The new accounts department is affected. There were some things that everybody had to go through—training on offering and requirements. My impression is that it didn't make a lot of difference." John Wright, assistant vice president of operations, said that the only change in standard operating procedures was a change in the frequency of interest payments. The account was done simply, within existing data processing and operations systems.

Design of the Innovation

Goals and Strategy

As with almost all the institutions, not offering the account was never seriously considered. As one manager put it: "There wasn't any question but that we would have to offer it. We didn't want to be in a position where everyone else is offering and we were not involved. We did them in consideration of our commercial accounts."

The larger goals for the NOW account were clear and simple. They were to provide service to the principals of the firms with whom First City did business. Part of First City's larger strategy was to provide its customers with excellent service rather than to focus on price. The NOW account was offered to provide that service to the bank's best customers. According to Mr. Wright, "Our philosophy is that we cater to businesses and the principals of those businesses. As for retail, we haven't gotten involved with money markets, small savers, or all savers. We offer them, but we don't solicit them. We're not trying to attract that kind of deposit. We offer these services in consideration of our principals." Their major criterion for success, then, was whether their principals were happy with their product.

With that philosophy as a guide, First City had a second goal for the NOW account: using it to discourage small-balance customers. Mike Houseman, the chairman, saw an opportunity to reduce traffic in the lobby, thus giving the principals better service. One other constraint existed. While they did not offer NOW accounts as a source of profit, they did want to break even on them.

These goals led to the defensive strategy similar to those of the other banks in this study. A minimum balance of $2,000 and a $3,000 average balance were necessary to avoid a service charge. The $2,000 balance was higher than that of any of the larger banks, reflecting First City's goal of offering the service to their elite cusotmers and discouraging small-balance customers. A special group of customers called "key executives" had the minimum balances waived. According to Mr. Houseman, this was one more way that First City made its best customers feel special and appreciated.

All the banks were concerned that paying interest on checks could cut into profits if the service were not priced properly. Even so, larger banks thought they could make a profit on balances of $1,000 to $1,500. First City, however, with its $2,000 minimum, did not see NOW accounts as a product contributing to profit. They were priced simply to break even. According to John Wright, they came up with the price "just to cover our cost. It's not a money maker; it's not going to lose money."

As for other retail products, advertising was almost nonexistent. They sent out a memo with statements, but they did not use a printed flyer. This low-key approach was similar to the way the bank approached most retail products, although for some retail products they even omitted the memo and gave no notice at all. Customers had to solicit the information. Commercial products, however, were marketed both through flyers and with personal contacts from marketing representatives. Overall, then, the strategy for NOW accounts was perhaps the most defensive of any of the banks, since there was no goal of using them to increase profits, to cross-sell other products, or even to retain retail customers.

Strategic Decision Process

The direction for the policy-making process came from the chairman, Mike Houseman. He took the initiative by analyzing data available to him and then proposing the policy in a brief memo to the controller, the assistant vice president in charge of NOW accounts, an operations assistant, the assistant treasurer of the second bank facility, and a vice president in data processing. The president also had input. After this group discussed the memo, Mr. Houseman rewrote it. His second memo was the final policy.

From the president's point of view, the major input came from the chairman, the executive vice president, and himself. A vice president concurred. All agreed that the major impetus came from the chairman, who himself said:

> When something like this comes up, I like to prepare figures. I don't like to just talk, to have a meeting just to be talking. I'd rather have somebody prepare an outline to provide direction to a discussion. I may not be as democratic; I believe in everybody having a say from the lowest person on

up. We try to have systems to make that possible. I wrote a memo; we discussed it and reached a conclusion. Then I amended it as a guide to people.

The decision process was one in which the data were selected and presented by a person at the top; others at lower levels had an opportunity to discuss it; and the top person made the final policy statement. While people below the chairman had the opportunity to make suggestions, no one at those levels indicated they had actually made suggestions or altered the policy. This meant that the decision was shaped almost entirely at the top, through the use of information as well as the chairman's position, though he was open to modifying his plan.

Search. Managers at First City did their own search of the environment for the information that influenced their strategic decisions. Compared to the larger institutions, their search was not extensive. They relied largely on articles that made use of data from Federal Reserve studies and articles that described what other banks were doing. They did not go to New England, attend seminars, survey the market, or hire consultants. Their limited search was consistent both with their limited goals and with the size of the organization.

Implementation of the Innovation

The very defensive strategy along with some decisions about operations resulted in an easy implementation process. First, the minimum balance was high enough to discourage customers from opening the account. By the end of February, there were only twenty to thirty accounts, leaving little to be done to accommodate the new accounts. Second, and probably most significantly, Mr. Houseman decided on a policy that would allow them to use their existing software with almost no modification. Therefore, there were few issues to be decided in implementing the NOW account at First City.

Internal Processes

The internal processes for implementation were essentially the same as for design. Mr. Houseman decided on the policy to use their current software package. There were no issues to be negotiated between departments, because the decisions about preparing statements, computing, and reporting interest were made at the top. They did not use new account numbers or new checks, so training new-accounts representatives and tellers simply involved discussing the new account and who was eligible for it. In sum, there was almost nothing to decide given the strategy and the decision to work with their existing software. There was considerable flexibility in that decisions were informal. The only written document was the one-and-a-quarter page memo from Mr. Houseman.

Complexity

The small banks were not holding companies; therefore, they did not have the structure of facilities with separate bank presidents and large departments. We expected much less complexity in these organizations, but First City, even though small, was quite differentiated with respect to NOW accounts. At the upper level of the organization, five different positions participated in planning the product: the chairman, president, controller, vice president-data processing, and assistant treasurer. Participants at lower levels of the organization included the assistant vice president-operations, assistant vice president-data processing, director of operations/banking, an operations assistant, new-accounts supervisor, new-accounts representatives, and tellers. In all, twelve positions participated in some way in the implementation of the NOW account. While this is less than at the large and medium banks, it reflected more differentiation than at the other small institutions in the study. It falls into the category of moderately complex.

Readiness

They were easily ready by the date NOW accounts became legal. Mr. Cohen explained the process of becoming technically ready.

> We had just gone to a new package. NOW accounts were in that package. It was pretty easy. There were a couple of minor changes to get a routine working or coding accounts to be interest-bearing. We were lucky. It was not onerous. It was a matter of writing a routine, testing it, and putting the accounts on. I figured there would be something that didn't work. But there were no problems. The system handled it like a charm. The big difference is that we had a package that handled it. The bank I had just left would have had a problem, because they would have had to put in a whole new system. Here we had a package and it worked.

There is little to say about the internal processes of implementation at First City, because there was so little activity. The few decisions that were required were made by the chairman during the strategic decision process. Thus, there was no need for managing conflicting interests, readjusting the plan of action, or working through unforeseen problems. The only change was to offer the NOW account to key executive customers without a minimum balance requirement, a decision made by the chairman. Finally, because it was defined as a minor product, the chairman found it too small to monitor its progress. He simply assumed it would go smoothly, as it did.

Internal Outcomes

Clearly, implementation was extremely smooth internally. Statements were accurate and on time. There were no reports of data processing problems, stress, overtime, or confusion among employees. They had no major difficulties implementing the NOW. It was ready on time and worked well. Because so few demands were put on the bank, no one reported any new learning about making the organization more effective.

Product/External Outcomes

First City Bank defined success as making their customers happy. Mr. Wright and Mr. Houseman agreed that they had done that, especially after waiving the minimum balance requirements for their key executives group. Just over a year after they first offered the NOW account, they had approximately 130 accounts, a very small number. At the same time, each account had a $12,000 balance on average. They were generally satisfied with these results. Chairman Houseman did make one slightly negative remark about the number of accounts. "If rates stay this high, we probably would have looked better if we'd priced lower, but not significantly better in relation to the total profit of the bank." Overall, though, he was happy with the results. He had hoped to encourage low-balance accounts to move, and they did.

> Whenever you price higher than everybody else you reduce volume. We did so to keep the lobby uncluttered, so you don't have to wait in line.
> Seven hundred accounts moved to other locations. We felt that was great. People who don't carry significant balances in their accounts cause the most difficulty in handling the accounts. They call for balances and create overdrafts; they're in the bank more frequently. We cut down significantly on activity. That left fewer people in the lobby, and everybody got better service. There were fewer checks at the end of the cycle. There were a lot of benefits. We had more time to devote to the customer.

Overall, people at First City Bank were pleased with the success of the product it offered and the way it was implemented.

Summary and Interpretation

First City defined the NOW account as a nonevent and made the necessary strategic and operations decisions to insure that it truly would be a nonevent.

Radical versus Routine Innovation

By defining the NOW account as almost irrelevant to the organization's success, the innovation became very routine. Like all banks, First City already had routines for check processing, so it would have been routine in any case. But since they also decided to offer it on such a small scale, it required extremely few changes in existing procedures to implement it.

History/Unique Characteristics

The bank's history was important in defining the NOW acccount as a nonevent. Their location in a poor neighborhood had made it impossible for them to be successful at retail operations, so they had found a different niche in commercial banking and transportation service. Therefore, all retail products were used only to bolster their commercial operations.

First City was dominated by the personality of the chairman; its culture was heavily shaped by his values. He was an aggressive entrepreneur who identified with the entrepreneurs who were the bank's customers. He believed in firing people who did not perform and sharing the profits with everyone else, including tellers and new-accounts representatives. He was very religious and liked his employees to share his religious views. He was success oriented, as was the whole organization. Perhaps because the chairman was so aggressive, the other people we interviewed were more reserved. Talking with people in this bank, we had the impression that the chairman's persona loomed large and dominated most events and decisions in the organization.

Goals and Strategy

There were two goals for the NOW account. The first was to break even. Since the account was not installed to make money, they had no profit goals for it, but they also wanted to guarantee that they would not lose money on it. The second goal was to provide it as a service to their principals to keep their principals happy. In order not to lose money, they required very high minimum and average balances, higher than any other institution in the study. They also did no promotion of the account. They found, however, that the high minimum balance did not please their principals, so they dropped the required balance for the key executives category.

Search

They determined this defensive posture largely on the basis of what they saw as their main business. However, they also used statistics compiled on the New England banks as a way of arriving at their minimum balances. They did not engage in an extensive search of their environment.

Complexity

First City was not a complex organization, but its approach to the NOW account was more complex than that of the other small organizations. With twelve positions having some involvement with NOW accounts at two facilities, a certain amount of coordination was needed to integrate these different functions. We describe it as moderately complex.

Flexibility

The organization was quite flexible because it was informal and communication among a small number of people is relatively easy. There were few written rules or procedures. With only two small facilities, everyone could easily talk with everyone else. Making the decision to change the minimum balance for key executives was reportedly done quickly and implemented easily.

Power Arrangements for Decisions

Both strategic and implementation decisions were made almost entirely at the top. While the chairman did solicit reactions to his proposal, his views were dominant because he had gathered the data and organized the information into a plan of action, giving others only the ability to react to his lead. Even there, people did not report suggesting significant changes in the chairman's proposal. With respect to NOW accounts, there were no conflicting interests to be managed, since the directives came so strongly from the chairman.

Readiness

The organization was extremely well prepared to implement the NOW accounts. Because it was a routine innovation, existing procedures made them ready for it. Moreover, their top-down decision process was efficient, so they had plenty of time to focus on implementation. Most important, though, they made the decision to offer the NOW account within the limits set by the software package they had purchased sometime earlier. Therefore, data processing was easily ready to manage the NOW account by the time it became legal.

Internal Outcomes

The implementation of NOW accounts was smooth at First City. Statements were accurate and on time; employees did not put in overtime and experienced no stress. The reason for the smooth implementation is clear. The innovation was defined as a nonevent and the chairman made the necessary strategic and operations decisions to insure that it truly would be a nonevent. They priced it at a higher level than their competitors, did not promote it, and, in fact, only communicated its availability in one memo. As a result, there were so few accounts that managing them would have been no problem, even if the account had required significant changes in standard operating procedures and software. However, such changes were not required, because the chairman deliberately chose policies consistent with their current software and SOPs. All this was possible because they had anticipated the need for software with a NOW routine and because they were not interested in designing a product with particular features that would appeal to their market. It was enough to have a simple product for their best business clients.

Product/External Outcomes

The product outcomes were exactly what the organization wanted. They lost a large number of small-balance accounts. After making a change for key executives, they made their principals happy with the product. The chairman expressed some regret at not pricing lower, since NOW accounts turned out to be profitable, but he saw the amount to be made from NOW accounts as minor in comparison to their main businesses of commercial lending and transportation service. Overall, people were pleased with the outcomes.

Second City Bank

Second City Bank was also a commercially oriented bank, with about 60 percent of its demand deposits in commercial accounts. However, its commercial orientation was not as strong as that of First City. It had nearly $105 million in assets at the time of the study, roughly the same as First City. Also, like First City, it had two facilities. Managers reported that they offered most of the products that became legal, but they did not see themselves as being innovators. They participated in whatever came along as a way of being competitive.

The bank's size and climate can be seen in the following comments by the president. "We don't have an organization chart on purpose. We are a small organization. We see each other every day. We have no problems delineating responsibility. We have a small number of officers. We have meetings of officers once per month. We try to keep it [the decision process] on a verbal level."

Our first contact at Second City was with the president, Joe McCall, who gave us a detailed description of the issues and decisions about NOW accounts. We then interviewed Harry Treman, vice president; Martha Kessler, a customer service/new-accounts representative; and Susan Miles, a new-accounts representative.

Routineness

The staff at Second City perceived NOW accounts as a routine innovation. According to Mr. McCall, "This is just a combination of two accounts we had been offering already." He said the tellers saw it as just one of the many accounts they offered. A new-accounts representative commented, "The NOW account hasn't changed anything." Everyone agreed that the change was minor, especially since they had already offered a zero-balance or automatic transfer account.

Design of the Innovation

Goals and Strategy

Second City's goal for NOW accounts was simply to protect themselves from loss of customers to their competitors. They did not see NOW accounts as having a high probability of contributing to profits. According to Mr. Treman, "We had to be competitive. We didn't think it was the greatest idea in the world, but we knew we had to do it. We didn't want to lose any accounts, and we didn't lose any." This view was also held by employees lower in the organization. For example, Martha Kessler said they started NOW accounts because of "competition with other businesses that had the NOW accounts."

Given this lack of enthusiasm for the NOW account, Second City Bank took it as a goal to limit the number of accounts they opened. As with other banks, they saw NOW accounts as paying interest on what had once been free money, so they felt that if they had to pay interest on only 15 percent of their deposits, they would be doing well. Mr. McCall observed: "As it turns out, we've got 11.5 percent; we got off a bit easier then we thought." In other words, they wanted as small a percentage as possible of their demand deposits in NOW accounts.

While all the banks studied took this defensive posture with respect to NOW accounts, the strategy fit particularly well for Second City because they were more a commercial than a retail bank. Thus, their primary goal was to sell other services than checking accounts and not to build their retail business. On the other hand, the president expected that retail services would account for a larger proportion of their total assets in the coming years. Nevertheless, this possibility did not seem to influence the strategy for the NOW account, which was defensive.

The defensive strategy was operationalized by requirements of a $1,500 minimum balance to avoid charges and $2,000 to accrue interest. Along with First City Bank, this was clearly the highest average balance required to earn interest. In addition, Mr. McCall reported doing only token advertising. "So much advertising is done by our competitors that we didn't have to do it. We sent out stuffers for our customers." They had one problem with their advertising. According to Ms. Miles, "whatever advertisements they sent didn't explain that there was a sizeable minimum balance, so people expected something different that what we were actually offering."

Strategic Decision Process

Although different managers provided slightly different interpretations of what took place, all indications were that the decision-making was done at the top. The president said that a vote was taken by three vice presidents and himself. "The officers had been meeting; the full committee was formed and reported back to the officers committee; the officers committee made a decision." However, members of the committee indicated that the other officers conformed to the president's views, so that de facto the decision was made by the president. Also, he indicated that there was no input at all from levels below department head.

Even though the decisions were centralized, information flowed freely. Everyone at the officer levels talked about it, even though they did not participate in making the decisions. Mr. Treman explained, "Everyone was involved. We're not big enough to have secrets in this place. We just talked about it." In sum, officers had an opportunity to give their views before the top management group met to hammer out a policy; the president's influence was so strong that it is reasonable to conclude that he made the decision.

Search. The information used for making these strategic decisions came from four major sources: newspaper and journal articles about the New England experience, materials from the American Banking Association, information from their correspondent bank, and comparisons with the large banks in the area. All information came from printed documents, with the exception of what they learned from local large banks. They did not contact New England banks or use consultants who had New England experience. Mr. Treman indicated the probable reason for their minimal search of the environment. "What is a $100 million bank to decide? All we have to decide is how we're going to do it. The only issue is what should the minimum balance be."

Based on the information they uncovered, Second City Bank chose a defensive strategy deliberately intended to limit NOW accounts to 15 percent of the demand deposit accounts they had at the time. Such a strategy meant few demands on the organization, few changes to be made, and few mistakes that would require attention if any problems should arise. In other words, far less preparation was needed for smooth implementation at Second City than was required in the larger organizations.

Implementation of the Innovation

Internal Processes

Because managers chose a strategy that put very limited demands for implementation on them, their existing internal organizational arrangements were adequate. Nevertheless, their organizational dynamics provide insight into implementation in small organizations.

The decision-making process did not separate strategy from implementation, largely because there were few implementation decisions to make. The major one was that they would use software from a computer vendor (one that did not have a program for NOW accounts until three months after they were first offered). That decision as well as other more minor implementation decisions were made by the top-level vice presidents and the president.

Second City operated rather informally, with the NOW account proving no exception. Mr. McCall commented on the deliberate lack of an organization chart and the efforts to keep communication verbal. For NOW account implementation, memos were written but there was no procedures manual. Mr. McCall said, "A summary plan was drawn up for the officers, written instructions were given to the departments. The heads of all departments were at the officers' meetings and they would write memos and procedures for their departments." Said Mr. Treman, "There is no big, fancy chart. Joe tells you a date, makes a note, and God help you if you don't have it done." In addition to its small size, one other element that might help to put the informal structure in its proper context is the long tenure of the officers. Mr. Treman observed: "We're one big family. This was the way Mr. Elman, the previous president, always had it. Most of the vice presidents here now were here when he died about fifteen years ago. Most of the assistant vice presidents have been here twenty years or more too."

Monitoring was also left informal. In Mr. Treman's words, "We didn't supervise people—we gave them the customer sign-up cards, and told them what numbers to use to classify the accounts." Mr. McCall observed: "Each officer just took his share of the responsibility to see that his people knew what to do. We had and still get a daily report to monitor." He stated that the NOW accounts were discussed at a few meetings after implementation, mainly during the following three months.

Complexity

Second City was not highly differentiated. Only seven positions were involved in designing and implementing NOW accounts. Four upper-level managers participated: the president, vice president-operations, a vice president who was a facility manager, and an unnamed vice president. At the lower levels, the positions involved were tellers, new-accounts representatives, and data processing staff. Even among these positons there was some blurring of duties, with tellers and new-accounts people doing each others' jobs as necessary, vice presidents often not being given labels associated with particular functions, and the president making the strong point that they deliberately avoid a formal organization chart as a way of keeping jobs fluid. In sum, structural arrangements involved little complexity.

Readiness

Two major aspects of the organization needed to be ready to implement this innovation. The first was the technical system; the second, staff.

In all cases, technical system meant data processing capability. This is because data processing was critical to preparing customer statements reporting the interest their accounts accrued.

Second City began considering the computer issues several months before January 1, 1981. However, it was three months after they first offered the account before they had a software package that could handle NOW accounts. They knew in advance that they would not have data processing capability by the time NOW accounts were legal. They had been obtaining their software from their computer hardware vendor. Since they had neither internal expertise nor an established external relationship for programming, they decided to wait until their computer company provided the NOW account package. However, the delay produced no problems at the time they started offering the account. Their president said, "Our key concern was getting it on the computer on time, and we did. By the end of April, it was completely on the computer." Most other organizations would have been in serious trouble if they had not had a NOW account package until April, but the very defensive strategy and the size of the company led to minimal problems. "For about three months, we did have to do some manual compilation on the interest accrued. We had no problem keeping up with the manual system because we only had thirty to forty accounts."

The second aspect of readiness was to give the staff sufficient knowledge about the new product. At Second City, there was no formal training. In addition to the cards Mr. Treman noted earlier, the extent of the preparation of the staff was a memo and a meeting. "The assistant vice president explained it all to us at a meeting. There was a written memo before the meeting, and the meeting was set up so we could ask questions and get answers." Most staff education came as a response to day-to-day problems. "There were instances of different kinds of things that came up daily that we didn't know about. It was embarrassing. We tried to get an answer and usually did get an answer quickly."

Thus, in two areas, managers at Second City were, in an absolute sense, unprepared. Yet they were not thrown into a crisis, because the number of accounts was so small that they could respond quickly and easily to immediate problems that arose.

Internal Outcomes

There were no internal changes because the number of NOW accounts was so small that little stress was placed on the institution and there was no need for change. There is no mention of any internal change in any of the interviews. No one mentioned stress, though customer-contact people did experience some frustration. Given their ability to process checks manually, they were able to get accurate statements out on time. Overall, implementation was very smooth despite a marked lack of preparedness.

Product/External Outcomes

Second City clearly met its goals for NOW accounts. It wanted to limit the number of accounts to 15 percent of their demand deposits; it "surpassed" this goal—it achieved 11.5 percent (300 NOW accounts). The average balance of $8,743 was very high compared to other banks and S & Ls in the area. Said Mr. McCall, "the NOW account is a profitable account. Even with the cost of checking services, it's profitable." Mr. Treman noted, "How can you come out bad at 5 1/4 percent interest? That's cheap money. I just paid over 14 percent on a certificate of deposit today."

There is a contradiction in these outcomes, of course. On one hand, they limited the number of NOW accounts they sought; on the other, the accounts turned out to be very profitable, at least during the period of high-interest savings accounts. Thus, like most banks that took a defensive approach to the NOW account, they probably could have made more money than they did.

Summary and Interpretation

Second City demonstrated how being small can make implementation easy. Although managers were quite unprepared for NOW accounts, their implementation process was smooth and unstressful, because their size allowed them to compensate for deficiencies in preparedness.

Radical versus Routine Innovation

As with all the other banks, interest-bearing checking was perceived to be just another checking account, requiring little in the way of internal changes in order to implement it. It was especially routine because they had already been offering zero-balance checking accounts, which were even more complex than NOW accounts.

History/Unique Characteristics

Many of the officers and even the customer-contact people had been at the bank for twenty years or more. They shared many memories and traditions that were important to them. In particular, they saw themselves as a bank that was solid and dependable. No one had ever lost any money in their bank. Furthermore, they tried to be a friendly bank. Being a solid and dependable bank, they did not see themselves as being innovators, but they did expect to offer new products that became available to them.

Goals and Strategy

The image of being solid, dependable, and not particularly innovative contributed to the managers' orientation toward NOW accounts, an orientation that was less than enthusiastic. Their goals were also determined by the bank's niche as a commercial lender, which led them to offer NOW accounts to protect themselves from the competition and not to gain more retail customers. They were concerned about pricing the account at a profitable level, so the defensive strategy was operationalized with a very high minimum balance and no promotion. Instead, they hoped to ride on the coattails of the promotion done by the larger banks in the city.

Search

Consistent with their size, the resources they put into the search for information about NOW accounts were not great. Nearly all of their information came from printed materials readily accessible to them, rather than from contacts with New England banks or consultants.

information came from printed materials readily accessible to them, rather than from contacts with New England banks or consultants.

Complexity

With only seven positions involved in NOW accounts, Second City was very simple with respect to this innovation. Even though they had their own computer, few specialized functions participated in either the design or the implementation of the new product.

Flexibility

While the bank did not modify its original plan, it had to remain flexible to process checks manually at first and then by computer. Furthermore, since it did not provide training, it needed—and had—the flexibility to respond to new-accounts staff's and teller's questions and problems. First, little was committed to writing. An outline of the product and some of the procedures were written in memos, but there was no procedures manual. This allowed the bank to adapt quickly without going through the time-consuming process of rewriting policy. Second, communication was informal and open. One manager said that everybody knew everything that was going on, indicating that they communicated freely with each other at all levels. This gave them the flexibility to make changes, moving in new directions quickly and with ease.

Power Arrangements for Decisions

Power was arranged hierarchically. As would be expected in a simple system with open communication, lower-level officers had an opportunity for input into decisions through their communication with the vice presidents of departments. Then the top vice presidents got together with the president to actually make the decisions about both policy and implementation. While a vote was taken among this group, the president was highly respected, and his views strongly influenced the outcome of the vote.

Conflicting interests were few since there were few specialized positions to have conflicting interests. Nonetheless, people did disagree, and that conflict was resolved by the department vice presidents in their meeting to decide the issues. It was an open give-and-take, with the final outcome apparently depending on the ability to persuade the president of the merits of an argument. Monitoring was accomplished through reports rather than personal supervision.

Readiness

While Second City had little complexity to manage and had the communication tools and the processes available for making decisions, the organization was nevertheless technically unprepared for implementing NOW accounts. This was not due to a lack in their internal processes, though; rather, they chose to process by hand because their computer manufacturer had promised them a software package shortly. Since they expected few accounts, this route seemed less likely to cause them problems than having a program written that they perhaps could not trust to work properly. They also were not ready in preparing their customer-contact staff through training, but their small size allowed them to inform and work with that staff on an individual basis, rather than going through a formal training process. As a result of their small size and the eventual availability of software from outside the organization, being unprepared had few consequences for them.

Internal Outcomes

Given their small size, they were able to implement smoothly. Statements were accurate and on time; employees did not experience overtime or stress. Organizational learning was not reported, because they attempted almost no modification of their existing procedures.

The lack of formalization, combined with minimal training, left their direct-contact people feeling confused, but it also potentially gave the organization more flexibility. In sum, implementation decision making also involved most department heads, but final decisions were made by top managers; the organization was quite informal. These qualities were advantageous in getting the views of many of those affected by NOW accounts, yet mobilizing the necessary support to get a decision made. The informality also made possible greater adaptability to make the necessary modifications after initial implementation. But these qualities were not necessary in an organization that had so few accounts during the first months of implementation.

Product/External Outcomes

Managers at Second City Bank surpassed their goal of keeping money out of NOW accounts, having few accounts, and maintaining high average balances. While they accomplished what they had hoped with their defensive strategy, they wondered in retrospect if they should have pursued them more aggressively, since the NOW account turned out to be much more profitable than expected.

The Small Savings and Loan Associations

The small savings and loan associations smoothed their implementation process by purchasing check processing and data processing from outside the organization. Like the small banks, they worked within the constraints of the software available to them, which limited their control over the design of their product. The combination of small size and external constraints made implementation easy, despite the radical nature of the innovation.

First Neighborhood S & L

With assets of $60 million in 1980 and twenty-eight employees, First Neighborhood S & L was considerably smaller than either of the two small banks. The organization was located in older, less affluent sections of the metropolitan area and had loaned money almost exclusively for older homes in the city. At the time NOW accounts became legal, they were attempting to reposition themselves in the market, as will be described. As with many savings and loan associations at the time, First Neighborhood was struggling financially.

Information about First Neighborhood came from three sources. Our first contact was with a vice president, George Crocker, whose brother was president of the association. We also talked with a teller supervisor, Pam Moore, and a teller, Elise Fuller.

Routineness

Their complete lack of prior knowledge about checking made it clear that this was a radical innovation. They had to make changes in forms, in data processing, in screening new accounts, and in interacting with customers. In comparison with the banks, these changes had to be developed from scratch rather then being adaptations of current standard operating procedures. As a result, implementation of the innovation was a more complicated process.

Design of the Innovation

Goals and Strategy

First Neighborhood's main goal in offering the NOW account was to create an image of themselves as a leading financial institution in the community where they had recently opened a new building. NOW accounts became legal just after they moved into a beautiful new multiple-story building several miles west of their previous headquarters. They hoped to use the NOW account to attract business to that location, which they saw as potentially more profitable than their previous headquarters location.

One the other hand, they were skeptical of the benefits of the NOW account. According to the vice president, Mr. Crocker:

> Originally, we didn't want to offer them. But we have three offices now. We were in the midst of planning this building here for a new office. If it had not been for building here in this part of the city, I doubt that we would have gone into it. We felt our two areas (a retirement village and a blue collar area) could both be checking areas. However, we didn't think we would capture that much of the market there. We felt this was going to be a much more viable market. We thought, if we're going to be putting up this building, we might as well have the service available. We made the decision to go with NOW accounts. We weren't happy, because we could not see making money at it. I guess one thing about this industry just now is that we're starting to learn that you have to make a profit.

First Neighborhood was purchasing data processing services from Third Commercial Bank. Many of their concerns about pricing and profitability were based on comments and recommendations from this bank, which (like most banks) was pessimistic about NOW accounts' potential profitability.

Mr. Crocker went on to say, "The first reason for offering NOW accounts was to look like we were a number one association in this new area. The second was profit. We wanted to be competitive when we came out here, so we made the decision to have them."

Developing this image as a number one association was important to managers at First Neighborhood because they wished to change the firm's image. Mr. Crocker observed:

> For years we had a reputation of being an inner city vendor. We got burned. We were losing $2 to $3 million a year because of this. We're not big enough to get into good housing, a mix of new and used. You have to be able to retain builders. You have to have a constant flow of funds. So we got into the secondary market. The controller has to take credit for that. Since 1974, we've been in the secondary market.

In essence, the vice president was indicating their desire to move away from their image as an inner city association and develop an image as an institution for middle class suburban customers. Their current market position had not been profitable. They wanted the NOW accounts to help them reach a new market segment.

In a very real sense, First Neighborhood had conflicting goals for the NOW account. On the one hand, they wanted it to be a loss leader so they could attract business to their new location. On the other hand, they wanted to make a profit. In determining their strategy, they agonized between the pull toward each of those two goals. Information from various sources indicated that NOW accounts had to be priced at a fairly high level in order to make a profit. According to Mr. Crocker, "All the information we were getting was that we were going to be butchered. Unless you price it well, you're going to get butchered. Everything was negative coming from the east coast. We knew the banks were having a minimum of $750 and up."

On the other hand, their decision to go with NOW accounts at all was due to the decision to give market share priority over profit, based on a belief that NOW accounts would not be profitable. Therefore, when they decided on their pricing strategy, they decided to price low.

> If we were going to capture the market, we would have to be lower than the banks. Large S & L A had no minimum at all for one year. We knew the average was $100 to $200; some were $500. We didn't want to fool with the average balance. We went in with a set balance of $200. $100 was too low, $300 was too high. If you're going to attract anybody, you have to have a lower price. $200 was an educated guess.

However, in addition to a low minimum balance, they also offered many free services. For example, Mr. Crocker said: "We don't have a charge for the checks. You can write all you want. For the saver who had $1,000 or more in savings, if the balance slips below $200, there is no service charge. Also a mortgage loan customer falls into the same category. [So does] anybody with direct deposit checking."

First Neighborhood took a number of steps to offset the cost of this new service. First of all, they hoped to offset costs by attaining a high volume of accounts. They knew that if they got 400 accounts they would be breaking even; if they got more than 600 to 700 hundred accounts, they would be making a profit. So their aim was to capture a large share of the market. Second, they decided to truncate [not return cancelled checks] for all customers as a way of reducing costs. They were in a small minority in choosing to truncate rather than return checks, but they felt it was necessary in order to reduce their operating costs and make a profit on a fairly expensive product. Finally, Mr. Crocker said they were also very hard on customers who wrote bad checks. "Our attitude is two bounces and you're out, unless there is a very good reason." All of these strategies were taken to balance their conflicting goals of increasing market share and changing their image on the one hand and making a profit on the other.

Given their size, they promoted fairly aggressively.

We sent mailings to the customers to inform them that we were having the NOW account and explain the program. We had a premium promotion; the first fifty checks were free. That's typical. We promoted in the newspaper. Let them [customers] know you've got them. Being small, we can ride on the coattails of the big companies' advertising. Particularly with NOW accounts we did local advertising. Checking accounts are localized. We did more office area advertising [direct mail to households near one of the firm's offices].

In sum, the NOW account strategy for First Neighborhood was an aggressive one, particularly when their size is considered. They priced it low; they offered special premiums; and they advertised to the extent that the budget allowed.

Strategic Decision Process

Even though First Neighborhood was a small organization, there was not a great deal of upward communication and lower-level participation in the decision-making process. As it was described by Mr. Crocker, the teller, and the teller's supervisor, only three people had input into the decision. Lobby employees had no involvement whatsoever. As Mr. Crocker described the process, "Implementation was assigned to myself, the controller, and the company secretary. It was pretty much the three of us using information we gathered from the outside. The president was included, but he basically left it up to the three of us. Getting down from the three of us, you get into the staff." When asked what the controller's involvement in the process was, Mr. Crocker answered, "He called people he knew, while I called people I knew. We'd get together, kind of mesh together, and come to a happy medium. We would sit down, state our definite opinions, and discuss them, but there was no great fight."

The decision-making process portrayed in these comments is decision by consensus among a small high-level group of association officers. When asked to what degree she participated in the planning, Ms. Fuller said, "I didn't really." Likewise, Ms. Moore described her participation as "not very much." This process was characteristic of both the strategy decision making and the more technical decision making necessary for implementation.

Search. In order to determine what their strategy would be, managers engaged in a rather extensive search of the environment. First, they went to a number of seminars given by the U.S. League of Savings Associations. In addition, they did an informal survey of approximately two hundred of their customers, asking them about their attitudes towards truncation. A third source of information was friends in the savings and loan business in the metropolitan area. Since many of these individuals were in the same situation of not knowing what they should do with NOW accounts, they were eager to exchange information. Finally, since nearly all of their staff had checking accounts at a bank, they asked those people to report to them on the minimum balances and fees charged by the banks. As a result, information from numerous sources was available to help them determine strategy.

Implementation of the Innovation

Internal Processes

As mentioned, decisions on implementation as well as strategy were made at the top; lower-level people did not participate. In general, the organization was not formalized. That is, any communication that was reported was done in meetings rather than through memos. The only formal manual reported was a procedures manual distributed by their data processing vendor.

There was an indication that the information flow was imperfect. In particular, there was some problem in communication between lower-level participants and higher-level managers, in part due to the move to the new building. Recall that lower-level participants had no influence whatsoever over the decisions made. In addition, both Ms. Fuller and Ms. Moore made reference to the physical separation of lobby employees from the top managers on the second floor of the new building. One said, "People like someone in authority in the lobby though, and that's harder now that the biggies are upstairs." The other said, in response to a question about management's attitude toward employees, "Some people can care less, but then again, that's probably why they're not down here on the first floor." There was also a noticeable paucity of statements indicating an open flow of communication—statements that had been made in other organizations.

To summarize, the internal process was fairly informal, with decision making limited to four high-level managers. There was little communication between the higher and lower levels, even though the organization was small enough to facilitate that kind of interaction. Fortunately, there were few reasons to modify the original plan, so flexibility and feedback from lower levels were not as important as in some organizations.

Complexity

First Neighborhood had a simple structure, with few positions participating in the planning and implementation of NOW accounts. Only four upper-level managers participated in NOW accounts. They were the president, vice president, controller, and secretary of the association. At lower levels, tellers and new-accounts representatives participated. In all, only six different positions were mentioned, suggesting little internal differentiation. Branch structure was not considered separately; there were only two facilities.

Readiness

First Neighborhood purchased outside services for both check clearing and data processing. They described their involvement with these outside service providers as quite simple—managers at First Neighborhood did what they were told. In other words, they accepted the services available to them from the outside without attempting to modify them. Instead, they modified the product that they offered to their customers based on what was available, particularly in data processing.

> We're going to do what Third Commercial Bank tells us to. They work very smoothly with us. They came to us and told us what their package would do. The check companies also came. They said "this is what we'll do." There again, it's just faith in the company. Superior [the check supplier] had been around a long time. They ought to know what they are doing. We did what they said when we set up credit and debit memos. We had guidance.
> We used Infocheck to check on people. Infocheck came in and held training sessions. I set up procedures with the team next door.

As a result, there was the general feeling that they were up and running on time. There were minor problems, they said, but no major problems. They did not specify what the minor problems were.

Training

The training was done primarily by the outside vendors. Representatives of the check vendor, Infocheck, and the data processing vendor came in and explained to the employees how to use their particular product. In addition, the three association officers who designed the NOW account held three to four training sessions with new-accounts people. The vice president indicated that training the tellers was left up to the head teller and branch manager. Overall, people were well trained and the organization well prepared through the use of outside expertise.

Internal Outcomes

Internal changes were few, probably because of the small number of accounts that the organization attracted. For example, the vice president remarked,

"We'd probably like to have a lot more accounts, because of their balances and the cost of money. We'd also like to have more so we could hire someone to take over the department, to ease things up for the secretaries." The head teller said, "Anticipating it, we had very big plans, perhaps plans for a separate department." However, since they did not get the business they had expected, there was no change in the organization structure.

Compared to other organizations, particularly the large savings and loan associations, the NOW account put relatively little stress on the employees of First Neighborhood. There was some extra work, particularly in the early stages, but never the kind of volume that put demands on people for long hours day after day. One respondent said, "I thought I would be more involved and busy."

In the beginning, there was some stress from the anxiety of a new product and not knowing how to implement it. According to the teller, "It was just seeing the form and how much information you had to get. It could be very confusing trying to get that information." Also, some anxiety was induced by the need to turn down customers whose credit checks were unacceptable and by explaining the procedures and guidelines relating to NOW account customers. These reported levels of stress were extremely mild, however, compared to the problems caused by extreme overtime, failures of data processing systems, and inadequate organizational systems reported in other organizations.

Finally, there were no reports of changes in the way the organization solved problems. Some organizations learned much about how to manage from their NOW account experience; however, people at First Neighborhood reported no such progress or changes. This is to be expected in an organization where the change made few demands of them internally, since they relied heavily on outside vendors.

Product/External Outcomes

According to their own assessment, the product was moderately successful. However, because we have contradictory data on the exact number of accounts that First Neighborhood obtained, it is difficult to determine the success of the NOW account. One respondent said that 400 accounts were necessary to break even and that they were almost at the point of making money. At the same time, there was an indication that they had between 800 and 900 NOW accounts at the time of the interview. The reported average balance was $1,100, considerably higher than their expected average balance. According to the vice president, "Right now we're shooting at average balances and total checking amounts of $1 million. If we can have that at 5 1/4 percent, that's cheap money. We're just about there. We probably would like to have a lot more, because of their balances and the cost of money. We're happy with what we have done so far." The head teller echoed their desire to have more accounts, and (like the vice president) expressed optimism that they would pick-up more accounts through their recent advertising campaigns.

Summary and Interpretation

Radical versus Routine Innovation

The innovation was radical for First Neighborhood. It had many procedures that had to be changed or added and little knowledge about how to make those changes.

History/Unique Characteristics

First Neighborhood was attempting to reposition itself in the market to serve more middle class homeowners. It had recently moved to a beautiful multi-story building in a different section of the metropolitan area and hoped to use the NOW account to lure those middle class customers and help it change its image.

Goals and Strategy

The primary goal for the NOW account, then, was to create the image of a respectable association, one attractive to the middle class in its new community. The secondary goal was to make a profit, and they were sensitive to the need to make a profit. Given the desire to enter a new market niche, they decided to require a low minimum balance and to market aggressively, hoping that they could make up for the expense of low-balance accounts with volume.

Search

Since they keenly felt the need for more knowledge about checking in order to make reasoned decisions, they engaged in a broad search within the limits of their resources. They went beyond the seminars of the U.S. League of Savings Associations, using vendors, other savings and loan associations, a survey of their customers, and information about banking minimums and fees that their employees brought to them.

Complexity

First Neighborhood had an extremely simple structure. Only six positions were involved in designing or implementing NOW accounts. There was little task specialization and little to coordinate or integrate to make NOW accounts operational.

Flexibility

First Neighborhood did not have occasion to modify its plan, probably because so much of the work for NOW accounts was done by outside vendors. However, had it needed to make modifications, it might have had some difficulties. While the organization communicated informally, aiding in its flexibility and adaptability to unforeseen events, it did not have open communication. In particular, it did not have good upward communication, which would have allowed it to adjust to customer complaints or processing problems if they had existed.

Power Arrangements for Decisions

All decisions were made at the top by a committee of three officers who reported to the president. In this case, the only middle-management group that existed was composed of two branch managers, and they did not participate in either policy or implementation decisions. Likewise, those lower in the organization had no input.

Readiness

Overall, First Neighborhhod was well prepared to offer NOW accounts. Their use of an outside data processing vendor and their willingness to tailor their product to the data processing constraints given by the vendor meant that they were easily ready technically. They used a bank for data processing, which meant that their vendor was under pressure to have a NOW account package ready by the January 1 deadline for themselves, giving First Neighborhood some assurance that the package would be ready for them also. Organizationally, they prepared themselves with training from the check vendor, the data processing vendor, and the officers.

Internal Outcomes

As a result of their preparation, they were able to implement smoothly. They did not give details but said that everything went well, and that problems were too minor to mention.

Product/External Outcomes

The firm apparently fell short of its goal for number of NOW accounts. The data are conflicting, but respondents indicated disappointment that they did not get more accounts and found to their surprise that NOW accounts were a relatively inexpensive source of funds.

Second Neighborhood S & L

Second Neighborhood S & L, with $65 million in assets in 1980, was almost exactly the same size as First Neighborhood. Again, size proved to be an important variable affecting managers' decision-making process and the smoothness of implementation. Second Neighborhood was a traditional thrift institution, catering to older people with passbook savings accounts. It was not aggressively seeking to take advantage of the new banking regulations, nor did people see their firm as being a community leader or innovator.

Our first information came from a joint interview with John Marshall, president and Michael Weaver, vice president. We then interviewed Barry White, another vice president, and Edith Aldo, the savings manager who was responsible for opening new accounts.

Routineness

The NOW account was a radical innovation for Second Neighborhood. Considerable organizational adaptation and learning were required. According to Edith Aldo, it was the first new product they had offered in years. Furthermore, when the accounts were first offered, the routines for the tellers changed due to different forms to fill out, clearing the customer's creditworthiness, and showing the selection of checks they offered. At the same time, people had little knowledge about how to make these changes. According to Mr. Weaver, "We assumed our people knew as little as we did."

Design of the Innovation

Goals and Strategy

Second Neighborhood's goal for the NOW account was simply to meet the competition. They perceived that their clientele, which was made up of older people, would not be attracted to checking accounts. They believed that their older customers preferred paying their bills and doing business in person and therefore would not be interested in having a checking account.

At the same time, they had customers asking about NOW accounts, so they felt they had to offer them in order to avoid losing current business. In the words of Mr. Marshall, "We figured everyone else would do it. It was defensive. We felt we had to protect ourselves. We felt initially that it would be of minimal benefit."

Unlike First Neighborhood, this thrift institution was not using the NOW account to change its market position or to create an image in the community. They simply wanted to prevent the erosion of their customer base.

To reach their goal of retaining current customers, the managers at Second Neighborhood adopted what they described as a middle-of-the-road strategy. They compromised among themselves on a minimum balance of $300. Said one, "If you make it too cheap, you get all the cruddy customers from banks. So we did not want to attract people who had low-balance accounts. They'd write overdrafts and bad checks." While managers saw $300 as a moderately high minimum balance, it was really quite low among the banks and S & Ls that we studied, though it was higher than at the more aggressive savings and loan associations. From our perspective, their price was fairly aggressive despite their perceptions that they had chosen a defensive strategy.

Also, their promotion was fairly aggressive for an organization of their size. They had no readily available funds to advertise the NOW account, so they diverted funds from other ads. They advertised through radio commercials, newspaper ads in their section of the city, and stuffers in statements to current customers. In addition, they gave gifts to customers opening new accounts. Toward the end of the first year of NOW accounts, they decided to promote them again, in their words "a bit more actively." They reported that their campaign had little effect, a finding that supported the beliefs of most of the people we interviewed that it was difficult to get people to move checking accounts once they had opened them.

The picture, then, is of an organization that perceived its pricing and promotion as defensive, but whose strategy (compared to the other banks and S & Ls in our study) appeared at least moderately aggressive. The aggressive stance is difficult to account for. On the one hand, they did not want NOW accounts. Nor did they expect to be able to attract them. On the other hand, they viewed their customers as rather inert. They felt they needed to offer the account to compete, but their degree of aggressiveness seemed inconsistent with their premises.

Strategic Decision Process

Second Neighborhood was an organization where everybody knew everybody and talked to everybody. Consequently, the NOW account was discussed and debated among all levels of personnel, from tellers all the way up to the association president, during the entire decision-making process. However, two vice presidents along with the president made both the strategic and the implementation decisions, and the board of directors then approved those decisions. Ms. Aldo explained the process: "Mr. Marshall would listen to them [members of the board] and he would listen to us, and then that would get discussions going." But she also described a process whereby she was told how things were going to be. She went on to say that people at her level or below were consulted because

> We might know more about it and make suggestions. They knew we had to deal with the people, so they asked for our suggestions. We are the ones dealing with the people. The customer comes first—we have to remember that. We have to work together—we listen to them and they listen to us. The men on our board had many, many meetings. And then they would relate to us how things were to be.

Within the committee of two vice presidents and the president, there were differences of opinion. Vice presidents sometimes persuaded the president to accept their position. According to Mr. Weaver, "John Marshall never would have touched the NOW account. He felt it would be a loss leader. Barry and I were all for it." Since they decided to adopt the NOW account innovation, it would appear that these two men were able to influence the president. The president and vice president also described an ongoing process characterized by debate of the issues, particularly those of the minimum balance and whether to truncate or return checks.

To summarize the data on the decision-making process, people at all levels were involved in discussing issues and giving input on policies. However, three men took that information and arrived at a decision through a consensus process among themselves. After they had arrived at a decision, it was submitted to their board, which then gave final approval. One important characteristic of this decision-making process was the informality of communication. The association had only one small branch so most people were together in the same place and had an opportunity to communicate face-to-face. The small size meant that participants lower in the organization were not isolated from higher-level managers, so that discussions around the coffee pot were possible between a teller and the president. One side effect of this informal communication process was that information from the lower level was readily available to those who made decisions.

Search. The search process used for determining the NOW account strategy was rather simple. Nearly all the information they obtained came from the U.S. League of Savings Associations. That group provided seminars and publications enabling them to perform a break-even analysis on costs. It also provided them with procedures for opening checking accounts. According to Mr. Marshall, "We followed their [U.S. League's] lead a lot—we knew nothing."

Several other sources were used. First, they had discussions with other savings and loan associations in the area. They exchanged information in an effort to find out what to do. They also reported having some discussions with local banks. They specifically chose not to buy a package on NOW accounts from consultants from the East Coast, believing they could learn how to do it without that input. Finally, their check vendor gave them some information about NOW accounts.

While managers did not do a wide search for information about NOW accounts, their small size made their reliance on information from the U.S. League a reasonable choice. The U.S. League tailored its information to the small savings and loan associations. The cost, of course, was that they had fewer alternatives from which to choose when deciding their strategy.

Implementation of the Innovation

Internal Processes

Because the decision process and the implementation process overlapped both temporally and with respect to the people involved, much of what is known about the internal process has been reported in earlier sections of this analysis. Communication was clearly informal and personal. The only exceptions were an outline that tellers were given to follow in explaining NOW accounts to the customers and a manual, which a vendor supplied, that explained how to use the computer tie-in. Otherwise, organization members seemed to function as a small group rather than as a complex organization.

This small-group or simple structure mode of organizing gave the association potential flexibility. Information could come up from the bottom so that the organization would have the knowledge necessary for making adjustments to their original plan. As at First Neighborhood, though, it is not clear how necessary organizational flexibility was. There were many constraints imposed by vendors and their reliance on external sources of information. This left less room for them to adapt to their customers. At the same time, it did make modification more possible within their constraints.

Complexity

Like other small organizations, Second Neighborhood was simple in structure, with most of the differentiation at upper levels. With respect to the NOW account, five participants at upper levels, including the president, executive vice president, vice president, vice president and savings manager, and treasurer were involved. The only lower-level positions involved were tellers. Overall, then, with only six positions involved, Second Neighborhood was low in complexity for the NOW account.

Readiness

All our data point to a system that was extremely well prepared for the introduction of the innovation. They had been using an outside data processing service, and they decided to continue to use that service as they introduced NOW accounts. That service already had a NOW acount program available, so there were no last-minute concerns about writing and testing programs. Part of the reason that this process went so smoothly was that they modified their strategy to fit the available computer program, while tailoring their product to the data processing services available. As a result, they were ready on January 1, when the NOW account became legal.

Training

In addition to being technically ready, they prepared staff for the innovation. The most extensive training came from their check vendor, who gave slide presentations on checks to everyone. In addition, there were meetings to give the overall picture of what the association was trying to do, and tellers were trained to recognize illegitimate checks. There were a total of ten people trained.

Internal Outcomes

Internal changes were few, which is a surprise even in this small an organization. Given that the innovation was radical, we might have expected to see at least a change in structure in which some person was designated to oversee checking accounts or to be in charge of processing checking accounts. Instead, there were no reported changes in the structure whatsoever. Also, no changes were reported in the planning process, even though the NOW account was the first of many innovations facing banks and S & Ls. Likewise, there were no reported changes in the power dynamics of the organization and no reported organizational learning from the NOW account experience.

For many organizations, the introduction of the NOW account was a stressful event, particularly for larger savings and loan associations. However, since Second Neighborhood adapted to the data processing capabilities available to it, internal changes were apparently small enough that anxiety was at a minimum. Their staff did report some stress about the new procedures they had to follow, but did not report being overworked. In addition, they had no problems with statement errors or delays, so there were few customer complaints to put stress on them.

Product/External Outcomes

In terms of product success, managers reported that Second Neighborhood exceeded its goals. By September 1981, they had already exceed their target of three hundred accounts. Moreover, the average balance was in excess of $1,500. They described the NOW account as profitable and said they were probably making a little money on it. According to the president, "Now that we have it, we are satisfied. I think it will be valuable for S & Ls. It's a benefit—it helps customers, it helps us. It has not proven to be a burden. Checking account dollars are now the cheapest source of funds we have."

Summary and Interpretation

Second Neighborhood managers surprised themselves with how smoothly they were able to introduce NOW accounts and how much money they made on them.

Radical versus Routine Innovation

For them this was a radical innovation, requiring them to engage in many new procedures. However, the number of new procedures required of them was reduced by using outside services rather than doing the work in-house.

History/Unique Characteristics

Second Neighborhood was located in a stable older community. They did not want to be innovators, perceiving that their customer base was not interested in new products in general and the NOW account in particular.

Goals and Strategy

Given their orientation toward the NOW account, they viewed it as a product they would have to offer to meet their competition but not something that would be profitable for them. They viewed the situation much as the banks in the study did. They had no clear goals other than to protect themselves from loss of customers and loss of money. Toward that end, they adopted what they perceived to be a middle-of-the-road strategy, requiring a $300 minimum balance and promoting through premiums, ads, and local newspapers. This strategy, which they perceived to be on the defensive side, was quite aggressive compared to the banks'.

Search

Their search process was limited. They relied almost exclusively on information from the U.S. League, though they did supplement that information with discussions with other savings and loan associations in the area.

Complexity

Only six positions were involved with NOW accounts. The organization was simple, therefore requiring little coordination and integration compared to more complex organizations. Furthermore, most employees worked in one building, with only a few in a small branch, so whatever coordination was required was faciliatated by ease of face-to-face communication.

Flexibility

The organization's flexibility was not tested, since it did not modify its original plan. The heavy reliance on services and expertise from the outside put some limits on its flexibility, while at the same time removing some of the problems that would have required modification. Had they needed flexibility, the organizational conditions were there for providing it. They had open communication among all levels of the organization. People at the bottom had regular and easy access all the way up to the president's level, so any customer or processing problems would have been readily known. Further, they committed little to writing and therefore had the ease of making changes without going through policy modifications.

Power Arrangements for Decisions

Influence was distributed throughout the organization. People at the lowest level talked about their views; in fact their views were solicited. The organization's vice presidents and president took that information as well as the wishes of the board of directors into account in working out the policies.

Yet, no one dominated, not even the president, and the group worked toward consensus. The board then approved their decisions.

Readiness

Through the choice of outside vendors, Second Neighborhood was well prepared technically, particularly since it put no demands on its data processing vendor to modify its programs for their product. They also trained their staff largely via outside vendors.

Internal Outcomes

Implementation was extremely smooth. There were no problems with employee stress or overtime, though some early anxiety was reported. Statements were accurate and timely. No organization learning was reported.

Product/External Outcomes

Second Neighborhood S & L exceeded its goal of three hundred NOW accounts. Its managers discovered that NOW accounts were profitable and regretted not attracting more of them. Further advertising attempts had less impact than they hoped. They reported no customer complaints.

Summary of the Small Organizations

Any comparisons of the smallest institutions with the others are dominated by differences associated with size. This is true for two reasons. First, the small organizations relied heavily on outside services and expertise. Even though the small banks did their own data processing, they did it within the constraints of the softwre available to them without modification. Their heavy reliance on outside services and expertise meant that fewer internal problems arose. It also meant less difference between radical and routine innovation, since the small S & Ls bought someone else's routines.

Second, the small organizations had few accounts to open and process. If something did go wrong, it went wrong for a few accounts, not a few thousand. Any problems were therefore easy to correct. Since the problems were not significant in any of these organizations, implementation was extremely smooth.

Looking at the list of factors potentially affecting NOW account implementation, only size seems significant. It did not matter if the innovation was radical or routine; what the goals and strategy were; what the search process was like; how complex the organization was (though none were very complex and complexity was clearly associated with size); how flexible they were; who made decisions; or even how well prepared they were. Most striking is that unprepared firms implemented as well as those that were prepared, because small size allowed easy use of temporary measures until they became ready with their data processing systems. In all, the small organizations had a distinct advantage in implementing change because they had fewer accounts to put demands on their systems and because they exported many potential problems to outside vendors for whom the innovation was routine.

Appendix
Summary of Case Studies

	Radical vs. Routine Innovation	History/Unique Characteristics
First Commercial Bank	Extremely routine.	Extensive experience with checking. Undergoing concurrent restructuring. Trust, commitment to resolving conflicts between functions.
Second Commercial Bank	Very routine.	Traumatic prior experience with automatic transfers led to significant organizational learning. Professional, centralized power and control via rational procedures at holding company. Decentralized day-to-day operations.
Third Commercial Bank	Very routine.	Powerful, central leadership; strong data processing; tradition of mutual adjustment at lower levels.
First National S & L	Extremely radical.	No relevant prior experiences. Flexibility, commitment, and respect, but inability to make decisions and overcome competing interests.
Second National S & L	Very radical.	No experience that would help implement NOW accounts. Oriented toward the hierarchy. Punitive.
First Regional Bank	Routine.	NOW accounts implemented simultaneously with conversion from in-house to external data processing.
First Capitol S & L	Radical.	Managers eager to try new products, explore different market niches. Flat structure, fuzzy job descriptions.
Second Capitol S & L	Perceived as routine, though required significant new procedures.	Aggressive but conservative in risk taking.
First City Bank	Very routine.	High commercial, low retail emphasis. Dominated by chairman. Entrepreneurial and aggressive.
Second City Bank	Routine.	Most personnel with bank for 20 years or more; respect for the bank's traditions. Dominated by president.
First Neighborhood S & L	Radical.	Image of lending to inner-city. Desire to use NOW accounts to enter more middle class market niche.
Second Neighborhood S & L	Radical.	Located in older community; perceived customers as not interested in NOW accounts and other new products.

Complexity	Flexibility	Power Arrangements for Decisions
High.	Very flexible.	Policy decisions based on inputs from all levels of employees; implementation decentralized to project team and banks.
High.	Adequate.	Most decisions by top-level holding company personnel, who sold their ideas to those below.
High.	Very flexible through open middle and lower level communication.	Decisions primarily by executive vice president; considerable influence by data processing. Middle managers and lower-level staff had the opportunity to react to and advise on operational aspects.
High.	Slightly formalized, very flexible.	Before consultants—decisions made by functional officers in committee of equals; power very diffuse. During consultants' intervention—project structure. After consultants—decisions made by ranking functional officers in project teams accountable to a project director; power more concentrated.
High.	Inflexible.	Most decisions, including implementation, made by consensus within top-level committee.
High.	Flexible but unable to change in ways that were desired.	Data processing unit less powerful than the senior vice president of operations and the banks, leading to difficulties in having the data processing viewpoint acknowledged.
Moderate.	Very flexible. History of implementing policies quickly; open communication among the different levels. Fuzzy job descriptions contributed to flexibility.	Chairman made all policy decisions, retained right to make implementation decisions, but delegated much responsibility to a vice president. Officers had considerable influence through preparing proposals from which the chairman chose.
Moderate.	Extremely flexible through delayed decision-making; open, informal communication.	Decisions by small group of high-level officers; little input from below. Punitive orientation toward monitoring.
Moderate.	Very flexible.	Most power resided with chairman.
Low.	Very flexible; open, informal communication.	Decisions made by a vote of the top vice presidents and president, with president having strong influence.
Low.	Moderate, informal but little bottom up communication.	Decisions by consensus of top-level officers.
Low.	Flexibility possible; open, informal communication.	All levels and functions contributed their opinions. President and vice presidents made decisions; board approved.

(continued on next page)

	Goals and Strategy	Search Process
First Commercial Bank	Defensive. Keep all customers, particularly high-balance customers. Moderate/high minimum balance ($1,000).	Extensive external and internal search. Substantial consultation with all concerned.
Second Commercial Bank	Highly defensive: high minimum balance, very little promotion. Profit on the NOW account on its own terms. High minimum balance ($1,500).	Extensive external search; little internal search.
Third Commercial Bank	Enhance image as a large commercial bank and retain current retail customers. Aggressive promotion to current customers and advertising to business. Moderate/high minimum balance ($1,000 with variety of contingencies).	Many external sources of information but heavy reliance on internal cost estimates.
First National S & L	Extremely aggressive marketing. Low minimum balance ($200).	Extensive internal and external.
Second National S & L	Become more like a retail bank, offer more services, gain market share, enter new market segments; risk short-term losses for expected long-term profits. Aggressive promotion. Low minimum balance ($200).	Primarily standard seminars, printed materials, U.S. League of Savings Associations.
First Regional Bank	Retain current customers; make a profit on each account. Little promotion. Moderately high minimum balance ($1,000).	Relied heavily on one banking analyst but also observed actions of local large banks, read trade journals, and attended seminars.
First Capitol S & L	Conflicting goals; offer the account defensively vs. increase market share. Little promotion; price slightly higher than the aggressive savings and loans. Low minimum balance ($300).	Very extensive and early.
Second Capitol S & L	Retain current customers. Aggressive promotion. Subsequent goal to increase market share via very low price and continuing aggressive promotion. Moderately high price relative to other S & Ls. Initial minimum balance $500.	Extensive, not unusually early.
First City Bank	Break even on NOW account, offer it as service to make business customers happy. No promotion. Very high minimum balance ($2,000 minimum/$3,000 average).	Not extensive.
Second City Bank	Prevent loss of accounts and make a profit on each account; no promotion. High minimum balance ($1,500 for account/ $2,000 to accrue interest).	Reliance on easily accessible printed materials.
First Neighborhood S & L	Change their image; make a profit. Aggressive promotion. Low minimum balance ($200).	Extensive for a small institution.
Second Neighborhood S & L	Keep current customers without losing money on the accounts. Moderately aggressive; aggressive promotion given size. Low minimum balance ($300).	Limited.

Readiness	Internal Outcomes	Product/External Outcomes
Extremely well prepared; ready early.	Accurate, timely statements; no overtime; little employee stress; much organizational learning.	Lost few accounts; profitable; customers satisfied; accomplished organization's goals.
Extremely well prepared organizationally and technologically.	Very smooth implementation.	Successful; very small number of new or lost accounts.
Generally ready by January 1.	Smooth implementation; few mistakes; little employee stress; no reported organizational learning.	Current customers satisfied; NOW accounts perceived to enhance commercial image.
Crisis level of unpreparedness before consultants. Well prepared after consultants.	Great individual and organization-wide learning; high levels of employee overtime and stress; high levels of exhilaration; accurate and prompt statements.	Large number of accounts; more profitable than expected; satisfied customers; initiation into retail banking; considerable cost to hire consultants.
Not prepared technically or organizationally.	Inaccurate and late statements; employee stress and turnover; little organizational learning.	Achieved targeted number of accounts and average balances; lost customers due to dissatisfaction with service.
Moderately technically prepared; organizational routines already in place.	Moderately positive. Inaccurate statements for four months; middle managers stressed, upper and lower levels satisfied. Data processing learned how to get more power by being proactive.	Lost few accounts, though did not gain new accounts. Accounts were profitable; some regret that they did not promote harder.
Sufficiently prepared though some gaps in preparedness.	Smooth implementation; problems easily managed. Organization learned checking by hiring a banker.	Profitable. Obtained fewer accounts than desired.
Very well prepared technically and organizationally.	Very smooth implementation.	Profitable; achieved number of accounts within expected range; developed other business through the NOW account.
Very well prepared organizationally and technologically.	Very smooth implementation.	Successful; business customers happy; lost many small-balance accounts; made profit on NOW.
Low but adequate both technically and organizationally.	Smooth implementation.	Few accounts as desired; some regrets for not having a more aggressive strategy.
Very well prepared.	Smooth implementation; little organizational learning.	Fewer accounts than desired.
Very well prepared.	Smooth implementation; little organizational learning.	Exceeded goals for number and profitability of NOW accounts; regretted not attracting more.

III
New Views on Implementation

12
Factors Contributing to Successful Implementation

Our study was guided by one fundamental question—what contributes to successful implementation of innovation in organizations? So far we have described what twelve organizations experienced in implementing the NOW account. Now, we will compare these experiences to see what general clues to successful implementation exist in our data. Our concern with implications both for students and for managers of innovation continues. For students we attempt to refine the concept of innovation and link our findings with the existing literature. For managers we present the basis for viewing implementation of innovation as akin to other processes rather than a totally unprecedented phenomenon as popular writers sometimes make it out to be.

When we began this study, we expected to find at least one component that would clearly distinguish the more successful from the less successful organizations. For example, we expected that, controlling for size, organizations that attracted the highest number of accounts and served them most profitably would have employed different structures and processes than those that attracted the fewest customers and served them less profitably. We now see that such expectations were unrealistic in several ways. First, with respect to what each firm hoped to achieve, all the firms had some success; the variance was not as great as we had anticipated. Second, success could not be assessed commensurately across the organizations because they differed from each other on several important dimensions, beginning with the fact that they had different goals for the NOW account. Third, the firms differed so markedly from each other with respect to history, contemporaneous developments, and technical competencies that, at least with a sample of only twelve firms, there were far too many variables to isolate simple relationships. In short, because the firms started from different places, encountered different events during implementation, and sought and achieved different ends, it would be surprising if general correlates of success appeared.

In more abstract terms, we conclude that innovation is best understood when it is conceived as a process that is both equifinal and multifinal (Ramaprasad, 1982). A process is equifinal to the degree that there are a variety of paths to the same end state. For example, given some combination of unique starting points, systemic properties, and environmental events, organizations might achieve identical outcomes by following diverse paths.

On the other hand, a process is multifinal if two or more systems can do similar things, yet arrive at different outcomes. In this chapter, we consider the multifinal aspects; in chapter 14, the equifinal.

Multifinality—Variations in Meaning of Success

We used four criteria to evaluate implementation: (1) each organization's achievement of its own goals, (2) the costs that the organization confronted in achieving its goals, (3) the smoothness of the implementation phase, and (4) outcomes that are best labeled by-products (such as organizational learning and employee motivation that resulted from the innovation but were not specifically intended). Two other possible standards are the degree to which the goals set for the innovation were "the best" ones in an absolute sense and the extent to which the means used to implement were the best ones for achieving other objectives of the organization. Although we have no information bearing directly on these matters, our data did provide some insight about how organizations might select less than optimal goals. However, we have no way of evaluating whether what appeared to be successful implementations could have been substantially more so. What is clear, however, is that there were many ways to define success.

Organizationally Specific Criteria

The twelve organizations defined the success of their NOW accounts in diverse ways. At the extreme, some wanted to lose some checking accounts and others wanted to get as many accounts as they could. As we saw, the banks sought mainly to defend themselves against losing large customers, paying interest on money that previously was "free" to them, and dealing with troublesome small accounts. However, even among the banks (including individual banks within the same holding company), objectives varied. For example, Third Commercial Bank wanted to use the NOW account to send the message "We are a large bank, too" to current and potential constituents. Generally for the savings and loan associations, the primary measure of success was attracting a large number of accounts—even if, as in the case of Second National, it meant short-run losses. Not all the S & Ls shared this goal. Most notably, First Capitol S & L, because real estate ventures were much more important here than at other S & Ls, was quite defensive and, in fact, almost did not offer the NOW account.

Costs of Implementation

Although we recognize that organizations differ in their objectives, we suggest that it may still be useful to assess implementation partially through absolute standards. One of the most important factors for managers is cost. It is obvious that there are costs associated with implementation, but little research on innovation has been concerned with them.

Our study suggests that analyzing the relationship between costs of implementation and other organization characteristics may be useful. For example, size was positively associated with costs of implementation. For the smaller organizations, implementation was not expensive in terms of either staff time or abnormal expenditures on consultants, additional staff, technology, and materials. On the other hand, generally the larger organizations found implementing costly. The high cost of the consultants at First National S & L was the most obvious expense, but even routine innovators incurred substantial costs. Executives and middle managers devoted considerable time to searching, planning, and meetings to educate and persuade. Materials had to be developed; staff had to be trained. Even at Third Commercial Bank, where a highly centralized and nonbureaucratic approach was used, special meetings and training sessions were employed. At First Commercial, a great deal of time was spent in discussion at all levels.

Our point is not to suggest that the large organizations were somehow less efficient; perhaps time spent per capita was no greater than in the small organizations. However, they were more complex and doing many more things; there were more specialists and more line personnel to deal with. Nor are we suggesting that the meetings were wasteful. What we do wish to suggest is that measures of implementation success must take into account a full array of costs. While we do not have data to show what the relative costs were, the cases demonstrate the need to collect such data in order to evaluate alternative approaches to implementation. For example, we viewed the organic processes at First Commercial as extremely successful; but if we had some way to estimate the full costs and could compare them with the incremental benefits that they may have produced, the relative advantages of the organic system might be diminished significantly. Or we might discover that their costs were no greater than those of less successful organizations or that the long-term benefits outweighed the costs. These concerns require further investigation.

Two other implications of this argument, beyond the obvious ones for researchers attempting to conceptualize successful implementation, deserve mention. First, once variables such as cost are included, the link between innovation research and organization theory will become stronger, because they will consider the same set of dependent variables including total costs and efficiency. Second, once costs are factored in, managers may be in a better position to see the importance of preparing their organization for innovation ahead of time. As we argue later, investments in the organization prior to innovation may be far more cost effective than an equal pool of resources spent during implementation.

Smoothness of Implementation

Usually, other things being equal, the less the implementation process disturbs other aspects of the organization, internally and externally, the smoother and more successful the implementation can be said to be. While there is overlap between the costs of implementation and smoothness, analytically it is useful to separate them. For the most part, the elements of smoothness are less tangible and/or less apt to be measured in terms of dollars or resources devoted directly to the innovation.

We found a number of dimensions useful in describing the smoothness of implementation. One indicator of smoothness was a low number of people leaving the organization because they were unhappy with the way things were done. Smoothness also was indicated by low levels of employee stress, unresolved tension, and conflict. Damaged relationships with customers, suppliers, and other groups outside the firm indicated an implementation that was not smooth. Finally, failure to complete the work on schedule and systems that produced many errors indicated less smooth and hence less successful implementation.

Although smoothness is a rather imprecise construct at this point, and we have indicated only a few of its components, the criteria it suggests are relevant for defining success, and therefore are both theoretically and practically important. Most organizations are doing many other things while they are engaged in a specific innovation. Other things being equal, reducing the disruption of these other routines and objectives is a positive feature of an implementation program. Of course, the degree of impact will differ depending on the nature of the required interdependence (Thompson, 1967). Some innovations may have only a pooled interdependence with other elements in the organization, whereas others may be related more intensively— sequential or reciprocal interdependence. Still, the point remains—measurements of implementation success need to include the effects of the innovation elsewhere in the organization. To date, little research has done so.

By-products

A fourth criterion concerns other indirect effects of the innovation within the organization. Innovation is part of an organization's ongoing history; whether it succeeds or fails, it changes the organization. Many of these by-products can be classified under the headings of organizational learning and impact on employees' motivation.

Organizational Learning. To some degree, our results support the intuitively appealing proposition that the more radical the innovation, the more likely individuals are to learn and the more the organization as a whole will have wider competencies and perspectives. At the individual level, people at several of the S & Ls learned new vocabulary and behaviors, while coming to think more like bankers. The most dramatic evidence of organization learning was at First National S & L, where even before the consultants arrived, managers reported they had learned a great deal about the NOW account and about banking in general. Once the consultants entered, managers reported learning more than just how to run the NOW account. They imitated the consultants' project management style in managing other projects and were confident that they had learned so much, that if anything like the NOW account were to be introduced in the future, they could handle it. Project management represented a change in the patterns of influence people saw as legitimate to accomplish interdepartmental tasks.

However, radicalness did not always produce such individual learning. In fact, little or no individual learning was reported at some S & Ls. Whether or not individual learning was reported seemed to depend on the process the firm chose for implementing and hence on how radicalness was mapped into the organization. For example, while both First National S & L and Second National S & L sought the same ends and faced rather similar demands, endogenous events produced different amounts of learning. The crisis at First National S & L resulted in extraordinary responses, including the very visible and effective one of hiring the consultants. At Second National, the crisis was not perceived as strongly, no new models were added, and less learning was reported.

Similarly, at the small and medium S & Ls, little personal learning was reported because of the way the innovation was introduced and the existing nature of the firm. At the two small S & Ls, radical innovation produced little in the way of perceptions of change; no crisis was perceived and no extraordinary responses were taken. At Second Capitol, two aspects of the approach to implementation made an objectively radical innovation seem routine. First, as with the other medium and small savings and loan associations, Second Capitol purchased all of the necessary services externally. This meant that little learning of new procedures or technologies was required, particularly since they designed a product compatible with the services available to them. However, some S & Ls bought external services and still perceived NOW accounts as radical. The critical difference appeared to be Second Capitol's previous pattern of unusual flexibility, here a willingness to reverse decisions as often as necessary based on continually updated information, especially from customer-contact people. Few procedures were routinized; therefore changing did not require agonizing shifts that uprooted long-standing routines. (This is not to say that Second Capitol did not have any long-standing routines, but rather that change was an accepted, though sometimes frustrating, way of life for this organization.)

The means used at First Capitol resulted in greater organizational competence but again, little individual learning. Here, the outsider who was brought in became part of the organization and developed a department to run the operation. Thus, the organization as a whole did have new capacities, but because so few changes were required of other participants, little learning was perceived. In sum, the ways that organizations define and respond to implementing a particular radical innovation, not just the objective qualities of the innovation, influence the type and degree of organizational learning. It also should be noted that routine innovation produced learning. There was, for example, evidence of job expansion and learning at the middle levels of Second Commercial Bank and Third Commercial Bank and, of course, learning from the automatic transfer at First Commercial.

When learning is considered to be increased competence of the total organization, both radical and routine innovation are associated with it. As expected, radical innovation almost always increased the competencies of the S & Ls, sometimes by changing the way managers thought about their business and sometimes by adding the skills and orientations of new employees. However, routine innovation could spawn similar outcomes, as the experiences of two of the large banks reveal.

The experiences of Second Commercial Bank with the automatic transfer—a routine innovation by our definition—resulted in considerable learning; the project management framework that managers learned resembled those that managers at First National S & L reported in connection with the NOW account. In addition, significant learning from the NOW account was reported at First Commercial. Recall that the holding company was introducing a new structure in anticipation of future requirements. The NOW account provided examples of possible future problems and a chance to observe how the new structure would cope with them. The bank presidents reported that this experience helped them to understand the new structure and to become comfortable with it. In essence, the innovation helped the organization learn by legitimizing parallel changes in organizational processes and structures.

Finally, both routine and radical innovation helped many of the organizations to discover organizational deficiencies. These discoveries were particularly noticeable in the data processing area and were not restricted to radical innovation. Both Second Commercial Bank (with the automatic transfer) and First Regional Bank experienced problems similar to those of the large S & Ls. Several organizations dealt with these problems by replacing key members of the current staff. (As Nystrom and Starbuck, 1984, would have it, sometimes learning requires unlearning; one way of unlearning is to remove previously key people.) In addition, organizations discovered structural and communications problems while implementing. Again, Second Commercial Bank's experience with the automatic transfer and First National S & L's total experience with the NOW provided the clearest examples. In both cases, high-level managers discovered that either important information was not getting to them and/or they were discounting information inappropriately. Comparing just these two organizations reveals some interesting similarities. In both cases, significant personnel changes in data processing took place and more influence and resources were allocated to data processing. Implementing an innovation helped the organization discover deficiencies and correct them, thereby avoiding problems that were quite likely to occur in the future.

Overall then, we see that both routine and radical innovation can result in either little or great amounts of learning, and in either similar or different types of learning. Using the ideas of Downs and Mohr (1976), such a mixture of outcomes is expected. The effects of the innovation will be more a function of the nature of the requirements members of the organization perceive than of the objective routineness or radicalness of the innovation. In addition, the patterns we observed point to the importance of considering the multiple ways organizations learn—adding and subtracting personnel, using consultants, creating and staffing new departments, developing current personnel, altering influence patterns, and legitimizing new structures and ways of thinking. At First National S & L in particular, people began to think of themselves differently; they were more like bankers than before. These conclusions point to the importance of a broad perspective of organization learning of the type advanced by Duncan and Weiss (1979). Organization learning reflects more than the aggregate of individual knowledge; it reflects changes in the nature of knowledge that is accepted as a basis for action: increments in individual knowledge, removal of unwanted perspectives, addition of people with new perspectives and skills, and changes in ways of thinking about the requirements of the business and how to manage it.

Participant Motivation and Satisfaction. Other possible by-products of implementation include changes in the motivation and satisfaction of employees. Our results generally paralleled the findings on organizational learning. In only a few cases were any changes reported, and high levels of satisfaction and motivation were widely reported in only two firms—First Commercial Bank and First National S & L. The greater emphasis these two firms gave to employee involvement and commitment and the extension of these traditions to implementing the NOW account seemed to be associated with these differences. Conversely, the only report of consistent dissatisfaction was at Second National S & L, which employed rather hierarchically driven procedures and had a punitive orientation toward employees both historically and for the NOW account.

The only other reports of significant dissatisfaction were at the middle levels of First Regional Bank; these feelings were related to managers' inability to influence top management and each other on certain critical matters. At the other organizations, the innovations did not seem to be associated with any special motivation or satisfaction. Perhaps for a variety of reasons they were perceived to be a nonevent, were handled by a new unit, or involved few changes.

Overall, in the few cases where individual learning was reported, employees saw themselves as confronted with new demands, while managers acknowledged the importance of employee inputs and needs in meeting those demands. Positive benefits were absent both where no new demands were perceived and where they were perceived but where employees' opinions and needs seemed to be discounted by managers. In somewhat similar fashion, the level of involvement generated by past practices and the extension of these efforts to the NOW account seemed positively associated with employee satisfaction. These patterns are consistent with the conclusions of advocates of organic structures and participative management that high levels of involvement contribute to learning and motivation. However, because the firms simply extended their normal approaches to the NOW account, these patterns cannot be interpreted as showing that a shift to more involvement during the implementation process alone would produce such benefits.

Conclusion

The varieties of objectives and criteria mean that evaluation of implementation needs to proceed from the view that it is a multifinal process. The multifinality we encountered complicated our search for clues to successful implementation. Moreover, as our discussion in chapter 13 of the contingency factors will show, there are many possible explanations for the differences and similarities we found in both approaches and results. Therefore, we do not assert that we have established generalized causal relationships. However, we still believe we progressed toward our objective. Our major purpose was not to establish causation; our objective was to discover clues to success.

Given this objective, the large number of variables operating to make each organization unique could turn out to be an asset. If, in view of all this diversity, a uniform process could be distilled that seemed to be associated with successful implementation across all the cases, one might expect that the process was a robust one. In fact, we think we found some of the essential components of such a process.

Summary of Successes and Failures

Combining these four criteria for success, we have classified the twelve firms into four categories of success. These are shown in table 12–1. Our classifications involve considerable judgment because goals differ, and because the firms implemented NOW accounts in qualitatively different ways, so their successes or failures were qualitatively different. There were no clear configurations of variables distinguishing the more successful from the less. Ordering organizations along a continuum of success in implementation masks some of the qualitative distinctions and is subject to errors of judgment because the success of some of the organizations was easier to categorize than the success of others. Still, commonalities can be found and they are helpful for understanding what organizational structures and processes were present in the more successful banks and savings and loan associations.

Very Successful

Several banks and one savings and loan association fell into the "very successful" category. The easiest to categorize was First Commercial Bank.

Table 12–1
Classification of Firms on the Basis of Degree of Success in Implementation

Very successful
First Commercial Bank
Second Commercial Bank
Third Commercial Bank
Second Capitol S & L
First City Bank

Moderately successful
First National S & L (after consultants)
Second City Bank
First Neighborhood S & L
Second Neighborhood S & L

Moderately unsuccessful
First Regional Bank
First Capitol S & L

Unsuccessful
First National S & L (before consultants)
Second National S & L

Note: The ordering *within* classes is not intended to reflect a ranking of success.

This organization was ready to implement a month before the NOW account became legal. Employees were knowledgeable and reported high levels of satisfaction and no major stress. The data processing system was virtually error free after a week of operation, so statements were accurate and timely. The organization learned from the innovation, even though it was routine. Its strategic goals were accomplished; implementation was clearly successful. Second and Third Commercial Banks were also successful. Second Commercial had previously been unsuccessful with automatic transfers but had almost all the positive outcomes that First Commercial had with NOW accounts, although personnel reported less learning and there was less satisfaction than at First Commercial.

Third Commercial had somewhat more problems with data processing errors and customer complaints, but these were minor and handled quickly and easily. Overall, it was similar to the other large banks in other measures of success, and therefore categorized as very successful.

Implementation at First City Bank was also highly successful. Data processing was virtually error free, little stress was put on the organization, and strategic goals were met. No significant organizational learning was reported, though.

Finally, implementation at Second Capitol was highly successful. Although it attracted fewer accounts than managers hoped, it did so because the original strategy required a moderately high minimum balance, rather than because there were implementation difficulties. Further, Second Capitol moved very rapidly to modify its strategy to increase the number of accounts. The data processing system produced few errors, and statements were timely. Employees liked the product and felt little stress.

Moderately Successful

Second City Bank and three of the savings and loan associations were moderately successful. While they had difficulties of various sorts, they were able to overcome those difficulties quite well.

Second City Bank deliberately chose a data processing package that was unavailable until three months after NOW accounts became legal. The result was that interest computations and statements had to be done manually. In addition, some employees complained about not being well enough informed and prepared. At the same time, accounts were processed accurately and on time; strategic goals were met.

Both small S & Ls were moderately successful. They did not meet their strategic goals, but they processed accounts on time and with a minimum of errors. Employees seemed to manage the innovation with little stress and no overtime, but little organizational learning was reported. Their slower reaction to the number of accounts they attracted put them in the moderately successful category, compared to the categorization of Second Capitol as very successful.

Finally, *in the end*, First National S & L fell into this category, even though we have also put it in the unsuccessful category. At considerable cost and with the help of outside consultants, First National S & L was highly successful in accomplishing its strategic goals, attracting more NOW accounts than any other financial institution in the state. The data processing system was up and running in time and provided mostly accurate and timely statements. Employees were exhilarated. However, there were many standard operating procedures still not finalized when NOW accounts were first offered in January 1981, and employees reported high levels of stress.

Moderately Unsuccessful

Two organizations were moderately unsuccessful in implementation. First Regional Bank's data processing systems were not ready and there was considerable unresolved conflict at middle-management levels. However, people at the top and bottom of the organization were satisfied with the process and the firm accomplished its original strategic goals, though managers had some serious regrets about not attempting to increase their market share.

First Capitol S & L implemented smoothly for the most part, but a technical problem caused embarrassing errors. It failed to meet its strategic goals, largely because the strategic decision process bred competition and delay among top managers. Thus, the strategic decisions were not entirely consonant with the explicit goals. Implementation pressures were great, because the organization was so late in starting the process. Once it began implementation, though, it was effective in defining the standard operating procedures, preparing line employees, and getting statements out.

Unsuccessful

The two large S & Ls fell into the "unsuccessful" category, a finding that is not surprising given the circumstances. First National S & L was headed for complete failure before bringing in the consultants. At the root of the problems was the almost nonexistent data processing capability. Moreover, managers were unable to develop this capability due to internal conflicts and lack of expertise. The absence of a data processing framework fanned out to many other areas, so many operating decisions had not been made two weeks prior to NOW accounts being offered. Employees were highly stressed and overworked. Had the consultants not been successful, First National would not have been able to overcome these deficiencies in time. Moreover, purchasing consultants' services made implementation very expensive.

Finally, Second National S & L was least successful in implementing NOW accounts. Although it surpassed its goals for NOW accounts, the firm lost many customers and continued to have numerous dissatisfied customers for many months after first implementation. Moreover, employees were still stressed and overworked eighteen months after initial implementation and data processing problems continued.

Conclusion

Looking at the pattern of success, implementation of NOW accounts was clearly least problematic for the large banks and most problematic for the large savings and loan associations. The small and medium institutions generally but not always fell into the two middle categories.

Successful Implementation: Four Requirements

The twelve cases revealed a variety of ways that organizations can successfully implement a new product. Even though this was a borrowed innovation in a mature industry (albeit one more turbulent than in the recent past), there were wide variations in objectives, search, technical and social readiness, implementation approaches and problems, and outcomes.

Within all this diversity, though, successful implementation efforts had several common features that were different from efforts of the less successful implementers. And, while there is some confirmation of existing theory about innovation in organizations, the cases reveal some novel patterns as well. In short, even though at the concrete level, the process is accurately described as being both multifinal and equifinal, at a more abstract level, certain generalizations are possible.

The Larger Firms

First consider the larger firms—the large and medium-sized ones. (The small organizations have a different pattern that will be treated separately.) Four characteristics were present in every successful and moderately successful large or medium organization: The three large banks, First National S & L (after consultants), and Second Capitol. They are flexibility, concentration of power, access to technical competence, and attention to the views of those directly responsible for implementation. Not only did these four characteristics emerge from interorganizational comparisons; they also appeared to make a difference within individual organizations.

Flexibility. Flexibility was manifested in modifications of decisions and patterns of communication to permit mutual adjustment, and in supple role boundaries and the ability to transcend precise job descriptions in order to get the job done. Flexibility, however it was gained, characterized the successful innovators. Lateral and/or upward communication was the major component of this flexibility, because it allowed information about a wide spectrum of unanticipated problems to flow to the people who had the skill and authority to make changes.

The contribution of flexibility to implementation in our study is consistent with the findings of Beyer and Trice (1978) and contradicts previous conclusions including those of Zaltman, Duncan, and Holbek (1973) and Tornatzky and Klein (1982) who have viewed implementation as a process of carrying out predefined policies or programs. The organizations that implemented most successfully in this study demonstrated clearly that even in routine innovation, the implementation phase required continual redefinition of the policy as well as tactics for implementation. For example, many of the problems at Second Commercial Bank (automatic transfer), First National S & L, First Regional Bank, and First Capitol S & L were associated with traditions that hindered mutual adjustment across departmental or hierarchical boundaries. Successful implementation at these organizations, when it occurred after initial failures, was also characterized by flexibility. Overall, successful implementation almost always was associated with such flexibility.

It is important to note, however, that the sources of flexibility were not the same in all cases. In First Commercial Bank and Second Capitol S & L, traditions of seeking information from a wide spectrum of organizational members and unconstrained communication patterns were important; by contrast, at Second and Third Commercial Banks, the adjustments were orchestrated more centrally and formally via project plans and managerial control. Also, some important sources of mutual adjustment and flexibility at Third Commercial Bank were due to informal patterns that lower-level participants had evolved to help each other. Thus, flexibility is necessary if the organization is to adapt successfully to the surprises it encounters as it tries to effect a new product or procedure, but the methods of achieving flexibility are many.

Flexibility alone was not sufficient, though. First National S & L, for example, had long-standing patterns of informal communication and ad hoc adjustments. Yet, it was only when some sort of project structure and redistribution of power took place that the patterns of open communication and flexibility proved productive for radical innovation.

Concentration of Power. Concentration of power somewhere in the organization was also necessary to achieve successful implementation. Traditional wisdom from structural theories of adaptation and change (Burns and Stalker, 1961; Thompson, 1967) holds that power should be pushed down to lower levels, to those who deal directly with the environmental element causing the need for change. First National S & L showed us that power could be too diffuse, while two large banks, Second Commercial and Third Commercial, provided examples of successful implementation with power concentrated in the hands of a senior vice president. Yet the highly successful patterns at First Commercial Bank concentrated considerable power in the hands of a project manager at a level below vice president.

Taken together, these various success stories show that it is *not* necessary to push power down, formally. Although pushing power down as First Commercial did was associated with some beneficial outcomes, such as high employee commitment and rapid mutual adjustment, appropriate alignments of power were achieved in other ways. For example, employees at Third Commercial made adjustments across functional lines, because they knew they were accountable to the top for any problems that resulted from not making those adjustments.

In fact, difficulties resulting from a failure to move decision-making power to lower levels were minor compared to the problems associated with First National's failure to concentrate power at a level where implementation policy could be defined. Equals with competing interests could not reach agreement, so no action was taken. In some cases, such a stalemate can be overcome by commitment to common organizational goals, as Burns and Stalker (1961) and Ouchi (1980) have suggested. Considering that First National S & L had a clearly defined and familylike culture, it seems unlikely that commitment to the organization alone can be counted on to direct actions toward common goals. At First National, something else was needed to move the organization. The stalemate was ultimately overcome by the concentration of power at the top through the consultants and the subsequent delegation of that power to an appropriate project team.

First Capitol S & L also demonstrated the importance of some concentration of power for implementation. Traditionally, decisions were made by the CEO alone. In the case of the NOW account, though, he was completely removed from the process until he made his final policy decision. Meanwhile, vice presidents had different views and each vied to have his position selected by the CEO. Because there was no concentration of power during the design phase, energy was diverted from achieving a speedy mandate for action. Once a strategy for the NOW account had been decided, the CEO concentrated power by putting one vice president in charge of NOW accounts. From that point, implementation proceeded smoothly and efficiently.

Organizations that were less successful also had concentrated power. At Second National S & L, it was concentrated in the hands of vice presidents, with an understanding that the vice president of savings was responsible for implementation. At First Regional Bank, it was concentrated in the hands of the vice president of operations. Obviously, concentration of power is not enough. We have already shown that flexibility was one of the other factors required. There were still others.

Access to Technical Competence. Technical readiness and access to technical competence constituted a third set of characteristics shared by those who implemented successfully. Competence to introduce and manage the innovation had two components. First, a technical side had to do with the substance of the innovation. The organization had to know what technology to use, how to use it, and how to judge its effectiveness in using it. Second, a social side had to do with the ability of the organization to activate and coordinate its resources. An organization needs to be able to divide the labor in appropriate ways, to motivate performance, and to integrate activities to achieve desired outcomes.

Due to some combination of previous activities and anticipation of future ones, several of the routine innovators had both elements of readiness. First Commercial Bank had bought a software package that included NOW accounts five years prior to the legalization of the account. Moreover, all of the large banks were experienced in data processing after years of processing their own checking accounts and selling their data processing services to smaller banks and savings and loan associations in the area. In contrast, the large S & Ls were facing a radical innovation of major proportions. Compared to that of the medium and small firms, the volume anticipated by the large S & Ls made it attractive to do their own data processing; and in contrast to the banks, they had had no prior need to purchase demand deposit software. Therefore, not only did they lack previous experience with any software that would have included routines for the NOW account, but they had small data processing units. The consultants brought the necessary expertise to First National S & L, while Second National S & L did not achieve the required technical proficiency. After an unsatisfactory attempt at purchasing data processing services, managers at Second National decided to provide their own and struggled to achieve internal data processing skills. The medium savings and loan associations were also encountering the need for new types of technical competence. Managers at First Capitol S & L attempted to manage their technical unpreparedness by purchasing data processing services. To their dismay, the service they chose did not provide the level of competence they needed, so they eventually went to in-house processing. Managers at Second Capitol S & L, in contrast, were able to purchase the technical competence they required.

The lack of technical readiness was self-perpetuating. Organizations lacking technical readiness were unable to recognize these inadequacies.

Managers did not know what questions to ask, how to ask them, and whom to ask. In addition, the technical people in the organization lacked the ability to recognize what the requirements would be. It seemed to take a crisis to produce a corrective response.

A second type of competence, ability to handle what respondents called the "business" issues, was also important. After all, the organizations were in the financial business, and knowledge and skills particular to banking (such as customer relations and strategy) were also important. Obviously, neither of these competencies alone would suffice—success depended on the integration of these different skills. For the most part, successful implementation occurred when the technical resources were available and simultaneously guided by the "business issues" such as customer responses. The mechanisms that enabled diverse expertise to be applied effectively when and where needed constitute the second general form of competence—social competence.

Social competence is derived from some combination of personal skills in working with others and structures that aid integration. We suggest that social competence was one aspect of what Lawrence and Lorsch (1967b) observed in high-performing firms that were able to integrate highly differentiated units. In our study, social competence appeared to be one very important element that distinguished the implementation successes at First Commercial, Second Commercial (for the NOW account), and Third Commercial Banks and First National S & L (after the consultants entered) from the problems at Second Commercial Bank (automatic transfer), First Regional Bank, First National S & L (before the consultants), and Second National S & L. As we saw it, this synergy was produced in a variety of ways—through centralization at high levels (as at Third Commercial Bank), through an organic process (as at First Commercial Bank), by a project structure coordinated at high levels (as at Second Commercial Bank), and by being introduced by the consultants at First National S & L. Some of the greatest successes (First and Third Commercial Banks and First National S & L, after the consultants) occurred through a form of constrained centralization—power was concentrated in the hands of a technical specialist who understood the business issues. Whether this finding is because technical issues were especially problematic for NOW accounts, because technical people in the successful organizations were particularly attuned to business issues, or because of political processes within individual firms, cannot be determined here since we studied only one innovation so most of what we know about each organization was revealed in connection with its approach to this innovation. In any case, this finding gives some support to the emphasis given in the ambidextrous model to coherent direction during implementation, although the ambidextrous model sees the coherent direction as less flexible and more predetermined than we found to be the case.

Many of the most serious problems seemed to occur when social competence was lacking and, as a result, a representative of the technical issues lacked appropriate resources and/or influence. First Regional Bank provided an example of these problems even for routine innovation.

What constitutes social readiness, of course, depends upon the requirements of the innovation. For example, innovations could be classified according to the degree of differentiation and integration required; organizations could be classified according to their initial standing on these dimensions. Such initial classifications could be used as a basis for predicting success as well as for examining what processes organizations use to cope with varied degrees of fit between structure and innovation requirements. Some innovations (such as the NOW account at the S & Ls) may require that a particular organization develop a shorter and more uniform time orientation. Other innovations may demand that some organizations adopt longer and more diverse time orientations. There is no reason to assume that these two changes require the same approach within the same organization, much less the same approach for different organizations. Social readiness must be assessed so as to reflect the ability or an organization to match its influence processes to meet idiosyncrasies. Future research needs to get closer to the social and political processes that determine why some people and some perspectives come to exert different degrees of influence over the direction of the innovation. Such research might help to provide one set of secondary attributes on which, following Tornatzky and Klein (1982), theory could be built.

More generally, conceptualized in this manner, readiness may lead to recognition of two distinct approaches that successful innovators may pursue. On the one hand, some firms may follow a homogeneous course and select innovations that have similar requirements, such as long time orientations. On the other hand, organizations may select innovations according to some "absolute" criterion (such as profitability) and consequently experience contradictory pulls from the diverse requirements of the innovations they attempt. (For example, some innovations may require longer time orientation than others.) These firms will in essence be engaged in serial radical innovation and constantly need to build new sources of technical and social readiness. However, it is important to note that even the homogeneous innovations may face different requirements over time. Moreover, experience with heterogeneous innovations may result in a generalized competence for innovating. For example, as managers become experienced with a particular form of innovation, they may develop routines for even radical innovation (such as adding a new, quasi-autonomous unit for each new effort). Whereas establishing this approach initially may have required a strong leader or a very decentralized structure, running it may have quite different requirements.

In sum, social as well as technical readiness is important for implementation success. However, what constitutes readiness depends upon the nature of the innovation and the requirements that it presents for a particular organization. There are a variety of paths to achieve technical and/ or social readiness, depending on where the organization has been, is, and wants to go. A taxonomy of requirements and a taxonomy of states of being might foster theory to be built in the manner suggested by Tornatzky and Klein (1982).

Listening to Staff. Attention to the views of those directly responsible for implementation was the fourth characteristic of the successful implementers. Support for this assertion came from two types of evidence: reports of success linked to its presence and reports of problems linked to its absence.

The significance of attention to the views of those responsible for implementing was clear throughout the experiences of First Commercial Bank and Second Capitol S & L. There was also some evidence of this in Second and Third Commercial Banks, although the information flows in these two seemed to be somewhat more constrained than at the previous two firms. Conversely, inattention to various perspectives led to problems. In particular, at Second Commercial Bank (with the automatic transfer), First Regional Bank, First National S & L (prior to the consultants), Second National S & L, and First Capitol S & L, there were instances of failure to be responsive to signals from specific departments. Second National S & L stands out as being particularly impervious to feedback from the ranks. In several of these cases, the problems were similar; the time and resource requirements were not given appropriate weight in overall planning. Moreover, in two firms, Second Commercial Bank (automatic transfer versus the NOW account) and First National S & L (preconsultants versus postconsultants), readjustment of the information flows to give more weight to messages from certain groups was associated with substantial improvements in implementation.

The Small Organizations and the Four Requirements

Through all stages of the innovation, the small organizations relied on informal processes. The simple structure of these organizations allowed direct supervision and mutual adjustment (Mintzberg, 1979) to serve as adequate coordinating mechanisms. Implementation relied heavily on interpersonal, informal communications; there was little evidence of any formalized processes that would be expected of mechanistic structures. Yet, given their goals, all of these organizations innovated successfully—their objectives were achieved and few problems of any kind were reported.

The small firms were qualitatively different from the larger ones, as Tornatzky et al. (1983) indicated is often the case. However, it is worth noting that for the most part, they shared the attributes that we propose are important for implementation success. Flexibility was present in all of the small organizations—they all changed at least one major aspect of policy or implementation. Their small size made mutual adjustment easy, and the mutual adjustment contributed to flexibility. Power was concentrated at the top. Technical expertise was obtained through purchase of software or a data processing service to which they adapted, rather than trying to adapt the software to their requirements. Further, the limited number of accounts made it easy to compensate for technical failures. The importance of the fourth attribute, attention to the views of those charged with implementation, was not as clearly demonstrated by the small firms. Little evidence that attention was given to those implementing was reported in these small organizations. Of course, the influence of technical people was less critical; the absolute demands on these systems were not great and the process was not complex. Perhaps an even more important reason that evidence of such attention was not found was that those who made the decisions were either the same people as, or were very close physically and organizationally to, the implementers. Thus for example, customer reactions could be directly known by top managers. In a sense, integration was an intraindividual act; it took place in people's minds and hence left few traces for an outside observer to see.

These four characteristics were the heart of successful implementation in the large and medium organizations we studied. None of them alone accounted for success; the less successful organizations had one or two of these characteristics. However, only the successful implementers had all of them. In addition, with one possible exception, these four processes also characterized implementation at the four smaller successful organizations.

Ironically, sometimes having one attribute may make it more difficult to have one of the others. For example, the second attribute speaks of the value of concentrating power whereas the fourth attribute points to the importance of influence from diverse sources. We postulate that while successful implementers are apt to have all four attributes, there will be differences among them with respect to how these competing requirements are managed. In some organizations, the process may be sequential—the firm can do one and then another. More important, however, we are not asserting that any of these attributes must be maximized. Rather, we are asserting that all play an important role and some amount of all four is needed. We expect that the patterns and means through which they are obtained will vary across organizations, and that among the successful implementers such differences and patterns may be associated with different degrees of success. At this point, all we assert is that these are four clues to success; more detective work is required before the clues can be assembled into a complete scenario.

The Design Phase

Although the four attributes and the major emphasis of our research center on implementation, we did collect a good deal of information about the design phase. One question this information allowed us to pursue was: Would organic structures and processes be superior during the design stage while mechanistic structures and processes would be better during implementation? Contrary to existing theories that suggest the need for organic structures during the early stages of innovation, we found that the design process at seven of the eight large and medium firms was centralized at high levels in the hierarchy, and that in most cases the results were positive. Only First Commercial Bank seems to give substantial support to traditional theory; and all things considered, it was perhaps the most successful and also the most organic early on. The design process was orchestrated centrally, but the firm's tradition of consulting all relevant parties was followed in developing the new product. However, it is important to note that the emerging product was similar to that of the other large banks and conformed to the approach advocated by opinion leaders in the banking community. Therefore, although a different process might have led First Commercial Bank to another decision, it seems unlikely. In other words, the organic process resulted in the same type of product as developed by other organizations. Thus, at least for this innovation, the design process was handled quite successfully either by one or a very few individuals at high levels in the firm's hierarchy or by a centrally orchestrated search that drew openly and heavily on inputs from many levels and units within the firm.

The process used during the design phase did have important consequences nonetheless. For this innovation, and perhaps other borrowed ones, achieving a "meshing" or "fit" with the organizational strategies and other activities appeared to be important during the design phase. Two aspects of fit are especially relevant to analysis of implementation of innovation. The first we term "consistency;" it refers to the relationship among the means used to design and implement with existing structures, processes, and other characteristics of the organization. The second aspect we call "fit." It concerns the degree to which the methods and systems used are consistent with the requirements for getting the tasks accomplished. Our data revealed much more about consistency than about fit.

For the most part, achieving consistency with the existing fabric appeared to be a major concern during the design phase, particularly for routine innovation. Consistency was accomplished predominantly through centralization at high levels in the organization, in combination with a pattern of consultation that was typical and expected in each particular organization. Centralization seemed to fit the task requirements for searching successfully, advancing a defensive strategy (one aimed mainly at preventing the loss of business), and developing a product consistent with other organization objectives ("commonizing"—creating products common to all banks). As always, however, many specifics limit the generalization of such an argument; three qualifications are most important. First, because it was a borrowed innovation, centralized search was feasible. Second, organization members from the presidents of the individual banks on down expected leadership from holding company executives on such issues. Third, the process used was quite consistent with past practices—high degrees of consultation and participation at First Commercial Bank, meetings of the presidents with rather limited influence at Second Commercial Bank and First Regional Bank, and decisions heavily influenced by one person at Third Commercial Bank. Because none of the routine innovators deviated from existing routines (or, in the case of First Commercial, from routines being introduced for other purposes), we cannot determine how critical the consistency with existing routines was. Intuitively, it seems reasonable to assume that in a complex interdependent system that is working well in most respects, it is best to design routine innovations to minimize impact on other subunits. Therefore, we speculate that, other things being equal, the more a routine innovation is consistent with existing or expected procedures, the more effective it is apt to be. If these procedures are centralized, a centralized process may be quite satisfactory.

Our findings, then, revealed that decentralization during the design phase was unnecessary for successful innovation. While such results appear to be at variance with a portion of the Zaltman et al. (1973) and Duncan (1976) ambidextrous model, it is quite possible that, despite the apparent concentration of power, the processes we reported were in fact flexible. For one thing, we found little evidence of formalization at this stage. Following Mintzberg (1979), we argue that simple structures with their high concentration of power at the top can be very effective for tasks with modest complexity (tasks whose information-processing requirements are simple enough that "one mind" can process it). They also can be very flexible. In short, one way to achieve the four requirements was to revert to a simple structure within a larger structure. If the person in charge knew how to access the technical competence and the concerns of actors in key roles, the simple structure like arrangements allowed for the needed flexibility and concentration of power.

However, there is a major caveat. Recall, we studied a borrowed innovation. The design process did not demand enormous complexity or sophisticated information. In essence, it was a task well suited to a simple, centralized process—the type of process Mintzberg (1979) argued is performed optimally by a simple structure. Nevertheless, although most of these organizations were large complex systems, they used a form analogous to a simple structure to design the NOW account.

Conclusion

This chapter is far more complex than the one we wanted to write originally. In fact, the complexity is a direct outcome of our approach; our effort to understand a few organizations in depth yielded many apparently unique factors. Perhaps if we had included a few more organizations, more systematic patterns would have emerged. On the other hand, more elements of multifinality might have emerged as well. Overall, the complexity is consistent with the previous literature summarized in chapter 1. Organizational innovation is contingent on many variables. While in some ways, contingency theories can become so ad hoc that they are poor substitutes for sound theories, these variables must be known and described before better theory can be built. In the next chapter, we treat some of the contingency factors that seemed to have the most important effects on implementation in the firms we studied.

13
Contingency Factors

I n Chapter 12, we examined the multifinal aspects of the implementation of NOW accounts. In this chapter we consider the equifinal aspects.

To label a process "equifinal," there must be multiple paths for achieving the same end state. Among other things, equifinality implies that the consequences of a given act depend upon the state of other variables in and around a system. These other variables we call contingency factors. Chapter 1 highlighted some contingency factors that previous research found affected innovation. In this chapter we treat the contingency factors that were particularly important in the firms we investigated.

Implementing Routine versus Radical Innovation

Routine Innovation

Achieving Consistency. We have shown the general patterns for all twelve organizations. Despite some rather clear similarities, there were differences between the radical and routine innovators. In designing and implementing the NOW account, managers at the four largest banks were routine innovators and gave considerable attention to meshing the product and procedures with existing patterns of relationships with member banks, correspondent banks, and customers, as well as with overall strategy. In chapter 12, we referred to this accomplishment as consistency. Managers at the banks generally assumed (correctly so except for Second Commercial Bank's experience with the automatic transfer and First Regional Bank's data processing problems) that their organization had the necessary specialized skills and a social structure that would allow the various specialties to integrate with each other effectively. Rather than focusing on their technical and organizational skills, they devoted more attention to achieving consistency.

We also found that, while integration was important for achieving consistency, the mechanisms used to achieve integration were not all the same. For example, the process at First Commercial Bank was less centralized and, where power was concentrated, its focus was at a lower level than at the other two large banks. Still, at the four largest banks, there were structures that delineated the various subtasks and time requirements, processes that facilitated communication among the various parties needing to be involved, and means for feedback to trigger adjustments as things moved forward. The problems that arose were created when these mechanisms failed to elicit needed corrective actions. For example, when managers at First Regional Bank decided to use outside data processing, the organizational routines shifted significantly; but because the NOW account was the vehicle for establishing the new routines, the needed communication process took time to evolve. As a result, the trial-and-error process that occurred in the critical data processing area resembled that of radical innovation: smooth methods of operation and problem solving did not yet exist. Overall, however, all the routine innovators had a structure that made it possible to know to whom to assign something, whom to consult, and whom to hold accountable for implementing policy. Implementation required primarily using and modifying existing components.

Moreover, the demands that the defensive strategy placed on the routine innovators were minimal compared to what a more aggressive posture might have caused. A highly priced account with little promotion placed few demands on all parts of the system, whereas the requirements generated by an aggressively promoted low-priced product could be substantial. In addition, if the strategy permitted the firm to draw services and/or technology without modification from its environment, demands could be reduced greatly. For example, those organizations that simply used existing outside data processing services had fewer data processing issues to be resolved. The combination of defensive strategies and ability to employ outside services without modification were particularly helpful to the small banks. When a small firm pursued a defensive strategy, the demands that the innovation placed on the system were so slight that few changes in resources or basic procedures were needed.

The combination of routine innovation and defensive strategy suggests that, except for First Regional Bank, the banks had little to do to implement the NOW account because they made few changes and put relatively little energy into aggressive marketing. This is true in comparison with the large S & Ls; but it may understate the demands on the banks because defensive innovation, even if routine, still must be introduced in a way that does not upset existing relationships.

While a defensive strategy could reduce demands on an organization, the design of a defensive strategy raised problems in a large, complex system. Most important, a marketing approach needed to be developed that would not disturb major customers whose checking accounts might be only a minor portion of their relationship with the bank. These people had to be informed of the NOW account and served in a manner that caused them minimal inconvenience. On the other hand, managers did not want to encourage smaller customers (who had non-interest-bearing checking accounts) to switch to the NOW; and they were not interested in attracting many new, small accounts. Therefore, normal mass media would not be useful; more pinpointed personal approaches to the major customers were needed. Such approaches often relied on personal telephone calls and necessitated special staffing and training. These special approaches for the defensive strategy needed to be designed in ways that would be consistent with other things the firm was doing.

Although no one at the organizations spoke of attempting to achieve a fit with the existing fabric, current practices tended to be followed. We have seen how the design decisions were made by the upper levels through processes that were typical for the individual organizations.

Similarly, as implementation progressed, managers used procedures that were normal for the particular organization. Again, these varied widely from organization to organization and, with only minor exceptions, individuals reported accepting the roles they had been given and feeling that they had been adequately prepared to play them. All four of these routine innovators were generally successful implementers. However, First Commercial Bank's tradition of high levels of communication, training, and participation was associated with more favorable reactions at the lower levels.

Consistency during implementation was achieved in several ways. First, the holding companies took primary responsibility for designing the overall procedures. Second, some of the holding companies consulted managers from the individual banks in designing forms, training procedures, and other materials to make the NOW account operational at the individual banks. Third, managers at individual banks played a major role in training their staffs, thereby allowing each bank to follow a process consistent with its normal operations.

While it cannot be concluded that consistency was a goal or a necessary step to achieve success, it can be said that an implementation format that fit with existing routines was quite helpful for achieving at least the short-term goals. Consistency allows a stable context for change; we speculate that for routine innovation, implementation success will be positively correlated with the degree of fit with existing practices, because start up costs and disruption of other subsystems are apt to be minimized. Indeed, often routine innovation may be implemented best when it is defined as a routine problem.

This conclusion may have special importance given the current concern over the inability of U.S. industry to innovate and the attention that firms attempting to innovate through nontraditional structures seem to receive. People often conclude that the economic system's viability depends on traditional firms behaving in very nontraditional ways, so that they can innovate. Our findings suggest that at least sometimes they need not. The excitement generated by the nontraditional firms may lead them to be overrepresented in the popular and academic literature. In this regard, an observation of Karl Weick (1979) is most germane. At the end of his path-breaking book that drives the reader to think about very nontraditional ways to keep organizations open, Weick noted: "Enthusiasm for open systems models should not divert attention from also understanding the ways in which organizational inertia and organizational attentiveness to one's own past experience can continue unpunished for surprisingly long periods of time" (p. 239). Although in the long run, inertia may lead to problems, for many years firms may be very successful *because* they do routine things well. Consequently routine innovation and managers who achieve it successfully may deserve more research than they have received.

This conservative scenario is not applicable for all routine innovation. In fact, the problems at First Regional Bank and Second Commercial Bank (with the automatic transfer) were similar to those faced by the two large S & Ls in attempting radical innovation. In all four cases, problems resulted from a failure to recognize the inadequacy of existing routines and personnel, and were associated with the absence of several of the four basic conditions we suggested are required for implementation. Taken together, the experiences of these two routine and two radical innovators suggest that some of the problems of routine and radical innovation can be very similar.

Motivation and Learning. Except for DP problems at First Regional Bank, few problems appeared at the larger banks. They were ready on time and technically prepared; direct costs and employee stress were not problems; the reaction of customers was as desired. There were, though, differences among them in employee commitment and learning. Here, consistent with much of what is believed about the outcomes of organic structures, the opportunities for individuals to have input and responsibility seemed to be associated with favorable outcomes. Such benefits were greatest at First Commercial Bank, where people learned much by seeing up close the relationship between the NOW account and other changes. Theory would also suggest that the strong team spirit at First Commercial was a function of the frequent consultation. At Second Commercial Bank, little was said about learning or commitment, although so much had been learned from the crisis of the automatic transfer that perhaps there was little additional to learn from a product that was so similar.

The pattern at Third Commercial Bank was more complex. Lower-level managers who felt responsible to learn and to find flaws seemed highly committed to making the NOW account successful, even though they reported no learning. These managers and lower-level personnel felt that they were accountable for their own preparation, even though some reported being treated like school children. This responsibility and the fear of error seemed to reinforce the existing interdepartmental relationships that might be useful for coping with problems in the future. While it is hard to think of Third Commercial as an organic system, giving employees responsibility for successful task accomplishment generated personal involvement and appeared to create the potential for some learning. At First Regional Bank, the only reports of learning stemmed from the crisis around DP. In general, middle managers were dissatisfied because they experienced so little control over the process. Customer-contact people, who had been offered an opportunity for input during training sessions led by the holding company vice president of operations, were very satisfied.

Overall, the positive side effects from implementation of this routine innovation were primarily the satisfactions that occurred when people were consulted. Other positive side effects were limited. When they did appear, they either emerged around a crisis, were associated with responsibility for the task's success, or arose when the relationship between the innovation and other changes was perceived.

Radical Innovation

Doing while Learning. We have suggested that routine innovations may benefit considerably from existing competencies and organizational relationships. In contrast, radical innovation is more likely to require that new capacities be developed and sometimes that previous organizational patterns be abandoned. In addition, at least in the case of the NOW account, new ways of thinking about many aspects of the business—new paradigms—may be required. To complicate matters, the need for reorientation emerges as ad hoc adjustments to a series of problems prove to be inadequate. For routine innovation, it is useful to view the organization as adopting the innovation; for radical innovation, more emphasis needs to be given to how the innovation adopts the organization.

The problems spawned by the need "to do while learning" appeared at all levels of the two largest S & Ls. First National S & L approached the entire innovation more flexibly than did Second National and was considerably more successful on several dimensions. It is very difficult, however, to know what role the initial approach played in ultimate success, given the enormous changes in technical and organizational skills that the consultants introduced at First National S & L. (Indeed, it is hard to envision how, without the consultants, First National could have avoided a major catastrophe, let alone attain even the moderate achievements of Second National S & L.) Still, some tentative statements about clues to success can be advanced. The fact that two such different organizations came to face similar problems during radical innovation gives us some insights into the nature of radical innovation. Moreover, we can see what allowed one firm to solve the problems better than the other one did. The experiences of the two medium S & Ls can be used to amplify both matters. The contrasts are clearest if the design and implementation phases for the four larger S & Ls are considered separately.

Design. The S & Ls, like the banks, used their normal procedures to begin work on the NOW account. First National S & L approached the problem as it approached most problems—with a group decision procedure and no clear accountability. The other three of the four larger S & Ls centralized the design decisions at high levels. Also, two of them added someone with special skills from outside the organization either before the NOW account was formally being considered or at a critical juncture during the design stage.

With respect to the design of the product, the decision process appeared to produce few differences among the four larger S & Ls. All S & Ls decided to be aggressive, although the medium ones were defensive early on. The major strategic difference among the firms concerned their data processing (would it be internal or external?), and this was more a function of other factors—such as size—than of the way the firms were organized. Perhaps the only instance when the organization's structure had distinct consequences during preadoption was at First Capitol; there the high degree of centralization at the level of the president, combined with the president's ambivalence, slowed the process so that when a strategy did emerge, it was too late to implement it fully before the legal date for the product. The experiences of First Capitol after the banker took over also suggest that if combined with needed expertise, concentration of power can produce very positive results, even during the design phase of a radical innovation.

From these experiences, we suggest that contrary to much existing theory and consistent with our findings on routine innovation, the design phase of innovation—even radical innovation—does not require a decentralized process. All organizations arrived at the same decision; in three of the four, power was concentrated at the top while complexity was low. In fact, instead of general transorganizational requirements, we see how the outcomes of various structural arrangements are apt to be relative to the state of the particular organization. For example, First National probably would have been better off with greater concentration of power in the hands of Ms. Smith. Second National would have been better off if managers and lower-level members had been given more influence. First Capitol benefitted from concentrating authority and Second Capitol did extremely well with a centrally directed process that was flexible and open to inputs from all sources.

Again, the caveats we have stressed must be recognized. In particular, because this was a borrowed innovation, the design phase was less important than it would be for many other innovations. Also, the borrowed nature may have permitted search and design to be accomplished by a very small number of people, whereas being the first to design an innovation may require less concentration of power. Thus, even though we conclude that substantial concentration of power was quite compatible with effective design,

Zaltman et al. (1973), Duncan (1976), and others who have postulated the importance of organic structures during this phase might still be correct for innovations where the design stage is more critical and complex. In addition, as we have noted, the processes used, while centralized and not especially complex, were not formalized. Three of the firms seemed to use a simple structure for this particular task—a structure Mintzberg (1979) argued is organic.

Implementation. Each of the four critical elements played a major role in accounting for success or failure at the four larger S & Ls. Technical readiness was clearly essential, and the other three elements were important for assessing, creating, and utilizing the technical capacity. One key factor turned out to be the degree to which power over issues related to the NOW account was concentrated in the hands of one or a few individuals who had enough knowledge at least to diagnose what was needed. Many of First National's problems (particularly for implementation) appeared to be associated with Ms. Smith's lack of influence. Even though the process involved substantial face-to-face discussion of those charged with implementation, the needed mutual adjustment did not occur. Among other things, when the consultants entered, they concentrated power and linked it to technical competence. First Capitol did not seem to be able to plot a clear course until Mr. Walters came on board and was given authority to do what was needed. Second National remained centralized at high levels; this centralization, paired with reliance on normal formalized procedures, seemed to inhibit needed information flows. Had the information flowed more readily, perhaps the problems could have been detected earlier and addressed. Alternatively, had the "banking expertise" existed centrally, it might have made the need for the flow of information less critical.

Some of the clearest contrasts emerge from comparison of the two largest S & Ls. First National S & L had a long-standing familylike atmosphere. Individuals at all levels were loyal to the organization; management routinely went a long way (too far in the minds of the consultants) to accommodate individual employees. This loyalty seemed to be an important resource. During the crisis, employees were willing to give extra, even extraordinary effort to avoid the firm's being embarrassed.

The family atmosphere led to open communication during implementation. Mechanisms were introduced to allow branch employees direct access to headquarters personnel. This system helped to reduce employee stress as well as provide a channel for information to flow upward. Even though branch personnel did not always know what to do, this access was important in reducing the pressures they felt. We speculate that their direct access to the policymakers had symbolic value as well. Clearly, at headquarters the presence of the president during the crisis had symbolic value. At the branches, the special amenities (such as dinner and parties) provided during the crisis contributed to group morale. Overall, the employees' memories of the enormous pressures were interwoven with feelings of exhilaration, accomplishment, pride, and realization that they had learned a great deal.

In contrast, Second National approached implementation of the NOW account in a more formalized, hierarchical manner. Employees were told what to do and expected to do it. Upward communication was not encouraged; problems reported upward tended to be discounted. As a result, problems remained unsolved for a long time and employees reported stress and frustration. Whereas First National was a stronger social system following the crisis, Second National was not.

However, not all aspects of First National's family culture were beneficial, as illustrated by the problems with data processing. Relative to bureaucracies, families are apt to find that it is more difficult to alter power relationships to correspond to environmental demands. At First National previous social relationships dominated. Without clear and forceful messages from the head, newcomers were treated as outsiders; their expertise was not influential. The delay in confronting problems that had been visible to some people for months seemed to be linked to the same set of factors that produced the loyalty to the organization. Only when the consultants entered with a clear mandate from the president could power be realigned appropriately. Prior to the entrance of the consultants, the social structure interfered with the effectiveness of the communication system.

Second National's more formal social structure, with top-down communication, also interfered with information flows. Thus a strong family-type culture and a strong hierarchical orientation produced similar results—much information was not used appropriately. In both cases, the social processes made implementation less effective, although First National reaped the benefits of high levels of commitment and morale.

The impact of an altered social structure can be seen at First National S & L after the consultants entered. In addition to providing critical technical resources, the consultants changed the social structure. They removed the communication barriers embedded in the preexisting social relationships both outside and inside the firm. They gave greater access to key actors in the external environment; their clear position of authority, their demonstrated expertise, and the project management structure they implanted realigned the internal influence process.

The project management structure was similar to what First and Second Commercial Banks had come to earlier. In this structure, power was more concentrated than it had been in the committee, but the structure was also highly flexible in allowing power and resources to flow to the appropriate places for task accomplishment. The use of PERT charts and enforced schedules increased formalization, although it was still a long way from a hierarchical, mechanistic system. What was centralized was a system of scheduling and of making people accountable; in addition, information was channeled to one central point. Members of the organization did not view it as a formal, rule-driven, autocratic process. What they reported were feelings of pressure to perform their particular tasks, confidence that someone was structuring things in a way that would work, and access to resources they felt their tasks demanded. In short, the new structure provided a coherent focus; while more centralized and formal than the previous mode of organization, it was far from a mechanistic system. This structure and process made implementation possible—most implementation was achieved in about seven weeks.

These "before" and "after" experiences at First National, in the light of Second Commercial Bank's automatic transfer experiences and the success of First Commercial's project management approach, suggest that the project management structure was useful for this innovation. Moreover, its absence at Second National was associated with continuing problems. Of course, the experiences of Third Commercial Bank and Second Capitol S & L indicate that it was not a necessary structure and its use at First Regional Bank indicates that it was not a sufficient structure.

Comparison of these three "deviant" cases suggests why the project structure might work the way it did when used successfully. The project structure operationalized a holistic view of the implementation requirements and their interrelations. It allowed information to flow and be channeled toward task accomplishment. Third Commercial Bank had mechanisms that did this, including a centrally developed project structure, upward communication on potential problems, and lateral communication to deal with ad hoc matters. Second Capitol S & L had centrally orchestrated coherence, mutual adjustment, and flexibility. First Regional Bank had a project structure, but, like Second National S & L, failed to respond in a timely manner because signals of problems from data processing were ignored, and power was not concentrated in the hands of the project manager.

Overall, the requirements for implementation of radical innovation had much in common with those of routine innovation. In both cases, the four implementation requirements seem to be needed. In addition to technological preparedness, there must be some structure to achieve focus. There must be flexibility and some means to allow persons at lower levels in the system (or in departments that previously were less critical and less influential) who are essential to making the innovation operational to be taken seriously by those in charge. Consistent with Hage and Dewar (1973), such upward communication does not require participation in decision making by lower-level participants. Decision making is only one of the forums for communication; many other channels exist. More generally, there are a number of organizational stuctures that can achieve a variety of ends. Some (such as those at the small organizations and Third Commercial Bank) can be centralized; others (such as those at First Commercial Bank) appear to occur at lower levels and involve a greater dispersion of power. However, in no case did we find much support for the predictions of the ambidextrous model that mechanistic structures characterized by high formalization, centralization (at high levels) and functional specialization were especially useful for implementation. The pattern was more mixed. Certainly, coherence and concentration of power were important and could be provided by centralization. On the other hand, sometimes centralization got in the way of attention to important signals. Moreover, mutual adjustment and attention to the needs of those charged with implementing often required some ad hoc arrangements that centralization and formalization might have retarded. Project management provided the appropriate mix. So too did the simple structure like arrangements at the medium-sized S & Ls.

Learning and Motivation. Overall, there were surprisingly few reports of individual learning and heightened motivation. Only at First National S & L were these mentioned frequently. There, some combination of crisis, successful coping, the models provided by the consultants, open flows of information, and social support seemed to produce a climate for learning and involvement. At the three other larger S & Ls, several of these conditions were absent. Of course, all four of these S & Ls had increased their competence, had altered their paradigms a bit and hence, in the broad sense Duncan and Weiss (1979) suggest, had learned. Overall, however, we conclude that the degree to which radical innovation generates individual learning and motivation is more a function of the way the implementation process is managed than of the radicalness of the innovation per se.

Conclusion. In discussing routine implementation, we drew on Weick (1979) to suggest the importance of understanding the processes by which organizations quite appropriately draw on their own past experiences. In attempting radical innovation, drawing on the organization's past raises general problems: there is no relevant experience to draw on, and what is mistakenly drawn on will be misleading or not relevant for the problems at hand. To the degree Weick is correct in asserting that "Experience is the consequence of activity" (p.148), we see the major problems facing radical innovators in a new light; they have to do something in order to develop meaningful experience. When the problems are complex and the stakes are high, the learning from doing can be a very risky approach because it is so dependent upon costly trial and error approaches. Often there may be no alternative; in such a case, the creative strategies offered by Weick and the advocates of structures that promote risk taking, experimentation, and so forth have much to recommend them. That is, structures that make it possible to adapt quickly to knowledge gained through trial and error should aid radical innovation. The overall result is apt to be that the experience with the innovation becomes mapped into the new arrangements. It is in this sense that a radical innovation adopts the organization.

Other Contingency Factors

Strategy

All twelve organizations adopted the NOW account fully in the sense that they offered the product and, in order to do so, made all parts of the system operational. Differences in strategy were not reflected in differences in adoption or nonadoption, as suggested in much of the diffusion research. In this case, they were reflected in the posture toward a fully implemented innovation. In other words, meshing with overall strategy called for variations in design of the NOW account, rather than making a decision about whether or not to adopt it.

We have seen how an organization's strategy influenced the definition of success and thereby had a major impact on the demands placed on the firm during implementation. Strategic considerations made the NOW account almost a nonevent in several organizations. These organizations adopted a defensive stance and designed an inert product that would neither help nor hurt the organization and that placed few demands on any part of the organization. Others followed an aggressive strategy that placed great demands on them. The same innovation produced diametrically opposed approaches in different firms (such as high versus low volume of account sales). As we have seen, the banks tended to define success as preserving the status quo—only slowly and minimally shifting money from standard checking accounts to NOWs and retaining major customers. The S & Ls wanted to become more like retail banks and believed that attracting checking accounts was a major requirement. Therefore, they tended to be aggressive and defined success in terms of NOW account volume. Both approaches could be successful, depending on the firm's strategy and ability to implement.

Aggressive and defensive strategies were implemented through different approaches to pricing and promotion. Although for the most part, an aggressive strategy placed greater demands on the organization, the defensive approach placed the greater demands on promotion. An aggressive strategy was consistent with mass marketing, which can be done through fairly well established channels. On the other hand, defensive strategies were intended to keep many customers inactive. Defensive marketing requires a more precise approach: certain people (for example, large customers) need to be contacted and dealt with personally; other people need to be excluded. Consequently, the larger banks needed to be more innovative with respect to promotion than did the large S & Ls following a more aggressive course. Generally, however, aggressive strategies were associated with the most implementation problems, although it must be remembered that in our study, aggressive approaches were partially confounded with radical innovation.

Aggressive approaches placed enormous demands on some organizations and required them to make substantial changes to respond to the environment. For example, whereas no changes at the level of new-accounts personnel were needed for implementation at First City Bank because its strategy required little interaction with retail customers, the extremely aggressive strategy of First National S & L resulted in lines of customers and ad hoc procedures to manage them. In this respect various strategies activated different sets of environmental events that produced diverse requirements. Consequently, we conclude that strategy differences imply choices about the parts of the environment an organization must respond to, and hence about what is required for successful innovation. This conclusion supports Child's (1972) and Miller's (1979) cautions to organization theorists about the hazards of considering bivariate relationships between structures and environments without attending to such matters as strategy.

Variations in strategy meant that firms differed in other goals they were pursuing besides those related directly to the NOW account. The impact of these differences in shaping the process of implementation was most noticeable in the large banks. All three large banks wanted to position themselves to be able to use mass media for marketing the NOW and other products in the future. This desire made offering a common product for all banks a constraint within a geographic region. Even if they had rural banks that wished to be more aggressive (for example, by charging a lower price for NOWs), they had to offer an identical product if these communities were in the range of the mass media. Even in organizations that were geographically dispersed, offering a common product required centralized policy decisions.

Similarly, we have suggested that the banks, especially the larger ones, were concerned with the consistency between the NOW account and other services and routines. In part, this emphasis stemmed from the nature of their strategies (and to a degree the history of the financial industry), which entailed offering a greater variety of services than the savings and loan associations did. The banks had more opportunity for and more to gain from synergy than did the S & Ls.

Strategy also affected the process of implementation indirectly. This influence was most apparent in First Commercial Bank, where a strategic decision to emphasize cross-selling had led management to introduce personal bankers to handle all the contacts with individual customers. Because personal bankers were responsible for communicating with key customers, First Commercial needed no new or ad hoc procedures to inform its customers. Similarly, First National S & L had established the Electronic Funds Transfer Committee to handle an earlier service that required integration of many departments. Because the NOW account required similar interactions, it was assigned to this group.

Comparable to our discerning the need for organizationally specific criteria to evaluate success, our findings concerning the idiosyncrasies resulting from strategy point to the need to consider each innovation in the context of a particular organization. We suggest, however, that the diversity of criteria among organizations may vary from innovation to innovation. Other innovations may yield more common objectives across organizations than the NOW account did, but the commonality needs to be determined empirically; it cannot be assumed. One of our most important conclusions is that the definition and measurement of success of innovation must be specified in the context of the organization's strategy and of other objectives the organization is working toward simultaneously. While this point has been recognized in the previous literature (for example, Rosenbloom, 1978; Ettlie, 1983, 1984; Ettlie, et al., 1984), most research on initiation as well as implementation has not sufficiently incorporated organizationally specific criteria.

Size

Organizational size was another contingency factor that appeared to have important consequences for approaches to successful implementation. While it is often convenient to treat organizational size as a cause of certain processes, considerable caution needs to be exercised. As chapter 1 indicated, size is a correlate of many other variables and these other variables, more than size per se, are properly treated as having causal effects on implementation. Also, as Kimberly (1976) observed, there are many different aspects of size, and the various aspects differ according to what variables they are more or less closely related. Moreover, since in our particular study the banks tended to be larger than the S & Ls, size was confounded with our operationalization of radicalness. Therefore, our study provides only limited causal inferences about the role of size. Nevertheless, it does suggest some relationships between size and innovation that deserve special attention. Specifically, we suggest a distinction among four issues: the pressures placed on the organization to cope with the external environment, certain internal requirements, the resources available to the organization, and the requirements for making decisions about and implementing the innovation within the organization.

Size and Environmental Pressures. Managers of larger firms reported giving more attention to the external environment than did managers of smaller ones. However, this relationship did not appear to be linear. Managers of the very largest firms reported giving considerable attention to influencing organizations with whom they had a temporary alliance (their action-sets, Aldrich and Whetten, 1981), but managers of the medium and smaller firms seldom if ever expressed any such concerns. For example, managers at First Commercial Bank indicated they considered it important that their decisions did not lead other banks down the wrong track. Several large banks were concerned with influencing their correspondent banks to set productive approaches. First National S & L was concerned about avoiding the embarrassment of failure. Third Commercial Bank was concerned with demonstrating its position to the community. Overall, the large organizations were visible and, recognizing that they were being (or hoping that they would be) observed, their managers were concerned with the impact of their actions on their environment and on subsequent perceptions of themselves.

In addition, because the larger banks served their correspondent banks and diverse customer bases, their environments were more complex. Consequently, to achieve sufficient consensus and coherence without disturbing other goals such as common advertising within regions, these firms faced problems that the S & Ls and the smaller banks did not. They had two methods of response. One was incorporating diversity into their routines. Another was buffering the organization from the effects of the diversity, such as by influencing all their own banks to offer an identical product. None of these issues arose in the small and medium firms.

This finding is consistent with the view that size reduces the ability of a firm to employ what Munson and Pelz (1981) classified as a "packaged" innovation. However, the influence of size on the ability to use packaged innovations may be moderated by other relationships, such as the degree to which an organization is similar to other organizations of its type. The more similar an organization is to others of its type, the more easily it can relate to members of its organization set, including suppliers and trade associations. For example, S & Ls that were similar to most other S & Ls were more apt to find suppliers who had developed technologies and materials that could be readily adopted. In contrast, the significant discrepancies in size between First National S & L and most other S & Ls made it difficult for First National's managers to use information provided either by trade associations (because the information was not relevant) or by local banks (because First National believed the banks would see them as a potential competitor and might mislead them). Likewise, to the degree that size was positively related to complexity, the larger organizations would be involved in a broader spectrum of activities than would the smaller ones. As a result, if vendors and other units in the environment are oriented to the average firm, their services may not fit the large firm. Both large S & Ls in our study experienced such problems because they offered services (outlets in supermarkets for First National and telephone bill payments at Second National) that made them unable to use software developed for the average S & L.[1]

The small and medium firms had another advantage in dealing with their environments; they could rely on the large ones to set the norms about issues such as price. Their search for information could be minimal because they decided what to do on the basis of what others in their immediate environment did. Moreover, the small (and to a degree the medium-sized) firms could rely on the larger firms to educate the general public about the NOW account. Consequently, they needed to engage in only limited promotion. Finally, the very small organizations could wait for firms with stronger technological needs to experiment with and refine the technology.

In short, the requirements for innovation at the smaller organizations were qualitatively different and quantitatively less than those of the larger firms. The large firms attempting radical innovation faced the most stringent requirements.

Size and Endogenous Demands. In several ways, the larger organizations also faced more demanding requirements due to endogenous elements. Size-related requirements appeared to be critical in making radical innovation much more difficult for the large S & Ls than for the medium and small ones. The larger S & Ls needed to have their total systems operational because of the enormous volume and the corresponding costs of late processing. The smaller organizations could make do, if they had to (and one of them did), with a manual ad hoc back-up system. Moreover, the large S & Ls were more complex, primarily because of the services they offered that other S & Ls did not. Consequently, as we have suggested, they needed not only a fully operational system, but one developed to their own specifications.

Size and Resources. At least under some conditions, size was related to the resources the organizations had at their disposal. For example, the three large banks had developed sophisticated computer systems. First National S & Ls ability to hire a Big Eight accounting firm was linked indirectly to its size—indirectly because the financial resources it could spend were made available by previous success, not size per se. Nevertheless, size did seem to be associated with the capacity to cope with actual and potential problems spawned by the NOW account. However, size alone cannot account for resource availability, as Second National S & L illustrates; it was the lack of resources that its managers gave as a reason for their problems. As we will discuss later, the resources may need to be perceived as "slack" if they are to aid innovation.

Size and Decision Process. Finally, size was associated with quite different internal processes for implementation. Here, if a dividing line were to be drawn, it would most likely separate the four small organizations from the rest on the basis of divergent social processes used to design and to implement.

Although there were considerable differences among the large and medium firms, as a group their design and implementation processes were far more complex and prolonged than those in the small firms. Decisions in the small organizations were typically made in one or two meetings at which only a few people were present, and typically the firm's highest ranking member's views dominated. The decisions were implemented by verbal instructions—either directly to people who would meet customers or perform other related functions, or to one other person who would communicate them personally to the operatives. In contrast, the medium and large organizations differed from each other far more than the small organizations did. Typically, however, they had numerous meetings both to decide on strategy and to communicate decisions and the required actions to others. They developed a variety of new forms and procedures and devoted at least some time to training their members—even people who would be affected only occasionally. Their decision processes tended to be diverse internally— different things were handled in different ways. (For example, coordination of the development of training materials might be done by someone in the holding company, but decisions about how to administer them might be left to the individual banks.)

The small organizations ranked about equally on our somewhat crude measure of complexity; usually about six positions were involved in design and implementation. The large and the medium firms revealed higher degrees of complexity. The range of complexity among these firms, too, was restricted: from a high of twenty-two positions for Third Commercial Bank down to sixteen for both medium S & Ls. These results suggest that above a certain size (and perhaps below some other size that none of the firms we studied had reached), size was not strongly related to complexity. Perhaps there was a certain scale of operations needed to design and introduce a NOW account in an organization above a certain threshold size. Once this scale was reached, within the range of size encompasssed in our study, no additional skills or orientations were needed. Finally, the narrow range of complexity could have been an artifact of how we measured it—by counting the number of job titles our respondents said had been involved. The large banks reported involvement of nearly the same number of titles as the medium ones, but in the large banks, there were more people holding any given title.

Together, these findings suggest the value of attempting to integrate the ideas of Tornatzky et al. (1983) on organization size and innovation with some of Kimberly's (1976) observations. On the one hand, our findings support the assertion by Tornatzky et al. that at some point there is a qualitative difference between small and large firms with respect to how they innovate. However, we would add that where this point occurs is not the same for all matters. For example, with respect to decision process, the medium and larger firms were quite similar to each other but very different from the four small ones. On the other hand, with respect to relations with their environments, the medium and small firms appeared to be very similar to each other but very different from the large firms. This research supports Kimberly's (1976) assertion of the dangers of treating size as a monolithic construct and helps to explain why correlations between size and some overall measure of decision making may be small.

Finally, size may be a very misleading indicator of the social processes that organizations use to innovate. Recall that Rothwell and Zegveld (1982) suggested that small organizations may have advantages over larger ones in innovating because they are better able to respond quickly and efficiently to environmental changes, but the larger ones are apt to have superior resources. We observed that the larger firms also had greater demands and that some of the larger firms were able to behave somewhat like small firms—they centralized control in the hands of one or a few individuals and, to a degree, operated as simple structures (Mintzberg, 1979) existing within a larger organization. In some ways, the project teams served as another device for achieving many of the benefits of simple structures. We conclude, therefore, that size may be associated with both more demands and more resources but that, even in mature industries, larger organizations can obtain many of the advantages of smaller ones if they choose the appropriate structures. In Pinchot's (1985) words, there "is a way to have the advantages of both bigness and smallness at once" (p. 4). Similarly, Kanter's (1983) parallel structures achieve such conditions, although we suspect that such structures may be more advantageous for implementation than she does.

Slack

Bourgeois (1981) defined organizational slack as a cushion of resources that allows successful adaptation to internal and external demands. While it is difficult to know precisely at a given time whether a particular resource is a cushion in the sense that it is not necessary for functioning effectively, the concept does orient us to the existence of discretionary resources in organizations and to how these resources can facilitate innovation (Bourgeois; Cyert and March, 1963; Hambrick and Snow, 1977). Often, it is thought that slack provides resources for creative and innovative activities, and therefore its most positive effects on innovation occur during the preadoption phases, where creativity is assumed to be most important.

Our data on the role of slack are sketchy. The concept is difficult to operationalize and we did not collect data about it systematically. However, slack did appear to aid implementation in three ways.

First, in all probability, slack contributed to technical and organizational preparedness. For example, First Commercial Bank's development of its ability to process NOW accounts approximately five years before it could offer them reflects the use of some slack resources. The organization had invested heavily in training and communicating with its personnel and developed a social system that aided communication and promoted commitment to the firm. In essence, these prior expenditures helped First Commercial to be well prepared both technically and organizationally. Similarly, previous expenditures at First National S & L seemed to contribute to employee loyalty that allowed the firm to make extraordinary demands on its people in a crisis. Those investments in people also resulted in employees' high level of ego-involvement, which was expressed in their desire to keep the firm from being embarrassed. While it might be argued, as the consultants did, that the familylike style of management was inefficient, it was associated with a culture that was extremely helpful during the NOW account crisis. It is in this sense that we suggest the way First National used slack at an earlier time helped it survive the NOW accounts crisis.

Second, Galbraith (1974) argued that one way organizations employ slack is to lower performance standards, such as by extending deadlines forward in time. Lowered standards can reduce the amount of information that organizations need to coordinate their subunits. In this sense, many of the firms we studied used slack to aid implementation. Low levels of aspiration permitted some organizations (particularly the small ones) to temper the impact of the innovation. Higher goals would have placed many more demands on many of these systems.

Third, slack was used to acquire resources that aided implementation. This use of slack was shown most clearly at First National S & L, particularly in comparison with Second National S & L. First National's financial resources allowed them to purchase the managerial and technical resources of a prestigious consulting firm, and thereby avoid a major disaster. On the other hand, managers at Second National reported that they could not implement their marketing strategy for a protracted period of time because they did not have the resources to hire adequate personnel—not even relatively inexpensive clerical staff. Because slack is a function of perception of priorities relative to resources, it is possible that managers at Second

National just had other priorities. All we can say for sure is that if cash reserves and other uncommitted resources are perceived to be available, they provide an opportunity for managers to improve implementation if they wish.

In short, our data suggested that slack can play an important role in implementation, over and above any role it might play in stimulating creativity and experimentation. These results are consistent with Meyer's (1982) analysis of the role slack plays in responses to environmental jolts. Consequently, it would seem that both empirical and theoretical work on innovation needs to attend to this variable as both a contextual factor and an element of the innovation itself. An attempted innovation might succeed in one organization and fail in another solely as a function of differences in behavior due to variations in actual or perceived slack. Therefore, inquiry might begin by investigating what determines the perception of slack. Of course, how perceived slack is used, not just its existence and amount, will be of critical importance. Thus, it may be productive to consider ratios such as the amounts of slack expended to the benefits achieved or the smoothness of innovation as indices of successful implementation. Again, conceptual and operational problems may limit the value of slack as a construct. Nevertheless, some consideration of the availability and utilization of discretionary resources throughout the innovation process seems essential.

History and Concurrent Events

History and contemporaneous events in organizations and industries present a host of contingency factors. A few examples are reviewed here to demonstrate how organizations' histories influence implementation and to show why the organization's past deserves careful attention in innovation research.

First, consider the context in which Second City Bank's highly centralized decision making and informal implementation took place. In view of the tradition of centralized decision making and long tenure of most employees, it is not surprising that the approach worked well, at least for a routine innovation.

Second, history contributed to the different strategies employed by the banks and S & Ls. The fact that banks already had large amounts of money in interest-free checking accounts and S & Ls did not made a defensive strategy far more attractive to the banks. Historical conditions made for a different set of payoffs from the same product.

In addition, we saw how the overall commitment of First National's members was a valuable resource and how Second Commercial Bank's experience with the automatic transfer affected its capacity, processes, and ability to think about the NOW account. The difficulty that managers at

Second Commercial had in keeping the automatic transfer and NOW accounts distinct in their minds and their use of experiences with the former as standards of comparison for the latter reveal how history can influence the perception of an innovation. Moreover, we saw how the major commitment of First Commercial Bank to participation and personnel development was associated with high levels of employee participation and decentralization. Also, we found that had the NOW account been delayed for a few months, some of the process might have been treated quite differently, in view of the ongoing restructuring.

Similar statements could be made about the influence of the past and present on implementation at almost every organization. Consequently, the discovery of clues to successful innovation demands incorporating distant and recent events in and around a given organization. Our findings indicate that history also has major implications for implementation. However, these dynamics cannot be understood from a distance, such as by counting the number of previous innovations a firm has accomplished. Knowledge about the past and how it is expressed in current beliefs and structures is needed.

The importance of history and concurrent events poses a dilemma for understanding innovation. On the one hand, it indicates that researchers must collect data about these elements and interpret their findings accordingly. On the other hand, such data collection is extremely expensive and is less amenable to interpretation through normal statistical techniques—partly because the large number of variables will require an enormous sample size. Most cross-sectional studies will sacrifice the needed depth; most studies such as ours will suffer from an insufficient sample size and problems of aggregating while still dealing with all the idiosyncratic nuances appropriately. Moreover, in many cases the only feasible approach will be to reconstruct organizational history from current participants. Given its validity problems, such reconstruction may sometimes provide a distorted picture of the past on which to base an understanding of the present. In short, dealing adequately with organization history poses a major problem for the study of innovation.

Conclusion

The roles played by these contingency factors make it clear why the implementation of innovation must be viewed as an equifinal process. In complex systems such as organizations, many things interact to determine the consequences of a particular approach or action. Clearly, this conclusion is consistent with the perspective of Downs and Mohr (1976). However, as chapter 12's discussion of the general clues to successful implementation indicated, we believe that, despite substantial differences among organizations, a small set of general requirements for successful implementation can be abstracted. To be sure, because organizations differ widely in key dimensions, different organizations will have to do different things to meet the general requirements. Consequently, our conclusions are also consistent with Tornatzky and Klein (1982)—a transorganizational theory of innovation is possible if the meaning of these contingency factors is interpreted in the context of the particular innovation. Moreover, it is possible to provide general guidance to managers seeking to implement innovations. The final chapter presents the implications of our findings for theory and practice.

Note

1. This point would hold up only for firms below a certain size. For example, Pfeffer and Salancik (1978) observed that a firm may be so large that, for practical purposes, it is the environment for suppliers. Such an organization has many suppliers gearing their efforts to discovering and providing what the dominant firm wants.

14
Old Understandings and New Directions

In this chapter we assess what our findings mean for students and managers of innovation. For students, we suggest some modifications of existing concepts concerning design and implementation of innovation. We also introduce some new concepts and suggest ways for improving research. For managers, we propose a set of guidelines for implementing innovation based on our findings and previous research. The chapter is divided into four major sections: implications for theory and concepts, implications for research methods, advice to managers, and conclusions.

Implications for Innovation Theory and Concepts

Our findings suggest several extensions and refinements of concepts and theory used to direct the study of organizational innovation. Perhaps the most direct and important ones concern the ambidextrous organization.

The Ambidextrous Organization: Some Qualifications

Our findings suggest that the ambidextrous model as normally used is simplistic and misleading. We have seen that for both routine and radical innovation, a variety of paths were associated with both successful design and implementation.

Design. In many cases design was aided by seemingly mechanistic elements (such as concentration of power and search by one or a few people). We found little support for the view that structures and processes that generate widespread participation are required for the preadoption phase. These findings are consistent with Marino's (1982) critique of the ambidextrous model: organic structures may be less important in preadoption phases, during which the generation of new ideas is not critical. Still, despite considerable centralization, important aspects of design in all twelve cases were at least somewhat organic—they clearly were not formalized.

Implementation. Implementation was aided by organic processes that fostered mutual adjustment and the free flow of information. These findings are consistent with those of Greenwood et al. (1975) and Beyer and Trice (1978), who found that organic structures are useful for implementation. Again, we find a mixture of organic and mechanistic. Flexibility, open communication, and mutual adjustment were helpful, but so was concentration of power. In the four requirements for successful implementation we presented in chapter 12, we find that elements of *both* organic and mechanistic structures can lead to their fulfillment.

Subtasks during Design and Implementation. Some of the problems with the ambidextrous model stem from inadequate analysis of the subtasks that must be managed during each of the general stages of implementation. When the stages are examined closely, we see that each is composed of a number of subtasks and that accomplishment of each subtask could require a unique process. This latter point can be seen most clearly if we once again ignore the smaller firms.

In the larger, complex organizations, a number of people were doing various subtasks. Those subtasks differed in their requirements and therefore were often accomplished by different approaches within the same organization. For example, the search process and strategic planning (for this particular innovation) could be done by one or a very few people—high concentration of power and low complexity were appropriate. On the other hand, achieving internal consensus and designing a product that allowed variations in the environments faced by different parts of the organization required more input from various parties, and hence more constrained centralization, decentralization, and complexity. However, because uniformity in product design was often a requirement, even this step seemed compatible with substantial influence from a single source, whether a project manager or a high-level executive.

At later stages, again different subtasks required different processes. For example, at Third Commercial Bank, where there were high degrees of technical readiness and a good understanding of the business requirements by technical personnel, substantial centralization in the systems design aspects was possible. Similar conditions tended to hold at the other large banks. In these systems, however, the design of training materials and the training of new-accounts personnel seemed to benefit from decentralization. Such differences were less apparent at the S & Ls, where nonroutine elements increased the need for mutual adjustment. However, even here, certain tasks such as search, strategy formulation, and the design and ordering of checks could be routinized without cycles of mutual adaptation. Other aspects of implementation (such as integrating DP with other parts of the organization) benefitted from more communication and mutual adjustment. Again, the exact structures needed in each case were a function of the task requirements for that organization and the competence and influence of various participants.

In essence, the innovation process in any organization is composed of a number of subtasks; not all of these subtasks require the same type of structure and process. Moreover, the required structures and processes are apt to be influenced by individual differences: competence, managerial skills, and power in a particular system at a particular time. The task of integrating the various subtasks will also vary depending on the nature of the subtasks, individual differences, and the quality of the relationships among key departments and individuals.

Also, it is reasonable to expect that each subtask, to the degree that it is new to the organization, is itself an innovation and therefore has its own substages of design and implementation. For example, while the search process is usually considered part of the design process, it too must be both designed and implemented.

The ambidextrous view and the stage models such as Pelz and Munson's (1980) can easily obscure the variations required within each phase. Of course, when Zaltman et al. (1973) and Pelz and Munson used the term *implementation,* their unit of analysis was the total innovation, not the subtasks necessary for designing and implementing. For many purposes, such a unit is appropriate; we only wish to suggest that if attention is not directed to the various subtasks, the chances of making overly simplistic statements about the structures and processes associated with success are high. Our findings that *both* successful design and implementation were a mixture of presumably organic and mechanistic elements point to the need to refine the ambidextrous view accordingly.

Importance of Managers' Perceptions of the Demands Placed on Organizations

As we argue in more detail later, our findings support the views of Yin (1978, 1979) and others: the innovating firm must be studied in depth if we are to understand the innovation process. We believe that other comparative case studies of similar organizations attempting similar innovations can be useful. Still better would be studies that, in addition, compare the same organizations doing different innovations—different at least in terms of their primary attributes.

What may be even more valuable are studies that treat the demands placed on the organizations as secondary (perceived) attributes. Drawing on the management/organization literature, these demands can be specified in terms of the functional requirements they impose on a given organization— for example, greater differentiation, integration, or technical readiness. Such a step would strengthen Downs and Mohr's (1976) point that innovation is not a unique process requiring special theories.

Similarly, the emphasis on functional requirements would reduce the need for and temptation to create an array of special ad hoc models or techniques (such as ambidextrous structures and parallel organizations) to account for success. Instead, any given innovation becomes viewed as a family of tasks for an organization. These tasks, like any task, require a fit among appropriate technologies, resources, people, and social structures, with *appropriate* being defined in the context of the special situation.

In addition, such an approach would draw the organizational and innovation literature together (as Becker and Whisler, 1967, urged long ago) and help us move toward theoretical development in a manner analogous to what Tornatzky and Klein (1982) suggested. They argued first, that organizational innovation must be understood from analysis of the ways individual organizations perceive an innovation's characteristics, and second, that theory can be developed by systematic study of such perceptions. We agree, but we also believe that their perspective can be a useful basis for linking innovation research to organization theory by postulating that organizations will respond to a given set of perceived characteristics by translating them into a set of functional requirements. Organizational innovation can be understood by examining how these functional requirements are defined and how these definitions are operationalized in an ongoing system. Over time, it ought to be possible to develop theoretical statements about how perceived characteristics are translated into functional requirements. Also, it ought to be possible to systematize how various functional requirements can be best achieved in known organizational contexts. Because organization theory makes it possible to analyze functional requirements, understand the means to achieve them, and classify contexts that influence success of the various means, a productive synergy of organization and innovation theories seems likely.

Our research supports the arguments of many writers that such a merger will be extremely valuable for improving our understanding of innovation. In addition, Staw (1984) argued that the study of organizational innovation is "probably the best current candidate for progress in integrating micro and macro research" (p. 659). Delineation of the functional requirements and analysis of the ways organizations achieve and fail to achieve them would seem to be a useful framework for such inquiry.

Our data also support the view derived from Downs and Mohr (1976) that innovation types, such as routine and radical, must be treated as secondary attributes. For example, we saw how Second Commercial Bank's experience with the automatic transfer paralleled that of First National S & L with the NOW account. Moreover, we saw how First Capitol S & L perceived what a priori would be a radical innovation to be a routine one. A priori classifications may often lead to confusing results.

Problems with Organic/Mechanistic Concepts

Although we drew heavily on the organic/mechanistic terminology, our experiences tell us that it may be productive either to abandon these terms or to become much more precise in using them. This suggestion is based more on our efforts to use the concepts than on our data per se. First, it is important to recognize that Burns and Stalker's (1961) concepts are multidimensional. Yet we know of little research that has attempted to see how these dimensions are related to each other, how they should be weighted to determine how mechanistic or organic an organization is, or how various combinations of the dimensions may be related to different types of outcomes. The tendency in the innovation literature (as well as in organizational behavior literature more generally) to treat organizations as being either mechanistic or organic is counterproductive. Second, Burns and Stalker were explicit that organizations "oscillate between the two forms" (p. 122). The pattern of oscillation may have important consequences and hence deserves special treatment. Third, not all parts of a system are apt to be (or ought to be) equally organic or mechanistic. As we have shown, innovation is composed of many subtasks, each with its own requirements. Considering the pattern and variance of these requirements may be more productive than basing conclusions on some measure of central tendency. We found that a mixture of the elements existed in most of the larger organizations and that various mixtures were useful in different contexts.

For smaller organizations, however, it may be more useful to speak of some overall standing on the mechanistic-organic continuum than it is to refer to larger organizations in this way. Just as the word culture may be more helpful in understanding social life on a small Pacific island than in a complex nation such as the United States, so may the mechanistic/organic dimension be more helpful in understanding smaller organizations.

In any case, precise use of these words requires more than just summation of scores on the subdimensions. We would need to know how these scores should be combined and weighted to achieve an overall standing or else subdivided to yield various classifications. Without such precision, "organic" and "mechanistic" structures are apt to be useful only as general, orienting concepts that lull people into a false sense of comprehension. We suggest that case-by-case analysis of how organizations achieve certain functional requirements will yield the much-needed fine-grained analysis from which more useful generalizations may be built. Finally, it should be noted that, if the notions of organic and mechanistic are as problematic as we suggest, so are the various stage models constructed on them (for example, ambidextrous organization and parallel structures) by Duncan (1976), Kanter (1983), and Rogers (1983).

Additional Dimensions for Classifying Innovations

Chapter 2 revealed many of the ways that innovations differ from each other. Our study revealed ways to improve this taxonomy both by suggesting refinements for existing categories and by calling attention to some additional variations. In particular, we found four types of innovation that we believe have not been noted previously: defensive and oblique, time-driven, core-function, and joint payoff innovations.

Defensive and Oblique Innovation. Managers at all the banks, and to a degree at one of the S & Ls, felt that the NOW account was not apt to be profitable but that they needed to offer it to avoid losing large customers and to avoid being perceived as "behind the times." They engaged in what we call defensive innovation—their primary motives for innovation were concerned with outcomes the innovation would *prevent*. As we saw, this meant that the success of the NOW account could not be measured as we had originally hoped—by recording the number, the dollar deposits, and profitability of NOW accounts. In fact, because some organizations sought to slow down the rate at which their current customers switched to NOW accounts, success would have been negatively correlated with the number of accounts and the number of dollars deposited.

Defensive innovations are part of a larger set that we call "oblique innovations." Oblique innovations are those undertaken for other reasons than an intent to benefit directly from the innovation per se. Organizations can adopt an innovation to achieve many goals that are only indirectly related to the innovation itself, including establishing a presence in a particular niche, becoming familiar with a technology, and appearing to offer a complete line or be on the cutting edge. The success of defensive and other oblique innovations cannot be measured only by evaluating a particular innovation by itself. Previous research has failed to recognize that because oblique innovations can be successful without being used very much and perhaps without being fully implemented, their success cannot be measured on the same criteria (such as frequency of use) as nonoblique innovations.

Recognition of oblique innovation is important for conceptual and theoretical work. First, we expect that it occurs far more often than the existing innovation literature reflects. The failure to recognize the frequency of oblique innovations may be due to a number of reasons, including the "pro-innovation bias" (Rogers, 1983) and the fact that either they have not been studied or they have been investigated but not separated from nonoblique innovations. Separating nonoblique from oblique innovations may help remove an important source of error embedded in previous research. Second, the recognition of oblique innovations would reveal the inappropriateness of Tornatzky and Klein's (1982) "tentative" suggestion that degree of utilization be used to measure implementation in future research. Some innovations are not introduced in order to be used directly. Third, the success of oblique innovations may be less likely to be tightly linked to any organizational structures or processes than is the success of nonoblique ones. Defensive innovations place fewer demands on the organization than nondefensive ones. Consequently, the requirements to achieve success (as defined by the managers in a particular organization) are very different. For example, there is no reason to expect that the factors leading to successful innovation for a defensive innovator, such as First City Bank, would be the same as those leading to success at any organization attempting to introduce a more ambitious effort—including, of course, a more aggressive First City. In short, the obliqueness of innovation moderates the relationship between organization characteristics and successful innovation.

Time-Driven Innovation. A second dimension of innovation has major consequences for implementation but also has received litle attention to date. This is the degree to which implementation is time-driven. While all the organizations were free to introduce the NOW account at any point after January 1, 1981, all of them (even the defensive ones) believed that they had to offer it on the first day. Although pressures to be an early innovator are present in many cases, some innovations may in effect exert more pressure to offer them at a specific time than do others. While initially the importance attributed to time may have been perceptual (in that the law did not *require* anyone to offer the NOW account), it led to decisions and commitments that made it necessary for the organizations to be ready by January 1. These commitments created much of the crisis, especially for the large S & Ls. Clearly, innovation that allows the organization to set its own timetable is apt to allow more latitude than innovation that is time-driven.

Core-Function Innovation. A third classification dimension emerging from our data is the degree to which an innovation affects a core function. Managers from several organizations told us repeatedly that the NOW account was different from other innovations in that the demand deposit function was "the spinal cord" of a bank; not only was it located in an extremely critical function but it also required effective coordination of the operations of several different units. Because we have no data on other innovations (except for the similar automatic transfer), we can only speculate about the implications of these aspects. In all probability, the criticality and the required coordination increased the pressures people experienced and the amount of liaison needed. Moreover, the combination of the two features that define radical core-function innovations make them especially difficult. Because they involve a core function, they require tight integration with a wide spectrum of the organization; because they are radical, they are apt to threaten existing routines and demand integration among units that have had little reason to work together previously. For the most part, however, the banks had little difficulty because their existing routines meshed well; but for the S & Ls—particularly the large ones experiencing the demands of high volume—the absence of effective integrating structures to get changes made within existing units proved to be a major problem. Had the innovation been less of a core function, and/or less radical, fewer changes in ongoing operations would have been needed.

Joint-Payoff Innovation. For some innovations, almost all participants are apt to perceive common or joint outcomes—that everyone succeeds or everyone fails. For others, different participants (for example, members of various departments) may perceive the outcomes to be more separable. The different payoff structures mean that motives for cooperation cannot be assumed to be uniform across innovations; consequently different processes for successful implementation may be needed.

In many innovations studied to date, participants appeared to view the consequences as separable. For example, in Sapolsky's (1967) study, those initiating the changes and those who were supposed to use them apparently had conflicting goals. Similarly, in innovations involving personnel practices (for example, Beyer and Trice, 1978), it may have been possible for those who designed the system to experience success (by perceiving that they had designed an excellent program, for instance), even if the system was not implemented. Whether or not it was used, their job could be considered done, and those who did not use it were at fault for resisting change. Similarly, the Radnor and Neal (1973) research on operations research and management science innovations often seemed to describe cases where one unit was imposing change on another rather than units working together toward mutual accomplishment. In such situations, although win-win outcomes were possible, all parties could perceive positive outcomes even from noncooperation. No resolution between the parties was required; any given outcome, even nonutilization, could be acceptable to all.

The core nature of the NOW account produced high levels of reciprocal interdependence. Without some mutual adjustment, everyone was apt to perceive that they lost. For example, if the computer program did not serve the needs of the "business side" of the organization, it needed to be redone or everyone would look bad. Similarly, if the marketing manager placed unnecessary demands on the DP function, everyone was apt to fail in this or in other tasks in which they had interdependent or joint outcomes. Although these joint outcomes may not have always been perceived (as in the case of the DP manager at First National S & L), the task requirements fostered the view that everyone involved succeeded or failed simultaneously. While the NOW account may not represent the most extreme case of joint consequences, the fact that it had greater potential for joint payoffs than many other innovations discussed in the literature suggests separability of outcomes as an important dimension for classifying innovations.

Interrelation among these Four Dimensions. While we suggest that obliqueness, time-drivenness, joint payoff, and the degree to which an innovation involves a core function are conceptually unique characteristics for classifying innovations, in practice they may be correlated. For example, it is more likely that core innovations will have joint payoff structures than will noncore ones. Oblique innovations may allow the organization to ignore conflicts among competing interests, at least in the short run, and consequently may be less apt to be perceived as involving joint payoffs.

*Organizational Environments and Innovation: Some
Extensions*

Previous research has shown that the relationship between organizations and their environment plays an important role in innovation activity. Our investigation highlighted a number of elements that sharpen our understanding of these relationships.

Borrowing and Organization Sets. The fact that this was a borrowed innovation helped to make the relationships with other members of the organization sets—such as vendors, trade associations, and the New England banks and thrifts—very important and different than would have been the case had the twelve banks and S & Ls been first users. Contacts with a variety of these organizations were valuable. They provided data on all aspects of the innovation so that planning could proceed on a solid foundation. Moreover, the industrywide consensus about how to approach the NOW account made it possible to proceed confidently. On the other hand, such a consensus on a borrowed innovation could lead the current innovators to be victims of pluralist ignorance (i.e., an erroneous, yet widely shared, consensus). For example, during the period of extremely high interest rates, NOW account money was a rather cheap source of funds that the banks took little advantage of because they were committed to a defensive strategy. Moreover, there appeared to be some regions where a more aggressive strategy for the large banks may have been well advised, but the industrywide consensus was so strong that challenging the defensive approach successfully was difficult. To be sure, we are not saying that the banks should have been more aggressive. We only wish to suggest one potential problem that may affect organizational innovation. The impact of consensus in an organization set may be particularly important for borrowed innovation because the organization tends to rely more heavily on external sources than on its own problem-solving efforts. In sum, our findings support the view that interorganizational relationships have important effects on innovation and suggest that the role played by organization sets may be somewhat different for borrowing than for other types of innovation.

Organization Networks. Our data revealed how organization networks as well as organization sets (Aldrich and Whetten, 1981) affect innovation. For the organizations we studied, a leadership pattern had been established. Smaller organizations looked to several large banks to set the norms on pricing. Moreover, managers of the large banks, aware of their roles in pattern setting, tried to influence the overall pattern within legal constraints. The importance of these networks and organization sets indicates that major aspects of innovation and the reactions of organizations implementing them can be better understood by thinking of an interlocked set of organizations than of unconnected individual ones. Weiss (1983) came to a similar conclusion.

Government as a Major Actor. The fact that this particular innovation was affected by a key environmental actor, the federal government, introduced several interesting aspects. First, the NOW account was made possible by a law that set a legal starting date. The date was a major factor contributing to the time-driven character. There was one specific day when all one's competitors would be apt to innovate; each organization felt it needed to be ready at precisely that time. Second, the environment could change as a result of decisions of legislators and regulators. These changes could occur rapidly and were difficult to anticipate. For example, a minor change in a regulation (such as a tax law) having no direct relationship to the NOW account could result in the need for considerable reprogramming and require that some of the larger firms, which relied heavily on routines including forms and training, revise what they had already designed and redesigned. Such revisions are costly and time consuming and introduce new possibilities for error. Consequently, implementation may be aided by the ability to influence political entities to refrain from changing even apparently minor details. This aspect of innovation appears to add to the importance of the distinction between entrepreneurial and organizational innovation noted by Schumpeter (1961).

Boundary Spanning and Position in Input/Output Sequence. We observed that the environment, the nature of the innovation, and the organizational type influenced boundary-spanning activities. For one thing, this particular innovation required boundary spanning to occur at several levels in the organization. As with many innovations, high-level executives did the main boundary spanning in developing strategy; middle-level managers played more important boundary-spanning roles on technical issues. In addition, because these organizations employed a mediating technology (Thompson, 1967), the NOW account required lower-level participants to be boundary spanners during implementation—tellers and new accounts personnel were the primary contact with a major component of the organization's environment, the NOW account customers. Mistakes here could reflect poorly on the organization. Consequently, it was important that these employees understood the procedures to open a NOW account and could respond to customers' questions. However, because customers' questions could be variable and unpredictable, mechanistic procedures may have been less useful to prepare them for their roles than would be the case when lower-level participants were required to interact mainly with a more predictable and perhaps more forgiving internal environment. More generally, we speculate that approaches to implementation may be a function of the locus of their impact. If, for example, only the work of people who are far removed from contact with the environment is affected, then relatively routinized, mechanized approaches may be adequate. However, if the work of people at the organization's boundaries is affected, highly organic processes that promote flexible responses may be needed, particularly if the environment they confront is nonroutine and unorganized (Jurkovich, 1974).[1]

Similarly, if the innovation affects customers directly, implementation may require different approaches than if only an organization's employees are affected. When effective implementation requires managing customers, new problems emerge. In comparison to employees, the customer is loosely coupled with the organization. Having less control over its customers, the organization must anticipate and attempt to influence what the customer is apt to do in ways other than using the legitimate authority it often relies upon to control employees. For example, the NOW account required a new format for customer statements, while managers felt they needed to help their customers to understand the new statements. They attempted to reduce the education required in a variety of ways including careful design of the statement; they attempted to meet the needs directly by training new-accounts personnel to inform the customers when opening an account and to provide good answers to customer inquiries. Similarly, customer behavior forced some internal adjustments. For example, Second Commercial's initial system relied on customers to report how many checks they had outstanding on their old accounts. However, managers soon learned that customers did not keep appropriate records, so a special internal system was needed to distinguish the old from the new checks. In addition, several organizations complicated their check-processing operations to avoid requiring customers to use new checks. In short, customers introduced variability that the organizations needed to anticipate and respond to. The locus of the direct effects outside the organizations' boundaries introduced pressures for a flexibility in implementation. In some cases, flexibility was accomplished by training lower-level personnel to prepare the customers; in other cases, by complicating but not disturbing routine systems.

Boundary Spanning and Routine/Radical Innovation. The nature of boundary spanning was not the same for radical and routine innovation. For routine innovation, the banks required few changes in boundary spanning. In fact, although the design phase did involve the development of contacts with the New England banks, relationships with the environment seemed to be unchanged during implementation, except for the responses to customers just noted. On the other hand, in attempting radical innovation, S & Ls faced many new elements and problems. First, there were new organizations to deal with, including check printers and software vendors. Second, much internal learning was required for the organization to be able to access its environment effectively. For example, organization members needed to learn new jargon in order to communicate with vendors; much needed to be learned before even the right questions could be asked. Third, the S & Ls had become potentially more competitive with banks. Some managers, particularly those at the largest one (First National), wondered if they could trust the advice of the bankers for services they bought from them much as they had in the past. Finally, the relationship of S & Ls with their customers had changed. Previously, customer service personnel had been able to respond fully to customer requests. Now, however, customer requests could entail considerable time when, for instance, people who had dealt with the firm for many years needed help to balance their accounts. Moreover, personnel now had reason to fear that customers might try to take advantage of them via bad checks. Thus, some forces existed to give customer relations a more distant and/or bureaucratic character. Similarly, serving customers now demanded more in terms of lobby capacity, parking space, and teller time. Radical innovation required considerable expansion and reprogramming to achieve desired relationships with customers.

Inert Segments of the Environment. We have seen how a defensive strategy reduced the demands the innovation put on some organizations. At least for the NOW account, the defensive approach and its success rested upon the belief that many customers would be passive or inert: without special encouragement, they would not open a NOW account, and unless provoked, they would not move their business elsewhere. More generally, we suggest that certain environments, because they are inert, make implementation easier. In such environments, the organization can succeed simply by not disturbing certain external actors (or by working to keep them from becoming proactive). So while most treatments of innovation seem to center attention on how the organization needs to reprogram itself to deal with a changing environment, we suggest that for *some* innovations, successful implementation may depend upon making an accurate assessment of what portions of the environment are inert and then keeping these segments that way. Theorists and managers need to distinguish these conditions from those that pressure the organization to change.

Conclusion. Because the NOW account was a borrowed innovation, the environmental relations we reported are not likely to generalize to early users. Relationships with components of environments may be more routinized and hence easier to see in borrowed than in initiated innovations. In any case, our data revealed quite clearly that the requirements for successful implementation are a partial function of the interaction between the nature of the innovation and actors in the environment including suppliers, regulators, competitors, and customers. In fact, considerable interorganizational cooperation and coordination were involved at several levels. At the national level, organizations from another region of the country were willing to provide substantial amounts of information. Normal market relationships linked vending and consulting firms to users. Professional organizations also played major roles. At the local level, information coordination and cooperation among firms that were in some ways competitors were apparent.

If the observed degree of interorganizational cooperation and coordination in implementing the NOW account is common to other innovations in modern society, our discussion of Schumpeter in chapter 1 takes on special importance. Recall that Schumpeter (1961) suggested that the referent of the word *innovation* changes over time—innovation may involve quite different activities in one era than in another. If integrated and cooperative activities, both within and among organizations, are as critical to innovation as our results suggest, we see how obfuscating certain past connotations of the word *innovation* may be. Often, the innovator is assumed to be the "rugged individual." To be sure, such people have an important role to play. On the other hand, to the extent that researchers', managers', and policymakers' focus on innovation is driven by such images exclusively, they are apt to overlook personal and structural factors that produce the integration that appears so critical for innovation in an organizational society. Moreover, we see how even using an organization as the unit of analysis for innovation can be misleading. Guided by inappropriate images, scholars and managers will be ill prepared to understand and manage innovation. As society evolves, those who seek to understand and influence innovation are apt to benefit from analysis of transorganizational systems (Cummings, 1984), which combines insights into social structures and processes from the study of interorganizational relationships with social problem solving.

One matter we have not considered so far in our analysis of organization environment and innovation is the possibility that the organization may import portions of the environment to aid in implementation. As we argue in the following section, while importing has received little attention in the innovation literature to date, it can play a major role in successful implementation.

Importing, Contracting, and Implementation

Our current study was designed in a tradition of research on implementation which seems to have given little attention to the role of importing and subcontracting. Following the research we reviewed in chapter 2, we expected that implementation would be accomplished through the application and modification of existing structures and the deployment and development of current personnel. However, these expectations were not confirmed. The failure in this and previous research to find consistently strong correlations between organization structure and successful innovation may be because, in fact, the two are not always related to each other. A firm need not be technologically or managerially competent ahead of time with respect to a particular innovation if it can import the capacity or can contract with an external provider. When one of these routes is taken, prior competence is not apt to be as highly correlated with success as intuition might suggest. Similarly, if the structural requirements can be introduced by implanting (for example, by hiring bankers and making them part of the firm, as several S & Ls did) or by putting an entire structure in the core of the system on a temporary basis (as First National did), prior structure might have little relation to success. In fact, it might be that a very inappropriate structure drives the firm to import or subcontract, and therefore we would find a negative correlation between the assumed appropriate structure and success. If a particularly troublesome function can be contracted out, the firm is in essence hiring a structure (i.e., the structure of the subcontractor) appropriate for the task and therefore has little need to modify its own or to worry that its structure will cause problems. Although it is quite possible that certain structures may make for more effective importing and subcontracting, there is no necessary reason to believe that these are the same ones that would make a firm able to perform the requirements of the innovation internally. In essence, importing and contracting out can reduce the effects of previous history and thereby greatly diminish the relationships between structure and task demands that structural contingency approaches lead us to expect.

These processes played major roles in some of the firms in our sample. Consequently, we came to view importing and subcontracting as major techniques for successful implementation. These techniques have important implications for theory because, to a degree, they enable an organization to separate its ability to innovate from its prior state of being.

Importing and Design. Almost all the organizations imported information during their search process. The mechanisms they used varied, but because this was a borrowed innovation, many of its parameters could be anticipated. Such importing is the essence of borrowed innovation and therefore is well known in the innovation literature. However, other types of importing and the role of subcontracting have received little attention.

Some of the most interesting aspects of importing appeared in the cases of radical innovation. There were three major forms: importing personnel with relevant experience as permanent employees, employing consultants as temporary employees, and buying established systems.

Importing Personnel. It has long been standard practice for organizations to hire appropriately trained people from outside to obtain the competencies they need but have not had the occasion to employ in the past and/or have not invested in developing internally. However, for the most part, the innovation literature seems to have focused more on reorienting current employees than on hiring new personnel.

New personnel contributed to successful implementation in several of our organizations. All the large and medium-sized S & Ls hired individuals with banking backgrounds as back-room operatives. First National S & L and First Capitol S & L hired managers with banking backgrounds, but Second National S & L and Second Capitol S & L did not. While Second Capitol experienced few problems with implementation, their size had allowed them to use the guidelines and services of the Federal Home Loan Bank Board, thereby reducing the need for internal expertise. As a result, their need for a banker in a management position was minimized. Second National had too much volume and too much product complexity to do that, and was in sore need of expertise which was never imported. In contrast, many early problems First Capitol experienced disappeared with the hiring of a banker and centralization of the process under him. On the other hand, First National imported the necessary technical competence and orientation by hiring Ms. Smith; unfortunately, however, she was not able to influence the process in a timely manner.

We conclude that importing personnel can be critical, but its effect depends on the organization's ability to use the expertise of the "outside" people effectively. Although it would be hazardous to generalize from just two organizations, we speculate that successful importing may be aided by allowing a new person (or unit) to operate as a self-contained entity, thus reducing the need to establish a political base in order to achieve the necessary integration. Where importing worked at First Capitol, the new manager was given a clear charge from the president and the process was centralized under him. On the other hand, at First National, neither was clear support of the president given to Ms. Smith nor was the process centralized in her hands. Again, we see how aspects of a centralized yet flexible system may aid implementation. Such systems may have more in common with a Mintzberg (1979) simple structure located within a larger organization than with the mechanized structures postulated by Zaltman et al. (1973).

Temporary Importing. A second and much more dramatic form of importing was the use First National S & L made of the consultants. In essence, First National achieved technical and organizational readiness by temporarily implanting part of another organization; giving virtual line-authority to managers from another organization added a new dimension to the normal use of consultants. We call the structure used for this temporary importing an "implanted" organization.

This implanting accomplished a number of things simultaneously: the needed technical skills were added, the skills of project management were provided, and the power needed to dislodge entrenched interests and facilitate information flows was introduced. While one could argue that the project management process employed was organic in a number of ways, the creation of the implanted organization was instituted centrally and it functioned in a way to replace a committee that had proved incapable of forcing needed actions. Although implanting part of another organization could work for a variety of reasons, in the context of First National these changes helped because they concentrated power and added expertise.

It is difficult to know how widely the implanted organization can be applied. It did help First National to achieve technical readiness, a common focus, coordination, information flows, access to resources when needed, monitoring, and an efficient decision-making process, all of which proved vital. Moreover, it provided access to key parts of the environment—especially the software vendor. Perhaps, it also served the symbolic function Nystrom and Starbuck (1984) postulated to be a catalyst for dramatic change—a belief that finally things would really be different. A formerly powerful individual was removed from the process and came to appear as a scapegoat. Overall, then, it appears that the implanted organization created many conditions thought to aid innovation.

The similarities of some of these achievements with those of Kanter's (1983) parallel organization suggest possible generalizability. The innovating unit was buffered from normal pressures; the consultants could do the specific project without the need to worry about long-standing social relationships. Unlike the parallel organization, however, it was part of the regular organization structure. Still, it must be stressed that the implanting took place in a particular context. The system had struggled with the NOW account for over a year and much learning had already taken place during the struggle; also, a crisis was evident, people had high levels of commitment to the organization, and the innovation was borrowed. While no claim about general applicability can be made from the one case reported here, it is clear that the implanted organization represents one additional way some organizations can reduce the constraints of their previous structure, competencies, and history.

Purchase of Established Systems. The third form of importing was the purchase of established routines and technology, or what Munson and Pelz (1979) called "packaged innovations." All the organizations met some of their requirements by purchasing, but some organizations found it easier to import established routines than did others. In particular, Second Capitol S & L and both small S & Ls purchased the necessary technology, while Second National and First Capitol S & Ls and First Regional Bank purchased outside technology but had difficulty adapting it to their needs. Several factors seemed to account for differences in abilities to import.

One was the similarity of the organization to others; the more dissimilar an organization was to other organizations on key dimensions, the more difficulty it faced in importing. For example, First National was much larger than most other S & Ls in the country; it did not find information from S & L trade associations to be relevant to its problems. Likewise, its on-line teller system and Second National S & L's telephone bill payment system required tailored programs, making it difficult for them to import from the environment. Thus, similarity mediates the relationship between requisite structure and environment for innovation. In fact, the ability to import in general may be a function of certain organizational characteristics that are generic rather than particular to any one innovation.[2] To the degree that this is so, we expect quite different approaches before, during, and after implementation might be equally successful. Moreover, for firms that rely on importing, success ought to be positively correlated with their similarity on key dimensions to other organizations in their environment. What these key dimensions might be remains to be discovered.

Importing was also affected by how urgent it was that the firm take action. Large organizations that had promoted aggressively needed to handle a large volume on the very first day; this ability required a qualitatively different technology than was demanded to process a lower volume. For example, small firms that had not promoted aggressively could handle the small volume by manual procedures. They could wait, as Second City Bank did, until the right software package was available.

Finally, ability to import seemed to be influenced by managerial preferences and judgments. Some organizations accepted the limits of purchasing software or external data processing, whereas others wanted the freedom to design their product as they deemed necessary.

Subcontracting. Contracting with an outside firm for a service is closely related to importing, particularly importing through the purchase of established routines. All our organizations did this to some degree—for instance, none printed their own checks. For several firms, subcontracting played a major role in reducing the demands for check processing. Subcontracting then, like the various types of importing, allows the organization to be less dependent on its previous operations when innovating. It too deserves a more central place in the innovation literature than it now has.

Conclusion. Our data revealed that several forms of importing can play important roles in the implementation process. Variations in the capacity to import may be introduced by structures and processes that are different from those thought to affect internally developed innovations. These variations and the dynamics of importing are worthy of future study. Importing is yet another process that may reduce the strength of the relationships between organizational configurations and their ability to innovate. Finally, although Second Commercial Bank did some importing in coping with the automatic transfer, importing was most varied and interesting for radical innovation. In those cases when importing was successful, it was characterized by rather centralized authority around the tasks required for the NOW account, it often brought in technical expertise, and it created a setting where the people whose skills were needed gained influence and other resources. In short, importing may be a major tactic for radical innovation.

Methodological Implications

In interpreting our findings, we so far have suggested some ways to refine inquiry about organizational innovation focusing mainly on conceptual matters such as the dimensions for classifying innovations. We now turn to research methodology.

Need for In-Depth Research

First, and most important, our understanding of organizational innovation will benefit greatly from methods that permit researchers to interpret their data in the context of the organization as an ongoing social system. Although case studies may not be the only vehicle for reaching such understanding, obviously this assertion is consistent with the appeals for in-depth case studies by Yin (1978), Pellegrin (1978), and Gibson (1975). We now attach greater importance than when we started to Gibson's observation that, even though the process through which longitudinal case research is generated and tested is a slow one, seemingly more efficient cross-sectional methods alone will not suffice.

Gibson argued that even though it entails considerable disadvantages in developing and testing theory, the methodology required to study implementation of innovation needs to begin with multiple case studies. Knowledge will accumulate as the instruments and results from one site are tailored into working hypotheses and instruments for research for the next study. However, this approach is congruent with the phenomenon. In Gibson's words:

> *To the extent that implementation is indeed best conceived as a process, taking place over time, and as a complex, multivariate process of interpersonal influence, then the longitudinal, case-by-case, action research methodology is most appropriate.* Moreover, if one believes as I do that the state of implementation theory leaves much to be desired, the exploratory and grounded-theory nature of this methodology is more likely to yield valid constructs and relationships for eventual theory (p.71).

Although our study was cross-sectional and we collected data after the fact, the degree to which our understanding was furthered by inquiry into the history of the firm convinced us of the merits of Gibson's position.

However, we suggest that Gibson's reasoning has merit even if implementation is not primarily an interpersonal process, because the approach he advocated is helpful in uncovering the influence of history, strategy, and size on the idiosyncratic patterns of action and interpretations of events. Critical aspects of the process may involve micro-level actions that cannot be seen easily from a distance. For example, it would have been easy to miss the fact that implementation at Second Commercial Bank was facilitated by managers bringing their secretaries, who occupied central positions in information flows, to meetings at the holding company. Similarly, it could have been difficult to uncover how the process at First Commercial Bank was aided by Mr. Wayman's judgments about what were the real priorities of the business managers and how he could realize his own objectives by proposing certain trade-offs. Of course, interpersonal relationships did play a major role in our organizations, as they did in Gibson's. These relationships too were often of a micro nature and could easily be missed without close contact with the people involved. Implementation is indeed a rich social process and it demands a rich methodology to study it.

Perhaps most important, our findings indicate the need for such a rich approach to understand what the innovation means to the organization. As we indicated, the criteria of successful innovation are organization-specific and therefore vary among organizations. Consequently, measurement of success must be expanded to include the diversity and to reflect possibly unique objectives. Both requirements may be difficult to meet without in-depth probing in an organization, particularly since some of the outcomes may be long-term and only indirectly related to a particular innovation.

Unfortunately, in comparison with cross-sectional studies where the researcher does not explore beyond the immediate impact of the innovation, data collection will be more expensive and analysis will be more problematic because the data will be richer and less readily quantifiable. Nevertheless, given the nature of the phenomenon, such expense will be necessary if we are to understand it.

Necessary Confounding of Size and Method

Methods used to study innovation might need to vary as a function of the size of the units involved. In our study, the small and large organizations functioned in qualitatively different ways. In the large organizations search, decision making, and implementation left traces—there were formal training materials, written action plans, and notes on meetings. Moreover, a number of people had played specialized roles and voiced deliberate strategies for influencing their counterparts. Consequently, the process appeared somewhat formal and it was possible to validate individual interviews through archival records as well as other interviews. Efforts to achieve integration left traces visible to an outside observer. By contrast, in the very small organizations, few traces were left. Decisions were often made by individuals or in a small group meeting and were implemented via oral communication. Integration was not as problematic as at the larger firms. In short, knowing what transpired in the large organizations required organizational analysis as well as consideration of personal and interpersonal factors; the events in the smaller organizations could have been described adequately by focusing on interpersonal (and intrapersonal) dynamics.

In general, it may be difficult to use one method to study implementation when the organizations involved vary widely in size. In designing the current study, we unconsciously had larger organizations in mind. For example, we expected that there would always be written materials to compare with the interview data, but this was not true. Moreover, we planned multiple interviews to allow us to reduce our dependence on the recall of one person. This luxury is less available in small organizations. Because many factors normally expected to be present in formal organizations (formally differen-tiated departments and written rules and procedures, for example) were largely absent in the smaller organizations, it seems reasonable to assume that interpersonal and group dynamics may have played a relatively greater role here than in larger organizations. Consequently, it might have been much more important to watch the process first-hand (by being a group process observer) than it would have been at the larger organizations. In the latter, in fact, key events were apt to be so diffuse that they could not feasibly be observed save by having someone be with every possible actor all the time. As a result, our understanding of the smaller organizations may have been more adversely affected by the ex post facto nature of our study than was our comprehension of the larger organizations. Method and size may be confounded in research on organizational innovation as well as in research on organizations in general.

Preliminary Advice to Managers

For the manager, the message from this research is to search for and/or design structures and processes that: permit needed flexibility, concentrate power sufficiently, ensure that inputs from those who are close to the innovation and are apt to know what is needed are effective, and provide appropriate technical and organizational readiness. Parallel structures, matrix designs, and project teams become mere models that achieve these requirements in some contexts, rather than "the way" to innovate. We conclude that the manager needs to analyze the organization's technical and social competence vis-à-vis such factors as the organization's goals for the innovation and its past experience with similar products or processes. As a result, our guidance to managers consists of a list of *items to consider*, not a specific program of action.

Some of the eight items on this list are well known in the management literature and are apt to strike most managers as being intuitively obvious. Although we doubt that such congruence means that organizational innovation is a well-understood process, it does support out view that often innovation is not as exotic and unique as other writers have suggested. A few elements on this list are less widely known; some we think are new. We hope they will expand the set of ideas managers use to approach innovation. Implicit in each item is the view that organizations can be prepared for innovation ahead of time.

Achieving Technical Competence

The organization must have, or have access to, sufficient technical competence to introduce and run the innovation. This competence can be addressed in a variety of ways. Obviously planning and anticipation, although not always possible, can be extremely valuable. Organizations such as First Commercial Bank that engage in continuous long-range planning and are willing to commit resources to personnel development and technology well in advance of innovation are apt to benefit greatly. In addition, previous research has shown that access to professional networks and diversity facilitate innovation.

Our study suggests that these resources can be useful in implementation as well. As many managers have realized, investing in the general professional development of their people can be extremely profitable. First Commercial benefitted substantially from such investments.

These results are consistent with the modern human resources approach to management (Miles, 1975). Related investments oriented to building loyalty to the organization, such as those we observed at First National S & L and First Commercial Bank, may serve as a reservoir of good will with employees and customers that can help during crisis.

Building an Organization Capable of Innovating

Building capacity for innovation is a continuing process that the organization needs to invest in over an extended period of time. A variety of approaches exists. Most approaches are geared to individual development. If the organization has done the type of planning just suggested, then the criteria for such development can be better assessed. Because much important learning can occur when individuals have the opportunity to observe others, it may be useful to consider employing individuals who have particular skills and placing them in positions of high visibility even before the particular skills are critical for the organization. Also, managers can be encouraged to develop their people. Such efforts need to include but go beyond standard training programs. For example, Bradford and Cohen (1984) urge managers to consider the development of employees as well as current performance in day-to-day supervision.

This approach can be extended to the organization level. For instance, organizations might choose oblique innovations that involve them primarily in activities to learn things potentially useful in preparing the system and its members to innovate in the future. Some organizations already do this when they work on a new product or employ a new process primarily to gain experience with a technology. Of course, resource allocations of this sort are limited; but the general idea of giving some weight to the question "What can we learn?" in deciding upon alternative activities may help an organization prepare itself for innovation in the future.

Integrating Effort through the Management of Organizational and Social Processes

Creating and managing organizational structures and social processes take on special importance for implementing innovation. The basis for this conclusion was pervasive in our findings. Here we highlight only three interwoven aspects: (1) creating organizational arrangements, (2) distributing influence to mesh with the task requirements, and (3) managing expectations.

While all of these are intuitively obvious, a few words about each in the context of our work may be helpful in contemplating implementation.

Creating Organizational Arrangements. As our organizations demonstrated, integrating tasks and functional areas could be achieved in a variety of ways. Some, such as scheduling and project management, are well known and have been useful in many contexts. In most but not all of our larger organizations, project management proved to be a useful approach. Its value seemed to stem from the fact that it laid out the requirements in sequential fashion, developed a schedule, and assigned accountability. When done well, it also was flexible—making it possible to add new routines and people and to readjust the parts to fit emerging requirements. To be sure, there are a number of alternative ways to achieve these things in various systems, but the project structure seems to add direction to the process and brings together people from different levels in the hierarchy and various functional areas.

Similarly, concentration of power in the hands of one person for projects of limited complexity (as in simple structures) is neither new nor difficult to put into operation. What is more difficult is achieving coherence when tasks are more complex and/or less capable of being routinized, because it often requires winning agreement of high-level managers who have their own agendas to promote. These tasks require agreed upon concepts, strategies, and visions. In our study, homogeneity at the top levels was aided by a vision or a set of beliefs and images that were developed and actively promoted by high-level executives. What was being done with the particular innovation made sense because it was consistent with a given framework. Generally, successful implementation is apt to be aided when the concept itself can be shown to be consistent with other things the organization is attempting to do.

Perhaps one advantage that organic type systems have in innovating is that the more holistic orientation that exists among their members may make it easier for congruence to be demonstrated. This theme is a central one of recently popular treatments of organization culture (for example, Peters and Waterman, 1982; Ouchi, 1980). Building on Kerr and Jermier (1978), we argue that such shared assumptions, values, and beliefs serve as partial substitutes for leadership in complex systems that are too large for face-to-face-interaction and direct monitoring. Similarly they may serve as partial substitutes for structures that cannot be instituted because the process they would guide is only clear after the fact. In short, managers can help their organizations to innovate by developing shared conceptions among members ahead of time. The development of shared strategies and values takes time. It should be treated as an investment and be part of a long-term strategy for preparing an organization for innovation. When members of the organization have common orientations and can see how a particular innovation is consistent with pervasive long-term means and ends, a working consensus can be achieved even without any special structures.

Of course, it is clear from our study that such homogeneity can also be achieved by concentration of power. This was apparent in the small organizations, where one or a very few people had almost total control. In fact, even in large organizations such as Third Commercial Bank, homogeneity can be achieved through strong leadership. In several firms where one individual or a small group of managers had sufficient technical expertise and a strong sense of the business requirements, centralization (both high-level and what we have called "constrained centralization" where power was concentrated in the hands of managers below the very top levels) aided implementation. First National S & L made it clear that shared assumptions and values may not be enough when power is too diffuse.

To summarize, these firms were aided by a variety of approaches; many of them seemed related to Mintzberg's (1979) simple structures. The particular project and the skills of important actors made it possible to process informaton and to direct action centrally.

It is important to note that such arrangements can be very flexible. Because they require so little formalization or group consensus, they can also be inexpensive to develop and operate. However, because they depend on managers who can comprehend and respond to the *whole* problem, prior investment in hiring and developing such people is required. Organizations must continue to seek ways to develop a core of managers well versed in both technical and business elements. Such people may prove invaluable for innovation because they allow the organization to benefit from some of the advantages of a simple structure. In other words, the capacity to achieve the requisite integration is built into the organization ahead of time via its managers.

However, such people and structures do not guarantee success. For example, Mr. Friedman at First Regional Bank was a talented man with a strong managerial and technical background. The problems encountered stemmed in part from his making decisions for data processing without the needed information. Even extremely able people can make mistakes when, for whatever reason, the information flow fails to function effectively. Integrating the business and technical issues also requires the ability to create appropriate information flows.

We suggest that while innovation depends upon the somewhat rare individuals we have been describing, often such people may be systematically screened out of organizations. It is probable that many individuals who could play such roles may become frustrated by the standard operating procedures that organizations often find most effective for their ordinary circumstances. They may either leave the firm or not be recognized by the firm until it is too late. We have no simple resolution for this dilemma except to suggest that developing innovative capacity be treated as a long-term investment that provides an overarching logic for experimenting with modifications of today's practices to develop tomorrow's capacity to innovate.

The problems our organizations faced in integrating the business and technical requirements and the critical role played in several firms by one person who combined these two orientations indicate a critical need for a special type of manager for innovation. Organizations and society need ways to develop what Victor Thompson (1965) called "technical generalists." At a national level, business and engineering schools may have much to offer through joint programs or other mechanisms to prepare students in undergraduate, graduate, and executive programs to play such roles. However, many managers will not be able to wait for such programs to develop.

What can firms do to develop their own technical generalists? What distinguishes organizations that have the appropriate generalists available? Our study offers a few clues. First, long-range planning and continuing cross-area meetings and projects (as at First Commercial Bank) seem to be important. Second, by-products from work that the firm does in the normal course of its operation may play a major role. The major by-product noted in our study was the sophisticated DP capacity that the large banks had developed through the services they had provided for some time. In other words, opportunities existed that demanded and hence led to the development of joint orientations. As we suggested before, oblique innovations may be attempted in the hope that they yield such results.

Third, rather traditional human resource functions—planning and development—may be crucial. Structures, no matter how exotic, will be only an inadequate substitute. Firms can do much to improve their capacity to implement future innovations by anticipating the management skills that will be needed and developing people who have them. It is probably more than coincidence that successful First Commercial Bank stressed its training function, or that Mr. Wayman, who played such a central role in getting both sides integrated, was a technical specialist and enrolled in an MBA program.

One nontraditional aspect, however, may be warranted. In many cases, the integrating efforts are apt to have a much stronger technological emphasis than has been needed in the past. From our study, it appears that developing the business orientations of technical specialists is a viable approach; it may well be that managers geared to business issues can develop the needed technical sophistication as well.

Redistributing Influence. Managing implementation requires that the distribution of power be aligned with the needed expertise. Particularly for radical innovation, this may require redistributing power because currently powerful people are not apt to be those with the expertise required for the innovation. Management may need to take special steps to enhance the power of some people and reduce the influence of others. In some cases, these steps can be taken ahead of time. Managers can predict what type of orientations must be influential and support their development. In other cases, realigning influence may well be the most important role for top management to play during implementation. Using Zaleznik's (1977) distinction between leaders (people who shape ideas and develop options) and managers (people who operate established procedures), we postulate that leadership has a most important role to play in implementation, especially of radical innovation. During radical innovation, previous routines are being destroyed and new ones have yet to be established. It is here that leaders may be the only element capable of providing direction, coherence, regimentation for new roles, emotional support, and confidence.

Of course, there are alternatives; the ones that work will depend on existing conditions. In some cases where the appropriate groundwork has been done, these needs may be met by procedures, personnel, and climate ingrained in the organization and "spontaneous" adjustments within the groups charged with implementation. In other cases, personnel changes and/ or training in such skills as project management may be needed. In yet other cases, as Hage (1980) suggested, innovation will require the creation of a new organization.

Managing Change by Following and Leading Expectations. Underlying much of what happened in the twelve organizations were expectations people had about what was being done and why, and how change of a particular sort should be introduced. At First and Second Commercial Banks, the presidents of the subsidiary banks were willing to follow the defensive strategy advanced by executives from the holding company because they expected strategic leadership from these people. Similarly, the perception by lower-level participants in many organizations that the innovation was a nonevent seemed to be linked to the fact that management was following expected patterns. To be sure, the patterns were not always the same across the systems—in some cases people expected to be consulted and in other cases they did not. What was common was that their expectations were met.

Based on our data, we cannot say that violated expectations cause problems, because the firms were so consistent with their standing approaches. (The only major inconsistency we observed involved the breakfast meetings at Third Commercial Bank, which were simply forgotten.) However, because so many people reported that the consistency with expectations appeared to be important, we speculate that such consistency was a background factor that happened to characterize the firms we studied. We suggest that implementation benefits when the processes used are the ones expected by those affected.

It is important to note, however, that we are not suggesting that expectations should never be violated. In fact, violated expectations may be needed to "unfreeze" attitudes and beliefs, and thereby to make change possible. Thus, leaders of innovation may sometimes find it useful to violate expectations deliberately.

In essence, we suggest that innovation can be guided by a sensitivity to and management of expectations. Many potential problems can be avoided if people are treated in ways they have come to expect. Managers who know what is expected and who act in accordance with these expectations can avoid unnecessary problems. On the other hand, sensitivity to the expectations may allow managers to know when violating them may be necessary to make a system able to innovate. For example, the magnitude of the crisis at First National S & L might have been reduced had the president acted to counter the norms of committee decision making by showing that the NOW account required a different means of operation. In short, implementation may be aided by a sensitivity to expectations—plus the knowledge and skills to avoid violating them unknowingly and unnecessarily but to violate them effectively when necessary.

Integrating Effort—Some Additional Thoughts. Clearly then, no general statements can be made about how to achieve the appropriate integration of effort. The procedures that can be used to achieve the appropriate alignment will be a function of the organization's history, culture, and leadership style. However, it should be clear that managers must anticipate and orchestrate the needed alignments. Such efforts require a sensitivity to organizational processes that many managers either lack or are unwilling or unable to act upon.

It is interesting to note that we found no evidence of inquiries about structural arrangements in any of the search activities. Moreover, we found little awareness of the potential impact of the existing distribution of influence on implementation. In many cases—particularly in the small organizations— the lack of this information seemed unimportant. As we saw, however, many of the problems that did occur could be traced to the inability of actors with relevant expertise and information to have an appropriate degree of influence. These findings give some support to applied behavioral scientists who have argued that managers are well advised to take action to create the alignments needed for successful change. The chances that managers will do so are increased if they examine the organization requirements for the change and then ask themselves "Who needs to be influential to actualize these requirements?" and "Do these individuals or units have the appropriate amount of influence?" As a correlate, sometimes managers may be well advised not to attempt a particular innovation because the required realignments are judged to be too costly, too unlikely to succeed, or too inconsistent with the current fabric; there may be some instances where it is prudent to allow structure to determine strategy.

Borrowing Ideas and Prototypes

Borrowing and imitation, perhaps because they have pejorative connotations in a society oriented by a pioneering spirit, have not been considered systematically by theorists or practitioners. Yet borrowing, imitating, and purchasing can be vital processes in innovation and should be considered deliberately.

However, not all firms will be equally effective borrowers. Implementation is likely to be affected by the networks of relationships between organizations and their environments. These relationships can influence the procurement of needed information, technology, and other resources and the ability of the organization to learn from observing others. Organizations vary in how similar they are to other organizations and how well they mesh with potential suppliers. Many potential problems in borrowing can be anticipated and perhaps avoided if, early in the planning stages, these issues are taken into account. It is possible to become a better borrower if the process is considered analytically.

Importing Competence

We suggest that ways to import competence be considered as a viable tactic for implementation. Permanent importing, such as hiring new staff, is a well-established practice and can be improved by anticipation of and attention to power alignments. Temporary implanting represents a more intensive use of outsiders, such as consultants, than is traditional. The experiences of First National S & L suggest that radical innovation can be done quickly, circumventing the existing social structure, by incorporating another organization on a temporary basis. Such an arrangement aids radical innovation by introducing a somewhat intact unit and avoiding the delays encountered when the human beings who have populated an organization for a long time attempt to accommodate each other. Obviously, such an approach runs many risks and may work only under a severely constrained set of conditions. Nevertheless, we have clear evidence that it can be extremely effective.

Reducing the Demands of an Innovation

Managers are well advised to seek ways to reduce the requirements that the innovation places on the organization. We suggest that sometimes what has

been termed the pro-innovation bias (Rogers, 1983) may produce dysfunctional consequences by propelling the organization to create the "perfect" rather than the optimal level of innovation. As Galbraith (1974) pointed out, under some conditions, lowering standards is a better way to manage information requirements than is attempting to process more information. Our organizations revealed that innovation can vary in the level of performance required. Some of our organizations reduced their risks and implementation problems substantially by defining the innovation in a way that demanded little change initially but more later on.

More generally, organizations have choices as to standards they wish to hold up for a particular innovation. The strategy of the organization as well as its established capacity to handle a particular innovation ought to be used to help decide upon the level of the innovation. Innovation need not always be all or none. Managers ought to evaluate the level of an innovation that fits their organization. Similarly, organizations can reduce the requirements they face by taking advantage of parts of their environments that are inert. We saw the banks do this by recognizing that many customers were passive and would not change their accounts unless stimulated to do so. Consequently, a defensive strategy could be effective. Managers may foster successful implementation by knowing what parts of their environment are not changing and by responding accordingly.

Flexible People and Organizations—The Comparative Importance of Communication and Participation

Our study—along with those of Beyer and Trice (1978) and Greenwood et al. (1975)—demonstrated the importance of flexibility and mutual adjustment for implementation, even at lower levels of the organization. While these are outcomes normally attributed to organic structures, we saw that there were many ways to achieve them. In fact, there are so many possible alternatives that we found it necessary to specify four generic requirements (concentration of power, attention to signals from those charged with implementation, flexibility, and technical readiness) and suggest that these can be actualized in different ways depending on the context.

One reason why organic structures have been seen as likely to encourage flexibility is that they allow widespread participation, which leads to informed and committed personnel. However, of the four generic requirements for innovation, only the second and third suggest possible benefits from high participation by lower-level participants.

In our study, most lower-level participants were not consulted at all, although this posed no problems. Whether these individuals were consulted or not, whatever complaints they had focused overwhelmingly on the fact that they were not confident that they knew what to do. In this light, we speculate that for lower-level participants, the communication function served by participation may be at least as important as the motivation function that many behavioral scientists have stressed. Clearly, certain seemingly mechanistic processes (such as procedures manuals, forms, and "close" supervision) can serve the communication function (although they do not allow for the necessary feedback loops). As Hage and Dewar (1973) noted, participation is only one means to aid communication.

On the other hand, participation may be a particularly good form of communication for implementation because it makes mutual adjustment and redesign more possible. The experiences of First Commercial and Second Commercial Banks showed the utility of designing procedures manuals and forms using input from those familiar with the demands of the users and suggest that certain organic approaches may aid the information flow. Motivational effects may have been most important for the middle-level managers responsible for adapting the guidelines set by the holding company for use by their units.

We conclude that managers need to approach the issue of participation in change more carefully than we behavioral scientists often encourage them to do. We believe that there are many benefits and potential benefits from participation, but they may have as much to do with communication as with power. Moreover, they are apt to be quite dependent on the consistency of the approach and what people have come to expect.

Encouraging Upward Communication

Finally, systems designed to permit lower-level participants ready access to those who can deal with any problems at the moment they arise appear extremely useful. Such access may be required most often in radical innovation because there are more unanticipated events and because the social parterns are in flux and/or are inappropriate for the problems that occur, but it seems important to those involved in routine innovation as well. In a way, such backup systems are really alternatives to specification. Managers therefore may be well advised to center attention on the development of procedures to solicit constant feedback and make changes regularly, allowing employees to get answers when they need them. These requirements can be achieved in a number of ways in different systems. Once again, we found evidence that communication was critical in overcoming resistance to change more because it provided needed information than because of its benefits in terms of human relations, such as commitment and motivation.

Conclusions

This book was written with two audiences in mind—students of innovation and managers of innovation. While we did not attempt to give equal attention to the interests of both groups, we believe that several of the most central themes we developed are common and equally important to both groups.

First, our findings are consistent with the observations of general systems theorists: in complex social systems, you can never do just one thing. Managers attempting to increase their organizations' innovating capacities need to recognize the continuous interplay between actions explicitly directed at innovation and other activities. They would do well to consider how activities during apparently static phases can be modified to prepare the organization for future innovation. For example, routine innovation can be accomplished in different ways. Some paths will promote more learning than will others and, all else being equal, may be selected for this reason. Similarly, managers need to recognize that any given innovation will have a variety of outcomes. With this in mind, they need to allow multiple criteria to influence their decisions about what innovations to attempt, how to implement the chosen ones, and how to evaluate their success.

Students of innovation also can gain by emphasizing the idea that organizations never do just one thing. By doing so, students will benefit from a wider set of criteria to evaluate implementation than they have employed in the past. How frequently an innovation is used can be a misleading index of implementation. As we have suggested, some innovations are undertaken with little intention to use them. For example, a given defensive or oblique innovation can be very successful and of great benefit to an organization even if there is little evidence that it was used. In fact, the less it was used may sometimes mean that it was more rather than less successful.

Second, our findings point to another observation of general systems theorists: organizations are complex social systems; such systems are both equifinal—there are a number of paths to achieve similar ends—and multifinal—the same processes may produce different ends. Managers of innovation will benefit from this recognition if it discourages attempts to introduce a particular approach that has worked in other organizations and encourages them to examine their particular organizations. Mintzberg (1979) observed that there is no one best overall organization structure, but there may be one best structure for a particular organization at a particular point. Similarly, the best structure for innovation is idiosyncratic; managers need to find the one that fits their system best for a particular innovation.

Theorists and researchers would do well to recognize the same point. Understanding implementation will be advanced by recognizing the particular end state an organization seeks, specifying the functional requirements needed to achieve given outcomes, and examining what conditions influence the particular steps necessary to achieve these outcomes. Such a relativistic perspective is preferable to seeking and proposing general models about how to innovate or attempting to find a set of variables associated with successful innovation. Structural contingency theories are limited for pointing to correlates of successful innovation if, as we found, certain informal modes of operation are important and if organizations are able to import and implant, thereby freeing themselves from their existing structures. In this way, our overall conclusions have much in common with Meyer's (1982) findings that structures provide only weak constraints on responses to "environmental jolts." He found that strategies and what he termed "ideologies" were much more influential than structure. We suspect this argument applies to innovation as well.

Finally, we believe that both managers and theorists will benefit if they think about the underlying similarities between innovation and other things organizations do. In attempting to compare the organizations we studied, we gravitated to some common, general requirements: searching, decision making, developing needed integration, differentiation, technical and organizational readiness, and aligning power and expertise. These are requirements for most planned organizational events, not just NOW accounts and not just innovation. While in comparison to a more stable situation, innovation may permit an organization to give a quantitatively different emphasis to some of these requirements, we suggest caution in assuming that qualitative differences are involved. Our findings lead us to conclude that implementing innovation can be understood and accomplished using concepts well known to organization theorists and managers. Of course, these conclusions must be tempered by the fact that our study focused mainly on the implementation stages of a borrowed innovation. On the other hand, many innovations that modern organizations are apt to attempt will be of this type or at least involve a number of borrowed components. After all, by definition, the number of first users of anything will always be small.

Notes

1. In personal communication Jane Dutton noted that locus of the effects in the input–output sequence might be equally well treated as yet another dimension for classifying innovation. We treated it as an environmental issue because in our study its importance emerged at the organization–environment interface rather than elsewhere in the sequence.

2. What may be equally crucial is the organization's ability to import the relevant personnel and routines and integrate them into the organization. To our

knowledge, the conditions and structures aiding such importing have received little attention. Our findings suggest that importing may be an important factor for successful innovation and that research into the borrowing process may be fruitful.

Appendix A:
Interview Schedule for Managers

Our questions deal with three general topics: (1) the decision to introduce the NOW account, (2) the process of implementing it, and (3) [name of bank/S & L] as a whole.

I. Decision to Introduce

1. First, we are interested in getting a complete picture of how [name of bank or S & L] went about deciding to introduce the NOW account. As you recall, when did [name of bank/S & L] first begin to consider the NOW account? Early in the process, how did you go about deciding what to do? (*Be sure to get names and roles of people involved, criteria employed, and weights given.*)

2. As things progressed, how was the decision reached to go ahead? *Possible follow-up questions:* Who actually was involved in making the decision? Were they all equally enthusiastic about the decision?

3. Were other people consulted? Did they make any suggestions or have any reservations? *If yes, probe for details.*

4. Were there people or departments whose work would be affected by the NOW accounts who were not directly involved in the deliberation? If yes, who were they?

5. Overall, was the procedure followed in deciding to introduce the NOW account typical of how decisions to introduce services are made? Give key similarities and differences.

II. Implementing

6. Once the decision to go ahead with the NOW account was made, what was done to make it operational?

   a. Did you have any written action plan? Could you describe it?

   b. What problems were anticipated?

   c. What things were done to deal with anticipated problems?

   Ask d and e only for top-level personnel.

   d. Who was responsible for implementing? Give people, departments, and relationships within organization.

   e. How was their progress monitored?

   Ask f and g for middle- and lower-level supervisors.

   f. Which of your employees were involved in NOW accounts in some way?

   g. How did you monitor their performance?

   h. What other people or departments were involved?

   i. Were there any new personnel?

   j. Was there any training?

   k. Were there any new SOPs?

   l. What written materials did you give people to communicate policy and procedures?

   m. Were there criteria stated in advance for evaluating the success or failure of the NOW account? If yes, what were they?

7. When was the first NOW account (automatic transfer account) opened?

8. At first, some changes go very smoothly; some are experienced as involving a lot of hassle. How did this one go? *(Probe for specifics.)* Why?

   a. Describe the nature of early problems. Were they anticipated? What problems did you have with any computing services you purchased?

   b. How were these problems dealt with?

9. When did you feel the process was running smoothly? Did it take longer than you expected to reach this point? Why?

10. Some changes of this magnitude are viewed differently by various members of the organization. For example, high-level managers may see the change quite differently than people at lower levels in the hierarchy. Or people in some departments may see the change more favorably than do members of other departments. Was there any indication of such difference in perceptions or feelings here? *If yes, probe for: Who was involved, the nature of differences, how resolved.*

11. We've looked at the history of the introduction of NOW accounts at [name of bank/S & L]. Now that you've been doing it for a while, how successful has it been? What criteria are you using? *Probe:* You did not mention [a–e below]. How is it going on this dimension?

   a. Profit

   b. Costs

   c. Number of accounts, customer reaction

   d. Account size

   e. Employee satisfaction

12. If you had to do it over again, would you do it? *Probe:* What would you do differently?

III. General

13. Does [name of bank/S & L] envision itself as any particular type of bank/S & L? Does it have any special niche? If yes, what type?

14. As you look to the future, what major innovations are financial institutions such as [name of bank/S & L] apt to be considering?

14a. Are you working on any of these now? If yes, could you briefly describe what you are doing?

15. We have discussed a number of things. Are there questions I should have asked to better understand how the NOW account was introduced at [name of bank/S & L]?

16. How many people work at [name of bank/S & L]?

17. How many branches (banks) do you have?

18. May we have a copy of the organization chart?

Appendix B: Interview Schedule for New-Accounts and Customer Relations Personnel

We're studying NOW accounts in banks and savings and loans. I would like to get your impressions about what happened with NOW accounts here. We have divided the interview into three sections. The first asks you to describe the steps that were taken to get the NOW accounts off the ground. Then I will ask how they affected you personally. Finally I will ask you to talk about how you saw them affecting other people at [name of bank/S & L].

I. General Description of Implementation

1. Tell us what you do in connection with NOW accounts.

2. Why do you think they were started?

3. To what degree did you participate in the planning?

4. If you were not involved in planning, how did you find out that [name of bank/S & L] would be having NOW accounts? (*Probe for more than one source of information.*)

5. What things did you and your coworkers have to do differently in order to get the NOW accounts started? (*Probe for: changes in duties, and people who were transferred, lost their jobs, or were retrained.*)

6. How is it going now?

II. Personal Reactions to Implementation

7. At the time, what did you expect about how this was going to affect your work?

8. What led you to expect that?

9. How has it affected your job?

    a. Do you have new duties?

    b. Do you have new contacts?

10. Do you think the people around you see your job as being different?

11. Has it turned out the way you expected?

III. Reactions of Others

12. How did other people feel about the change at the time?

13. What do they feel about it now?

14. Were there any problems between people?

    a. Were there difficulties with coordination?

    b. Were there disagreements among people? (*Probe for delays and changes in plans that resulted from disagreements.*)

IV. Summary Questions

15. If [name of bank/S & L] were to do it again, what should be done the same and what should be done differently?

16. Is there anything I have not asked about that would be helpful for me to know? Is there anything you would like to add?

References

Abernathy, W.J., Clark, K.B. and Kantrow, A.M. (1981). The new industrial competition. *Harvard Business Review*, *59*, 68–81.

Adams, J.S. (1980). Interorganizational processes and organization boundary activities. In B.M. Staw and L.L. Cummings (eds.), *Research in organizational behavior* (Vol. 2, pp. 321–55). Greenwich, Conn.: JAI Press.

Aiken, M., Bacharach, S.B., and French, J.L. (1980). Organizational structure, work process, and proposal making in administrative bureaucracies. *Academy of Management Journal*, *23*, 631–52.

Aiken, M., and Hage, J. (1979). The organic organization and innovation. In M. Zey-Ferrell (ed.), *Readings on dimensions of organizations* (pp. 263–279). Santa Monica, Calif.: Goodyear.

Aldrich, H., and Whetten, D.A. (1981). Organization-sets, action-sets, and networks: making the most of simplicity. In P.C. Nystrom and W.H. Starbuck (eds.), *Handbook of organizational design. Vol. 1. Adapting organizations to their environments* (pp. 385–408). New York: Oxford University Press.

Baldridge, J.V., and Burnham, R.A. (1975). Organizational innovation: Individual, organizational, and environmental impacts. *Administrative Science Quarterly*, *20*, 165–76.

Barnard, C.I. (1938). *The functions of the executive*. Cambridge: Harvard University Press.

Basch, D. (1976, November/December). The diffusion of NOW accounts in Massachusettts. *New England Economic Review*, *14*, 20–30.

Becker, S.W., and Whisler, T.L. (1967). The innovative organization: A selective view of current theory and research. *Journal of Business*, *40*, 462–69.

Beer, M. (1980). *Organizational change and development: A systems view*. Santa Monica, Calif.: Goodyear.

Bennis, W.G., Benne, K.D., Chin, R., and Corey, K.E. (eds.) (1976). *The planning of change* (3rd ed.). New York: Holt, Rinehart and Winston.

Berelson, B. (1954). Content analysis. In G. Lindzey (ed.) *Handbook of social psychology. Vol. 1. Theory and method* (pp. 488–522). Cambridge, Mass.: Addison-Wesley.

Berman, R., and McLaughlin, M.W. (1978). *Federal programs supporting educational change: Implementing and sustaining innovations*. Santa Monica, Calif.: Rand Corporation. R-1589/8 HEW.

Beyer, J.M., and Trice, H.M. (1978). *Implementing change*. New York: Free Press.

Blau, J.R., and McKinley, W. (1979). Ideas, complexity, and innovation. *Administrative Science Quarterly, 24*, 200–17.

Bourgeois, L.J., III (1981). On the measurement of organizational slack. *Academy of Management Review, 6*, 29–39.

Bradford, D.L., and Cohen, A.R. (1984). *Managing for excellence: The guide to developing high performance in contemporary organizations*. New York: Wiley.

Burns, T., and Stalker, G.M. (1961). *The management of innovation*. London: Tavistock.

Carroll, J. (1967). A note on departmental autonomy and innovation in medical schools. *Journal of Business, 40*, 531–34.

Centre for the Study of Industrial Innovation. 1972. *Success and failure in industrial innovation: Report on project Sappho*. London.

Chandler, A.D., Jr. (1962). *Strategy and structure: Chapters in the history of the American industrial enterprise*. Cambridge, Mass.: MIT Press.

Chandler, A.D., Jr. (1977). *The visible hand: The managerial revolution in American business*. Cambridge, Mass.: Harvard University Press.

Child, J. (1972). Organizational structure, environment and performance: The role of strategy choice. *Sociology, 6*, 2–22.

Corwin, R. (1969). Patterns of organizational conflict. *Administrative Science Quarterly, 14*, 507–22.

Corwin, R.G. (1972). Strategies for organizational innovation: An empirical comparison. *American Sociological Review, 37*, 441–54.

Crane, D.B., and Riley, M.J. (1978). *NOW accounts*. Lexington, Mass.: Lexington Books.

Cummings, T.G. (1984). Transorganizational development. In B.M. Staw and L.L. Cummings (eds.), *Research in organizational behavior. Vol. 6* (pp. 367–422). Greenwich, Conn.: JAI Press.

Cyert, R.M., and March, J.G. (1963). *A behavioral theory of the firm*. Englewood Cliffs, N.J.: Prentice-Hall.

Daft, R.L. (1978). A dual-core model of organizational innovation. *Academy of Management Journal, 21*, 193–210.

Daft, R.L., and Becker, S.W. (1978). *Innovations in organizations*. New York: Elsevier.

Depository Institutions Deregulation and Monetary Control Act of 1980. U.S. Senate Report no. 96-368, March 28, 1980.

Downs, W., Jr., and Mohr, B. (1976). Conceptual issues in the study of innovation. *Administrative Science Quarterly. 21*, 700–14.

Duncan, R. (1976). The ambidextrous organization: Designing dual structures for innovation. In R.H. Kilmann, L.R. Pondy and D.P. Slevin (eds.), *The management of organization design* (Vol. 1, pp. 167–88). New York: North-Holland.

Duncan, R., and Weiss, A. (1979). Organizational learning: Implications for organizational design. In B. Staw (ed.), *Research in organizational behavior* (Vol. 1, pp. 75–123). Greenwich, Conn.: JAI Press.

Ettlie, J.E. (1983). Organizational policy and innovation among suppliers to the food processing sector. *Academy of Management Journal, 26,* 27–44.

Ettlie, J.E. (1984). Implementation strategy for manufacturing innovations. In M. Warner (ed.), *Microprocessors, manpower and society* (pp. 31–48). New York: St. Martin's.

Ettlie, J.E., Bridges, W.P., and O'Keefe, R.D. (1984). Organization strategy and structural differences for radical versus incremental innovation. *Management Science, 30,* 682–95.

Ettlie, J.E., and Rubenstein, A.H. (1980). Social learning theory and the implementation of product innovation. *Decision Sciences, II,* 648–68.

Evan, W.M. and Black, G. (1967). Innovation in business organizations: Some factors associated with success or failure of staff proposals. *Journal of Business, 40,* 519–30.

Eveland, J.D. (1981). Evaluating the implementation of organizational technology. Paper presented at Annual Meeting of the Evaluation Research Society, Austin, Texas.

Galbraith, J.R. (1974, May). Organization design: An information processing view. *Interfaces, 4,* 28–36.

Gamson, W.H. (1966). Rancorous conflict in community politics. *American Sociological Review, 31,* 71–81.

Gerwin, D. (1981). Relationships between structure and technology. In P.C. Nystrom and W.H. Starbuck (eds.), *Handbook of organizational design. Vol. 2. Remodeling organizations and their environments* (pp. 3–38). New York: Oxford University Press.

Gibson, C.F. (1975). A methodology for implementation research. In R.L. Schultz and D.P. Slevin (eds.), *Implementing operations research/management science* (pp. 53–73). New York: American Elsevier.

Goodman, P.S., and Pennings, J.M. (1977). Perspectives and issues: an introduction. In P.S. Goodman and J.M. Pennings (eds.), *New perspectives on organizational effectiveness* (pp. 1–12). San Francisco: Jossey-Bass.

Greenwood, P.W., Mann, D., and McLaughlin, M.W. (1975). *Federal Programs Supporting Educational Change. Vol. 3. The Proceedings of Change.* R-1589/1. Santa Monica, Calif.: Rand Corporation.

Greiner, L.E. (1972). Evolution and revolution as organizations grow. *Harvard Business Review, 50,* no. 4, 37–46.

Gross, N., Giacquinta, J.B., and Bernstein, M. (1971). *Implementing organizational innovations.* New York: Basic Books.

Hage, J. (1980). *Theories of organizations, form processes, and transformation.* New York: John Wiley and Sons.

Hage, J., and Aiken, M. (1967). Program change and organizational properties: A comparative analysis. *American Journal of Sociology, 72,* 503–19.

Hage, J. and Aiken, M. (1970). *Social change in complex organizations.* New York: Random House.

Hage, J., and Dewar, R. (1973). Elite values versus organizational structure in predicting innovation. *Administrative Science Quarterly, 18,* 279–90.

Hambrick, C.D., and Snow, C.C. (1977). A contextual model of strategic decision making in organizations. In R.L. Taylor, J.J. O'Connell, R.A. Zawacki, and D.D. Warrick (eds.), *Academy of Management Proceedings* (pp. 109–12).

Harvey, E., and Mills, R. (1970). Patterns of organizational adaptation: A political perspective. In M.N. Zald (ed.), *Power in organizations* (pp. 181–213). Nashville, Tenn.: Vanderbilt University Press.

Jelinek, M. (1979). *Institutionalizing innovation. A study of organizational learning systems.* New York: Praeger.

Jick, T.D. (1979). Mixing qualitative and quantitative methods: Triangulation in action. *Administrative Science Quarterly, 24,* 602–11.

Jurkovich, R. (1974). A core technology of organizational environments. *Administrative Science Quarterly, 19,* 380–94.

Kanter, R.M. (1983). *The change masters.* New York: Simon and Schuster.

Kerr, S., and Jermier, J.M. (1978). Substitutes for leadership: Their meaning and measurement. *Organizational Behavior and Human Performance, 22,* 375–403.

Kimberly, J.R. (1976). Organizational size and the structuralist perspective. *Administrative Science Quarterly, 21,* 571–97.

Kimberly, J.R. (1979). Issues in the creation of organizations: Initiation, innovation, and institutionalization. *Academy of Management Journal, 22,*437–57.

Kimberly, J.R. (1981). Managerial innovation. In P.C. Nystrom and W.H. Starbuck (eds.), *Handbook of organizational design. Vol. 1. Adapting organizations to their environments* (pp. 84–104). New York: Oxford University Press.

Kimberly, J.R. and Evanisko, M.J. (1981). Organizational innovation: The influence of individual, organizational, and contextual factors on hospital adoption of technological and administrative innovations. *Academy of Management Journal, 24,* 689–713.

Knight, K. (1967). A descriptive model of the intra-firm innovation process. *Journal of Business, 40,* 478–96.

Lawrence, P.R., and Lorsch, J.W. (1967a). Differentiation and integration in complex organizations. *Administrative Science Quarterly, 12,* 1–47.

Lawrence, P.R., and Lorsch, J.W. (1967b). *Organization and environment.* Boston: Harvard University.

Locke, E.A., and Schweiger, D.M. (1979). Participation in decision-making: One more look. In B.M. Staw (ed.), *Research in organizational behavior* (Vol. 1, pp. 265–339). Greenwich, Conn.: JAI Press.

Malecki, E.J. (1977). Firms and innovation diffusion: Examples from banking. *Environment and Planning A, 9,* 1291–1305.

March, J.G. and Simon, H.A. (1958). *Organizations.* New York: Wiley.

Marino, K.E. (1982). Structural correlates of affirmative action compliance. *Journal of Management, 8,* 75–93.

Massie, J.L. (1965). Management theory. In J.M. March (ed.), *Handbook of organizations* (pp. 387–442). Chicago: Rand McNally, 1965.

McClelland, D.C. (1961). *The achieving society.* New York: Free Press.

McClelland, D.C. and Burnham, D.H. (1976, March-April). Power is the great motivator. *Harvard Business Review, 54,* 100–10.

Membership Directory of Members of the Federal Home Loan Bank System. (February 1980). Washington, D.C.: Federal Home Loan Bank Board.

Metcalfe, L. (1981). Designing precarious partnerships. In P.C. Nystrom and W.H. Starbuck (eds.) *Handbook of organizational design. Vol. 1. Adapting organizations to their environments* (pp. 503–30). New York: Oxford University Press.

Meyer, A.D. (1982). Adapting to environmental jolts. *Administrative Science Quarterly, 27*, 515–37.

Miles, R.E. (1975). *Theories of management: Implications for organizational behavior and development.* New York: McGraw-Hill.

Miles, R.E., Snow, C.C., Meyer, A.D., and Colemen, H.J., Jr. (1978). Organizational strategy, structure, and process. *Academy of Management Review, 3*, 546–62.

Miller, D. (1979). Strategy, structure and environment: context influences upon some bivariate associations. *Journal of Management Studies, 16*, 294–316.

Miller, D., and Frieson, P.H. (1984). *Organizations: A quantum view.* Englewood Cliffs, N.J.: Prentice-Hall.

Mintzberg, H. (1979). *The structuring of organizations.* Englewood Cliffs, N.J.: Prentice-Hall.

Moch, M., and Morse, E. (1977). Size, centralization and organizational adoption of innovations. *American Sociological Review, 42*, 716–25.

Munson, F.C., and Pelz, D.C. (1979). *The innovating process: A conceptual framework* (3rd version). Ann Arbor: University of Michigan.

Nadler, D.A. (1983). Concepts for the management of organizational change. In J.R. Hackman, E.E. Lawler, III, and L.W. Porter (eds.), *Perspectives on behavior in organizations* (pp. 551–61). New York: McGraw-Hill.

Neal, R.D., and Radnor, M. (1973). The relation between formal procedures for pursuing OR/MS activities and OR/MS group success. *Operations Research, 21*, 451–74.

Nelson, R.R., and Winter, S.G. (1977). In search of useful theory of innovation. *Research Policy, 6*, 36–76.

Nelson, R.R., and Yates, D. (1978). *Innovation and implementation in public organizations.* Lexington, Mass.: Lexington Books.

Normann, R. (1971). Organizational innovativeness: Product variability and reorientation. *Administrative Science Quarterly, 16*, 203–15.

Nystrom, P.C., and Starbuck, W.H. (1984, Spring). To avoid organizational crises, unlearn. *Organizational Dynamics, 12*, 53–65.

Ouchi, W.G. (1980). Markets, bureaucracies, and clans. *Administrative Science Quarterly, 25*, 129–41.

Pellegrin, R.J. (1978). Sociology and policy-oriented research on innovation. In M. Radnor, I. Feller, and E. Rogers (eds.), *The diffusion of innovations: An assessment.* Evanston, Ill.: Northwestern University Center for the Interdisciplinary Study of Science and Technology.

Pelz, D.C., and Munson, F.C. (1980). A framework for organizational innovating. Unpublished paper. Ann Arbor: University of Michigan.

Pennings, J.M. (1975). The relevance of the structural-contingency model for organizational effectiveness. *Administrative Science Quarterly, 20*, 393–410.

Pennings, J.M. (1981). Strategically interdependent organizations. In P.C. Nystrom and W.H. Starbuck (eds.), *Handbook of organizational design. Vol. 1, Adapting organizations to their environments* (pp. 433–55). New York: Oxford University Press.

Peters, T.J., and Waterman, R.H., Jr. (1982). *In search of excellence*. New York: Harper & Row.

Petersen, J.C. (1976). Organizational structure and program change in Protestant denominations. *Organization and Administrative Sciences, 6,* 1–13.

Pfeffer, J. (1981). *Power in organizations*. Marshfield, Mass.: Pitman.

Pfeffer, J., and Salancik, G.R. (1978). *The external control of organizations*. New York: Harper & Row.

Pierce, J.L., and Delbecq, A.L. (1977). Organization structure, individual attitudes and innovation. *Academy of Management Review, 2,* 27–37.

Pinchot, G. (1985). *Intrapreneuring*. New York: Harper & Row.

Polk's World Bank Directory (1980, Spring). Nashville, Tenn.: R.L. Polk.

Radnor, M., and Neal, R. (1973). The progress of management science activities in large U.S. industrial corporations. *Operations Research, 21,* 427–50.

Ramaprasad, A. (1982). Revolutionary change and strategic management. *Behavioral Science, 27,* 387–92.

Robertson, T.S., and Wind, Y. (1983). Organizational cosmopolitanism and innovation. *Academy of Management Journal, 26,* 332–38.

Rogers, E.M. (1983). *Diffusion of innovations* (3rd edition). New York: Free Press.

Rosenbloom, R.S. (1978). Technological innovation in firms and industries: An assessment of the state of the art. In P. Kelly and M. Kranzberg (eds.), *Technological innovation: A critical review of current knowledge* (pp. 215–30). San Francisco: San Francisco Press.

Rothwell, R., and Zegveld, W. (1982). *Innovation and the small and medium sized firm*. Hingham, Mass.: Kluwer-Nijhoff.

Sapolsky, H.M. (1967). Organizational structure and innovation. *Journal of Business, 40,* 497–510.

Schultz, R.L., and Slevin, D.P. (eds.), 1975. *Implementing operations research/ management science*. New York: American Elsevier.

Schumpeter, J.A. (1961). *The theory of economic development*. Cambridge, Mass.: Harvard University.

Schwenk, C.R. (1985). The use of participant recollection in the modeling of organizational decision processes. *Academy of Management Review, 10,* 496–503.

Shepard, H.A. Innovation-resisting and innovation-producing organizations. *Journal of Business, 40,* 470–477.

Simon, H.A. (1957). *Administrative behavior: A study of decision-making processes in administrative organizations*. New York: Free Press.

Simonson, D.G., and Marks, P.C. (1980, November). Pricing NOW accounts and the cost of bank funds. Part 1: Break even analysis of NOW accounts. *Bank Administration, 63,* 28–31.

Smircich, L. 1983. Concepts of culture and organizational analysis. *Administrative Science Quarterly, 28,* 339–58.

Smith, S. (1980, September 15). NOW accounts. What bankers are planning. *Bank News, 78,* 9–12, 92.

Staw, B.M. (1984). Organizational behavior: A review and reformulation of the

Field's outcome variables. In M.R. Rosenzweig and L.W. Porter (eds.), *Annual Review of Psychology* (pp. 627–66). Palo Alto, Calif.: Annual Reviews.

Stein, B.A. (1973). *Size, scale, and community enterprise.* Cambridge, Mass.: Center for Community and Economic Development.

Stein, B.A., and Kanter, R.M. (1980). Building the parallel organization: Creating mechanisms for permanent quality of work life. *Journal of Applied Behavioral Science, 16,* 371–88.

Szanton, P.L. (1978). Urban public services: Ten case studies. In R.R. Nelson and D. Yates (eds.), *Innovation and implementation in public organizations* (pp. 117–42). Lexington, Mass.: Lexington Books.

Thompson, J.D. (1967). *Organizations in action.* New York: McGraw-Hill.

Thompson, V.A. (1965). Bureaucracy and innovation. *Administrative Science Quarterly, 10,* 1–20.

Tornatzky, L.G., Eveland, J.D., Boylan, M.G., Hetzner, W.A., Johnson, E.C., Roitman, D., and Schneider, J. (1983). *The process of technological innovation: Reviewing the literature.* Washington, D.C.: National Science Foundation.

Tornatzky, L.G., Fergus, E., Avellar, J., and Fairweather, G.W. (1980). *Innovation and social process.* Elmsford, N.Y.: Pergamon.

Tornatzky, L.G., and Klein, K.J. (1982). Innovation characteristics and innovation adoption-implementation: A meta-analysis of findings. *IEEE Transactions on Engineering Management,* EM-29, 28–45.

Trist, E.L. (1981). The evolution of sociotechnical systems as a conceptual framework and as an action research program. In A.H. Van de Ven and W.F. Joyce (eds.), *Perspectives on organization design and behavior* (pp. 19–75). New York: Wiley.

Tushman, M.L. (1977). Special boundary roles in the innovation process. *Administrative Science Quarterly, 22,* 587–605.

Weberman, B. (1980). If it looks like a bank and acts like a bank . . ., *Forbes, 33–34.*

Weick, K.E. (1979). *The social psychology of organizing* (2nd edition). Reading, Mass.: Addison-Wesley.

Weiss, A.R. (1983). *The effects of interorganizational relations on the process and consequences of innovation.* Unpublished doctoral dissertation, Northwestern University, Evanston, Ill.

Whittle, J.W. (1979). NOW accounts, S & Ls, and pricing. *American Banker,* 4–9.

Wilson, J.Q. (1966). Innovation in organizations: Notes toward a theory. In J.D. Thompson (ed.), *Approaches to organizational design* (pp. 193–218). Pittsburgh: University of Pittsburgh Press.

Yin, R.K. (1977). Organizational innovation: A psychologist's view. Unpublished paper presented at "Assessment of Current Developments on the Diffusion of Innovations," a workshop at Northwestern University, Evanston, Ill.

———(1978). Organizational innovation: A psychologist's view. Chap. 9 in M. Radnor, I. Feller, and E. Rogers (eds.), *The diffusion of innovations: An assessment.* Evanston, Ill: Northwestern University Center for the Interdisciplinary Study of Science and Technology.

———(1979) *Changing urban bureaucracies: How new practices become routinized.* Lexington, Mass.: Lexington Books.

———(1981). Life histories of innovations: How new practices become routinized. *Public Administration Review, 41,* 21–28.

———, Heald, K.A., and Vogel, M.E. (1977). *Tinkering with the system.* Lexington, Mass.: Lexington Books.

Zaleznik, A. (1977, May-June). Managers and leaders: Are they different? *Harvard Business Review, 55,* 67–78.

Zaltman, G., Duncan, R., and Holbek, J. (1973). *Innovations and organizations.* New York: John Wiley and Sons.

Zaltman, G., Kotler, P., and Kaufman, I. (eds.) (1972). *Creating social change.* New York: Holt, Rinehart and Winston.

Zand, D.E. (1974). Collateral organization: A new change strategy. *Journal of Applied Behavioral Science, 10,* 63–89.

Index

About the Authors

Walter R. Nord is a professor of organizational psychology at the School of Business Administration, Washington University-St. Louis. His published work in academic journals has concentrated on the application of behavior modification in organizations and the development of a political economic perspective for organizational behavior. In his efforts to develop the political economic view, he has explored job satisfaction, organizational development, organizational effectiveness, and social power. Currently, he is investigating the development of work values. He has edited several books, including *Making Organizations Humane and Productive* (with Hyman Meltzer) and *Organizational Reality: Reports from the Firing Line* (with Peter Frost and Vance Mitchell). He received his B.A. from Williams College, his M.S. from Cornell University, and his Ph.D. in psychology from Washington University.

Sharon Tucker is an associate with the St. Louis office of the Hay Group, Inc. She consults in the areas of organization design and change, productivity, performance planning and appraisal, and pay for performance. Prior to joining Hay, she was on the faculty of the School of Business at Washington University for five years and at Southern Illinois University at Edwardsville for one year. Her research has been varied, including investigations of political influences on organizations, social influences on women's positions in work organizations, and the nature of helping relationships. She received her Ph.D. in social and organizational psychology from the University of Chicago.

DATE DUE